The Best *of* Hal Lebovitz

Merry Christmas
Dear Paul

Love,
Lorraine
2015

THE BEST *of* HAL LEBOVITZ

Great Sportswriting from Six Decades in Cleveland

GRAY & COMPANY, PUBLISHERS
Cleveland

This book is dedicated to my team—my beloved bride, Margie, and my son, Neil, and daughter, Lynn—and to my dear friends and co-workers who supported me along the way.

The columns and feature stories in this book dated between 1955 and 1959 first appeared in the *Cleveland News*. Those dated between 1960 and 1984 are © *The Plain Dealer* (all rights reserved) and are reprinted with permission (except "How Gamblers Move In On Baseball" and "Paul Warfield: Cleveland's Prize Rookie," which first appeared in *Sport* magazine.) Those dated between 1986 and 2003 first appeared in *The News-Herald*.

Library of Congress Cataloging-in-Publication Data
Lebovitz, Hal.
The best of Hal Lebovitz / Hal Lebovitz.
p. cm.
1. Sports—United States. 2. Newspapers—Sections, columns, etc.—Sports. I. Title.
GV707.L43 2004
796'.0973—dc22 2004010541

Gray & Company, Publishers
www.grayco.com

ISBN-13: 978-1-59851-023-2
ISBN-10: 1-59851-023-1

Printed in the United States of America

First Printing

Contents

Foreword

"Don't ever cut a boy!" The headline is synonymous with Hal Lebovitz, who wrote that column in 1964. How do *I* cut more than fifty-five years' worth of the best sports writing in Ohio history to just ninety examples summarizing a Hall of Fame career? More than enough pieces were left out of this book to fill a second and probably a third collection that would be just as good.

Ask Hal the Referee . . . Don't knock the Rock . . . the Deli Gang (the Maven, the Occult, Ira the Recruiter, the Tire Kicker, Ta-Ta-Ta) . . . My generation learned about sports from reading Hal every day in *The Plain Dealer*. Hal saved the Indians from moving out of town on at least four different occasions. He helped bring the Cincinnati Royals to the Cleveland Arena for several games a year, leading to the arrival of the expansion Cleveland Cavaliers. He was directly responsible for Grandstand Manager Night, Bat Day, and Ball Day at Cleveland Municipal Stadium.

You probably know about Mitch Albom's book *Tuesdays with Morrie*. For the past ten years, I have spent "Thursdays (or Fridays) with Hal." From 1994 to 1996 on radio, and from 1996 through the present, Hal has been more than a regular guest on my show, *More Sports & Les Levine*. He didn't want to do it at first when his friend Armond Arnson suggested the concept of "The Guys in the Know," but he did it for his friend, who soon became seriously ill. Members of Armond's family told me that looking forward to the weekly show added at least six months to his life, before he passed away in 1996. As for Hal . . . he was flattered that he was still remembered as a local treasure. We agree, we disagree, we fight, we laugh. But through it all there is total respect. It's almost like a marriage, although nothing like the one he has had with his beloved Margie for more than sixty-six years.

Hal sometimes doesn't understand the effect he has on people. Respected local journalists like Terry Pluto and Dan Coughlin say he was the greatest mentor and boss they could have ever had. Over the years he has fielded hundreds of calls from strangers in the middle of the night to settle sports arguments that arose after one or two too many beers were consumed. And what could be more impressive than having the phone ring in his University Heights home in the middle of a

World Series game, when producers from NBC or Fox would call to get an interpretation of a ruling that just occurred during the game?

Never thinking of retirement, Hal digs harder for stories than others a half century younger. I have given him information on certain things over the years for his Sunday notes columns, and always before I see them in the paper, he's made some changes after getting two or three confirmations or denials.

On July 23, 2000, Hal took his rightful place in the Writers Wing of the Baseball Hall of Fame in Cooperstown, New York. I was there. There couldn't have been anyone more proud of him on that day, other than Margie, his daughter, Lynn, and his son, Neil. My ten years with Hal have been great. Another ten would be greater.

— Les Levine

Postscript

It's never good news when the phone rings after midnight. Such was the case at my house in the early hours of October 18, 2005. It was news I expected but still wasn't prepared for, the news that Hal Lebovitz had just passed away at the age of 89.

Most people would take the kind of deal Hal had. Until the last couple of months he had a very healthy 89 years, 67 of them while married to his beloved Margie. Nationally and locally acclaimed as one of the top sportswriters in history, he continued to write his incredible notes column in the *News-Herald* and *Lorain Journal*, and appear each week on my television show, until three weeks before his death.

But Hal wanted more. He hadn't been able to write about a championship in Cleveland since the Browns won in 1964. He wanted to taste it again. As a man with a life-long devotion to his Jewish faith, he must have felt like Moses, who wandered the desert for forty years without getting to see the Promised Land.

Since Hal died, scores of men and women, from teen-agers to his contemporaries, have made me aware of how much they miss his columns and appearances. So I was honored when the publishers of the *News-Herald* and *Lorain Journal* asked if I would be interested in taking over the vacant Sunday column. After consulting Hal's son, Neil, and Margie, I agreed. But of course everyone understands that *nobody* can replace Hal Lebovitz.

Preface

I never expected to be writing this preface to a collection of my outpourings. For years I fought the suggestion whenever someone flatteringly said, "You ought to put together some of your pieces in a book."

I never was enamored with my stuff and I didn't think it would sell. Besides, I didn't want to go through the files and decide which pieces should be included. There simply was too much written—pieces from *The Cleveland News*, *The Plain Dealer*, *The News-Herald*, and the other dailies in Ohio who carry me: *The* (Lorain) *Journal*, *The Mansfield News-Journal*, and *The Dover Times-Reporter*, plus the many magazine pieces that have been published.

But my sweet daughter, Lynn, kept bugging me: "Why don't you write a book? All the stories you've been telling us—put them in a book." She even bought a tape recorder and urged me to start recording.

I continually turned her down, with, "I've already written them. I don't want to write them again."

Then David Gray, of Gray & Company, called and said he'd like to talk to me about compiling a book from all the articles I had written.

This time I hesitated instead of saying no. It would make Lynn happy. The timing might be right.

I said I'd be interested if I had nothing to do with the project other than saying yes. I didn't want to be part of the selection process.

Now my son Neil got into the act. He volunteered to find as many of my columns and articles as he could and pick what he thought were the most readable.

Poor guy, he didn't know what he was getting into. Neil is a former athlete and still a sports buff, but now he had forced himself to become a judge of his dad's writings. I don't know how many pieces he read before he produced a workable package of a four hundred, which he sent to the publisher.

Four hundred was too many for the book, so Gray turned Neil's collection over to an editor—Les Levine, a knowledgeable TV sports host—to make the final selection of about ninety.

What's inside is a trip through the world of sports—mostly Cleveland—as these eyes saw it, starting in the late 1940s, when I first joined the sports staff of *The Cleveland News*.

The book is really a family affair, from Lynn to Neil to my bride, Margie, who has been my personal editor all these years, fixing my grammar and advising on content and subject matter.

I have been extremely fortunate. Ever since I was eight years old I knew what I wanted to become when I grew up: a schoolteacher and a writer. I taught school for eight years in Euclid, Ohio, where I also coached, giving me a unique background when I took the job at the *News*. I loved teaching, but the salary was one-third of what the *News* offered, so I found it easy to jump to the other vocation I cherished.

The *News* had only a small sports department—four men—although these four put out a daily package the paper heralded without argument as the "Best Sports Pages."

These four men, Herman Goldstein, Ed McAuley, Howard Preston, and Ed Bang, honed me from teacher to journalist. I owe whatever success I have had to them and to Gordon Cobbledick, who, as sports editor of *The Plain Dealer*, hired me the day the *News* folded, January 20, 1960, a day that would have lived in infamy for me, if not for Cobby.

My "teachers" stressed one thing: "Write simply. Always keep the reader in mind."

Each time I put a piece of paper in my typewriter—or now punch out words on my computer—I think of you, the reader. I may not always have succeeded, but at least the words, I hope, have been sincere and clear—no razzle-dazzle trying to make you think I'm clever.

For me, being forced to read these selected pieces has been a cobweb duster, truly a trip down memory lane.

I had remembered writing "Please Don't Cut a Boy," because rarely a week passes that a request from a school official or a parent doesn't come in for a copy. They arrive from all over the United States. Also, I have a file I treasure of letters from boys who say the article saved them from being cut. Many went on to become top-drawer college players. (Are you listening, coaches?)

I remembered, too, the column when Luke Easter died because I advocated a tribute to him, such as naming a park in his name. The former Woodland Hills Park is now called Luke Easter Park.

And I'm reminded of the piece on Clark Kellogg because he was the LeBron James of his day and my strange mind has intertwined them.

Otherwise, reading the rest of the stuff was like opening a door to a forgotten past. How fortunate I am to have been a close observer of the fun and games that give us the needed outlet from the stress and strain of daily life. I've met so many interesting people (yes, I met Babe Ruth), been a spectator at so many major events.

Inevitably, I found some repetition of facts and anecdotes. They were appropriate for the respective articles and a compilation had not been anticipated.

It's been a good life and I'm eagerly awaiting the chapters I'll be covering today and tomorrow. Hope you enjoy the following pages and share the pleasure of my awakened memories.

Incidentally, my son just uncovered a number of files he hadn't seen before. He says they're filled with good stuff. He and the publisher are already talking about a Volume Two. If this book finds a receptive audience, they already have my permission.

STRONG WORDS

Did you ever cut a boy?

August 23, 1964

Consider this an open letter to every high school coach, principal, and superintendent:

Football practice is now under way. The boys have reported; they have been issued uniforms. This is what happened to one boy some years ago:

The boy had just entered high school. All summer he looked forward to the opening of football practice. He enjoyed contact. He had tossed a football around almost from the day he left his crib. His dream was to play on the high school varsity.

On August 20 he reported for the first day of practice. "You'll have to furnish your own shoes and you'll heed $7.50 for insurance," the junior varsity coach told him. The boy rushed out to buy a pair of shoes. Cost: $20.

He returned the next day carrying them proudly, paid his $7.50 insurance fee, did calisthenics with the squad and at the end of the session he was cut.

So were several other boys—all dropped from the squad after one session of calisthenics.

The boy rushed to the telephone and called his dad's office. Unable to withhold the tears, he sobbed, "I was cut."

"Go back tomorrow," the father suggested gently. "Maybe there was a mistake."

The boy returned, finally summoned sufficient courage to ask the coach for another chance. "Come back in two weeks," said the coach.

Two weeks later the boy carried his new shoes back to practice. "Sorry," said the coach. "We haven't time to look at you now. Come back after school starts."

The boy did. This time the coach apparently had no alternative. He gave the boy a uniform. Within a week he cut the boy once more.

The boy was crushed completely. The father advised, "Try next year, son."

"No," said the boy. "I don't want to be humiliated again."

The boy never did try out again. He never followed the team. His interest in school was never the same. The cleats on his $20 shoes are slightly worn—from football on the neighborhood lot. They remain the heartbroken memento of his brief high school football experience.

Later the father checked with the coach. "We can't handle 60 boys," he offered lamely. "We didn't want your son to get hurt."

If you are such a coach, I strongly urge you to quit. Mr. Principal and Mr. Superintendent, if your school has such a coach, get rid of him fast. Either that, or drop football, a game in which anybody's son can get hurt.

I speak as a former football coach who never cut a boy. I firmly believe there are lessons to be learned on the football field that are valuable carry-overs in life.

Doyt Perry, who, until his retirement, was one of the state's most successful coaches, in high school and later at Bowling Green State University, never cut a boy.

"I didn't care if 100 came out, and we got almost that many," he said. "If they want the football experience, they should have it. At Ohio State, Woody Hayes never sent a boy away, no matter how green or how puny."

Fortunately, most high school and college coaches have the same philosophy.

Football takes stomach. A boy who doesn't have it will quit of his own accord. The fields are big. They can accommodate large squads. Let the boy hang around. Let him do calisthenics. Let him run until he's out of breath. Let him scrimmage with the fourth and fifth teams after the regulars are finished.

But don't cut him. If he hasn't got it, he'll cut himself. If he has, he'll stick it out. He'll be a better man for the experience and by the time he's a senior he'll surprise you. He'll help make you a winner.

So, Coach, hold that knife. Why plunge it into a boy's heart.

Editor's note: This column drew a huge response from readers and was subsequently reprinted, almost annually, under the revised headline "Please don't ever cut a boy." That headline was later updated to

"Please don't ever cut a boy . . . or girl." Most readers who still remember it fondly—and there are thousands—refer to it simply as "Never cut a boy." We chose to run it here under its original headline.

Whose game is it?

May 28, 1972

A good friend and Plain Dealer associate said, "I met a guy who says he knows you. We met under strange circumstances."

"Strained" circumstances would have been a better description.

That's what Little League baseball does to parents.

Both men had sons involved in a practice game. The fellow who said he knows me was umpiring.

There was a runner on first. The batter grounded to the second basemen who transferred the ball to his bare hand and tagged the oncoming runner with his empty glove. The umpire called him out.

My friend at the PD couldn't restrain himself. He walked up to the umpire and said, "You know the kid tagged the runner with his glove, but he had the ball in his other hand. That's not a legal tag."

"Don't tell me the rules," shouted the ump. "I've been around. I played a lot of ball. What do you know about the game?"

The PD man stood his ground. "I'm from Brooklyn," he said, which is the ultimate reply explaining everything. "I saw a lot of games at Ebbets Field."

"I played there," retorted the ump. "They throw garbage in Ebbets Field."

The PD man took this as a personal insult. The words grew louder. Finally, in exasperation, the PD man said, "I know Lebovitz," a frightening declaration indeed.

"I know him, too," shouted the ump, completely unimpressed. "I'll bet you any amount you're wrong on the rule. Go ask him."

So that's how I got into the act.

The ump, whose name I won't disclose to prevent further bloodshed (mine), had been a National League ball player. Nevertheless, he blew the rule. It wasn't a legal tag. A tag must be made with the ball, or with the glove while the ball is securely held inside.

He should have known better.

A mature adult, he also should have known better than to get into an argument with a neighbor over such an insignificant incident and he's sheepish about it today.

The PD man is sorry, too. "I promised myself," he said "not to become a Little League father. I was just going to go to the games, watch and enjoy—and keep quiet.

"But before I knew it, I got involved in the game. I felt compelled to correct the umpire. We were silly to carry on like that in front of our children. From now on I'll keep my mouth shut."

It won't be easy. I know. I was a Little League father, also an umpire and a commissioner. Little League brings out the worse in parents.

The kids are great. It's the papas and mamas who take the fun out of the game for the youngsters. It's no longer their game. It belongs to the adults. We run it. We do everything but hit the ball and we burn when the kids can't even do that.

My suggestion is to give the game back to the kids and each time I make it, it's as though I'm blasting motherhood or the American flag.

Before you start writing that nasty letter, ask yourself these questions:

Is your son playing because he wants to or because you want him to?

If your son isn't the pitcher or the catcher, doesn't he stand around most of the time watching the action?

Are you putting any pressure on your son during the games?

Do you criticize him after the game for his failures?

If you are the manager, do you unconsciously favor your son?

If you are not the manager, do you question the way the manager is handling your son?

Isn't it true the manager really doesn't know much about the game?

Do you forget that you once made errors and struck out?

Is Little League forcing your son to become a beggar, going house to house or standing on street corners, asking for money so he can wear a big league uniform?

Do you want to shout, "Stand in there" when that big kid pitching throws a fast ball over the plate and your son backs away?

Do you get irritated by the other team's manager or the umpire because things aren't going your son's way and do you let your anger show? Do they become your momentary enemies?

Can you attend the games in a relaxed fashion?

Can you forget about the game after it's over or do your son's mistakes continue to bother you hours later?

Are you more wrapped up in the game than your son is?

Are you trying to recapture your childhood through him?

Are you and/or other adults in the community more involved in the program than the kids are?

Is there a good chance his present Little League experience will turn your son away from wanting to play baseball within a few years?

If the answer to most of the above questions is "yes," you will have to admit that changes definitely are in order.

Therefore, I hope you will agree with this four-point plan:

ONE—As much as possible, let the kids run their own league. Let it be *their* experience, not yours. Let them elect their own captain. Let the kids serve as base coaches. A knowledgeable parent can act as the head of the league in the manner of a leader or scoutmaster, but let the kids do as much work and organizing and maintaining of grounds as possible. Once the adults set up the structure, turn it over to the kids.

TWO—Bring in knowledgeable men from the community—the high school baseball coach, for example—to conduct clinics on fundamentals for the players. High school and college players can serve as managers and umpires. If parents *must* serve as managers, do not permit them to manage teams on which their sons play. If they really are dedicated and want to help the kids, they will gladly volunteer to coach another team. But, as much as possible, turn the game over to the kids. Let them take on the responsibilities. Keep the parents on the sidelines—as far, far back as possible.

THREE—Eliminate the big league uniforms. Caps, T-shirts and jeans are good enough. The kids should be playing for the fun of it, not for the uniforms. If they're big leaguers at age ten, what do they have to look forward to when they're fifteen? Under the present Little League structure, too many youngsters are finished with the game once they pass the LL age. Moreover, it will cut the cost of the program to a minimum. It will reduce the demeaning begging for funds.

FOUR—Start the kids off with slow pitch softball. This puts ALL the kids in the game. There's hitting, running, throwing, no standing around. Even the right fielder gets into the game. Meanwhile, there's greater exposure to all the fundamentals. Most of all, in slow pitch they don't become frightened of the ball. They don't develop the bad habit of backing away. When the kids get a little older, they can advance to hardball. They'll be more eager for it when they're physically ready.

Several communities have adopted these suggestions in recent years and, happily, they report highly successful results. I have letters on file as proof.

Try it, you might like it. More important, the kids will.

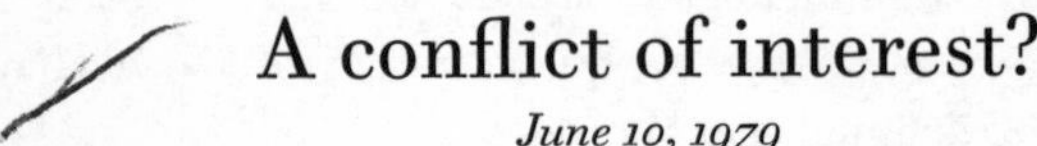

A conflict of interest?

June 10, 1979

Put yourself in this picture: You are the official scorer at a major league game. You also cover the home team for the *Daily Bugle.* The pitcher on the home team is rolling along. No hits in the first five innings. None in the sixth. None in the seventh.

The crowd wants the no-hitter. Everybody in the press box is thinking about it, even whispering.

No one is more aware of it than you, except perhaps for the pitcher himself. You laugh nervously at comments from fellow scribes. No question about it—your pulse is beating faster. You say to yourself, "I hope the first hit is a clean one."

One out in the eighth. Two outs. The next batter hits a medium speed grounder down the third base line. The third baseman moves toward the ball, reaches as far as he can for it. The ball glances off the tip of his glove and goes into the left field corner.

Your mind immediately clicks, "Hit," and you give the signal.

The no-hitter is over. It proves to be the only hit the pitcher gives up.

The game ends and you no longer are the official scorer. You are now exclusively a reporter and you must go into the clubhouse to talk with the pitcher.

Can you talk to him as reporter-to-player, or will he now look at you as player-talking-to-official-scorer?

I pose this situation to you because it's real, not hypothetical. It happened last Sunday in Pittsburgh, and I think it is the beginning of the end of baseball writers also serving as official scorers.

In Tuesday's *Pittsburgh Press*, the editor, John Troan, a devout sports fan, announced that as of the end of the 1979 season his paper will not permit sportswriters to serve as official scorers. "I would invoke the ban right now," he said, "but it would be unfair to the league for us to change the rules in the middle of the season."

It was Dan Donovan, the *Press'* baseball writer, doubling as official scorer, who called the base hit that ended Pirate pitcher Bruce Krison's bid for a no-hitter against San Diego. (Donovan, incidentally, grew up in Lakewood and went to St. Ignatius briefly before moving to Pittsburgh. He has many relatives here.)

"Earlier this year," Troan said, explaining the ban, "some Pirate players criticized Donovan for charging shortstop Frank Taveras with an error on a play they thought should have been scored a hit. Now it's the other way around. Some are complaining because he credited a San Diego player with a hit rather than charging Phil Garner (Pirates' third baseman) with an error when Bruce Kison was within four outs of a no-hitter. It's obvious that they don't want an official scorer who calls 'em as he sees 'em.

"It is equally obvious that a baseball writer who doubles as official scorer places himself in a position where he cannot possibly avoid a conflict of interest. That's why it's time to end the arrangement."

On the same day the *Pittsburgh Post-Gazette* also announced its baseball writer no longer will serve as official scorer, effective today.

The baseball writer for the *Post-Gazette* is Charley Feeney. Unlike Donovan, a relative newcomer to the assignment, Feeney has been on the major league baseball beat 30 years. He covered for the *New York Journal American* until that paper folded. The *Post-Gazette* then hired Feeney. For 25 of those 30 seasons he has been an official scorer. Today is his last day at calling the plays.

I phoned Feeney, rather than Donovan, because he can be totally objective about the "hit" call in the game Kison pitched last Sunday. I've known Feeney from his rookie days. He always levels, no matter who gets hit between the eyes.

"I'll tell you exactly how I saw the play," he said. "Barry Evans was the San Diego hitter. He hit a grounder inside the third base bag. Phil Garner takes a step, maybe two, to his right, then leans to backhand the ball as far as he can and it goes off the tip of his glove into the left field corner.

"Danny called it a hit right away. Evans rounded first and went to second. Danny immediately said, 'Double.' I mean there was no hesitation—all the way.

"There was disappointment among the fans that the no-hitter was broken, but they didn't show any reaction to the press box. They stood up and cheered Kison's effort.

"And in the press box there was no negative reaction at all. I mean nothing. Nobody thought it was an error.

"I understand there was a wire story account that Kison made some gesture to the press box and that the players in the dugout did, too. If that's the case, none of us saw it.

"At the end of the game about 20 of us, writers and broadcasters, went down the elevator to the clubhouse. Not a single one of us was thinking there might be a controversy about the call. When I got in the clubhouse somebody said, 'Kison's mad.' We were stunned. It was such an easy call, I couldn't believe it.

"We couldn't get to Kison right away because he was being interviewed for San Diego radio. When he came into the clubhouse he saw me and said, 'Charley, I wish you were scoring today.'

"I told him, 'Bruce, I would have called it a hit.'

It was obvious he was angry—restrained anger, I would call it—and he clammed up after that.

"I said, 'You've got to talk about it.'

"He said, 'In other towns they would have favored the home team.' He asked Donovan, 'Didn't you have any doubt?'

"'None at all,' Donovan told him.

"I must tell you Kison's behavior was uncharacteristic of him. But he ached for that no-hitter.

"The last thing I wanted to do was to have Kison think we official scorers were ganging up on him, protecting ourselves by sticking together. I wanted to give him exactly what he was asking for, the benefit of the doubt. I went to at least a dozen people who were in the press box and took a poll. Everyone said it was a hit.

"I talked with two Pirate officials, Pete Peterson, the executive vice president, and Joe Brown, who was the general manager and is now a scout. Both of them said, 'Hit.'

"The Philadelphia Phillies' scout, Fred Goodman, was at the game. I asked him. He said, 'Even Mike Schmidt (the Phillies' third baseman) couldn't have fielded the ball.'

"The man closest to the play was Doug Rader, San Diego's third base coach. I checked with him. He said, 'If it had happened in the first inning, nobody would have paid any attention to it. For Kison to be saying anything now looks like he's looking for a cheap no-hitter.'

"I'll put it this way: If Garner had come up with that ball we would have written, 'The third baseman saved the no-hitter.' Now I ask you—should that type of ball be ruled a hit?"

And it was that type of ball that spelled the end of scoring for Charley Feeney. He has no regrets.

Feeney's boss, John Craig, editor of the *Post-Gazette,* received a call from Troan, the editor of the afternoon paper. Troan told him of his decision to ban *Press* sportswriters from scoring, beginning in 1980.

Craig called in Feeney. "I knew what he wanted to talk about—the scoring. We had talked about it before—whether or not the baseball writer should do it.

Feeney was right. "Sure, it's a conflict of interest," Feeney told his boss. "You make a call on a guy and he doesn't like it and then you have to do a feature on him. It's got to be uncomfortable."

"I'm glad you agree," said his editor. "There will be no more scoring after this year, but we'll compensate you for the money you lose. How would you feel if we quit the scoring now instead of waiting until the end of the year?"

"If it's a conflict of interest next April," said Feeney, "it's a conflict of interest now."

So the *Post-Gazette* decided to put an end to it today.

I asked Feeney, "Being an honest guy, why did you score up to now if you thought it was a conflict of interest?"

"Because they don't pay you enough in this job to give up the money," he said.

Now, you can't be more honest than *that*.

And that's why all of us who worked the baseball beat became official scorers. It came with the territory. Initially, it was the baseball writers who set up the scoring code and handled the major league statistics. This was long before baseball became so sophisticated and there was nobody else to keep the records.

It then became a simple matter for the American and National Leagues to continue to use writers as official scorers. It was convenient and inexpensive. At first scorers got a few dollars per game; now it's $50 per. Usually, two or more scorers split the season, so a writer can make as much as $2,000, a pittance in these inflationary times.

Not only must the scorer call the plays, he also must send a complete box score to the league. To qualify as an official scorer, one must have seen a certain number of games each year for several years. Newspaper editors, knowing baseball writers got this extra scoring money, often figured it was part of their salaries and consequently paid them as little as possible. This was a rip-off, for the baseball beat is by far the toughest job on the paper.

In fact, when I became baseball writer for the *Cleveland News,* the scoring income was mentioned by my superiors as an incentive to take the job.

But now, at long last, editors are beginning to realize their baseball writers are underpaid. And those papers that have put a ban on scoring have made up for it—as the *Post-Gazette* did in Feeney's case—and, I understand, the *Press* will do for Donovan next year.

Incidentally, our baseball writer, Dan Coughlin, doesn't score Indians' games. Russell Schneider, our football writer and former baseball writer, is the official scorer. Feeney thinks Bob Smizik, the football writer for the *Post-Gazette* who once was a baseball writer, will replace him as the official scorer.

There is no conflict of interest, in my opinion, when the writer isn't on the beat and doesn't have to talk with the players. Umpires don't have to walk into the dressing room to defend themselves after a call. And writers shouldn't put themselves in that position, either. This includes columnists.

It isn't a question of ethics. I never have seen an unethical scorer. But it definitely is a conflict of interest for it makes the job as a writer more difficult—and sometimes impossible.

Feeney gave me the perfect example.

"During the season when Lou Brock was on his way to the stolen base title, an official scorer didn't give him a hit when Brock thought he should have had one. Brock didn't talk to the guy the rest of the season. Now, Brock was the biggest baseball news that year. You had to talk to him if you were the baseball writer, and this guy couldn't. And it wouldn't have happened if he hadn't been an official scorer."

In my dozen years of scoring I had a few skirmishes with the players. Fortunately, none prevented me from getting the news. Still, I did hear the same Kison-lament over and over again: "Scorers in other towns favor their players. Why don't you?"

Even some of the Pirate players who admitted Donovan wasn't wrong in calling the hit last Sunday came weakly to the pitcher's defense with the feeble begging for a home town decision.

The "homer" rap is inevitable. Officials always are suspect, even if they're pure at heart.

Last year, Bob Forsch of the Cardinals got a no-hitter when the scorer charged an error on a wickedly hit ball. Naturally, it was said that he favored his home team.

Some years ago, John Drebinger of the *New York Times* called an early hit. When that proved to be the only one Allie Reynolds gave up, he asked Phil Rizzuto afterward if the shortstop should have handled the ball. If you know Phil, you could have bet your life on the answer. He gladly gave his pitcher a no-hitter by saying, "Sure, I should have made the play." Drebinger changed his call and the no-hitter is now in the record books.

Years ago there was a no-hitter here by Wesley Ferrell in which the local scorer kept giving second baseman Bill Hunnefield questionable errors (or so it seemed to several impartial fans)—he had three—to preserve it.

It makes no sense for a baseball writer to put himself in the position of being suspected as a homer, of trying to curry favors, or even of leaning over backward to avoid being one. I'm sure Drebinger would have asked the visiting shortstop if the rival pitcher missed a no-hitter on that call. But why should a writer be doing that? It's not part of his job and clearly interferes with it. He becomes part of the story, rather than covering it.

I understand Kison is now contrite. He says, "I never said it should have been an error. I just mentioned what happens in other towns."

Since he really is a decent sort, he must not be happy that he was the cause of the ban now being put into effect by the Pittsburgh papers. He likes both Donovan and Feeney and they happen to like him.

But he shouldn't bleed. It was coming. Kison merely hastened it. And by so doing, he did the writers—and readers—a favor. It's high time those of us who write about the ball players and ball games get out of the official scoring business.

What about Brown's book?

September 23, 1979

Paul Brown was one of the greatest football coaches, if not actually the greatest, in the history of the game. During his prime he had no equal in the pros.

He was far ahead of his time as an innovator, motivator, organizer, teacher, strategist . . . in almost every facet of the game That everyone began to copy him is the greatest tribute to his genius. It took years for his peers to catch up to his methods. He revolutionized pro football. A portion of the success it enjoys today is due to him.

Having paid him the ultimate tribute, I wish it was not necessary for me to discuss his latest effort, his book, *PB: The Paul Brown Story*, excerpted on these pages last week and scheduled for the book stores Oct. 16. It's not pleasant to dispute a legend.

But Paul asked for it. He wrote the book, one of the most self-serving autobiographies I have ever read. Being the resident critic behooves me to comment on his book, much as I would prefer to ignore it.

I was disappointed in Paul's literary effort, which is the most polite thing I can say about it. For a man who has achieved so much, attained the pinnacle of his profession and great wealth through it, the gross amount of back-patting is unnecessary and redundant. If there was some contrast, it might be more palatable. There is none.

Whenever he has stumbled in this life—and we all do—it is never his fault. He tries to vindicate himself and is vindictive against those over whom he failed to gain complete mastery.

Perhaps that's what it takes to be a success—total autocracy, complete control and those you can't run over become your enemies permanently. But it doesn't make for happiness. The bitterness in Paul is painfully evident. Too bad.

Jack Clary, the professional writer who worked with him, obviously put a tape recorder to Paul and let him spill his innards, and that's what Paul must have wanted. It's his book. The greatest indictment of the book is that it contains little warmth, or humor, or excitement. There could have been so much of the latter, for his life has been filled with thrilling and fulfilling moments. His teams gave us so much pleasure. Yet, that spark is missing. There is no drama whatsoever on the pages.

At least that's how it hit me. For Paul's sake, perhaps you will find it otherwise.

Admittedly, my eyes are different from yours. I know most of the characters intimately. I lived through the Paul Brown period here, covered it and had personal knowledge of some of the incidents he relates, two of which concerned me directly. That his mind has distorted both of them completely leads me to wonder about his interpretation of other incidents and about his memory concerning the actual facts.

A simple instance of that fuzziness: While he was coaching at Great Lakes, Arthur McBride signed him to a five-year contract with the Browns. He writes, *"My salary was to be $25,000 per year, plus five percent ownership of the team and a monthly retainer of $1,500 for as long as I stayed in the Navy."*

I have a copy of his contract, along with other ledgers from those McBride days. Brown got only $1,000 a month and one percent of the stock, not five, and he forgot that he also got 15 percent of the team's net earnings before taxes. That 15 percent is a big number and should not have been so easily forgotten. I'm sure Paul didn't try to twist the facts. His memory is merely playing him tricks and leads to a question of its credibility in other areas.

But in the two instances in which I was involved he did twist them. He saw only what he wanted, thought only what he wanted and to hell with the truth.

With respect to his dismissal by Art Modell in early 1963, he writes:

"A newspaper strike in Cleveland at the time played perfectly into Modell's hands because most of our fans got very few details about what happened, so the subject never was aired in a prolonged public forum. The announcement was timed to take advantage of the news blackout, and Modell had organized a full-scale publicity force to back him up. He had hired out-of-work sportswriters from the struck newspapers and they put out a pamphlet that was supposed to present all sides of the story. It was nothing but a 32-page justification for Modell, with selected comments from the players and a vague attempt to be objective with a couple of excerpts favorable to me from out-of-town columnists.

"The tenor of the pamphlet was struck when it quoted team captain Mike MacCormack as saying, 'The Browns cannot win the title with Paul as coach,' when what Mike really said was, 'The Browns cannot win a title with Paul as coach AND MODELL AS OWNER.' That was typical of Modell's method of using the media for his own purposes . . ."

Here are the facts and I defy Paul to prove otherwise. I put out that magazine. Modell had *nothing* whatsoever to do with it.

During the newspaper strike Bernard E. (Buddy) Rand, who still is one of our town's more prominent citizens, called me and asked if the writers would be interested in giving their views on the firing of Paul Brown. He owned Prompt Printing Company on West 28th St.

and Detroit Ave. The booklet would provide a small payday for each writer. He thought it would sell. He had no affiliation whatsoever with Modell. He asked me to serve as editor.

The sportswriters were rehearsing for our annual Ribs and Roasts show at the time. I asked them if they would be interested in writing for such a project. They agreed. Subjects were assigned and each was told to write exactly what he thought, let the rocks fall where they may. Not one word of their copy would be changed.

The result was the 32-pager titled "Paul Brown—The Play He Didn't Call." It sold for 25 cents; 50,000 were printed and 50,000 were sold. It is a collector's item today.

Incidentally, Modell was far from overjoyed with our product. He came in for his share of criticism. It definitely was not a whitewash by any measure.

As for Mike MacCormack's statement to Paul Brown, for whom he now works as a line coach, his quote was not the simple one Brown excerpts. It was nine rather fat paragraphs, some of which were extremely favorable to the coach. But in them he made the same statement *twice*, the second time being, *"I don't think we ever could win under Brown."*

The other incident in which I personally was involved is covered on Page 260 of Paul's book:

"The biggest change was ostensibly scrapping our messenger guard system and allowing quarterbacks to call their own plays. The furor over the play-calling system and our use of audibles had carried over from 1961, with the same tired and erroneous reasoning, and it was fueled again by Modell who by that time had some Cleveland sportswriters doing Jim Brown's radio shows and sports columns, as well as blasting away on his own."

I wrote the Jim Brown radio show. Unquestionably, Brown and Modell had different views on the freedom of speech for the players. Brown wanted no public spokesmen among them. Modell, who grew up in TV, disagreed, believing the more exposure the team got the better it was for the product. At present, Lyle Alzado and Reggie Rucker, among others, have radio shows. Until Modell came along, however, players had better keep it quiet or else. And indeed, for years they were afraid to talk.

In any event, Jim Brown was working for Pepsi Cola as a goodwill ambassador during his years here with the Browns. Pepsi decided to have Jim do a five-minute radio show each week, to be carried nationally. Batten, Barton, Durstine and Osborne was Pepsi's advertising agency in New York and their Cleveland representative, Robert Carr, who still lives here, came to me and asked if I would work with Jim and do the writing.

It was strictly Jim Brown, Pepsi, the agency and myself. Art Modell was not involved in any way. He was never mentioned. I would sit down with Jim; he would tell me what he wanted to say. I would condense it; he would check the copy and make whatever changes he desired and then he would cut the records in a New York studio. The show first was aired while the Browns were in training camp in Hiram.

One show was critical of the manner in which Paul Brown was handling his quarterback, Milt Plum. Jim had a high regard for Plum's ability.

Jim believed that Paul's play-calling and handling of Plum was undermining the quarterback's confidence and said so for his radio program. I mentioned to him that these were strong words and that there might be repercussions.

Jim said his words were honest and might have a beneficial effect. Apparently Paul Brown didn't hear the record the first time it was played. Nothing was said.

The Cleveland outlet was WGAR radio. An astute executive at the station reran the record the day after the Browns lost a tough one to the Giants. He decided Jim's comments seemed even more timely after that loss.

Moments after the five-minute show ended my phone rang. It was an unhappy Paul Brown. He didn't think it was right for me to allow Jim to say such things. He made disparaging remarks about Jim's character and said I should know better, etcetera, etcetera.

"Paul," I said, "I just put down Jim's words. It's his show. Why don't you tell him?"

I then phoned Jim Brown and told him of Paul's call. "You'll be hearing from him," I said.

"That's fine," he said. "But I don't think so."

And he never did.

That wasn't the old Paul Brown I knew, the one who challenged any player who crossed him. He had changed.

I also know something about the Ernie Davis situation. In the book, Paul says Modell wanted him to play the halfback, who was dying from leukemia. The University Hospital specialist brought into the case was Dr. Austin Weisberger, a recognized authority on the disease. He was my neighbor. Dr. Weisberger became very close to Ernie and his efforts led to a remission of the disease.

Dr. Weisberger and I often talked about Ernie. He told me Ernie's great wish was to get into at least one game for the Browns. "I'd like to see him get in on a kickoff," the doctor said. "It would do him a lot of good mentally and it wouldn't hurt him at all physically. He's going to die anyway."

Modell, who had become almost like a father to Ernie, tried to push the desire of both the player and the doctor onto Paul. I don't blame Paul for not playing him. Another doctor had cautioned against it. If I were the coach, I don't know what I would have done.

Although Paul's "interpretations" of the above incidents, for whatever reasons, are disturbing, what really bothers me most about the book is the cold, calculated brush-off he has given Blanton Collier. No finer, sweeter man ever lived. During the building years of the Browns he was Paul's right hand. Paul once told me, "He's the only assistant I wouldn't want to lose."

Many of the innovations during the Browns' great years were implemented by Collier. Otto Graham, in his book, wrote, "I want to pay my sincere respects to Blanton Collier, our backfield coach with whom I work quite closely. He is the man in whom I have complete confidence and tremendous respect as one of the finest technical football men in the game. He taught me a great deal about T-formation quarterbacking."

Yet Collier is scarcely mentioned in Paul's book, and certainly not in a laudatory manner. Apparently, Paul is still bitter that Collier replaced him—and successfully. When Collier took over after Paul was fired, retaining all of Paul's assistants, the old coach seemingly viewed this as an act of disloyalty, if not actually of treachery.

Yet Collier never would have taken the job if Paul had asked him not to. Collier, in fact, went to him for advice and Paul said to him, "You owe it to your family to take it."

I can forgive the inaccuracies, the slurs and innuendos concerning the writing fraternity, but I find it difficult to forgive the cut he has given Collier, that fine gentleman who doesn't have a disloyal breath in his body. I know how hurt Blanton will be when he reads the book. It's almost purposely cruel.

The crowning irony of the book comes in Paul's recitation of his dismissal of Jim Daniell, the Browns' first captain. Daniell, Mac Speedie and Lou Rymkus were arrested after an altercation with police following some night revelry. Only Daniell, now a highly successful industrialist, was released. He is still angry at Brown.

Brown writes, "I suppose his resentment and bitterness stemmed from my not dismissing the other two players, but there was no reason to. It's too bad that something like this should cause a man to be bitter for so many years . . . "

Why then, Paul might well ask himself, is he so bitter after all these years?

I feel a real sense of sorrow for Paul. It's sad to see a man so big remain so petty.

From another planet?

January 23, 1979

I want to apologize for 23 fellow members of the Baseball Writers Association of America.

They must have been living on another planet. Or they're jerks. That's about as kind as I can get.

Those are the 23 who didn't put Willie Mays' name on their Hall of Fame ballots, the 23 who didn't make his election unanimous.

What more could they want from a player? What is there in the game that Willie didn't do?

Run? He was an outstanding base stealer and runner, getting every possible extra base.

Field? I never saw a better center fielder.

Throw? He could get the ball quicker to the infield than anybody I ever saw.

And he did it all for years and years, rarely missing a game until the seasons caught up with him.

Dan Coughlin, our baseball writer, may have nailed the reason at least some of those 23 omitted him.

"You're lucky," said Dan. "You knew Willie when he was young and easy to approach. After he became a super star he treated some of us like dirt. We would ask for a minute of his time and he would get downright nasty."

Admittedly, I never saw that side of him. But, so what? The Hall of Fame vote is for accomplishments on the baseball field, not a citation for diplomacy or for the social graces. Ted Williams never would have made the Hall if it depended on his relations with writers. You couldn't exactly call Ted a sweetie pie.

Happily, both Willie and Ted were so brilliant they overcame the petty few who indulge in personalities. And 409 writers did recognize Willie's peerless talents at the very first opportunity to do so. Shame on the 23 who didn't.

I voted for Mays, Duke, Snider, Enos Slaughter and Gil Hodges. I saw them play, studied their records and judged these men to be of Cooperstown caliber.

And then, as a gesture to their remarkable accomplishments, I added the names of Roger Maris and Maury Wills. I didn't expect these two to get many votes and I doubt if they ever will. Yet, I felt that their historical home run and base stealing feats, respectively, deserved some special recognition.

Still, I can't quarrel with anyone who says one brilliant season isn't enough to merit joining the all-time greats.

Nor can I argue vehemently about the relative near-misses of my other candidates. They were fine players, but not in Mays' class. So few are. I wish Slaughter had made it for this was his last chance in the BBWAA vote. I think Snider will make it on next year's ballot.

The trouble with Halls of Fame is that some guys always get in who don't belong and others much better are left out. The records show this. I can name several in the shrine who couldn't carry Slaughter's glove. He knows it—and it hurts.

Of course, there is no perfect way to conduct Hall of Fame elections. The pro football Hall does its selecting by a small committee and for some unexplainable reason each year they overlook and deeply wound former Clevelander Benny Friedman, who contributed as much to the game in those early years as men already enshrined.

Because the pain is so deep in those who don't get in. I'm not big on these Halls. The buildings in Cooperstown and Canton would be just as attractive as historical museums for their respective sports without the Hall of Fame hoopla. Art museums are highly successful without being a Hall of Fame for the artists.

There is too much politics involved in the selections; personalities play too great a part. I was against the new Cleveland Sports Hall of Fame for these reasons and each election reveals a strong basis for my opposition. Some of the voting borders on the ridiculous by any standard.

Since Halls of Fame never will be abolished, it behooves all who vote to do so with total objectivity. A man belongs, or he doesn't, exclusively on his performance. I'd like to hear the explanations from our 23 members for not voting Willie in. Again, as a member of the Baseball Writers, I apologize for them. They can have no valid reason.

Doesn't baseball owe us one?

August 9, 1981

Baseball owes us one.

If baseball's executives want to play square with Cleveland they will schedule a real, live, legitimate All-Star Game at the Stadium at the earliest opportunity.

The classic has been awarded to specific cities for the next three or four years. But as soon as these commitments run out, baseball should make up for the charade being foisted on our community.

It's so easy to visualize the brainstorming in baseball's high places that made Cleveland fans the victim:

The long strike was ending and Commissioner Bowie Kuhn and his advisers agreed a big event was needed to bring baseball before the nation's sports fans again. Get their minds off (ugh) football.

Ah, the All-Star Game on TV. On prime time Sunday night, before the season resumes. That would be perfect.

It costs nothing to watch on TV. Should have a high rating. Would NBC go for it? Does a peacock have feathers?

So what if an 8:30 P.M. starting time would be an inconvenience to Cleveland fans who would have to get up early the next morning to go to work? So what if the players hadn't played a game for two months? So what if all the plans Cleveland had made for a gala would be wiped out? The money was in the bank, almost $1.5 million. Take it and run.

Sure there would be some refunds, but with 75,000 tickets sold, a big crowd was guaranteed.

This is a show strictly for TV. That's what baseball needs now. And what's good for baseball is good for the nation. To hell with Cleveland.

Of course, the players aren't objecting because the money goes into their pension fund.

So ready or not, the ripoff will be played tonight.

And that's why Baseball owes us a bona fide All-Star Game, one with all the festivities intact, one with stars who are ready to play, one worthy of the name All-Star, at the earliest opportunity.

One executive, who asked not to be identified, apparently does have guilty feelings over how Cleveland is being used.

"I'm all for returning the game to your town as soon as possible. Cleveland deserves it."

The nation will see that tonight when the all-time attendance record, already established by Cleveland, will be broken.

I won't be among the crowd, even though I have a free press seat. Nor did I attend the sumptuous free bash put on by Commissioner Kuhn last night. I'm not trying to be a hero or a martyr. But feeling as I do about the farce it would be hypocritical of me to attend. It's no big deal, but I figure if I, as a sports editor, don't show in my own home town it's got to have some slight impact on baseball officials, just in case they are too calloused otherwise to realize the high-handed manner in which they have taken advantage of us.

A friend thinks I have been too harsh and am letting my personal anger take over my reasoning. He also says I'm being childish.

I'm really not angry. My blood pressure hasn't gone up a notch. But as the opinion-writer for these pages, I must call 'em as I see 'em, and I think charging $15 and $20 for this game after a strike of two months is a ripoff.

I know the All-Star Game is an exhibition at its best, but I can't remain silent when the game at its worst is crammed down the pocketbooks of our fans—at top prices yet. As for being childish in not attending, maybe so. But in good conscience I can't go.

"Won't you be surprised if it's a good game?" asked my friend.

"Not at all," was my reply. "You can get a fine game on the sandlots when kids choose up sides. They should be evenly matched, since both squads are unready."

My friend came back with, "What are you going to say when 70,000 people are there and you're home? You're going to be mad because they didn't listen to you."

Not at all. I can understand why fans will be there tonight. It's a happening. They bought their tickets in advance. Their kids who have been looking forward to it will be disappointed if they don't go. They don't want to bother with the refund. They don't want to lose the $2 service charge. They want to be part of the scene. They want the memories.

Fine.

It *will* be a happening and will set several firsts—the first to be played so late, the first to start a second season, etc. It will be hashed over for years.

Also it will be the first time one Stadium has hosted the game four times. We should make it five in the not-too-distant future, if baseball officials want to prove they really are fair-minded.

I did attend the other three games and personal memories of them will have to suffice.

The first All-Star Game played at the lakefront Stadium was on July 8, 1935. I sold candy bars in the stands that afternoon and was more involved in making a buck for my college tuition than in the exploits of the stars. But I did sneak in as many looks as possible.

It was the time of the Great Depression and I had been hustling at League Park, where most the Indians' games were played. But the All-Star Game was too big an event for the cozy park at E. 66th and Lexington.

A call went out for vendors to augment the small staff that easily covered League Park. The newcomers decided to make the most of this opportunity. They doubled the prices on drink, ice cream and popcorn. Off went the price stickers that had been stuck in our caps.

I was selling Baby Ruth candy bars, a 10-cent item at ball parks, twice as much as at candy stores. We got a 20 percent commission. I saw other vendors selling them for 15 cents to the crowd of 69,812. The fans were too star-struck to complain, so after fighting with my conscience for a while I followed suit.

I have had some pangs of guilt ever since. Perhaps it has made my conscience stronger.

The All-Star Game had been introduced two years before, the brainchild of Arch Ward, sports editor of the *Chicago Tribune*, the money to go to various charities. The fans did the voting and the *Tribune* counted the ballots. But even then there was controversy over the selections. So in 1935 the vote was taken away from the fans and the two rival managers, Mickey Cochrane of the American League and Frankie Frisch of the National, had the awesome burden of picking their squads.

Two members of the Indians were on Cochrane's team: left fielder Joe Vosmik, a native Clevelander, and Mel Harder, the brilliant pitcher who had been the star of the All-Star Game the year before.

Vosmik played the full nine innings, singled in the fifth, went to third on Charley Gehringer's single—I remember Joe stumbling between second and third as the crowd caught its collective breath, but he made it—and then scored on Jimmie Foxx's single. Harder, once again, was brilliant, pitching the final three innings without trouble.

Cochrane, the player-manager for the Detroit Tigers, had told his players prior to the game that he would use the same plan Connie Mack had instituted in the first All-Star Game in 1933. If his team went ahead he would stay with the regulars.

The Americans jumped to a 2-0 lead on Foxx's blast deep into the left field seats in the first inning, and after that Cochrane did little substituting. Mickey, who had planned to start himself behind the plate, backed off for Rollie Hemsley when he saw a left-hander, Bill Walker, warming up for the Nationals. Mickey never did put himself into the game. So the other subs couldn't complain.

Hero of the game was the muscular Foxx, knocking in three of the four runs. The record-breaking crowd grossed $93,692.80, meaning the average ticket price was considerably under $2, revealing how great a depression we were in.

Incidentally, there was no outfield fence at the Stadium then. A friend, Bill Wotsch, who was sitting in the bleachers, remembers a drive hit by Lou Gehrig. It was caught near the track in dead center—a sure home run today. I missed that one. I was trying to sell a candy bar at the time.

I have a better recollection of the second All-Star Game played here, July 13, 1954, because I was covering it and because a Cleveland player was the hero and all our advance stories questioned whether or not he should be allowed to play.

Several weeks before the game, Al Rosen had broken his right index finger. Normally a third baseman, Rosen had been moved to first by Indians manager Al Lopez to get Rudy Regalado, a rookie who had had a torrid spring, into the lineup.

Playing that new position, Rosen fractured the finger while fielding a grounder. It was a severe, painful break. Rosen had difficulty gripping a bat.

That year the All-Star team was chosen in the same manner it is today, by a poll of the fans with the two managers, Casey Stengel for the Americans and Walter Alston for the Nationals, selecting the balance of the squad. Rosen was a big winner in the vote. Other Indians who were on the squad: Bobby Avila, Larry Doby and Bob Lemon. Stengel had chosen Mike Garcia, but he was injured and had to be replaced.

Would Rosen play? Should he ask to sit out and rest up for the balance of the season, inasmuch as the Indians were in contention? (That was the year they won a record 111 games and the pennant.)

The crowd of 68,751—bringing in the top gross of all the classics up to that time, $292,687—cheered mightily when Rosen was announced as the starting first baseman.

He responded in story-book style in a game many still consider the most exciting of all the classics. It even had a major argument. And Rosen was the star of the stars as the Americans won, 11-9.

He struck out the first time up, and it was thought that would be his token appearance, but Casey stayed with him to his great delight. In Rosen's next two at-bats he socked home runs and then finished up with a single, knocking in a total of five runs. Because the game was so close, Stengel kept him in until the final out, shifting him to third base in the ninth.

All the Indians did well. Avila had a perfect day, three-for-three, and Doby, pinch hitting for pitcher Dean Stone in the eighth, homered to tie the score and then finished in center field. Lemon pitched part of the fourth inning in relief.

The blasting began in the third inning when Rosen socked a three-run homer and Ray Boone, once an Indian, followed him with another. The Nationals kept pace and the lead continued to shift.

The drama heightened in the eighth inning. The Nationals went ahead, 9-8, and continued to threaten, putting runners on first and third with two outs. Stengel summoned Dean Stone of Washington from the bullpen to face Duke Snider.

As Stone started his third pitch, Red Schoendienst, who was on third base, surprised everybody, especially Stone, by racing for home. Stone hurried his motion. Catcher Yogi Berra grabbed the pitch and nipped Schoendienst at the plate.

The Nationals' two coaches, Leo Durocher at third and Charley Grimm at first, screamed to plate umpire Bill Stewart that Stone had balked. (I was certain he did, too.) But Stewart said no. A lengthy argument ensued, but ended the way all these arguments do.

Now the Americans trailed by one run. Doby's pinch homer tied it and then, after all those lightning bolts, a little blooper by Nellie Fox scored two more runs and that put the Americans ahead to stay.

Ironically, Stone, who didn't retire a batter and who almost balked, was the pitcher of record when the Americans went ahead. So he became the winner.

The third All-Star Game here, played July 9, 1963, was comparatively mild. The crowd, too, was a letdown. Only 44,160 fans were at the Stadium to see the Nationals beat the Americans, 5-3. What I remember most clearly about that game was a toothache. Alvin Dark, manager of the Nationals, had it. In the dugout before the game he asked me if I could locate a dentist. I knew of one, a Dr. Baden, who had a box seat near the dugout. Baden, an avid fan, said he would see Alvin after the game.

Once again the vote had been taken away from the fans and given to the players, managers and coaches. Jim (Mudcat) Grant was the only Cleveland player selected, which partially may have accounted for the limited local fan interest. And Mudcat didn't get into the game.

In one of the finest tributes ever accorded a player by his peers, Mickey Mantle was named starting center fielder for the Americans, even though they knew Mickey wouldn't be able to play because of a broken foot.

Ken McBride, Cleveland-bred pitcher and West High grad, started for the Americans and gave up one run in the second and two in the third. His teammates matched the tallies so he wasn't the loser. But that was all the scoring for the Americans while the Nationals picked up single runs in the fifth and eighth.

After the victory I drove Dark to the dentist's downtown office. The toothache cured, the manager was finally able to savor the victory.

Tonight's 1981 All-Star Game? Tell me about it.

Will the cheating ever stop?

January 17, 1982

When Moses Malone was a high school senior at Petersburg, Va., the seven-footer was coveted by almost every major college basketball team. Recruiters pounced on him everywhere he turned. The offers were unbelievable. One recruiter said for starters he would get a Cadillac.

That one Malone believed, for, as if by magic, a brand new Cadillac was parked in front of his door the next day.

While on vacation in Florida recently, the big story was Howard Schnellenberger. The coach has turned the University of Miami (Fla.) football around. Would he stay there? The stories said he had big offers.

Miami came up with an annual income for him, according to the headlines. He is staying at Miami. More power to him. Still, that's more than any professor at the university makes, or college presidents. It's more than many pro coaches receive.

Let's end all the illusions. Big-time college football and basketball are pro sports. Even in the most moral and sacred halls of learning, it's only a matter of degree.

It is expected that soon the NCAA will blow the whistle on the recruiting practices at Clemson, the nation's No. 1 football team. In recent weeks, both UCLA and Wichita State have been put on probation because of unethical basketball recruiting.

If the NCAA had the manpower and subpoena power and the threat of perjury to go with it, I suspect it would find questionable recruiting practices at the great majority of our big-time colleges.

The sad truth is that virtually no one is shocked. When Jim Killingsworth, the Texas Christian University basketball coach, was asked how his players reacted to the news that the NCAA had placed the school on probation, he said, "They turned up their stereos so loud when I told them, I couldn't tell."

In effect, that's what the public does too. Even alumni—make that especially alumni—greet probation for their school with indifference: "Just don't get caught next time."

There always have been unethical recruiting practices. But since the mad scramble for the best athlete is greater than ever now, because the rewards are so much greater, the cheating appears to have grown proportionately.

Bobby Knight, the brilliant Indiana University basketball coach who makes a passion of being beyond reproach in his recruiting and who is looked upon as an exception by many of his envious peers, thinks it's ridiculous for the NCAA champion to receive a prize of about $370,000. He says there should be a ceiling of $100,000, including expenses, for the winner and the rest of the pot divided among all the other Division I schools.

Television is the partner in the crime. The networks vie for the product. College basketball is much more attractive to the TV moguls than is the NBA. A college gets $50,000 and more for being on the basketball Game of the Week. In addition, there are cable networks and state networks eager to pay for the show.

Look what is happening in football now because of the big TV bucks. Several colleges are trying to break away from the NCAA Game-of-the-Week package and form their own schedule on another network so they can get a bigger portion of the ever-growing TV pot.

All this means a greater demand for the best athletes. They are the performers, no different than a singer or an actor who gets a high audience rating. So the college coaches check out every summer playground league. A white face is not to be seen near a New York ghetto except when there is a game on a Harlem playground which breeds stop players.

The "best" coach is the best recruiter however he obtains his talent. Pete Newell, who once coached the University of California to the national championship and finally got out of the college rat race because recruiting became odious to him, says, "Schools don't ask if a coach is a decent, moral man. They ask, 'Can he recruit? Can he sell?'"

That's what the coach has become—a salesman. There were few better than glib Al McGuire at Marquette. When he was recruiting Maurice Lucas, now with the New York Knicks, he said, "I'll get you on national television five times a year . . ."

That pitch appeals to a kid from the streets who dreams of getting exposure for his carefully nurtured moves and the dollars he might make some day in the pros. It also underscores an ancillary power TV is exerting on college sports.

All right. Let's accept college sports for what they are—professional. By jamming the stadiums and arenas, by giving high ratings to the big games, the public has condoned and encouraged the present practices no matter how stinking some of them have become.

We virtually ignore the games between the simon pure colleges—those in the Presidents' Athletic Conference and the Ohio Conference, for example, where the kids play just as hard—and opt for the distorted big-time charade.

Mainly, I am disturbed by the manner in which the "pro" colleges are using the kids, taking advantage of the disadvantaged for their own profit.

In a remarkable book just published, *The Breaks of the Game,* by far the best I have read about pro basketball and basketball in general, David Halberstam, the Pulitzer Prize author, quotes Wayne Embry on college recruiters:

"They're so smooth, so friendly, there's not a question they don't know the answer to. It's 'yes, yes, we can take care of that. We can fix that.'"

Embry, you may remember, was a poor Ohio farm boy who played for Miami (O.) University, then with the Cincinnati Royals, appearing here many times at the Arena. He became an executive with the Milwaukee Bucks and is now a highly successful fast food chain executive and still does scouting for the Bucks. He remembers when he was heavily recruited back in 1955. He was almost giddy about the thought of going to Ohio State. He felt a magic about the books and the brilliant professors.

It all vanished the night he was the dinner guest of a top state official. Embry was told he could study three times a week in that official's office and receive $90 a week in salary—big money in 1955—just for studying. At that moment, he knew that, for him, there was something terribly wrong with Ohio State. His parents always had drilled into him, "Expect to work for what you get. That's the time before college. That's the time after." Poor as they were, the Embrys were "outraged" by their son's experience at Columbus.

Miami offered tuition and room and demanded he work in the dining hall to help pay for it. This fit the philosophy ingrained in him by his parents. He has no regrets he chose Miami.

Embry, because of what he has seen during his own college days and as a pro, has helped steer prospects of his acquaintance to what he considers a school that will prove beneficial to the athlete—after he gets out. Too many colleges seem to be saying, according to Embry, "You can cheat on life as long as your jump shot goes on." He adds, "And that, my friend, is not as long as you think."

Embry's words should be burned into the brain of every kid who dreams that sports is his ticket to a brighter future. Merely going to a college, taking the offers, and shooting baskets too often can wind up a big zero.

Clinton Smith of John Adams High School already is being swarmed over by recruiters. The 6-5 Smith is considered by many basketball brains as the best guard in the state. If he and others in similarly enviable shoes want some valuable free advice, I recommend they listen to

Ira Novak, a local insurance executive who has made sponsorship of amateur basketball a hobby and, as a consequence, has become close to many of the top high school athletes in the area.

He has been involved in the college choices of six outstanding area athletes. Five of the six selected different schools, revealing Novak has the interest of the athlete solely at heart and is not hustling for any specific school.

He has seen the pressure recruiters put on star athletes. He knows how they can romance them. Here are some of his "commandments":

- "The NCAA allows six official visits to a college. The athlete should make unofficial visits on his own, without the coach's knowledge. Begin the visits in your junior year. Get a feel for everyday life on the campus.
- "Don't listen seriously to alumni if you or your parents don't know the individual. Many of them are Monday morning cheerleaders and name-droppers.
- "Talk to some of the players who dropped out of the school after they were recruited to see how they were treated by the coach.
- "You know your position. Find out who else is being recruited for that position. If you can't visualize playing by the first quarter of your sophomore year, go to another school. All coaches tell good players, 'You'll start for us.' Remember, that's a sales pitch.
- "Even if it's a lifetime dream, FORGET about pro sports. If you happen to make it, fine. But don't bank on it. The number of college players who make it is infinitesimal.
- "Go to a school where your name will benefit you in the future. A good name is your greatest asset." [As a personal note, my choice of Western Reserve University had the greatest influence on my future. It was the best move I could have made.]
- "Know the exact terms of the scholarship. Don't go with your hand out. Listen carefully and ask questions. Check every aspect of what the coaches tell you.
- "Can they help you get a meaningful summer job, one which will have a bearing on your future?
- "Does the coach have a history of showing an interest in his athletes after they graduate, such as Woody Hayes did? Study the coach's background."

Novak points out that many coaches have only a temporary loyalty to the school, especially the assistants who generally do the recruiting. They always are trying to advance to a head coaching position somewhere. Also, the head coach who is selling the school probably never went there and soon may be moving.

He advises parents, "It's your son's life they're playing with. The college of his choice and his objectives in life go hand in hand. Help him. One athlete last year visited a Big Ten school. The boy wanted to major in business. The assistant coach took him to meet the dean of the business school but didn't even know the dean's name. Both the parent and the boy were perceptive enough to eliminate that school immediately.

"The boy must come out of college with a means to earn a livelihood. He must have his degree in something he can use. And he's got to play for that from the first day he listens to a recruiter. He should use the opportunity his talents provide. If the school also uses him, at least it's a fair exchange."

I especially like the way Reverend Theodore Hesburgh, president of the University of Notre Dame, puts it: "A decade after graduation, almost everyone will have forgotten where and what they played. But every time they speak, everyone will know whether or not they are educated."

There is a solution which virtually would guarantee every recruited athlete an education. It is being pushed by Bobby Knight, who prides himself that 31 of the 38 players he recruited for Indiana now have their degrees. He explains his plan simply: "I have four seniors this year. For me to replace them with new scholarships, these four seniors would have to graduate within a prescribed amount of time."

This, he says, is the only way to stop the cheating, for it will force the coaches to recruit students with a chance to get a degree. Knight and a few other coaches have pushed for the plan to be adopted by the NCAA. It doesn't have a chance The hell with the kids. Too many colleges want to win at any cost.

Oh, by the way, Moses Malone didn't take the Cadillac. The pros offered him a more expensive car and money. He skipped college. He decided to be an honest pro.

Hall of Fame for a cheater?

May 11, 1982

I need your help.

Assuming Gaylord Perry won't pitch forever, he's going to be eligible for the baseball Hall of Fame five years after he retires. If I'm still around, I'll be getting a ballot.

Normally, there would be no question about a guy who won 300 games going into the hallowed Hall. His admission would be automatic.

But how about an admitted cheater?

A few years ago, when Ferguson Jenkins was picked up for having illegal drugs in his suitcase, I said I never could vote him into the Hall of Fame.

One of our editors said, "Would you have voted for Babe Ruth?" His point was that Ruth was reputed to be a carouser, yet belonged in the Hall. He said a player should make it on his baseball achievements alone and not be barred because of his off-the-field activities.

If Ruth had been convicted of anything illegal while he was an active player, I'd have knocked him out of the box, too. Ruth was a colorful character. But I know of no unlawful acts he committed. He always was great with kids and made every public effort to look good in their eyes.

Perry is the perfect citizen off the field; far superior to Ruth. He is a fine husband and father, hard worker and exceptional competitor. But he is an admitted cheat.

When he pitched for the Indians and was accused of throwing a doctored ball—supposedly, he applied some rapidly evaporating jelly to it—I asked him point blank and he denied it. Instead of a splendid spitter, he was throwing a splendid sinker.

His catcher, Ray Fosse, also said the pitches were legitimate. Even off the record, he said so.

Then Gaylord exposed himself in *Me and the Spitter*, an autobiography written with the aid of former *Press* columnist Bob Sudyk. Although Perry was careful to say he no longer was throwing one, he confessed he had done some cheating in the past.

And Fosse, after leaving the Indians, admitted he had fibbed when he defended Perry.

Now, here's why I come to you, dear reader. As a Hall of Fame voter, I believe I represent you, the fan. Those enshrined in Cooperstown are your heroes. Each year, when I vote, I try to cast my ballot for you. But maybe I'm too strict, too square.

Let's try to make a case for Gaylord:

He never was caught throwing the illegal pitch, at least not to my knowledge, by the umpires. If he had not made the public admission, I still would be convinced, trusting soul that I am, he never cheated.

Gaylord, while not saying he still throws the slippery ball, argues that hitters try to cheat. Some have been caught doctoring their bats, putting cork inside, etc.

There already are a number of cheaters in the Hall of Fame. After Whitey Ford was elected, some of his New York Yankees pals disclosed what hitters had suspected: In his declining years, Whitey threw a "cut ball." His catcher, Elston Howard, supposedly would slash the ball slightly with his sharp belt buckle. The Hall of Fame didn't collapse after Ford's cheating came to light and nobody asked for a recount.

Mike Garcia, the Big Bear who was a member of perhaps the greatest pitching staff of all time, once confided that, on a rare occasion, he threw the spitter. "Maybe a dozen in my life," he said. "I'm sure plenty of the great pitchers did."

Yesterday, I asked the former Indians pitcher if he'd vote Gaylord into the Hall of Fame.

"I don't think he throws an illegal pitch," said Garcia. "Cameras, umpires never caught him. I think he said it to worry the hitters. But I don't know if I'd vote him. Besides, I think the Hall of Fame is a lot of bull."

I called Bob Feller in Seattle, where he was last night for the Indians' cable telecast.

"I'd have to give this a lot of serious thought," said Feller, a true Hall of Famer. "Putting something on the ball is no different from sticking a needle in it. At first glance, I'd be inclined not to vote in somebody who was doing something illegal.

"But Gaylord might have written what he did just to sell the book. I think before I voted, I'd have to sit down with Gaylord and discuss it with him personally."

Today, Gaylord is saying he hopes people will talk about his achievement and not about "that pitch."

But some day, the good Lord willing, I'm going to have to vote. I agree with Garcia about the Hall of Fame being bull. But it's there.

I wish the spitter, not the grease ball, were legal, as it once was. But it isn't. And I wish Gaylord hadn't written the book. But he did—for the money. Should that cost him immortality? That's what it amounts to.

So how would you vote if you had my ballot? Should Gaylord Perry be in the Hall of Fame? Yes or no? (Circle and return, plus comments, if any.) I won't promise to change my view, but I'll listen. I want your thinking.

The void at City Hall

January 23, 1983

A teenager from a broken home was a constant problem to his neighborhood. He was especially destructive on the playground. He was in juvenile court 15 times.

John Nagy, Cleveland's recreation commissioner, thought he could be rehabilitated. He talked it over with the city's maintenance supervisor, and they decided to hire him.

That boy, a respected citizen today, is still working for the city. He even invented the vandal-proof park bench.

A basketball team won the district AAU crown, entitling the players to represent this area in the national tournament. The backer said he could afford no more than $1,000 for the trip. It would take $3,000. John Nagy got on the phone, soon had the money, and the players got the trip they earned.

A young athlete from a destitute family had difficulty hanging on in college, because he needed clothes and other items his scholarship didn't provide. Nagy gave him a summer job as a lifeguard. Today he is coaching in the National Football League.

The name? There are several. The late Don McCafferty, once head coach of the Baltimore Colts, was a Nagy "graduate." So is Carl Taseff, now with the Miami Dolphins. The list goes on.

"More than half the coaches in Greater Cleveland can thank John for where they are," says Andy Okulovich, the former East High and

Ohio State star who is still with the recreation department. "He took the athletes from the old neighborhoods and gave us our start as playground instructors or lifeguards. Today those coaches are helping other kids."

A few weeks ago on a holy day, Nagy was passing St. Philip Neri Catholic Church, E. 82nd and St. Clair, so he dropped in for the noon mass. The priest, Father Vavco, met everyone at the door after the service. He saw Nagy and threw his arms around him, "Ah, Commissioner Nagy," he said, "you are a wonderful human being. If it wasn't for you, I wouldn't be wearing these robes. You gave me a job at St. Clair Bath House. You kept a lot of kids out of trouble."

It would be impossible for a man in public life for more than 44 years not to have some enemies. No doubt John Nagy has a hidden few, for he has had to fight politicians and make decisions not pleasing to everybody. But if he were to cash in on his good deeds, the line of people in his debt would be much longer than the debtors of AmeriTrust.

One week from tomorrow he will receive the highest honor given at the annual Sports Media of Cleveland and Ohio (SMACO) banquet, the Pride of Cleveland Award.

As prestigious as this honor is, it is just one of many of equal or greater magnitude he has received as a humanitarian or for his national contributions in the field of recreation.

There no longer is any room for awards in his modest home on W. 63rd St., just above Nagy Blvd., the drive that threads between Rose and Elder softball fields in Brookside Park. Nagy was the force that caused those fields to be built.

Last Friday the Cleveland Baseball Federation threw a party for John. The parties probably will be endless in the coming weeks. He will be 70 April 29. Three days later will be his last in City Hall. He is retiring.

Nagy doesn't have to retire and nobody is pushing him. His departure will cause a great void in Room 8 of City Hall, the dingy basement office that houses the recreation department and from which Nagy has spread so much light.

"I've had enough," he says. "It's time for somebody else."

Fortunately for us, he isn't walking away entirely from sports and recreation. He has just been re-elected head of the Golden Gloves, secretary of the Cleveland Baseball Federation, and Commissioner of Softball for this entire area.

Unquestionably, his greatest achievement has been to survive the heat of local politics. He first worked under Mayor Harold Burton. Then came Edward Blythen, Frank Lausche, Tom Burke, Anthony Celebrezze, Ralph Locher, Carl Stokes, Ralph Perk, Dennis Kucinich, and now George Voinovich.

Incidentally, Voinovich, a Republican, is another who is indebted to Nagy, a Democrat. Party lines meant nothing to Nagy. He once gave a youthful Voinovich a job in the recreation department's warehouse.

Stokes also worked for Nagy. While in college, he was a summer instructor at Portland-Outhwaite playground. "He was a good worker and he could box. He had good discipline," Nagy recalls.

Nagy says he never had conflicts with the mayors but occasionally with their "stooges." When Stokes was mayor his personnel director wanted to take over all the hiring in the recreation department.

Nagy said no. He wanted the most qualified. His motto: "If you don't have good supervision, you don't have a program."

Stokes called in his personnel chief. "Let John alone," the mayor said. "He runs the best recreation department in the country."

Nagy rates Burke the best of all the mayors he worked under. "He had the most guts. We only had six swimming pools in the entire city. I said, 'Tom, we need 10 more, five on the East Side and five on the West.'" Burke called in his finance director. When told by Nagy the cost would be "a little over $1 million," the finance director said, "You're crazy."

"Find the money," ordered Burke and the 10 pools were built. The next year another 10 were added. Nagy's philosophy: "It's better to spend the money to keep the kids in healthy activities than in jails."

Says Nagy, "Do you know it costs less to send a kid to Harvard for one year than to house a prisoner for the same period?"

Nagy was asked to run for mayor many times. He recalls, "An attorney, Henry Gottfried, was so sure I could get elected he offered to put $50,000 in escrow. It would be mine, he said, if I lost. I'm glad I didn't run. The Hough riots came during the next administration."

Nagy is an attorney. He practiced for two years before joining City Hall and working his way up to a post involving his lifelong love—sports. At Ohio State he had pitched for the baseball varsity and was on the football squad. Son of a Hungarian immigrant father, he needed a job to get through college. He and Jesse Owens, the track great, worked as pages in the Ohio House and became friends for life. Nagy's roommate at Columbus was Jim Rhodes.

"Rhodes always said, 'I'm going to be governor some day.' We laughed at him," says Nagy.

After graduation Nagy was signed by the Detroit Tigers and had a fling in their farm system. In 1935 he went to spring training with the big club at Orlando, Fla.

"They had Hank Greenberg, Charley Gehringer, Billy Rogell, and other stars. The manager was Mickey Cochrane, the great catcher, but he was a little bit crazy, I think.

"I was there a week, pretty much standing around. I saw the batting cage empty so I went in. Cochrane ran up and yelled, 'Get out, you hamburger. Get on the bus and get the hell out of here!'

"In the clubhouse I got dressed and began to cry. Greenberg asked what happened. After I told him he said, 'Don't worry about a thing. You're going to dinner tonight with me and Gehringer.' They treated me great and told me to suit up again the next day.

"I did and Cochrane didn't even remember what happened."

He was assigned to the Atlanta farm team, managed by Paul Richards, now the general manager of the Texas Rangers.

"We called him 'god' because that's what he seemed to think he was," Nagy remembers.

"One evening some musicians from Cleveland entertained in our hotel. I listened to them and took the elevator to my room at 1 A.M. Richards was in it. He gave me holy hell. Right after that we played in Little Rock. The temperature was 112 and he had me pitch in the bullpen from the first inning to the ninth. My neck became so sunburned it blistered.

"He was trying to teach me a lesson. He taught me one all right—how not to treat people. Then he sent me to Bluefield, W.Va."

At Bluefield he was a passenger in a friend's old Ford. It hit a hole and Nagy went through the windshield, cutting his pitching elbow and ending his pro career. He came home, practiced law, pitched on the local sandlots, and eventually became sandlot boss.

Nagy has been an innovative commissioner. He boosted women's sports long before it became fashionable. When the Ridge Maintenance girls won the national slow pitch softball championship in Sheboygan, Wis., in 1967, they were given a huge salami as a trophy.

Grateful for the help and encouragement Nagy had provided, they presented it to the commissioner. He hung it over his desk at City Hall for a year before the staff ate it.

He organized numerous bowling leagues for city employees. Many still laugh about the time Nagy was bowling and his ball suddenly split in half before it reached the pins. That "trophy" remains in his home. Whenever he needs a chuckle, he merely looks at those two halves.

In his capacity as chairman of various amateur sports he has traveled the world. He went to Rome with the Olympic boxing and basketball teams in 1960, was in Mexico City as an official in the 1968 Olympics.

In Rome Nagy got to know Cassius Clay long before he became Muhammad Ali.

"Our boxing team went nuts in Rome," Nagy recalls. "They never had seen anything like that city and the minute they got out of our sight they went for a good time. That's the reason we won only three medals.

"Cassius won one of them. He wasn't like the others. He trained hard, would go to bed early, and read his Bible until he fell asleep. He had no specific religion then. He was just a Bible student."

Years later, when Ali refused to be drafted, stating he was a conscientious objector and was put on trial in Houston, Nagy went there as a character witness. "I told them about the young man I knew at the Olympics. Even then he told me he hated war."

The United States basketball team, with Oscar Robertson, Jerry West, Jerry Lucas, and others who became stars in the NBA, swept Russia for the gold medal.

"Robertson showed me something," remembers Nagy. "We were electing a captain and it was between Robertson and West. I was counting the votes and Robertson won. Oscar got up and said, 'This is a big enough job for all of us. Let's share it.' They became co-captains."

The Olympics in Mexico City were memorable for the "black power salute" three track winners gave during the playing of the national anthem. "Jesse Owens was on the committee with me," recalls Nagy. "He really told them off. He said, 'You ought to be glad you're an American.' They didn't say a word."

During his four decades as commissioner, Nagy has seen sandlot baseball fall from hundreds of teams to a few dozen. Meanwhile, slow pitch softball—he instituted the Softball Hall of Fame in Oklahoma City—has grown into a top participation sport.

"Several things happened to baseball," explains Nagy. "Once the American Legion sponsored Class E Unbacked. The kids played in T-shirts. No uniforms. We had over 100 teams in that division alone, and the kids advanced all the way to Class A.

"Then Little League came along. It was the real killer. The kids get everything in Little League—uniforms, the works. They got big league treatment so early there was nothing to strive for and they couldn't accept our sandlot format.

"Nobody strikes out in softball, so guys who still like the game go for it. We now have over 2,000 teams here. I see some renewed interest in sandlot baseball, but there is going to have to be some support from outside sources. Few backers are now available."

He says the two major problems facing public recreation here are insufficient facilities and supervision because of lack of money, and vandalism. "It's a vicious cycle," says Nagy. "If we had the funds to do the things we want, we could keep the kids busy at healthy activities. Now we do the best we can.

"People think most of the vandalism is on the East Side in the black areas. Not true. It's more prevalent on the near West Side and the mid-West Side. On the East Side the kids seem to appreciate what we give them and take more pride in it. It sickens me to see the damage the punks do to our pools and recreation centers and ball fields."

In a few months the vandals will be somebody else's worry.

Whenever possible, Helen Nagy, his wife of 41 years, accompanies him in his travels. Their daughter, Kathy, lives in New Jersey.

Helen is an avid racing fan. She gets to Thistledown about once a week and all the regulars know her. She screams and jumps up and down as she tries to root home a winner, usually unsuccessfully. Regulars find out how Helen is betting her $2, then avoid that horse.

John's recreation is to go along with Helen, usually on Saturdays. When he is at Thistledown, the word left at the City Hal switchboard in case anyone tries to reach him is, "He's at his farm."

Now he'll have more time to spend with Helen "on the farm." May they have nothing but winners.

Feel sorry for Schlichter?

April 12, 1983

"I can't work up any sympathy for Art Schlichter," I said, playing the Devil's Advocate to acquaintances Benny the Bookie and Sammy Salami, a fairly high roller.

Schlichter, the High Street hero, the quarterback who became the Baltimore Colts' second draft choice in the first round after he finished up at Ohio State, has been caught with his pockets hanging out. He had gone to the authorities when—after losing $230,000 in cash and owing $150,000 to Baltimore bookies—the bookies put the squeeze on him, seeking $10,000 a week in interest and threatening to expose him if he welshed.

"I've seen guys who had to join Gamblers Anonymous to get straightened out," continued this Devil's Advocate. "I know it's a sickness. I feel sorry for them, but this kid is different. He's a pro athlete. He knows he isn't allowed to bet."

"Hey, wait," said Sammy Salami, "he didn't bet on football. He bet on basketball."

"So what?" said the D.A. "In every pro baseball, basketball and football locker room there are signs posted by the league head, telling the players they are forbidden from betting on any sporting event."

"That's a joke," said Benny. "I can name you dozens of baseball and football players who bet at the race track."

"True," said the D.A., "but that happens to be legal. As a matter of fact it's common knowledge Schlichter was betting the horses while he was at Ohio State and his coach, Earl Bruce, is seen at the windows at Thistledown when he's in town. Maybe that's where the kid got the bug. College officials should do some thinking about the connection."

"Aw c'mon," said Sammy. "Everybody bets. Judges go to the track. In police stations you'll find football pools. You bet chocolate sodas."

"Cut the comedy. You're talking about fun bets. I'm talking about the real thing, about a kid who went off the deep end."

"I'm just trying to keep you from being so damn moral about betting," said Sammy. "It's illegal in some places, but is it immoral?"

"It is when a guy can't afford what he's losing, or if he's a pro athlete," said the D.A. "You're not trying to say Schlichter did nothing wrong, are you?"

"He was guilty only of being stupid, extreme ignorance," said Sammy. "Say it any way you want and it comes out D-U-M-B. Real dumb."

"You know what he was?" said Benny. "He was a country boy who got spoiled in high school and in college. Everybody spoiled him. He got traffic tickets. They got taken care of. The hero could do no wrong. He got to thinking he was smarter than the system. He never thought he had to pay the price."

"How could he have gone so heavy?" asked the D.A.

"That's easy," said Sammy. "The kid already was a gambler. He thought he knew basketball, which proves how naïve he was. He lost. He wanted to recoup. He kept increasing his bets. The bookies had a sucker. They gladly strung him along until he was tapped out."

"That's where I begin to smell something," said Benny. "When you have a big money guy betting with you the worst thing you can do is try to break him. You don't want to kill the golden goose. You try to keep him playing."

"Maybe they thought he had more money than he actually did," said Sammy.

"Or maybe," said the Devil's Advocate, "they wanted to get the kid in their debt. Get him where he could help them on Colts' and other NFL games next season, maybe give them information."

"Down the line it's a possibility," conceded Benny. "Otherwise, they had to be as stupid as the kid."

"But if that's the case," said Sammy, "why would they threaten to expose him? Why would they charge him $10,000 a week interest?"

"To scare him," the D.A. ventured. "To get him so shook up he'd say, 'Okay guys, I don't have the money. I'll do anything you want.'"

"And then he fooled them," said Sammy. "He went to the authorities first. They never figured on that. It took a lot of guts to put his life on the line. Guts and a basic decency."

"Decency?" said the D.A. "The bookies didn't hold a gun at Schlichter's head forcing him to bet. So because he had a compulsion to gamble the bookies are going to jail. And he, the gambler and dealer, will get off scot free, a good citizen. Is that justice?"

"The bookies should go to jail for extortion," said Benny, "and for being dumb. That interest rate was nuts."

"But what about Schlichter? You guys sound as though you feel sorry for him."

"I do," said Sammy. "He has my sympathy. He didn't kill anybody. He stood up to the blackmailers instead of going along with them.

He didn't hurt anybody except himself. With all that talent, now he's broke."

"I feel sorry for him, too," said Benny.

"You mean he's been punished enough? If you guys were Pete Rozelle you'd pat him on the head and say, 'Son, I hope you learned your lesson?'"

"Naw," said Benny. "He's got to suspend the kid for a year. He did it with Paul Hornung and Alex Karras. From a public relations position he's got to suspend the kid."

"Right," said Sammy. "But one year is enough."

"And then what?"

"He'll probably have to live on the farm the rest of his life," said Sammy. "A quarterback's got to be a leader. Who would want that kind of an ignoramus to quarterback their team?"

"Right," said Benny. "Not even the Colts. You can bet on that."

Mackey deserved his last hard kick

June 23, 1990

My bride, knowing I planned to write about the sordid Kevin Mackey story, said, "Be compassionate. Don't kick a guy when he's down."

Sorry, hon. I hope the basketball coach who flushed his career at Cleveland State University down the toilet eventually can straighten out his life. But if he were standing here I couldn't resist the impulse to kick him. Right in the rear. Cleveland State had to fire him.

In these pieces I try hard not to let emotions color my objectivity, but in the Mackey case I find it difficult to be truly rational. You have been fully warned.

Being a former coach myself, Mackey's behavior—boozing, womanizing, drugs—has made me downright angry. Talk about kicks, he kicked our profession in the groin.

As a teacher and coach, Mackey betrayed a trust, almost a sacred one. He betrayed his university, its students, his players, the fans, the supporting community.

In an effort to put some balance into this perspective, I talked with several coaches. They unanimously share my outrage. Many of them know Mackey personally. They want to give him the benefit of any doubt. They can't.

Every coach said Mackey owed it to his players to get out of coaching when he found himself breaking every rule for decent behavior.

One high school coach said, "Last May he spoke at our senior awards banquet. He told the kids about hard work and keeping clean and being role models. Now these kids are reading about all his gutter activities. What a joke. And don't you think that now when we tell the kids what's right they're going to wonder: 'Is my coach just another Mackey?'"

Mackey didn't make the hypocritical speech out of the goodness of his heart. He got paid for it.

"A healthy fee," said the coach bitterly. "He wouldn't come otherwise."

Sure. He needed the money to do what he told the kids not to do. He needed it to support his drugs, drinking, and womanizing. He probably went right from that speech to a crack house. Much as he made as CSU's coach, it's never enough to pay for a double life.

The next step, if he had remained at CSU, could have been betting on games and then substituting his players so that his team would win, or lose, by the margin he needed to obtain the payoff.

Am I straining? Doesn't the creepy, crawly Mackey story itself strain your belief? If he had allowed himself to fall that low, the pit was bottomless.

His firing could prove to be the life-saving jolt he sorely needs. Had he been allowed to get away with it this time, given a year's sick leave as he requested, Mackey conceivably would con himself into thinking he beat the system once again.

For that is what Mackey has been, the ultimate con man, fooling others, but mainly himself. He thought he could do no wrong. Success does that to some. It makes them feel invincible. Pete Rose is one. George Steinbrenner is another. They think they are so smart they eventually outsmart themselves.

One acquaintance of Mackey's says he became the king who believed he was untouchable after CSU upset the heralded Indiana Hoosiers in the NCAA tournament. "He stopped listening to people after that."

Those at CSU responsible for monitoring the coach must share some of the blame for allowing the Mackey saga to reach this sad conclusion. Not that they knew of his drug habit, or his other vices, although there was some indication of his drinking. They couldn't get any concrete evidence. He was a convincing liar. And no one suspected dope.

Even after he was arrested upon leaving the crack house one of his assistants said, "I'll bet my last dime they find him clean of drugs. That's one thing he'd never do." Famous last words.

I have little doubt Mackey fooled his own family. But his bosses at CSU did have clear proof Mackey was not to be trusted. He lied to the NCAA during its investigation of his recruiting. He lied to such an extent that the sentence became exceptionally severe.

Then there was the game, two years ago, in which he tried to have a player, about to shoot free throws, fake an injury so a better-shooting teammate could replace him. This is out and out cheating, a horrible lesson to his players.

At that moment he no longer could be a teacher or coach in my school.

But CSU, drinking from Mackey's heady success, had become fogged by the win-at-all-costs results and they tolerated him. Until now, and to their sorrow.

When the Browns' Kevin Mack was arrested last year, I felt a deep compassion for him. I wanted him taught a lesson, but I thought the judge was making political hay by jailing him, for the sentence he imposed on Mack was far more severe than others received who were caught for the first time.

Moreover, Mack is no Mackey, no con artist. He's a quiet, really nice young man, victim of a horrible habit. He merited compassion and a second chance.

No doubt, Mackey also is a victim of the habit. But Mackey was supposed to be a leader. That was his chosen profession. That's what he was paid to be. That's why he had to be fired without an immediate second chance.

Mack had been a follower all his life, the major difference between the two cases. I can be more compassionate of a passenger on a plane than of the pilot. Those in the plane are followers of the pilot. If he does drugs, he can take everybody down. After the crash, would you have compassion for him?

Mackey was CSU's scary basketball pilot. He has been grounded. I feel relief. That's all. Sorry.

How gamblers move in on baseball

August 1965

In all my years of covering baseball, one incident stands out more memorably than the most dramatic home run. It happened on a sunny Saturday afternoon in 1953. On my way to Cleveland Stadium to cover a game between the Indians and the Yankees, I stopped in the office to get my mail. There were no important messages. I checked the Associated Press wire. Noting startling. Simply a repeat of the pitchers for the afternoon: Early Wynn vs. Whitey Ford.

The office was less than two miles from the Stadium. Within ten minutes after I left the office, I pulled into the Stadium parking lot. Gametime was in 1½ hours.

A Short Vincent character (Short Vincent is a downtown Cleveland street noted for its Damon Runyon types) drove up alongside. I knew him and as he got out of his car, he said, "Too bad about Early Wynn,"

"What do you mean?"

"Oh, you don't know? His gout is acting up. He can't pitch today."

My heart sank. I must have been scooped by the rival paper. "Who's taking Wynn's place?" I asked.

"Mossi. It was a pick game, but when I found out Mossi is going, I put a package on the Yanks."

I saw Frank Gibbons, my rival, the baseball writer for the other afternoon paper.

"Did you have the story, Frank?" I asked, fearful of the reply.

"What story?"

"Wynn has the gout. Mossi's pitching."

"No kidding. I didn't know. How'd you find out?"

I pointed to the informer, who was heading toward the box office. Frank knew him, too.

"That guy's a better reporter than both of us," said Frank. "I wish I had his pipeline."

We went to the Cleveland clubhouse and talked to manager Al Lopez. He admitted the pitching change.

"How come you didn't tell us? How come the Indians' PR man didn't call the papers. How come we had to find it out from a stranger?"

Lopez was astonished. "A stranger?"

We told him the story.

"It just happened a half-hour ago," Lopez said. "Only myself, Wynn, Mossi, our coaches and the trainer know. Maybe they told the other players. A couple of things kept me busy. I haven't even had a chance to tell the front office."

"How did that gambler find out?" one of us said.

None of us could answer.

We puzzled over the "leak" for a long time but our investigations revealed nothing. Finally, on the last day of the 1954 baseball season, I found it.

It was the fourth game of the 1954 World Series, Indians vs. Giants. I went into the clubhouse for one last look-around before going up to the press box. As I came back out, the vendor selling pennants at his station just beyond the clubhouse door said, "How's it look, Hal?"

"Okay," I said.

"The boys think they can take it?" he asked.

"Hard to tell."

"Is Lemon still pitching?"

The light struck.

"No," I lied. "Lopez has decided to give Feller his chance to win a World Series game. It could be his last chance. Lopez has gone sentimental at the last minute."

I continued to walk toward the ramp. Then, when I reached it, I flattened out against the wall. The vendor rushed to the pay telephone booth, less than 25 feet from his stand. He kept the door open so he could watch his pennants. I swung around and moved within listening distance.

"Lopez has switched to Feller," I heard him say. I departed quickly.

Mystery solved. Leak plugged. The next year the vendor was gone.

This was a classic, unforgettable example of the extent to which the gambler will go in pursuit of the "edge." In the bettor's parlance, the "edge" is that little extra, the information that helps him overcome the established odds. When the Short Vincent character learned Mossi had replaced Wynn he got his bet down before the information reached the bookies—before the odds changed.

Baseball betting is big business and the men who know it best, the bookies, say more money is wagered on baseball than on any other sport. This, they say, includes horse-race betting away from the track. Individual baseball bets, they reveal, are generally larger than those on football and basketball and far greater than the racing wager. It's common for the "small" baseball bettor to put up $100 a day. The total runs into millions.

"You get the best shake for your money in baseball," one confirmed gambler recently told me. "It's absolutely clean. You never have to worry about a fix. Any edge we get, we have to get on our own."

The quest for the edge, sought by the professional and amateur alike, begins when the baseball season begins—in spring training.

Miami is a mecca for vacationing "sportsmen." This is where the Baltimore Orioles train and what better way is there to vacation than to sit in the sun and get a "line" on the Birds? And, meanwhile, place a bet or two on exhibitions because a gambler needs spring training, too.

"They'd stick their heads into the dugout," says Orioles manager Hank Bauer, "to check out my lineup. I had it posted at one end and they wanted to sneak in some advance information before they made a bet. So I moved the lineup card to the middle of the dugout. Then they'd give kids a dime or two to come onto the field and ask me who was going to play. Happens every spring."

Last March, shortly after the Indians reported to their spring base in Tucson, Arizona, Cleveland manager Birdie Tebbetts pointed to a pair of cigar-smoking gents standing behind the fence near the dugout at Hi Corbett Field.

"See those two guys," he said. "I'm convinced they're here to make a 'line' on our club."

Birdie said this was the third spring they had boarded the same plane he had in Chicago. "They seem to wait for me," he said. "They say, 'Hello Skipper,' and head with me to Tucson. And here they are, looking us over. I guess they figure if they say, "Hello Skipper,' I won't be so suspicious.

"Look at 'em. Don't they resemble two refugees from the Al Capone days?"

Armed only with suspicion, Birdie merely could keep an eye on the pair. But in the spring of 1964, another "spy" caused him to take action. The Indians were traveling with the San Francisco Giants in 1964, playing a series of exhibitions along the West Coast. "I see this character," said Birdie, "one I had seen hanging around us in Tucson. I see him in the hotel in Sacramento. He gets a seat near me and my coaches at the restaurant. Next day we go to Fresno and there's this guy, sitting as near as he can, trying to catch what we say.

"So I go up to him and accuse him of being a gambler looking for a little information. He doesn't deny it. I say, 'All right, you've got your line. Now blow, before I turn you in.' That was the last time we saw him."

There's nothing illegal about obtaining information in this manner. It's sneaky, but it breaks no law. It was not even illegal for the vendor to pass along gossip. Hotel clerks, waitresses, bartenders, even the policemen working in the ballpark, hear things and pass them along. Sometimes inadvertently, sometimes—the policemen excluded, of course—for a price.

What the gambler is interested in mainly is information about the pitchers. Specifically, who's pitching and, if possible, how's his arm?

The bettors study the newspapers avidly. Some of them buy papers from all the major-league cities. Many of them walk around carrying powerful transistor radios, twisting the dial from one station to another, waiting for such clues as, "Trafrax isn't pumping the ball today. He seems to be laboring."

Next time Trafrax pitches, the gambler, on the strength of poor pumping, may bet against him.

"They probably know as much about the teams as general managers do," says the Indians' president and general manager, Gabe Paul. "We're looking for all the information we can get, so we can make intelligent trades. We get it by reading papers, talking with reporters, listening to the radio. We have our paid scouts. They have their own grapevine."

In Cleveland there are fine eating places along Short Vincent, and Frank Lane, former Indians general manager, recalls street-wise men coming to him and saying, "I hear you're trying to get Hammerhead. Don't. He's got a bad arm."

"These guys," marvels Lane, "know more than a lot of managers."

The daily "line" now comes out of three key centers—Las Vegas, Miami and Minneapolis. For $25 a week, the bookie can get the official odds, established by an expert, at 12:15 P.M. daily. By 12:30 the bettor can call his bookie for the daily quote. It's like calling your broker for the stock market quotation.

One bookie told me he refuses to pay for the daily line. Considering himself equally knowledgeable, he makes his own.

"I figure a pitcher's earned-run average," he explained. "I don't care if he gave up a big score in his last game. It depends how the runs were scored. If they weren't his fault, I don't count it against him.

"The pitcher decides the price. He's the main thing. Take Koufax.

He's worth eighty cents. When Koufax goes against an average pitcher the price is $1.80 to $1.00. Now Mantle, he's a big ballplayer. Tops. But if he's out, it's worth only ten cents. Like for example: If the Yanks are $1.30 to $1.00 and Mantle is out, the price goes down to $1.20.

"Each pitcher has his own value. The rest of the players don't mean nothing, except the top guy and, like I say, he's just ten cents. The four tops in the National League, all 80-cent guys, right now (this was in June) are Koufax, Gibson, Drysdale and Veale. Veale, he's worth 30 cents more than Law.

"Now you take Chance, of the American League. He won the Cy young award last year. That don't mean nothing now. Not to me."

At the time of our conversation Chance had been hit hard in three straight starts.

"I'd bet against him," said the bookie. "You can get a good price, because he's the favorite yet,"

"You mean you bet as well as book?"

"Sure, why not? If somebody comes to me I set my own price, take it or leave it. But if some other guy has a price I like, I'll give him a little action."

Bets can be made two ways, by teams or by pitchers. If the Indians are playing the Orioles and the bettor says, "I'll take the Orioles," the bet stands, no matter who pitches. If the probable pitchers are McDowell against Pappas and the bettor says, "I'll take only one pitch, the bet holds. But they must start.

Often when a gambler names a team, he's betting on momentum—a streak. One system calls for staying with a hot club during a streak and then jumping off the instant it's broken. But, according to the bookies, even when a man bets a team you can be sure he's made a study of the pitchers.

When the Black Sox scandal caused baseball to hire Kenesaw Mountain Landis as commissioner, his first order to managers, in an effort to thwart the gamblers, was: "Don't reveal your pitchers until gametime." But reporters began to guess successfully and eventually they prevailed upon the commissioner to permit the manager to make his "probable pitcher" public.

Baseball bettors often turn to the "probable pitchers" box on the sports page before they scan the front page. Sometimes, the paper gives the probable as "Ford or Bouton." The gambler isn't interested in either-or, He wants to know which one and he'd like to know 24 hours in advance. To find out, he will call the paper or the manager.

Every manager in the majors has had this experience. A phone call early in the morning or late at night. "Hello, this is the *Associated Press*. Who's your probable pitcher for tomorrow?"

Joe Cronin, president of the American League, always had a stock reply when he managed the Boston Red Sox. "I never gave out the true pitchers to anybody," Cronin says, "I'd always say, 'It'll be either Bill Butland or Woody Rich.' Both were down in our farm system and the person who asked me wouldn't question it because he wasn't sure whether we had reacquired them or what."

Bill Rigney, manager of the Los Angeles Angels, admittedly gets numerous calls in which the voice of the other end identifies himself either as a representative of a wire service or a newspaper. Rigney plays games with them.

"I got this call once from Miami, Florida," Rigney recently said. "The fellow says, 'Hello, Bill, this is Barney.'

"'Barney who?'

"Barney Kremenko.'

Barney Kremenko covers the Mets for the New York *Journal-American* and is a close friend of Rigney's. "I knew it couldn't be Barney, because the Mets were in New York," Rigney said, "but I went along with it. I asked 'Barney' what he was doing in Miami. He said he was vacationing there with his family. Ten he asked me: 'Who's pitching tomorrow?"

"I told him, 'Bob Reynolds.'" Reynolds happens to be president of the Angels.

The caller got the message and hung up.

"Once," Rigney said, "a gal phoned and said she was from *UPI*. She wanted to know my probable pitcher. I could hear a typewriter in the background but on these fake calls you always can hear 'em. I told her I was going to pitch Bob Reynolds.

"Next day I nearly flipped when I picked u the paper and saw my pitcher was going to be 'Reynolds. Record 0-0.'

"In New York once, Dean Chance was scheduled to start against the Yanks but when I got this late phone call, supposedly from *AP*, I said my starter would be Bob Botts, a rookie.

"The next day all over the country our probable was listed as "Botts." The kid came to me a couple of days later and thanked me for the publicity. He said, 'My parents saw it and called me up. They were thrilled.'"

At the meeting of American League managers last winter, Minnesota's Sam Mele suggested the league furnish them with a list of the wire-service writers. "I don't want to withhold information from a bona fide writer," Mele said.

Chicago White Sox manager Al Lopez suggests every reporter be furnished with a code number to be used when he calls for the "probable pitcher." Meanwhile, the managers will continue to remain evasive until they can identify the callers as actual reporters.

Once they discover the true pitcher, some gamblers go a step further. Now they want to know if he's ready. They have been known to go to the pitching coach. Tom Ferrick, who has served as pitching coach for several clubs and now scouts for the Kansas City Athletics, reveals the call generally takes this form:

"Hello, Tom, I'm a good friend of Joe Trafrax. It's too bad about this arm. I'm worried about it. Is he getting any better?"

Ferrick has yet to be taken in.

One pitching coach told me that a gambler used a girl friend to try to get information. "Somehow they found out what beauty parlor my wife went to," the coach said. "Then they found out when her appointment was. The girl friend made one at the same time. She managed to sit next to my wife under the dryer and became chummy. Pretty soon she began to pump my wife about my job. She said she was a great fan and she asked several questions about the players.

"Each time my wife had a hair appointment this girl had one, too. Soon she began to call up. It seemed natural for a while, but one night when we were coming out of a downtown movie my wife happened to see the girl walking with a well known police character. She didn't see us. From then on my wife answered, 'yes, no and maybe' at the beauty parlor and after than, the girl found another place to get her hair done."

Part of the "edge" is to discover what time the pitcher goes to bed the night before he works—and in what condition. This is a relatively simple matter on the road. The gambler, himself, can sit in the hotel lobby, or a bell boy or an elevator operator can be spying for him. Bartenders and taxi drivers also make good tipsters.

With few exceptions, the present day ballplayer is a class athlete who takes excellent care of himself. It's the exception that the bettor wants information about, even though it often boomerangs.

"Abut ten years ago," a Cleveland taxi driver, who also books on the side, told me, "I picked up a Detroit pitcher. He was supposed to work the next day. I took him from one joint to another. He also got a couple of broads. Naturally, I bet against him. He shut Cleveland out.

"That taught me a lesson. When you're young you can get away with it, especially in baseball. I never bet on what a pitcher does the night before, although a lot of gamblers do. Not in baseball. But you take in football, if I find out a guy's had a bad night, it's a real edge. In baseball there's more standing around. He got more of a chance to recover. In tennis if you know a guy's carousing the night before, you got a real break—practically a sure thing."

"Information," once it's out, travels fast. One bettor tells his buddy, hoping the favor will be returned. "It's much easier to get information in football," a gambler told me. "I hear about a key injury three days before it's in the papers, especially among the college players."

Who are the baseball bettors? I personally know of the president of a large manufacturing company, an advertising salesman, an accountant, a tavern owner—all highly successful in their respective businesses—who bet regularly on baseball. They enjoy the game more when they have something going on it.

In some ballparks a different breed of bettor exists. During a day game at Fenway Park go out to right field, deep n the stands behind the foul pole. Here the same men sit, game after game. They bet on everything. Will the next batter get a hit? Will it be a ball or a strike? Most of the bets are silently made, by sign language. A man will raise his finger. Another will nod. The bet is on.

These gamblers never annoy the players. So nobody bothers them.

The betting set-up in Cleveland, says one gambler, is essentially the same as in other cities. "There are at least 50 bookies in this town," he says. "I know 20 personally. A lot of them are in it just for the vigorish. For example, if you want the favorite, the odds might be 8 to 5. If you take the dog, it's 7-5. So the bookie has a point going for him, if he can get action both ways. As a rule, in baseball, the betting is one way—with the favorite. In football, there's more play on the underdogs because they give you points.

"So because the lay is heavy on the favorite in baseball, the bets usually wind up with the bookies who have the most money. The little bookie is satisfied with a small commission.

"Most of the bookies work out of their homes, but a few have offices downtown. Suburban living has shifted much of the action to the suburbs. It's hard to beat the bookies because they eventually get back by raising the odds. I knew a guy, years ago who always bet on Walter Johnson. Johnson generally won, but the guy lost money because every time the bookie saw him coming, he raised the odds.

"Last year I know of two bookies who had to close up. The Mets killed them. They lost too consistently. I made $27,000 last year because the games were running true to form. But once the dogs start to win, the bettors are in trouble. This year the dogs are winning more games than they should. Too many upsets. Maybe it's because the teams are better balanced. Anyway, I'm getting killed.

"See, last year when I won, what did I do with the money? Did I put it away as a cushion? No, I bought my wife a fur coat; we took trips; we lived high.

"This year I've already lost so much I'm in debt. I've got to quit for a while and let my business make up my losses. But get this: I've never made a bet in baseball I felt I was cheated. It's an honest game—all the way. I may get mad at a dumb manager, yes. But the game is clean. That's why I stay with it."

Commissioner Ford Frick, retiring at the end of the season, would shudder at the thought of a plaque from the gamblers, yet it is a fine tribute. He has indeed kept the game clean and the commissioner's office as created essentially for that purpose. There hasn't even been a hint of a major league gambling scandal during Frick's reign as commissioner. Some ten years ago a gambling plot was uncovered in the minors. Frick cracked down quickly and players who bet on games were barred for life.

"The minors are harder to police," Frick says. "The players move around so much."

To police baseball, Frick has a staff of investigators and informers. The players would flip if they saw his files. He knows more about them than their wives do. He has a record of their nightlife and he has a record of every dive in every city.

Recently, Frick read us one report submitted a few weeks earlier by a team of three detectives and one informer. The report pertained to four players on a Midwest major league team. Withholding the identities of the players and the tavern, Frick read the report.

"Players A, B, C, and D came into this place, known as a hangout for gamblers, at 12:30 a.m., following their night game. Player A bought the informer a drink. (Frick revealed the informer once worked at the ballpark.) The players remained there for 30 minutes and left."

Frick pointed out that the report, in itself, contained no damaging information. "But that's a bad spot," he said. "We can't have our players there. It could lead to trouble. The next morning I forwarded the report to the general manager of the team. We've made spot checks at that place ever since and there hasn't been a sign of a ballplayer there. The club acted quickly."

Another report revealed an established star was living in a hotel of questionable repute.

"Our investigator said known dope pushers and loose women also live there," said Frick. "We notified his team. He moved out of there the next day.

"We get great cooperation from the owners. Some years ago, in St. Louis, we had a report of gambling from the ballpark. Right across the street from Busch Stadium was a little restaurant that took bets. The ushers would serve as messengers for fans, go across the street and place the bets. I called August Busch about this.

"He said, 'We own the real estate. We'll take care of it.' He had the building torn down."

Not too long ago, Frick's men suspected that bets were being placed directly from the pay phone in the clubhouse of a major league team on the east coast. He received permission to have the phone tapped. The suspicions proved correct. The clubhouse man was calling in personal bets and also wagers for other employees at the park. Frick's men kept the tap on the phone for several weeks and had the clubhouse man trailed constantly.

Clearly, the players were not involved in any manner. Fortunately, too, not one of the bets involved the home team. The clubhouse man and his friends, it developed, were betting on other games. Nevertheless, the man was suspended from his job.

As a result of this incident Frick ordered the immediate removal of pay phones from all clubhouses. Now every call going into—and out of—the locker room must be monitored through the front office switchboard at all parks.

"What we really do," says the commissioner, "is practice preventive medicine. We can't stop gambling on baseball, but we can police it to see that our people aren't involved in any of it.

When Frick first became commissioner he confesses he jumped every time he received an anonymous letter about a player. "I'd call him in right away," he says. "Most of the stories proved completely phony. Now we just investigate and don't call in the player unless there's a reason. I'd rather call in five players, though, and find everything proper rather than ignore one case and be proven wrong."

In addition to the commissioner's investigations, each league does its own policing. Warren Giles, president of the National League says, "We follow up on any crank letter in which gambling is implied."

Giles has a special investigator. "He's my personal troubleshooter. Nobody knows who he is except me. Not even those in my office."

Joe Cronin is even more mysterious about his police force. "It's a military secret" he says. "We have ways and means of picking things up. You can bet we check every complaint."

Both presidents agree that their principal task is to see that their umpires are holier than thou. "The secret," says Cal Hubbard, the supervisor of American League umpires, "is to get good men to start with."

Says Giles: "Before we even think of buying an umpire we have his whole background investigated—all the way back to high school. Sometimes we go to four or five cities to get the full report on one man. We hire a private investigating agency for this. Sometimes the check becomes very expensive, but it's worth every cent. The investigators even talk to his school teachers. We look for anything that might put a man in a compromising situation.

"A big thing is his credit. About eight years ago we had a fine umpiring prospect and we didn't bring him up because of debts accrued by members of his family. Not by him, mind you, but by relatives. We just couldn't take the chance."

Several years ago, a veteran American League umpire fell into debt. The league called him in, paid off all his bills, took a portion out of his paycheck regularly to cover it and warned him never to let it happen again."

"An umpire who owes money is vulnerable," says Hubbard.

Though they fully trust their umpires, the league, for its own protection, must make periodic checks. Hubbard tells his men: "If you want a cocktail go to a decent place. Don't hang around any bar stools. Sit down and have dinner. Be careful who you talk to and don't let anybody pick up the check. If anybody ever mentions a baseball bet, get away for him."

"I quit going to a barber in Philadelphia," says one umpire. "I switched because he would tell us about the bets he made. I liked him and he gave me good haircuts, but he wouldn't shut up."

Umpires have been ordered to report unusual occurrences on or off the field. Fortunately, two American League umpires, trapped in a blackmail attempt in Baltimore reported the embarrassing circumstances to the Cronin immediately. The plotters were arrested and the umpires saved their jobs by their complete disclosures.

One umpire, a few years ago, was ordered "to stop visiting certain people." He promised to obey, but didn't. Though he was one of the best umpires in the league, his contract was dropped.

"I got a call from the front office one day asking me why I stopped in at a certain hotel one night," an umpire told me. "I had to explain an old college classmate was in town and I promised to visit him after the game. I had to give the name of the guy, what room, everything."

The umpires must arrive at the field 1½ hours before game-time. They sit in the stands and watch the players. In the American League the players have been ordered not to talk with spectators. If they do, it's a $5 fine. This American League rule was born, oddly enough, because a National Leaguer once was photographed leaning over a box seat and talking with Al Capone.

Gamblers try to get the edge, baseball personnel try to stop them from getting the edge. A baseball writer I knew figured if anybody had inside information on the probable pitchers, their health, etc., he did. And he decided to cash in on it.

He began to bet on the games he was covering. When he won that day, regardless of what the home team did, his stories were pleasant, favorable to both teams. But when he lost, pity the poor manager whose strategy backfired, or the player whose error cost him cash.

The writer began to lose heavily and he wound up losing his job—and broke.

He fell off the edge.

GOODBYES

Cobby . . . Cobby . . . Cobby . . .

October 4, 1969

It was after midnight that the ringing phone shook one out of a sound sleep. Gordon Cobbledick, after a lengthy illness, had passed away in Tucson, Arizona, at the age of 70, was the message.

There was no return to sleep. The heart was heavy at the loss of a good friend, a mentor and former boss. And the memories, visual pictures and thoughts of him filled the mind.

Cobby . . . Cobby . . . Cobby . . .

Cobby, whose command of the language made his column "Plain Dealing" an English teacher's delight.

Cobby, who would say to the staff "Keep it short," and always set the example himself. Rarely would his columns be longer than two double spaced typewritten pages.

Cobby, who walked so straight, talked so straight and lived so straight, but always was understanding of the foibles of others . . .

Cobby, whose eyes continued to smile even after he suffered a paralytic stroke and was withering away . . .

Cobby, who was so respected by the athletes he covered that they never hesitated to confide in him, knowing he wouldn't break a confidence. And when the big story developed, the 1940 Revolt of the Indians against their manager Oscar Vitt, it was given to him for his exclusive treatment . . .

Cobby, who could write such clever satire that the tongue in cheek often escaped many believe-it-all sports page readers, causing him to say, "Never again." But the imp in him kept overcoming the resolution, and he did it again, and again and again, needling players, golfers especially, fans, and even women, when in reality he was fond of them all . . .

Cobby, who was so adored by the gals in the home economics department here that he was the only one they ever baked cookies for . . .

Cobby, who was such good company that his table was always the gathering place at lunch . . .

Cobby, who was a soft touch for the panhandlers who paraded into his office . . .

Cobby, who carried the torch for his high school sweetheart, Doris, throughout 46 years of marriage, each day the flame growing brighter . . .

Cobby, the belittler of his own efforts, but who proudly boasted of the accomplishments of his grandchildren . . .

Cobby, to whom an angry ball player said, "I read your column today," only to be silenced with the perfect squelch: "That's why I wrote it. For you to read it."

Cobby, the boss whose staff loved him dearly . . .

Cobby, the strong man, the humanitarian, the sweet guy, the big leaguer . . .

Cobby, who became enamored with Tucson during his first trip there with the Indians in 1948 and vowed he would live there some day and who died there and now is going to be buried there.

Cobby, who is gone now but whose deeds, writing and lessons will live on and grow even more indelible with time in the minds and hearts of those who had the privilege to know him.

Cobby . . . Cobby . . . Cobby . . .

Wasn't he amazin'?

October 1, 1975

It was a privilege to know Casey Stengel.

I knew plenty about him even before I met him. When Al Lopez managed the Indians and Tony Cuccinello served as his coach, they told Stengel stories by the hour. Casey had been their manager, back in the 1930s, when they played for the Brooklyn Dodgers and later for the Boston Braves. They may not have been too crazy about the manner in which he managed the teams but they enjoyed the man and they loved him.

They would tell outlandish stories about Casey: about the time he came up to home plate and when he doffed his cap to some booing fans a bird flew out. And about the time, in spring training, he talked Wilbert Robinson, an old catcher, into trying to catch a baseball dropped from an airplane. Except that Casey, who did the dropping, substituted a grapefruit and it splattered all over Robbie's face.

And about the time he fell into a fake faint at an umpire's call and the next time he came out to argue, the same umpire immediately flopped to the ground in a "faint" and Casey stood there speechless—perhaps for the only time in his life.

They told how Casey, on the advice of his wife Edna, invested wisely in oil wells and became a millionaire and how he passed the tips along to Lopez who also became independently wealthy.

The financial part I knew was true. But the stories, I was certain, were apocryphal. Yet after I met Casey and got to know him well, I wasn't so sure. In fact, I began to believe.

In person he was even more of a character, more colorful than the stories.

Never was there a sports figure more appreciated by writers. You merely had to say "Hello Casey," take out your pencil, write down every word and you had a highly readable story. Not that the story made any sense, or had any substance. But it always was delightful copy, "Pure Stengelese" as it came to be known.

"He really doesn't talk that way, does he?" friends would ask. Congress discovered he did when he appeared in Washington before the Senate Antitrust and Monopoly Subcommittee in 1958. Senator Estes Kefauver asked him whether he thought baseball should be exempted from the antitrust laws and Casey's reply was recorded for posterity in the minutes:

"Well, I would have to say at the present time I think baseball has advanced in this respect for the player help. That is an amazing statement for me to make, because you can retire with an annuity at 50 and what organization in America allows you to retire at 50 and receive money?

"I want to further state that I am not a ballplayer, that is, put into that pension fund committee. At my age, and I have been in baseball, well, I will say I am possibly the oldest man who is working in baseball. I would say that when they start an annuity for the ballplayers to better their conditions, it should have been done and I think it has been done."

The minutes also reveal that a totally confused Senator Kefauver asked, "Mr. Stengel, I am not sure that I have made my question clear."

Only once did Casey refuse to talk. In the 1950s, Stengel's Yankees and Lopez' Indians annually fought it out for the pennant and for several years the Yankees always prevailed.

Again in 1954 they were battling. The Yankees seldom lost that season and finished with Casey's all-time high, 103 victories. But the Indians lost fewer, winning a record 111. The climax came Sunday, Sept. 10, before a standing-room-only crowd at the Stadium. The Indians swept a doubleheader and that took away Stengel's first pennant as manager of the Yankees. He dressed immediately after the game, talked to no one, quickly departed from the clubhouse and lost himself in the crowd walking up the Stadium ramp. I'll never forget his departing, hunched-over figure.

Casey was elected into the Hall of Fame in 1966, along with Ted Williams. It was my high honor, as president of the Baseball Writers Association of America, to introduce them to the audience that spilled all over the grounds at the Cooperstown induction ceremonies.

Williams made one request. "Put me on first," he said. "Nobody can follow Casey."

Williams gave one of the finest speeches ever delivered at the Hall of Fame. He spent hours writing it himself. Casey, without a line in front of him, was just as good. He left the Stengelese home. He talked sense, told stories about baseball greats, demonstrated how Williams batted and, as usual, revealed himself as baseball's greatest salesman. Moreover, he was surprisingly short.

When Casey wanted to, in his gruff voice, he could say it loud and clear. That night he stayed on the hotel porch and talked to fans until three in the morning. Several times his wife attempted to get him to retire. "Don't bother me, Edna, I'm busy," he would say.

Casey called Joe DiMaggio "amazin'" and he called Yogi Berra "amazin'" and he called his Mets "amazin'", but the most amazin' baseball figure of all times has to be Casey Stengel. There can never be another.

The most unforgettable characters

May 15, 1977

Frankie Pytlak, who died last Sunday at age 67, was the smallest major league catcher within my memory. He was five-seven and weighed 160 and he wore his hair to fit his stature—extremely short.

I remember a couple of things about Frankie, besides what I read in the newspapers . . . concerning occasional shuffles back to his home in Buffalo whenever the urge hit him . . . and his salary bouts with the front office.

During his freshman season as the Indian' catcher, 1933, I sold peanuts at the Stadium. It was the first year the Indians played ALL their games at the new park. The Indians had a number of sluggers. Most of them hit long flies. There was no outfield fence and they became long outs. Pytlak, with his compact swing, got line drives for singles and doubles. He batted .310 that season. The little man had the highest average on the team.

I remember, too, Frankie always seemed to be getting hurt. In his first four seasons he rarely was around at the finish. It was either stomach problems or broken fingers. In 1936 it was worse.

The Indians were giving the frightening Yankees a fight for the pennant in August. At least it seemed that way to the 65,342 who were there to see a Sunday game. Many of them sat in the center field bleachers. In those days the middle area was not roped off, although there had been some efforts to get the club to do so. The hitters had complained that they couldn't see the ball through the background of white shirts.

Pytlak, being smaller than the other hitters, looked right into the white. The first pitch thrown by the Yankees' Monte Pearson just missed his head. He turned his head slightly on the second one and the ball caught him flush on the left side of his face. Yankee catcher Bill Dickey rushed up and tried to stop the blood. Pytlak suffered a triple fracture. He was through for the season.

So were the Indians. He was batting .321 at the time. Eventually the center field bleachers were roped off, as they are today.

The injury didn't scare Frankie. He was back next season, his first full one, and batted .315.

My only personal contact with Frankie was through the mail, long after he had retired from baseball and had returned to Buffalo where he became a sporting goods salesman. Occasionally, questions would come in to Ask Hal, pertaining to Pytlak. Whenever I wrote him he would reply immediately with a short, polite note, supplying the necessary information.

Frankie was one of the two Cleveland catchers who were at the foot of the Terminal Tower on Public Square, August 20, 1938, when Ken Keltner went to the top and threw down a number of baseballs. Hank Helf caught one. Pytlak another. All the rest hit the pavement and bounced high into the air. Reporters estimated the height of the rebound was 13 floors, or at least 100 feet. A scientifically inclined reader questioned this. Pytlak, in his letter, agreed with the doubting reader. He thought the balls bounded three or four stories. At the Terminal this would be a maximum of 80 feet, the first stories being the tallest.

The altitude catches by Helf and Pytlak have been substantiated to be about 680 feet, a record that remains to this day, to the best of my knowledge.

Mel Harder, the former Indians' pitcher and a teammate of Pytlak, remembers those catches. Harder, now living in Mentor, says he went to Public Square to watch.

"It was tough to judge the balls because of the wind factor," he recalls, "and Keltner had to throw the ball straight out and hard to be sure it would clear the building. It was sort of dangerous down below. There were a lot of people. Thinking back, I'm surprised nobody got hurt.

"Those balls came down fast. Did Frankie say anything after his catch? I remember his saying, 'Geez.' He never did say too much."

Which reminded Harder of another incident, occurring in 1934.

"Willie Kamm, Pytlak's buddy and roommate, was playing third base. A batter hit a high foul between home and third. Both Pytlak and Kamm went for the ball. They stopped and it fell between them.

"'Why didn't you yell, if you weren't going to take it?' Kamm asked him.

"Pytlak replied, 'Didn't you hear me motion?'"

Both Harder and Bob Feller recall Pytlak as an excellent catcher, quick behind the plate, and a good handler of pitchers.

"We had a bunch of characters on the club in those days," said Feller. "When we got Rollie Hemsley, it was at my suggestion so Rollie told everybody I was his special catcher. When Johnny Allen heard that he said he'd pitch to nobody but Pytlak. Frankie became his private catcher. None of it was my idea. I liked Frankie a lot and enjoyed pitching to him."

Feller, in fact, gives Pytlak credit for his 18 strikeouts against the Detroit Tigers, Oct. 2, 1938. It was the first time a pitcher fanned that many and the number has yet to be surpassed for a day game.

"Frankie was a breaking ball catcher," said Feller. "He called for a lot of curves that day and as a result I got plenty of called strikes with the pitch. The last hitter, Chet Laabs, took a called third strike.

"After the game I told Frankie to go downtown to B. R. Baker's where I had a charge account and buy himself a suit. Remember, this was during the depression, when prices were very low. He picked one for $150, the best suit in the whole city.

Pytlak was nearly ten years older than Feller. "He always called me Robert," remembered the pitcher. "He's the only one besides my mother who called me that."

Last week, "Robert" sent flowers to Frankie's funeral.

I've known a number of unusual writers in my time on the sports beat. There was one who would overturn the waste basket in his hotel room and beat it rhythmically, like a drum, most of the night. There was the *New York Post*'s Arch Murray who set fire to many a hotel mattress. I could go on and on. But perhaps the most unforgettable of all was Jim Schlemmer, the former sports editor of the *Akron Beacon Journal,* who died last Tuesday. He was 77.

Before I met Schlemmer his reputation had preceded him. His writing, I was told, was full of vitriol. It was mean, outrageous. Then I saw this cherub . . . short, round-faced, pleasant smile, wispy moustache. No ogre. Must be the wrong guy.

Quickly he destroyed the outward picture. I don't know what he wrote, because I never saw the *Beacon.* But his cutting remarks were not confined to his columns. I was his target—the new, eager kid on the beat. Mostly I ignored his words, which made him even more vituperative. He couldn't stand being ignored. Perhaps an inner inferiority complex caused him to employ a biting typewriter and caustic words to gain attention. But once, in a mellow mood, he confided to me, "It sells papers." The *Beacon* couldn't have had a better salesman. Always he was thinking about his readers . . . how to stir them up . . . how to make them talk about his sports pages.

Because of his acidic writing Schlemmer had been threatened many times. He told me of a time at the race track, Ascot Park, I think it was.

He had been zeroing in on some trainer, if memory serves. At the track, the man ambushed Jim in a dark corner, put a gun at his temple.

"I heard him pull the trigger," Jim related, "and I waited to die. Nothing happened. The gun jammed. You should have heard that s.o.b. curse."

Than there was the time K.O. Christner came after him. Christner was one of the world's leading heavyweights. He fought for the title. Christner, the hometown boy, may have been an Akron hero, but not to Schlemmer. The bigger they were the harder Jim hit and K.O. made a perfect punching bag for his typewriter.

One summer night while Schlemmer was pounding away in the fourth floor office at the old *Beacon* building, the enraged fighter came storming in

According to Schlemmer's account the fighter tried to get him to back off the bad words, which was like asking a bee to get rid of his sting. Christner, finally unable to contain himself, grabbed Schlemmer and tried to throw him out of the window.

"A drawer was open in my desk," said Schlemmer. "I wedged my foot in it, and K.O. couldn't lift both me and the desk. Finally somebody came in and pulled him off."

I never knew whether these stories were true or apocryphal. I leaned toward the former, for I was there when others felt nearly as violent toward him.

In 1950, Hank Greenberg's first season as the Indians' general manager, Schlemmer immediately went for the jugular. Spring training had just begun when he wrote, in effect, "Al Rosen and Hal Saltzman are certain to make the team because Hank Greenberg is general manager." That's all. Let the reader draw his own inferences.

Greenberg bellowed in anger. He took Schlemmer out on the balcony adjacent to the press room at the Santa Rita Hotel in Tucson. It was a couple of floors above the ground.

We watched through the glass doors as Greenberg sought to discover why Schlemmer would make such a comment. We couldn't hear what Schlemmer said, but his actions didn't appear apologetic. Nevertheless, Greenberg decided not to slug.

Schlemmer came off that precarious perch safely to continue swinging at Hank for years and years.

Then there was the meeting on the 30th floor of the Hotel New Yorker. The Indians had just been whipped by the Yankees, 15-1, and

Greenberg invited the writers and Manager Lou Boudreau to his suite to discuss possible lineup changes.

In the course of the conversation Greenberg asked Frank Gibbons, the late baseball writer for the *Cleveland Press,* about a note he had written. According to Gibby's item, the players had signed a petition asking that a certain player be removed from the ball club.

Said Greenberg, "It's an absolute untruth. Where did you get the information?"

Gibby, six-five and about 240, and at that moment having had his share of brews, pointed to Schlemmer and said, "He gave it to me."

Schlemmer declared that wasn't quite what he had said. Gibby rushed Schlemmer. There were about six of us in the room and we hurried to protect Jim. Gibby cooled off and sat down. He thought about it again and rushed Jim once more. Again we separated them.

Time after time Gibby would sit down, get hot, jump up, and approach Schlemmer. Each time the six of us would jump up and move toward the middle. The scene was a sight out of a Mack Sennett comedy. We laughed about it—Gibby and Schlemmer, too—for years.

During those days I did a number of magazine pieces and once suggested to the editor of *Collier's* that Jim would make a fascinating yarn. I told him of his escapades and suggested the little, "The Typewriter With Nine Lives."

"Marvelous," he said. "Send me a one-page outline."

A few days later he called. "We just had a story conference. Everybody loved the Schlemmer stories. What a man. But the guys think no reader is going to believe them."

Schlemmer found targets everywhere. When Doris O'Donnell was assigned by the editor of the late *Cleveland News* to accompany me on an eastern trip with the Indians and do a woman's- eye-view stories of the team, Schlemmer put on his most hostile front.

"A woman in the press box," he fumed. He did everything possible to make Doris uncomfortable, but she withstood his "act."

And act it must have been, for as rough as he was with me, he was an absolute sweetie pie to my wife. And he always spoke lovingly and proudly about his sons and his wife.

Schlemmer especially seemed to enjoy agitating public relations men. He gave Nate Wallack a hard time when Nate was the Indians' tom-tom beater.

Jim enjoyed his whiskey and could consume a glass of it in a couple gulps without showing the slightest effect. During one spring training the Indians stocked the press room cupboard with bottles of the same expensive whiskey sold at the famous "21 Club" in New York. The bottles bore the club's label.

Jim constantly harassed Nate, calling the Indians "cheap, telling him to bring out the "stooping whiskey." (He called the good stuff "stooping whiskey" because he figured it was hidden below.) Meanwhile he wouldn't touch the "21" bottles, much as he loved his drinks. Which reveals how far he would go to make his point.

Wallack got an empty "Old Forester" bottle, Schlemmer's favorite, and filled it with the contents of a "21" bottle.

Schlemmer saw it. He filled his glass. "Ah," he said, smacking his lips. "Now THAT'S stooping whiskey."

Next day he learned of the Wallack trick. He was twice as rough on Nate after that.

I can recall letting Jim get under my skin only once.

I don't remember what he said. It was in the dining room of the Santa Rita Hotel. I finally told him off.

Later that night Harry Jones, baseball writer for the *Plain Dealer*, said, "I've just been to Jim's room He's crying."

"You've got to be kidding."

"Absolute truth," said Harry.

I never got to know the real Jim Schlemmer. He wouldn't let me.

A memorial for big Luke?

Sunday, April 1, 1979

It was less than a month ago that I sat with Luke Easter in his car and he talked at length about his job as a steward at TRW. It was a private talk, not ex-athlete to reporter, friend to friend.

He talked about the young people under his jurisdiction at TRW and their problems. How he was trying to save the job for this one, how he was trying to figure out how to keep another's marriage together and how he worried about those who were taking dope and what could be done about it. He seemed to be carrying each one's burden.

Luke would frown as he talked about this crazy, mixed-up world and how tough it is for kids to grow up in this jungle.

And then he would light up the car with his million-dollar smile when he recalled someone who now was going straight and doing well at the job.

As Luke talked, I remembered what an executive at TRW had told me: "Luke is the best man we have in dealing with the problems of the workers. He knows how to relate. They know he's for them. They know he really cares."

As long as I knew Luke, he always was doing things for others. And ironically, that practice caused him to be gunned down in cold blood Thursday morning. He was doing a favor for his fellow workers, those he tried to help and advise and protect.

Knowing Luke and his courage, I can picture him when the two gunmen confronted him outside the bank after he had cashed the $40,000 worth of paychecks for the employees in his unit at TRW so they would have money instead of paper when they went home that day.

If it had been Luke's personal cash, I suspect he would have given it up without hesitation in the face of the sawed-off shotgun.

But it wasn't his and he was going to protect those hard-earned dollars of his friends. I can see him saying in his gravelly voice, "Hey, what do you mean, man?" And maybe he foolishly did go for the old pistol he carried. And just that quickly he was dead, killed perhaps by men he had once befriended at TRW, killed by the jungle that perplexed him so.

When he died, this city lost more than a fine man. It lost a true civic asset. Luke didn't make his impact as a ballplayer, as a slugger for the Indians. He was in an Indians' uniform too briefly for that, actually just four full seasons. He made it with his deeds.

Everywhere I've gone since Luke's death, men and women have told me how Luke touched their lives or the lives of their children. He always was so friendly. At the Stadium, he would talk to everybody, sign autographs, help kids who asked him questions. They told me of speeches Luke gave, of baseball clinics he attended, of fund-raising ventures he supported, of sick youngsters he visited. He was a director of the Wahoo Club almost from the beginning. He sold tickets for the Indians. He was active in the Cleveland Baseball Federation, constantly assisting the sandlot kids.

He was Big Luke, who never said no to anyone needing a favor, or any worthy cause—a man with a super heart, a man who gave more to others than they gave him.

It would be sinful for this city to forget Luke and his contributions. At the very least, his wife should be asked to throw out the first ball on opening day. Surely, Mayor Dennis Kucinich would gladly share the honor with Virgil Easter, Luke's wife. Perhaps opening day can be dedicated to him, as one reader suggested.

And there should be more. Much more. Some memorial which would help do what Luke tried to do, make this a little better place, would be appropriate. Perhaps a scholarship in his name and a recreation field built where we now have a jungle. What Luke did and what he stood for must not be forgotten.

If all this sounds corny or maudlin, so be it. Luke was a special man. He could light up anybody's life. Except for those moments when he worried about others, Luke was all laughs and smiles and fun. I'll remember the happy moments. I don't want to think he is gone. He was bigger than life.

I first met Luke the day he stepped off the plane from San Diego. Indians' chief Bill Veeck had signed him, at Globetrotters' owner Abe Saperstein's recommendation, to a contract with the Tribe's Triple A farm.

Previously, Luke had played in the Negro Leagues for Abe. But he hadn't played much baseball, actually. Until he met Saperstein, he had been a softball player in the Seattle area, as I remember.

He took to baseball as though it was just another kid's game. For San Diego, he socked the ball out over the railroad tracks behind the center field wall at old Lane Field. Twenty-five homers in just 80 games made Veeck and his vice president, Hank Greenberg, drool. They brought him up and I went to the airport to interview him and drove him to the Stadium.

He put me on from the very beginning. He wore a ring containing a huge diamond, almost as big as a bottle cap.

"Where did you get it?"

"Found it in the gutter," he said. Years later, he told me he won it in a card game. That may have been the truth.

Wally Bock, the Indians' trainer then and now director of athletic services for executives at A-T-O Corporation, remembers the ring.

"He never would put it in the valuables box," recalls Wally. "He always made me carry it in my pocket."

On that ride, I asked Luke about his age. "You've got to be at least as old as I am," said I, 33 at the time.

He screamed, "Haw, haw. You're an old man. I'm just 26."

A few years later, Bock had him on the trainer's table—Luke was there often because he had very bad legs—and the trainer said, "I can feel your bones. I know how old you are."

"Don't tell anybody," pleaded Luke.

Throughout the years, he always called me an old man. Then it came time for him to get his pension. Suddenly, he became seven years older and a year ahead of me.

Thus, he was actually 34 when he first joined the Indians and his baseball feats, considered under the light of the hourglass, become almost legendary. In his first full year with the Indians (1950), with scarcely any professional background and at the age of 35, he knocked in 107 runs and hit 28 homers. The next season, he hit 27 homers and knocked in 103 runs. And the following year, as his knees buckled—he had several operations—and his ankles wobbled, he socked 31 homers and had 97 RBIs.

Bock recalls a time when Luke was hit by his own foul tip and tried to walk it off. "I went out to check and saw his metatarsal bone was broken," he said "He wouldn't believe it. He wanted to keep on playing. I can't recall a player who had more courage. One spring, he pulled a hamstring during an exhibition against the Giants in Dallas. I called Hank Greenberg and he told me to send Luke home. Luke wouldn't go. He opened the season at first base."

After 1952, Luke no longer had the legs to play much in the majors. By 1954, he returned to the minors. He played Triple-A ball with Rochester until 1965, when he was 50 and still hitting homers. Incidentally, they still love him in Rochester.

One wonders what Luke's major league record would have been had there been no racial barrier in the majors and he had been able to start at a young age. With his power, no telling what records he would have broken. He had more power than anybody I ever saw.

He hit numerous tape measure jobs. I recall one that would have hit the bleacher wall in right center on the line, I'm certain, if Dick Weik, a relief pitcher who was seated in the Indians' bullpen—then located in the shadow of the bleachers—hadn't reached up and caught the ball.

And then there WAS the home run I did measure. It hit in the upper deck, above the auxiliary scoreboard. I obtained a large ball of string, tacked one end at home plate and the other end to the chair where the ball landed. Then the string was laid out on the field and checked with a tape measure—477 feet, the longest homer ever hit in the Stadium. The chair was painted red and is now part of the Indians' memorabilia. At least that's one memorial to Luke.

Mickey Mantle once hit a homer that bounced into the bleachers and a sports magazine now on the stands shows it to be 465 feet. No way. The wall in dead center is only 450 feet.

Luke was an exceptional team man. Once, when Al Rosen hit a game-winning homer, everybody ran out to greet him. Everybody but Luke. They found him stretched out on the dugout floor. The big man, in his glee, had jumped up, hit his head on the dugout roof and knocked himself unconscious.

The classic story about Luke, one related here before, deserves retelling in detail one final time, for it reveals his character. I'm glad I couldn't sleep on trains, otherwise this story would have remained the players' secret.

The Indians had finished a series in Boston and took the night train to Detroit. Attached to the regular train were several cars transporting soldiers to their base.

The soldiers went into the club car where several Indians were sitting around having a few beers and playing cards. Soon, the conductor chased them out, saying they didn't have club car privileges. Two strangers remained. Apparently, they boarded the train for the sole purpose of fleecing the soldiers. They became friendly with Early Wynn.

Soon, Wynn excused himself to get into the poker game with teammates Bob Lemon, Harry Simpson, Easter and a few others. Minutes later, the strangers asked if they could join. The players thought they were friends of Wynn and said okay.

Wynn lost a bundle quickly and became a spectator. He noticed the strangers were seated so they had the players trapped between raises. The strangers did most of the winning and Wynn suddenly was certain he saw one dealing from the bottom of the deck.

He screamed and grabbed the man. As soon as he did, the other stranger ran out of the club car. Wynn held his victim and appeared about to throttle him when big Luke stepped in.

"Hold it, Early," he said. "If you hurt this guy, you could get in trouble. Man, sit down. You and I are going to play gin."

The stranger had no choice. Luke sat opposite him while the others watched. In short order, Luke had won back all the money—and more. "Get out of here," he told the stranger. "Don't ever let us see you again." The man left—fast.

Luke asked Lemon, Wynn and the others how much they had lost and gave them back the precise amount.

Later, I asked him, "Luke, how could you play against a man who deals from the bottom of the deck and still be so sure you're going to win?"

He laughed. "I can deal from the middle of the deck," he said.

I wanted to write this priceless anecdote, but Luke asked me to hold off. "Al Lopez (the manager) won't let us play for more than a 25-cent limit," he said. "If you run it, he'll fine all of us. You can print it after I'm no longer with the team."

He finally gave me permission a year later.

Luke could have been a Babe Ruth in escapades as well as in hitting. He would walk into a party and say, "Big Luke's here. Everything's going to be all right." And it was. He would laugh and be the life of the evening.

After such a night during spring training, he arrived at the ball park hoping to rest on the bench. Lopez sat next to him during the exhibition game. Luke got a chair and put it alongside the dugout. "Here Al, would you like to sit here where you can see better?" suggested Luke.

The pleased Lopez said, "Thanks."

A few innings later, Lopez looked into the dugout and saw Luke fast asleep.

The manager momentarily burned, then he laughed. Nobody could stay angry at Big Luke.

His heart was so big, he was a soft touch. He literally gave his money away to anybody who had a sob story. He once opened a restaurant in the Majestic Hotel and, although it was popular, it proved a financial flop because Luke was too trusting of those who ran it for him.

Then he started the Luke Easter Sausage Company with the slogan, "If you want to hit like Luke, you've got to eat like Luke." The sausage was excellent and business flourished, but Luke eventually had to fold the enterprise. Somebody was eating up the profits—and it wasn't Luke.

Not until he married Virgil did he become stable financially. Mrs. Easter, a highly intelligent, warm, lovely lady, began to handle the finances. From then on Luke could give only his big heart to others, not the food off the family table, although there were times when a truly needy person got that, too, with Virgil's blessing.

As Bock said yesterday, "I've seen people die—but I never felt so badly as I did when I heard about Big Luke. He was just a lovable guy."

I loved him—like a brother. Anybody who knew him did. Cleveland lost a civic asset. Somehow, we've got to do something to perpetuate Big Luke's memory, to remind others of the good he did and the cruel waste of his death.

Somehow, this tragedy must be used as a lesson to make the streets less of a jungle—the jungle that consumed him. That's what Luke would want.

Remembering Jesse Owens

April 1, 1980

I tried to see Jesse Owens last week while I was in Tucson. The hospital said his condition was "guarded. No visitors."

He was losing the battle against cancer. It was only a matter of time.

One thing I knew. Jesse wouldn't be complaining. It wasn't in his character. Life was not always easy for him. For many years making a living had been a struggle. He was a super athlete during this nation's deepest depression. He got headlines but no money. His father was unemployed during the years of Jesse's greatest successes.

Yet, he always had a smile, a pleasant word, an inspiring one for those he could help.

Had he been born 45 years later, his photo would be on the cereal boxes today. He would be making TV commercials. He wouldn't have had to scratch.

He always had charisma and personality and these qualities, together with his ability, unquestionably would have made him as popular and as marketable as O.J. Simpson.

Still, no one ever heard Jesse talk about what might have been.

Our talk at the hospital, I envisioned, would be about the "good old days," . . . perhaps days he would smile about and momentarily forget his pain.

We were contemporaries, during his years at Fairmount Junior High, East Tech, and Ohio State University. I can shut my eyes now and see his slim, sinewy body move so fast he was at the finish line almost before the smoke of the starter's gun disappeared.

He would laugh, I'm sure, at the recollection of his junior high days.

Fairmount had no athletic facilities, and he had to practice the dashes on the pavement in front of the school, running down E. 107th Street, just north of Euclid Avenue, while his coach Charley Riley held a stopwatch.

We would talk again, as we had done before, about his desire to play football and basketball at East Tech, along with his dearest friend and classmate, Dave Albritton, the high jumper. But no, the track coach said, it would be foolish to risk his brilliant future on these other fields and Jesse uncomplainingly went along.

And certainly we would have talked about that unforgettable day, May 25, 1935, at the University of Michigan's Ferry Field when Jesse rewrote the track record books, setting world marks in the broad jump, 220-yard dash, the 220-low hurdles, and tying the record in the 100-yard dash.

I know Jesse would have chuckled about that day, or at least about what preceded it, for he laughed when he told me the story of it many years later.

On the 25th anniversary of that afternoon, I called him. He was living in Chicago at the time, a disc jockey for Station WAAF. He was now 46 and weighed 190, 30 pounds heavier than that record-breaking day. He was to achieve even greater prominence in the Olympics the following year, but the four gold medals he won in Berlin were over several days. What he did at Ann Arbor was accomplished in under two hours.

Yet, Jesse almost missed those glorious two hours. He had a sore back and leg. Jesse said, "There's a story behind that sore back that's never been printed." He proceeded to tell it.

Two weeks before the meet, he was returning to the Alpha Phi Alpha fraternity house after his late night job at the state office building in Columbus.

"I was looking forward to hitting the sack," he said. "But I couldn't. One of the guys had shorted the sheets and soaked the bed with water. I was sure Jimmy Tibbs, a guy from New Jersey, had done it because it had happened before. He slept on the third floor.

"I filled a bag with water, crept up to his bed and hit him on the head with it. He yelled and that woke up all the guys in the frat. They started to chase me."

No way they would have caught Jesse, except that he missed the top step and slid all the way down to the second floor.

"On my rear, I slid," he said, laughing. "Boy, did it hurt."

The next day there was a slight pain in his back and it got progressively worse. He didn't report it to the coach. He was able to compete in a meet against Northwestern, but on the final event, the hurdles, "I felt a shooting pain in my spine when I landed on my right foot." He had to tell the coach.

The next day he couldn't even bend to touch his knees. He spent his practice time on the trainer's table. He slept in chemical heating pads.

In the Huron Hotel at Ypsilanti, where the team stayed prior to the Big Ten meet, he sat in a bathtub of hot water until 11 A.M., when it was time to leave for Ann Arbor.

Two teammates had to carry him into Coach Larry Snyder's Hupmobile for the short ride to the big meet. Once they arrived, he had to be carried up the stairs to the dressing room where trainer Tucker Smith applied more "red hot" ointment.

He put on his sweatsuit and dejectedly sat under the flagpole as the stands filled up with 10,000 spectators.

"It was a lovely, warm afternoon," he remembered, "except I felt awful. Coach Snyder came over and said he was going to scratch me from the events."

"I begged him to let me try the 100. He finally said okay. Charley Beetham, our half miler, helped me off with my sweatsuit, slapped me on my sore back, and said, 'You'll do okay, kid.' I got to the starting line just in time for the last call.

"When the starter said, 'On your mark,' I scarcely could get down, the pain was so great. When he said, 'Get set,' it began to disappear. When the gun went off, it was like a miracle. I didn't feel a thing."

The rest is history. At 2:15 he won the 100 in 9.4 seconds, tying the world mark. Meanwhile, the broad jump was in progress. He decided to take only one jump, placing a handkerchief at the world mark of 26 feet, 2½ inches, held by Chubei Nambu of Japan. At 2:25 he hit the takeoff board and flew beyond the handkerchief. The announcer said, "26 feet, 8½ inches, a new world record."

At 3:34 he flashed down the 220-yard stretch in 20.3 seconds, beating the old world mark by a full three-tenths. And at 4 P.M. he completed the grand slam, going over the hurdles in 22.6, two-fifths of a second faster than the former world mark.

The fans cheered mightily at the announcement that they had just witnessed the greatest feat in track history. "I was feeling absolutely no pain afterward," Jesse said.

No doubt he would laugh about those shorted bed sheets and the water fight and that Day of the Miracle, if we had been able to reminisce about it in Tucson.

Unfortunately, no miracle took place in Tucson. He went from "guarded" to "serious" to his final breath.

I last saw Jesse a few months ago when he came to Cleveland to deliver a speech at an AAU affair. It was an impressive presentation . . . Jesse had become a gifted and inspiring speaker.

I remember that he smoked repeatedly that night, prior to heading for the speaker's table, and it was mentioned it seemed out of character for a man who was trying to tell youngsters how to live to be smoking so much.

"Yes," he said, "about two to three packs a day. Awful. Horrible habit. I wish I could beat it. I wish I could tell every kid, every person, never to smoke."

If I know Jesse, the best memorial a smoker could give him would be to stop. At least, if he didn't win the final race he would be helping others prolong theirs.

That was Jesse's creed—always helping others and never complaining about what life dealt him.

Someone missing at Browns' games

August 3, 1982

The Browns lost their 12th man yesterday. Abe Abraham, the Man in the Brown Suit, died in his sleep at age 74.

He had been in the hospital for two weeks with an ailing heart, but he pleaded with his family to keep it secret. He wanted one more year with his beloved football team and he feared that if the Browns learned of his problem they would put him on the disabled list permanently.

No longer will we see Abe rush onto the field after he had finished his other game-day duties, pump an arm into the air in cheerleading fashion and plant himself in the end zone ready to catch the field goals of Matt Bahr, just as he did for Lou Groza, Sam Baker, and Don Cockroft.

Fans would cheer his entrance even before he asked them to cheer the team. He was a spark and a symbol in that orange-brown suit.

Named the Number One fan by the Touchdown Club and only last year given a uniform with his name on it and the numeral 1, Abe's love affair with the Browns began the year they were born, 1946.

He was a clerk in the newsstand in the Leader Building where Arthur B. (Mickey) McBride, the owner of the team, had an office. Business manager of the Browns, Frosty Froberg, invited the friendly little man to an exhibition game.

Froberg showed up late. "You're too busy," said Abe. "You need help."

The following Monday, Abe received a call from McBride. He hired Abe to do errands for Froberg at the games.

During the fourth game of that inaugural season Abe had a message for a doctor seated in Section 30. He took a short cut, across the field behind the end zone. As he reached the goal posts he heard a guard shout, "Look out, Abe." He did just in time to see a Groza line drive go over the cross bar and head right at him.

He tried to catch it, but was knocked down by the force. The trainer, Wally Bock, had to tend to his bruises.

With that blow an idea was born. The 5-7, 140 pounder who came here at age three from Beirut, Lebanon, and developed into one of the town's best Charleston dancers, asked if he could become the retriever for all of Groza's field goals at the closed end of the Stadium. Permission was granted.

Lyon Tailors made him the first orange-brown suit that became Abe's trademark and he went through four of them, clothing stores begging for the privilege to suit him up. His last should be sent to the Football Hall of Fame, for it has become as much a part of Browns' lore as the historic field goals he caught.

Only once did he resort to another color. For a big game against Paul Brown's Cincinnati Bengals in 1971 Abe decided to switch to green because that color represented "Go" and would give the Browns a "psychological advantage," he said. He had one custom-made for $148 and ran onto the field before the blinking crowd, shouting "Go, go go."

The Browns won handily, so the following week he wore the green suit again. But when the Browns had a poor first half he changed to his original orange-brown suit, which he had brought along, just in case. The Browns perked up the second half and he never changed colors again.

He never failed to meet the Browns' plane after road games, always being among the first to say a kind word to the players. He became so widely recognized that fans seeking the players' autographs at the airport also asked for his.

When he met the team after the 1980 victory over Houston which clinched the Central Division title—thousands were there to give the Browns an uproarious welcome—the thoughtful players delayed their waves to the fans to give Abe a gift. They had voted him a game ball. It was the greatest moment of this life and he cried.

He'll be missed for more than his presence at Browns' games. He was one of the kindest and friendliest men ever put on this earth. "He'd shake my hand at least a dozen times at every game," recalls Leo Murphy. Abe delighted in doing favors for others, be they star player, lowly water boy or fan. And it was impossible to repay him for a favor.

He never had much money. He suffered financial losses when a rapid transit station was erected at a diner he had established, yet he would be insulted if you handed him a ten spot for something he did that required time and effort.

A few weeks ago, Nate Wallack, the Browns' vice president, wanted to give Abe a gift and was certain it would be returned. He asked Abe's son to find out what might be acceptable.

Abe was asked. "He just wants one thing. He has made just two trips with the team in 35 years. He went to the championship game in Green Bay and to another in Dallas. He'd like to take one more trip."

Wallack said, "Tell him to name the trip. He's got it."

Abe died yesterday. At least he had the pleasure of anticipation.

The phone has stopped ringing

January 31, 1984

It is 24 hours since I returned from a vacation in Florida and Nate Wallack hasn't called. It will take time getting used to that.

Please excuse me if this piece is too personal or maudlin, but I can't come back to this typewriter without thinking about my dear friend who died in his sleep—"kissed by God," the rabbi said at his funeral—a week ago.

There rarely was a day Nate didn't call me at least once. The Browns' veep would talk during the day and invariably each night he would call again.

Never a boring conversation. Just a "What's doing?" and perhaps a short review of something that happened that day.

I always suspected Nate had a nightly phone list, but when I accused him of that he merely laughed his pleasant "Heh-heh-heh." I know wherever he was he would call his wife, Ruth, and his sons, Stuart and Louis.

He should have had a telephone dangling from his ear. Once, when the Browns were in San Francisco, several of us drove to Carmel to walk around that handsome community. We took pictures of Nate in every phone booth in Carmel and later gave them to him. His response: the soft "Heh-heh-heh."

He gave true meaning to the phone company's slogan "Reach out and touch someone," and now telephone stock will pay smaller dividends. Whenever he saw an injustice he would make a phone call or fire off a letter in an attempt to rectify it.

Our lives were intertwined. He was a scorer at amateur baseball and basketball games when I first began officiating. Often from behind the backstop I'd hear someone yell, "You missed that one, ump," or "Open your eyes." And I'd look around to spot the heckler. When I finally determined it was Nate, he'd smile and give me his gentle "heh, heh, heh."

When he became the social worker at the Warrensville Workhouse he established the first Alcoholics Anonymous group there and proudly invited me to a meeting. The success of that endeavor was one of his most satisfying achievements.

To augment his social worker's salary he also worked weekends at the *Cleveland Press,* in charge of taking all the high school box scores. He asked me to help occasionally and from that exposure I gravitated from teaching and coaching into this profession. Similarly, when I officiated in the National Basketball League—forerunner of the NBA—and learned that the Cleveland entry was seeking a public relations director I recommended Nate. His skill advanced him to the football Rams, the Browns and then Bill Veeck enticed him to the Indians.

Finally, Art Modell brought him back to the Browns and made him a vice president and members of his board of directors.

He became so good at his work that one season the football writers from the three Cleveland dailies, Bob Yonkers, Harold Sauerbrei and Herman Goldstein, chipped in and bought him a handsome gift at the end of the season, an action unheard of in sports.

As much as Modell appreciated him he can't truly comprehend

how much Nate did for the Browns. It is no accident that the Browns have fewer season ticket cancellations than clubs with better records and smaller stadiums. Nate personally talked with every season ticket holder who had a gripe, tried to improve seat locations whenever possible, but mainly he let each one know that the Browns' organization really cared.

Whenever I criticized Modell, Nate would needle me, saying, "You're becoming a poison pen." And maybe he wouldn't call me twice that day. But that night he would say, "Nothing can hurt our friendship." Because we were so close often he was accused of giving me tips on stories. Never did he break a confidence or give me an exclusive.

Nate always said facetiously, "to know me is to love me." Those who didn't, really didn't know him.

Nate had a serious fault for one in his profession. In public he was reserved, and those who thought him aloof mistook his preoccupied mind for arrogance. He often passed friends without seeing them. Once he said hello to everybody at a table at the Stadium Club except me. That night he called and asked, "Where were you?" He forgetfully drove away from a supermarket more than once, leaving his wife inside.

He had a bouncy walk, pet expressions such as "that guy is a Nothingburger," and he was streetwise, a page out of Damon Runyon. In fact, some of his friends called him "Nathan Detroit," the Runyon character in "Guys and Dolls."

Nate was the Ta-Ta-Ta of my Maven deli stories, the guy who hummed every song and ended it with ta-ta-ta and who ate off everybody else's plate. All the deli characters were at this funeral, along with the bankers and athletes and the rest of us who crowded Fairmount Temple on that cold day a week ago. The boys at the deli tell me the Maven, who disliked the Browns and was Ta-Ta-Ta's adversary, still is crying.

But after the tears come the funny stories about Nate. And Nate enjoyed stories about himself more than anybody, no matter how embarrassing. There are so many. Like the time at a draft meeting when he wrote "4 CBs, 3 RBs and 4 LBs," causing a sportswriter who was looking over his shoulder to rush to the phone and tell his office, "The Browns are going to draft four cornerbacks, three running backs and four linebackers." Turned out Nate, who always thought of food, merely was jotting down his luncheon shopping list, four corned beef sandwiches, three roast beefs and four lox on bagels.

I can still hear Nate's "Heh-heh-heh" after that one.

I hope they have golden phones in heaven.

There'll never be another Bill Veeck

January 6, 1986

They buried Bill Veeck Saturday, but they'll never bury the memories . . .

I talked to him by phone two weeks ago and had hoped to see him soon—in Cleveland. He wanted to take over the Indians again.

The first time I saw him was on Euclid Avenue in June 1946. I had just become a full-time sports writer for the *Cleveland News*. All the papers had stories about Bill Veeck seeking to buy the Indians. He had a syndicate of Chicagoans, a few Hollywood moguls, including Bob Hope, but he had no money of his own and he needed working capital too.

He was 32, had unmistakable features and short, blond, wiry, curly hair, giving rise to his nickname "Burrhead." I saw that head bobbing up and down Euclid Avenue and, like a house detective, followed him.

He went into one bank, then another, and then another as I shadowed a few hundred feet behind. Ah, he was seeking the final loan. His stays in the banks were short, meaning, I thought, he was being shut out. Then he went into National City Bank. He stayed a long time. He came out smiling.

I had the story. The deal had been consummated.

Three and one-half years later, after he had built the Indians to world champions and saw his success begin to fade, he sold the club. For double the price his syndicate paid. He sold it because he needed money to pay for his divorce. He came in with almost nothing personally. He left with almost nothing. But he left the city with a legacy—the 1948 championship season.

Until he built a team, Bill made the news with his vaudeville acts on the field, his own flamboyance. But once the team began to win, he wisely stepped into the background.

While he was building he went everywhere to make friends for the team. He was magnetic, fascinating, and good company, so I often volunteered to drive with him on snowy nights to tiny towns all over the state. Some had as few as 200 residents and they would crowd into the town hall to hear Bill. He would tell them whiskered baseball stories and they'd love it. And they'd make arrangements to come to the Stadium that summer. And they did, breaking attendance records.

After the visit to this or that hamlet, we'd drive back. I'd drop Bill off uptown. He'd drink beer with a group of socialites known as the Jolly Set, and, after the party broke up, he'd sit around with Shondor Birns and other characters on the fringe of the law. He loved characters, and he'd swap lies and laughs.

When the sun came up, he'd go to sleep for a few hours. Then he'd be out hustling fans again. He was just two years older than I. I couldn't keep up. I still don't know how he did it.

It was difficult to top Bill. If you bought him a drink, he bought you two. He was especially lavish with sports writers.

After the 1948 season he gave expensive television sets—TVs were rarities then—to the sports editors and columnists as Christmas gifts. The editors of the three Cleveland dailies ordered the sets returned. Gordon Cobbledick of *The Plain Dealer* refused, telling his boss, "If you think I can be bought, you should fire me." He kept the set. He was the only one.

I wasn't among the upper echelon, but he often sent my bride and me gifts, usually large, expensive books. Each time we would send him a more costly gift in return.

Beer was his favorite liquid. A puff of a cigarette and a gulp of beer was the way he breathed. His favorite brew was an imported Dutch variety. Our gifts to him were usually a case or two. After we sent him several cases, the gifts from him stopped. We had topped him, finally, because he realized that, if this kept up, he'd be breaking a poor but honest sports writer.

My bride's most poignant memory of Bill was that sight in the Cleveland Clinic after his leg had been amputated. The ricochet of a cannon, while he was serving in the Marines in the South Pacific, banged against his leg and osteomyelitis set in. The leg had to come off.

After the surgery we visited him and expected that even the usually effusive Veeck would be affected by the trauma of losing a limb. Instead, he was sitting up in his bed playing with a Slinky and other assorted children's toys. A friend had sent him a boxful. No child could have enjoyed himself more.

A few weeks later he was dancing and playing tennis on an artificial leg. He was to have many more operations on that leg, each time removing more of it, until the stump was above the knee. Never once did he consider it a handicap. A remarkable example for complainers.

Bill had a love affair with the fans, except when he tried to get rid of Lou Boudreau.

They adored Lou, the boy manager, a brilliant shortstop, and a fine hitter. But Bill, who inherited him as a manager, thought Lou was a lousy one. He began to work on a deal with the St. Louis Browns—Boudreau for their shortstop, Vern Stephens. Bill wanted to name Al Lopez as his manager.

In the winter of 1948 it became an open secret that the deal was on the fire. Fans burned.

But Bill persisted. Then he returned from the winter meetings and began to talk to fans on street corners. They told him, "Keep Lou."

"Okay," said Bill. "The fans win. Boudreau stays."

Boudreau had his greatest season, and the Indians won the pennant and World Series. But it wasn't the fans who kept Lou. Bill told me later, "I couldn't make the deal. St. Louis wanted too much for Stephens. I would have made it even-up in a second if I could." So he turned it into a seeming victory for the fans. And they loved him all the more.

Bill broke the color line in the American League by signing Larry Doby. Then he brought in Satchel Paige.

The Doby signing created no howls, but the acquisition of Satchel did. "Now Bill has gone too far," editorialized the *Sporting News*, known as Baseball's Bible. Not because Satchel was black, but because he was *old*.

Veeck, himself, enjoyed saying Satch was at least 50, maybe 60, "but what difference does it make? He still can pitch better than kids who are 20."

Satch proved him right and fans broke down the gates every time he pitched. Stories about him sold newspapers, too, and the circulation of the *News* zoomed during an 18-chapter series I did on him.

One chapter dealt with his age. Satch, unlike Veeck, didn't want to be considered an old man. He told me he entered pro baseball with the Chattanooga Black Lookouts in 1927 at the age of 16, which would have made him "only" 37 in 1948. He offered $500 to anyone who could prove he played before 1927.

One reader did. Five hundred was big money then. The reader went to Chattanooga, checked out the public library, looked through all the box scores, and found one that listed a pitcher named "Satchel" in 1926.

"That's me," admitted Satch. "I must have slept out a year." Which made him 38 in 1948.

Bill paid the $500 for Satch. But he continued to say Satch was 50 or 60. Never let the facts interfere with a good story. Not if it brought more fans to the ball park.

Bill fell on hard times after he had to give up the St. Louis Browns. Nate Dolin, a major stockholder of the Indians and Bill's friend, gave him a job as a scout, at $15,000 a year.

Bill came into Tucson for spring training and the Santa Rita Hotel, where the Indians stayed, was booked. I offered to share my room.

Each night Bill would soak his leg stump in the bath while reading law books. He was a voracious reader and now he had decided to become a criminal lawyer. It wasn't necessary to get a law degree, just pass the bar.

At 3 A.M. one morning the phone rang for Bill. One of the Indians' pitchers was in trouble with the law. Bill had brought the Indians to Tucson originally. Could he handle this one? Bill dressed and left. He whisked the pitcher to a ranch in New Mexico where he stayed until Veeck cooled things off with a certain irate husband.

"Don't you dare print this," he told me. "You'd never know about it if we weren't roomies." I didn't, then.

Later Bill put together a syndicate to buy the White Sox, turned them into a pennant winner, sold the team and bought it back again when there was a danger the franchise would be moved out of Chicago.

Two weeks ago I called him. I had heard he was interested in taking over the Indians again. Yes, it was true. "But don't make waves in the paper," he said. "It's a ticklish situation. I don't want to hurt my chances."

But was he up to it physically? "For a guy with one leg, one lung, and one ear, and who can't see very well, I'm doing OK."

Three years ago he had finally given up cigarettes, after a lung had been removed. He repeated the old line, "If I had known I was going to live this long, I'd have taken better care of myself." Then he added quickly, "But I've had fun. No regrets."

He said he hoped to see me soon in Cleveland, and that anything I could do to help him come back would be appreciated.

I talked with a potential buyer who became excited about the possibility of Bill taking charge again. He thought the time was ripe.

I thought so too. Now he won't be coming back. Too bad for Cleveland. Too bad for baseball. So long, old friend.

End of an era brings bitter tears

December 18, 1995

Dear Diary:

Dec. 17, possibly the final pro football game at the Stadium and probably the last for this edition of the Cleveland Browns.

Diary, I've got to admit I cried.

I've seen it all and done it all in sports. Never before have I been so emotionally moved to the point of tears.

Yes, when the game against the Bengals at the Stadium was winding down I cried. Tears of bitterness and sadness.

Diary, I've been writing to you each time the team has played at home since Art Modell announced this club will be in Baltimore next year. This could be the final entry.

Chances are the city will get a pro team again—another Cleveland Browns. But when? An expansion team could be years away. And would it be in this Stadium?

I have so many memories of this old park, the players, the Hall of Famers, so many of them dear friends. And the employees. I hugged some of them goodbye today.

I'll save special Stadium memories for another day, but oddly as I drove to the park, only one game came back vividly, the 14-12 playoff loss to Oakland when "Red Right 88" cost the Browns a trip to the Super Bowl. Funny how a sad day stood out above all the glorious ones. That one hurt personally, not because of the loss, but because I knew I would have to rip Coach Sam Rutigliano, a truly fine guy. But he pulled a rock, in my view, and I had to go back to the typewriter and say so.

Heading into the Stadium today there was a different look and feel as compared to the previous weeks. At those other games, many fans seemed to have put away their Browns attire, as if to divorce themselves from the Art Modell product. This time almost everyone wore something that said "Browns," as if to proclaim proudly: "This is our name, and you can't take it from us."

The Dawg Pound, filled an hour before the game, was a sea of brown and orange, and the Big Dawg, caretaker of the Pound, proudly was signing autographs.

Unlike in the past games, the fans seemed to be there not only to say goodbye to the Stadium, but also a warm farewell to the players.

Thousands crowded above the Browns' dugout and cheered as the players came out for the pregame workout. When the players came out just before the kickoff, many ran to the Dawg Pound, slapping hands with the fans. Like old times, this was, only with more feeling.

Two signs stood out like sore thumbs, if you'll permit an appropriate cliché. Both were professionally painted and wrapped around the orange tarpaulins on the north side of the field, perfectly placed for the national TV cameras. One read: "Art, thanks for 34 exciting years," and the other: "Thanks for the memories, Art." Disgusting plants. Obviously put there by the ground crew on orders from the Browns' organization.

Thanks for the memories, Art? Ugh. You took most of them away when you pulled the plug on us.

The sun was bright on this crisp winter day. "Modell weather," we once called it. Never again. And the field looked better than usual at this time of year, reminding me, in contrast, of playoff days on muddy fields and snow. Far, far better days.

Another irony: For the final (?) game to be against the Cincinnati Bengals. The TV cameras zoomed in on Mike Brown, sitting in a loge. With his hat on, the Bengals owner was the image of his late father, Paul, the first coach of the Browns. A reincarnation And I remembered when, back in 1945, Arthur McBride, who started the franchise, asked us, the sportswriters, whom he should hire as the coach. Unanimously we said, "Paul Brown."

Mike Brown still speaks angrily about the firing of his dad by Modell, so the final confrontation here of the two teams seemed theatrically fitting.

However, the game was going to be incidental, I thought. The Browns had been playing poorly and the Bengals were still in the playoff hunt, having beaten the Bears last week.

Another "dead horse" performance by the Browns wouldn't have surprised me. Instead, the Browns fed off the fans emotionally, as well as their own desire to go out with a victory gift to their loyalists. Football, more than any other sport, is triggered by emotions.

The Bengals aren't a good defensive club, and today the Browns put everything together—running game, with Earnest Byner going 100 yards, and Vinny Testaverde razor sharp. The surprise, though, was the Browns' defense. The Bengals are a high-scoring team, and the Browns' D has been awful. This time the Browns' defense took over. Result: An easy 26-10 victory.

The Browns looked so good I began to wonder, "What if the courts do force them to play out their lease here and Modell would have to fly this team back to the Stadium on Sundays. Would these fans stay away?"

I don't know. These are the most avid football fans in the world. It wouldn't surprise me if they fooled the NFL and 50,000 came for games for a "Lame duck" team, hoping somehow their presence could keep them here forever.

I wanted to keep Byner here forever. And Matt Stover, Mr. Automatic, and so many others. Yes, even Andre Rison. Sure, he puts his foot in his mouth and he's flamboyant. But, strangely, I find his candidness refreshing.

In the press box, I sat next to a New York writer, here to do a Stadium obituary. He had no real conception of our pain. At one point he brought out today's Baltimore Sun and read a three-page account of how Modell secretly gave them our team.

There was a big, smiling picture of Modell on the front sports page. He was holding the football he was bringing to that city. I wanted to reach out and crumple it.

The press box became antiseptic, and with five minutes to go I went downstairs into the stands.

That's when it all got to me. The fans already had begun to stand up, and they remained standing until the final play. The better the team played, the more angry and bitter they seemed to become at Modell.

They loved the players and they hated him.

Whether it was their anger or their desire for souvenirs, several soon began to break up the seats. In the Dawg Pound, seats were flung onto the field. Near me they ripped chairs out of their moorings. A few firecrackers exploded, like bombs.

Security advised the officials to move the ball away from the Dawg Pound, and I began to wonder how the Dawgs would behave when the game ended.

Meanwhile, the emotions of the fans transfused into me. You could almost hear them saying. "Why does this have to be? Why is our team being taken away? What have we done to deserve this?"

And this is when my eyes began to water and I couldn't see the last few plays. But I heard the crowd shout, "Six . . . five . . . four" as the final seconds evaporated. Diary, I thought of the countdown on New Year's Eve, with the ball coming down on Times Square. This time the ball was coming down on us.

And then it was over and the players, spontaneously, ran to the Dawg Pound. "Unplanned," they said later. Some went into the stands where Dawgs were crying, too. Carl Banks said later, "I've never been in anything so emotional. Not even when I was with the Giants and we won the Super Bowl."

Diary, it was that kind of a moment. I'm not ashamed of my tears.

Several players huddled at midfield, and most of them seemed reluctant to leave it for the final time.

I hated to see the destruction in the Stadium. At least $50,000 worth. Fans were carrying out planks, chairs. The security was on the field, not in the stands. Maybe the fans thought they would start the refurbishing.

But there were no fights or violence. Just anger and sadness.

And hope. Hope, perhaps false, that this team, somehow, will be back. Another irony: Saying farewell might have been easier if they hadn't played so well.

Diary, as I drove east from the Stadium, a bright orange sun descended behind the old ballpark, silhouetting it in its glow. It brought tears again.

A good sign or The End?

Loss of Harder is great one for Tribe

October 21, 2002

Mel Harder's ashes will be scattered across Mel Harder Field in Chardon. That's what he wanted.

The field was his love, and when the folks in Chardon named it after him, he considered it the honor of his life.

The longtime Indians pitcher and coach died Sunday morning

peacefully after many months of fighting off illnesses, mainly difficulty with breathing and eating.

Through all his suffering, mention a baseball incident or ask a question about the game and his eyes would brighten and he would dip into that fine memory of his and offer pearls no other person had. He would say, for example, that Lou Gehrig was tougher to pitch against than Babe Ruth.

Harder's birthday was last Tuesday.

He turned 93. Russell Schneider, once my peer at *The Plain Dealer* and now a columnist for Sun newspapers, thoughtfully mentioned fans might want to send Mel a birthday card. He was inundated with them, and many carried warm personal messages of their recollections about this outstanding pitcher and special man.

Fortunately, he was able to have them read to him during the final few days of his life and to know how much we admired and cared about this exceptional pitcher and gentleman.

He was one of the greatest pitchers ever to put on an Indians uniform.

He came to the Indians at age 18 in 1928, pitched through 1947, and won 222 games.

Then he became the team's pitching coach.

Bob Lemon is in the Hall of Fame.

He always said Harder made him.

Early Wynn is in the Hall of Fame. He always said Harder put him there.

Bob Feller is in the Hall of Fame. He and Harder were teammates. During which time Harder often counseled the young pitcher at Feller's request, and later Harder coached him. Ask Feller about Harder, and he'll speak only in superlatives.

The fourth man of that Big Four staff—often called the greatest of all time—was Mike Garcia. Garcia, until the day he died, would tell me how much of his success he owed to Harder. And if Garcia had pitched long enough, he probably would be in the Hall of Fame today, too.

Al Lopez was the manager under whom Harder coached. Together, they led the Indians through several outstanding seasons, the climax of which was a record 111 victories and the American League pennant in 1954. Lopez often told me of Harder's brilliance as a teacher.

"He never pushed his ideas on the guys," said Lopez. "He would wait until they seemed eager for help and advice."

Lopez is in the Hall of Fame.

Harder should be, too.

One of the disappointments in his life was that he had yet to be elected.

There is no pitcher more deserving.

Joe DiMaggio told me more than once that Harder was the toughest pitcher he ever faced. I heard this from so many old-timers.

Ted Williams always found Harder a problem, and he campaigned hard, along with Feller and many of his fans here, for Harder to be elected.

It was not to be because the Veterans Committee was rife with politics and this year it was changed for that very reason, influenced in part by the fact that it was so unfair to Harder.

We thought we had enough votes for him in 2000. The group pushing his election talked with every member of the Veterans Committee and we were promised the votes to get him in. But we were double-crossed by those who had friends they secretly favored and thus were lying to us.

Harder, of course, had pitched long before many of those on the Veterans Committee became seriously involved with the game. They really didn't know him and Harder was the quiet type who never made headlines with quotes or pushed himself. You'd never hear him toot his own horn.

So the man richly deserving of the honor lost out. It's the Hall of Fame's loss. The new selection process, of which I am now a part, makes it almost impossible for any old-timer to receive sufficient votes. I just voted for him—No. 1 on my list—and I'll keep pushing because to be in Harder's corner is a labor of love, although now a seemingly hopeless one.

But he did have that Mel Harder Field and the Wahoo Club every year gives out its Distinguished Service Award in Mel's name. And he is in the Greater Cleveland Sports Hall of Fame, the Ohio Baseball Hall of Fame and many others.

There are a few of us around who saw him pitch. He pitched the historic opener at Cleveland Stadium. If memory serves, the date was July 31, 1932. It was Wes Ferrell's turn to pitch, but on game day he begged off for some mysterious reason. Roger Peckinpaugh, the manager, asked Harder, pitching out of turn, to take the ball.

Harder never would say no. Before 80,000 fans, he and Lefty Grove of the Philadelphia Athletics engaged in a brilliant pitching battle, Grove finally winning, 1-0. (Incidentally, Grove is in the Hall of Fame.)

Harder pitched mostly for poor Cleveland teams, yet managed to have two seasons of 20 or more victories, and to accumulate 222 victories with little hitting behind him reveals how great a pitcher he was. His exceptional curveball buckled the knees of the best hitters.

In 1940, the Indians had one of their better teams and rebelled against Manager Oscar Vitt, firmly believing his thoughtless, outspoken criticism of some players—one being Feller—was costing them the pennant.

Hal Trosky, the first baseman, was to be the team's spokesman when the players presented their complaints to owner Alva Bradley and to request the removal of Vitt.

On the day of the meeting, Trosky had to leave the team for Iowa because of an illness in his family. Harder was asked to be the spokesman. Although this was not his nature, again he didn't say no because it hurt him deeply to hear the manner in which Vitt, in front of everybody on the bench, cut up those on the field when a misplay occurred.

The "revolution" resulted in the team being called the Cleveland Cry Babies, and in a sense, Harder was left holding the bag, but he never regretted standing up for his teammates.

He always was a standup guy and ever the gentleman. Even against Vitt, he never was vitriolic or swore. I never have heard anyone, not even Vitt, say an unkind word against Harder. He lived and died without an enemy.

He was a super husband to his wife Sandy, who died many years ago, and a father of two daughters who idolized him.

And anyone who became acquainted with him became a permanent Harder fan and friend.

The Burr Funeral Home in Chardon is certain to be crowded Thursday from 1 to 4 and 6 to 9 P.M. for our last goodbyes.

If there is a Hall of Fame in heaven for the good and special people, Harder will be in it today.

Lord knows he belongs.

EVENTS

Colavito is "for real" pitcher now

August 14, 1955

The Indians now have lost five in a row. So who cares? Rocky Colavito finally made his major league debut as a pitcher. That's the big news.

"We kind of shook things up out there," said Joe Gordon afterward. "It was kind of exciting for the fans, wasn't it?"

It was indeed. Almost electrifying it was to see Rocky walk in from right field in the seventh inning of last night's second game.

But that's not why the imaginative Gordon called on the Rock, although it could have been reason enough. The 14,351 customers are glad they paid their way into the Stadium last night even though the Indians lost both games, 6-2 and 3-2.

Gordon called on the Rock to pitch because in the manager's mind this was the situation tailor-made for him. "I knew that if I ever was going to use him it would be with first base open, runners in scoring position and needing a strikeout," said Gordon.

Last night with the score 2-1 against the Tribe, Frank Billing opened the seventh with a single and Red Wilson's single sent him to third. Coot Veal was up and when knuckle-baller Hoyt Wilhelm's second pitch got through catcher Russ Nixon, Wilson scampered to second.

Gordon called time and walked to the mound. It was apparent he was afraid of another passed ball. When Gordon motioned toward the bullpen the taxi drove over to pick up Don Ferrarese. Instead Colavito sauntered in from right field.

"As soon as I saw the passed ball I made up my mind, to use Colavito," revealed Gordon.

"No, I wasn't surprised," said the Rock. "Somehow I sort of expected it."

"My intention was to have him get us out of the inning and send him back to right field," explained Gordon later.

So there was the Rock on the mound in a major league game, not an exhibition, with runners on second and third, and the count 1-1 on Veal.

Completely poised, Rocky fired a fast ball. Umpire Ed Runge called it a strike as the fans cheered mightily.

The next pitch was another fast ball. Umpire Runge called it a ball. Catcher Russ Nixon protested vehemently. So did the Tribe bench. Runge indicated it was several inches outside and then waved someone off the bench. The "someone," it developed, was Jo Jo White, who stayed there for a while, completely unaware that the umpire had thumbed him.

Veal flied to left on the next pitch, and Bolling scored after the catch. Rocky walked the following hitter, Herb Moford, and at this point Runge threw Russ Nixon out of the game.

Runge had told Nixon, "Don't try to show me up just because the fair-haired boy is pitching out there." And Nixon, using some choice words, accused the umpire of alibiing, and so was thrown out for the first time in his major league career.

Gordon steamed out of the dugout, and he, too, was thumbed, and Runge finally convinced White he had to leave, too. During the argument Rocky got an opportunity to warm up fully.

Except for the loud boos for Runge things quieted down after that as Rocky retired Harvey Kuenn and Reno Bertola without much trouble.

At the end of the inning Gordon asked Rocky, "How do you feel?"

"Fine," replied the Rock.

"Do you want to stay in there?"

"Yes sir."

So the Rock, after getting a triple to drive in the Indians' second run, returned to the mound and held the Tigers hitless in the eighth and ninth.

"I figured," said Gordon later, "it would be experience for next time if he got a few more innings under his belt."

So there will be a next time?

"If the situation again presents itself, yes," the manager replied. "He's a good looking pitcher. In my book he did what he was supposed to do. No matter what the umpire says he struck out Veal."

Nixon said the same thing. "The ball got a good piece of the plate," the catcher insisted.

Colavito, just before leaving the clubhouse, stuck his head in Gordon's office and was told, "Good job, Rocky. You're my man."

"That was a third strike on Veal. If it wasn't I'm a monkey's uncle," Rocky told the manager.

"I know it was, Rocky. As far as I'm concerned you got out of the inning without a run."

The Rock left with a grin.

Said Gordon, "You've got to give him a lot of credit, to come in there in a tense situation like that and pitch the way he did."

Rocky threw 49 pitches and only 18 were balls. In the ninth he shrugged his shoulders slightly with a man on first and that was a balk. Otherwise he looked as though he had been pitching all his life.

Umpire Runge volunteered, "He's not as fast as I thought he would be." And the Detroit players agreed. Said one, "He doesn't throw as hard as he does from right field because he can't get the hop, skip and jump."

Frank Billing added, "You have to be cautious, because when you've never seen him pitch before you don't know what to expect." The Tigers were surprised that Rocky has such a good curve.

Gordon also agreed that Rocky wasn't his fastest last night. "He was much faster that first night he pitched in Cincinnati," said Joe, "but he was fast enough. Don't forget he was in the park from 3:30 on, running, taking batting practice and playing 15 innings before he came in to pitch. All that had to take something out of him. He probably was a little tired."

"I feel great," said the Rock, as usual.

One Tiger's comment was "If I were Colavito I'd get to Frank Lane's office bright and early tomorrow morning and get this thing straightened out. I see he's got 71 RBIs. Is he going to be a hitter or a pitcher? That's what I'd find out if I were Rocky."

The answer is, mostly he'll be a hitter, but occasionally he'll pitch, too. The pay should be pretty good, too.

It makes for a great show. Ask the fans.

Rocky Colavito: "Can't believe it!"

June 11, 1959

Baltimore—Rocky Colavito was sitting back in the chair, relaxing. Along with a few teammates, he was having a midnight snack at the home of a friend.

He mumbled something to himself and grinned.

"What did you say?" he was asked.

"Oh, I was just saying to myself, "it's unbelievable." I really can't believe it happened."

As if to prove that it did happen, he dug into his pockets and pulled out the evidence, examining it carefully, almost lovingly.

It was a baseball, the ball he had hit into the stands an hour earlier, in the ninth inning of the Indians' 11-8 victory over the Orioles. There was a soft spot on the ball where the bat had connected to write baseball history. That homer was his fourth in a row, a feat previously accomplished in a nine-inning game by only two major leaguers.

Back in 1894, Robert L. Lowe of the Boston National League club hit four homers in one game in four trips to the batter's box and Lou Gehrig of the Yankees repeated the feat in 1932. Now 27 years later, Rocco Colavito, 24-year-old Bronx-born son of an Italian immigrant, has etched his name below Gehrig's in the record book.

Rocky excused himself from the dinner table to call his wife who was visiting her folks in Reading, Pa. Then he called his dad in the Bronx and his brother, Dominic.

"Everybody is so happy," Rocky reported upon returning. "My wife is overjoyed. She heard the game. So did my brother Dominic. My dad sounded sleepy, but he knew about it. A New York paper called him and they're coming over to his house tomorrow to take pictures. He sounded proud."

Rocky studied the ball again. To get the souvenir, his roommate, Herb Score, had tracked down the fan who caught it deep in the left field seats.

"I offered him an autographed ball for it," revealed Herb. "He said no, he wanted Rocky's autograph on the ball and wanted to keep it."

Spud Goldstein, the Indians' traveling secretary, came along and made a deal. For $25 and two autographed baseballs, the fan agreed to give up the prize.

"Frank Lane is going to have it gold-plated for you, Rocky," he was told.

"Great, I'll put it on the mantle," said the curly-haired, slim six-footer.

"You won't get a chance. That ball is going to the Hall of Fame in Cooperstown."

"Hall of Fame!" he exclaimed. "Are you kidding? Gosh, that would be something. I'm a fortunate guy. I've been thanking God all night, ever since it happened."

The deeply religious Rocky then talked about the final homer.

"I was standing in the outfield after my third homer," he related, "and I heard somebody yell, 'Break the record. Hit another the next time up.' Subconsciously, I was thinking of that, too. But I forced the thought out of my mind. I looked up toward heaven and said, 'Dear God, I'm not greedy, I'll be happy if I can get a single next time.'"

"I always talk to God. He's been good to me. He gave me whatever talent I have. The rest is up to me to use it."

This attitude eliminated all pressure from him as he walked to the plate for the final time. "I was just going for the single—swinging down the middle—just as I had done all night."

Before the game, Manager Joe Gordon called Rocky aside and told him, "Somebody has printed the rumor that you're being traded to Boston. It's a phony. I'd never trade you to Boston. You'd kill us there. I wouldn't trade you anywhere." The manager added with a laugh, "But if you don't start hitting, I'll send you back to Reading."

Rocky laughed, too, and said, "Reading's a good town, Skip."

He went to the bat rack and studied his weapons. He decided to discard the bat he had been using, explaining, "It's pretty dirty. The dirt might make it a little too heavy." So he selected a clean model and swung it. "I feel great," he announced.

"You always do," ribbed a teammate.

Rocky noticed a writer on the bench. "Don't look so downhearted," he said. "We'll start winning. We'll be back in first place soon." Then he ran onto the field for batting practice.

"That guy wouldn't sound so gay if he had to watch himself hit," grunted the writer grumpily. Rocky had been in a lengthy slump.

Soon the game got under way. Rocky drew a base on balls his first time up.

He came up again in the third inning, with the Indians leading 4-3. Vic Power was on base. Pitcher Jerry Walker threw a change-up.

Rocky swung and lofted a high fly toward left. It cleared the fence for his 15th homer of the season.

He was up again in the fifth. This time the pitcher was Arnold Portocarrero, who threw him a slow curve. For the past several weeks, the pitchers had been fooling him with slow stuff. Rocky hit the curve into the seats at least 420 feet away. It was an eye-popping sock.

The next inning he faced Portocarrero again. This time, he swung at the fast ball, "down and away." It left his bat wickedly, a low line drive, taking off toward left center like a golf ball. "I wasn't sure whether it would clear the fence," admitted Rocky later. But the powerfully hit ball kept rising, clearing the barrier easily and became his third homer of the night.

In the press box a Baltimore writer noted, "No team ever has hit more than three home runs in one game in this park. Rocky has equaled that record himself." He added unnecessarily, "This is the toughest home-run park in baseball."

Then Rocky came up a fourth time and personally broke the Baltimore record. The pitcher was Ernie Johnson, who brushed him back with the first pitch. The next one was a fast ball, high and inside. Rocky swung. There was never a doubt the moment it left that bat.

The fans gave him a standing ovation as he trotted around the bases. Ironically, earlier in the game, one of them had poured beer down on Rocky after he had made a catch in right field. Rocky was so angered he almost threw the ball at the beer-thrower, but he managed to control himself and heard the boos as he jogged off the field. Each homer changed more boos to cheers and Rocky forgivingly tipped his cap each time.

When Rocky reached the dugout after his historic blow, he leaped into the crowd of teammates awaiting the conquering hero. The Rock let out several yells, "Yippee!" "Wahoo," and repeated the screams as he shook hands with his teammates.

Billy Martin, who had been taking a shower, rushed out naked to the bench to shake Rocky's hand. Pitcher Gary Bell, knocked out of the box earlier, ran into the dugout with a towel wrapped around him.

"The boys were a little stunned by the homer," described Manager Gordon later. "Rocky made most of the noise." Rocky went into the clubhouse to see if there were other hands to shake. To everyone he saw, the clubhouse man, the usher, he said, "Give me five," encasing their hands in his crushing palm.

After the game the reporters streamed in.

"Did you know," he was asked, "that the only player in modern ball to do what you did tonight was Lou Gehrig?"

"Gehrig? No kidding?" said the slugger, genuinely surprised. "He was my favorite player when I was a little kid. My brother, Vito, was a first baseman and he loved Gehrig, so naturally I did, too. That was before Joe DiMaggio, though. DiMaggio became my idol."

"But DiMaggio never did what you did tonight," Rocky was told.

A teammate shouted, "From now on, we'll call you Babe Ruth."

"Ruth never hit four in a game," said a historian.

"Well, then we'll stick to 'Don't Knock the Rock,'" another suggested.

Rocky tore himself away from the interviewers and went to Gordon's office.

"I don't have to go back to Reading, do I, Skip?" he said with a grin.

"I'm proud to have seen you do it," Gordon replied.

"I'm proud to have done it for you and under you," said the Rocky. "I know I've been in a bad slump, but you never gave up on me. When things were rough, you kept us loose. I'll never forget you for that. You're a great manager to play for."

When Colavito left, Gordon was speechless. He finally managed to say, "Well, how do you like that?"

In the dressing room Gary Bell drew a laugh with "A guy had to put himself in the Hall of Fame to win a game for me."

Rocky, still grinning much later, mumbled to himself, "I still find it hard to believe."

Jim Brown quits football

July 14, 1966

Jim Brown is retiring from football, he revealed exclusively to *The Plain Dealer*.

His decision is final. One of the greatest football players in the history of the game—if not the greatest—is hanging up No. 32 permanently.

Henceforth he will devote his efforts to the Negro Industrial and Economic Union, his movie career and other business interests.

The man who broke all pro records as fullback for the Cleveland

Browns for the past nine years will make the formal announcement of his retirement today at a news conference in Markyate, England, during a luncheon break of the filming of the M-G-M movie *The Dirty Dozen,* in which Jim has a major role. London time is five hours ahead of Cleveland's.

He notified Coach Blanton Collier and Browns' president Art Modell by mail of his decision and he told *The Plain Dealer* he also talked with Modell by long distance phone late yesterday.

"I am leaving the Browns with an attitude of friendliness and cooperation," Jim said. "Once I return to Cleveland I'll do everything I can to help the Browns—other than playing. The Browns have a great organization and a great team. One man won't make the difference. I leave with great respect for Blanton and Art. I'll help them in any way I can."

He revealed he has been wrestling with himself over the decision to retire for some time.

"I had intended to play this year. My original reason for coming back was because Art wanted me to. Then, when it was pointed out by Art my reporting late put the team in an awkward position, my original reason for returning wasn't there any longer."

The regulars are scheduled to report to Hiram Sunday, but it became evident Jim would be late—how late nobody knew—because bad weather had delayed the filming of *The Dirty Dozen.* When Modell ascertained this he said Jim would be suspended and if he could report later a judgment on him would be made at that time.

"I could see Art's point," said Jim. "He didn't want to set a precedent and do anything to disturb team morale. It wouldn't be fair to Blanton, either. I'm not the kind of guy that would beg off from training. It's important to get in the right football frame of mind and there are so many things Blanton would want me to work on—and things I would want to work on too. I definitely was not trying to avoid training camp.

"Each day I kept hoping I could call Art and give him a date when the picture would be completed. But nobody knew. We still don't know."

What if, after the picture ends, the team needs him and Modell asks him back?

"No," he said. "This decision is final. I'm no longer preparing mentally for football. I'm committing myself to other things. One thing I want to get over: I'm not going to play again."

His chief personal commitment is to the Negro Industrial and Economic Union, of which Jim was one of the founders. This is not a money-making proposition for him. In fact, he has put plenty of money into it.

NIEU is an attempt to make Negroes help themselves by establishing businesses, getting the proper financing to become producers instead of merely consumers. It's looked upon as an "Operation Bootstrap" attempt in which the Negro will raise his economic standards through his own efforts. Brown already has signed up several pro athletes to work with him.

"Negro participation in the American economy is very important to me," he explained.

At present his own financial future appears to be as a movie actor. Reports from London are that his work in *The Dirty Dozen* has been excellent. M-G-M has given him another script to read and he has a firm commitment from Paramount for three pictures. He previously appeared in a successful western, *Rio Conchos*.

Jim also is involved in Mainbout, a closed circuit television company which has rights to Cassius Clay's fights. "It's becoming more interesting all the time and I think it can create some jobs for the N.I.E.U.," he said.

"I believe I have a fine chance to make a living in the movie industry," he added.

"But I want to make this clear: My greatest hope when accepting the assignment in *The Dirty Dozen* was that it would be finished in time to play the additional year that Art Modell expected from me. It just didn't work out that way."

Jim says he intends to continue living in Cleveland "for some time, at least" and will return here as soon as the movie is finished.

Discussing his decision he added, "I'm a funny kind of guy. I loved football, especially my last three years with the Browns under Blanton and Art. In that period I realized everything I wanted. Communication with the coaches and other players, the opportunity to create and to express my opinions. I thoroughly enjoyed every bit of it.

"But I have other ambitions, things I would like to do that mean a lot to me. I really didn't want to play this year, but had told Art I would and then that didn't work out. I finally decided the timing for my decision to retire was now.

"I had a good year in 1965. (He gained 1,544 yards to lead the league for the fourth consecutive year.) We won the division title and it was satisfying in all respects except for our final game against Green Bay.

To come back for personal reasons: there would be only two, the championship and the money. But a man has to retire some time. We did win the championship in 1964 and I think I can make a living through my other interests."

It is believed his football salary on the three-year contract which was to terminate after 1966 was $75,000 a season.

"I'm sure the Browns will be contenders this year," he continued. "Blanton is a brilliant coach and a wonderful man. With or without me the club has great talent and Blanton knows how to get the most out of it. I think Leroy Kelly is a great runner and he and Ernie Green will make a fine running-blocking combination."

Jim, now 30, joined the Browns in 1957 as their top draft choice and he immediately proceeded to establish himself as the greatest runner the game has ever known. He appeared indestructible. Only once did he have to leave a game temporarily because of injury. This would have been his tenth year with the Browns.

"I love football," he said yesterday. "I love all sports. I'll see all the Browns' games. I'll be rooting for them to win the championship. I'll help in any way I can, if the will want me to. Any way except play."

Did the bus ride do in the Browns?

September 18, 1966

From high-school days to the present, I have made hundreds of bus trips with athletic teams. But never have I taken a bus ride to compare with the trip with the Browns, Jan. 2 of this year.

It was only 27 miles, yet it was the longest I ever experienced. It may have been my imagination working overtime, but if I were a betting man, I would have put my bundle on the Packers by the time the bus deposited the Browns in front of the locker-room door.

It seemed a good idea at the time to house the Browns at the Holiday Inn in Appleton, Wisconsin, prior to their championship game with the Packers. Green Bay itself figured to be jumping with football celebrants the night before the big game. Include the New Year festivities and "Titletown, U.S.A." simply had to be a bubbling, noisy cocktail shaker of a community.

In contrast, Appleton figured to be peaceful and quiet, a perfect spot to prepare for the championship match. And it was.

The wide divided highway in front of the motel led directly to the Packers' ball park, less than one-half hour away, a comfortable, relaxing ride.

Everything was beautiful—until about 6 P.M. Then the cold front hit. It began to snow. It snowed and snowed and snowed. It refused to quit. On the afternoon of Jan. 1, the sun was shining, the farmland was golden.

On the morning of Jan 2d, the entire landscape was a deep blanket of white.

The Browns had their pregame meal and their pregame meeting. Then they boarded the two buses stationed in front of the motel.

And the ride began. The snow had turned the smooth, wide highway into an obstacle course. In our bus, the driver's windshield iced up and his defrosting fan couldn't cope with the moisture that started out as hot breath from football bodies and chilled as it hit the cold glass.

The driver kept scraping away to get a clear patch of vision. The players did the same at their seats. Cars from all over Wisconsin, bumper-to-bumper, were on the same highway, heading for the Stadium through the driving, deep snow.

It was start-stop-start-stop as the bus edged ahead, a few feet at a time. Cars with less traction and worse vision had gone off the road into deep snow embankments. There were skidding accidents that caused locked bumpers and brought traffic to a complete halt.

I watched the Browns. Some looked out the window. Others yelled advice to the bus driver. A few tried to sleep without obvious success. There were some weak attempts at jokes.

As the minutes sped by without noticeable progress, anxiety and jitters showed up in several of them. One veteran paced up and down, tried to make small talk but it came out juvenile.

Again, perhaps, it was my imagination at work, still this team which appeared emotionally ready as we boarded the bus, was now emotionally spent when we finally reached the ball park more than 1½ hours later. Those 27 dragging, disturbing, harrowing miles had taken away their concentration.

Out of the field, brushes were revolving constantly to sweep the snow off the frozen ground. Only when the snow finally stopped falling did they make real progress and by game-time the field was ready.

But the Browns weren't. The Packers' two bulls, Taylor and Hornung, ate up the yardage and the clock as the champs played their ball-control game to perfection.

On that day, unquestionably, the Packers were the superior team. No alibis were in order.

Yet, I can't help but wonder what would have happened under better conditions—if the Browns had had a routine bus ride, if the weather had been more suitable for football.

Yesterday, we discussed this with a couple of the veteran Browns. I said, "I thought you lost the game on the bus."

"No," replied one, "I knew we had lost it when I walked to the dining room at 6 P.M. the night before and saw the snow moving in."

It added up to the same thing.

Are the Browns up for today's game? No stethoscope has been devised to supply the certain answer. Morrie Kono, the Browns' equipment man ever since they came into existence, has his own measuring stick for "upness."

"It's the way they act in practice," he explains. "If the spirit and concentration are there."

And what does his yardstick say?

"They're up," declares Morrie. "Definitely, they're ready,"

But they were ready on the morning of Jan. 2, too. Then came the snow and that nightmarish bus ride.

Today, there'll be no snow—and no bus.

What if Lombardi's gamble had failed?

January 7, 1967

You are in a dark room, alone. It has two doors. You have been fighting for your life and you have only 16 seconds in which to make the vital decision.

The path to one door is clear. It's a simple matter to walk through it. Once out the door you are free. You must face your adversary again but this time in broad daylight and you have a 50-50 chance of beating him.

The path to the other door is heavily mined. The slightest slip and you're dead, blown to bits. Exactly where the mines are located you don't know. It's almost like walking blindfolded. But if you make that door you're free. The fight is completely over. Your foe will have vanished permanently. You will have won your battle.

Which path would you choose?

This is analogous to the corner in which Vince Lombardi found himself last Sunday as the Packers game against Dallas was about to end. He refused the safe path, the field goal that would tie the game and prolong it to sudden death. Instead he gambled on a quarterback sneak—and he won.

After the game we wrote of Lombardi's great courage. I said I look up to him in awe. What great confidence he had in the team his discipline had molded!

Yet, even after writing about the great decision I can't get it off my mind. Often writing serves as a catharsis. The incident is over and done. Not in this case. This was a provocative moment in sports that will go down in history as one of the greatest throat-pinchers of all time.

Those who saw the game on TV must be reliving that moment also. All week long the phones have been ringing, with the callers seeking a verbal replay of that final moment in an apparent effort to confirm what they actually saw.

Yes, the Packers had used up all their time outs and, yes, the clock undoubtedly would have run out if the sneak had been unsuccessful.

All of us, apparently, keep putting ourselves in that dark room. If I had been Lombardi, without hesitation I would have walked the clear path to the field goal door. Wouldn't that have been your decision, too?

On that one play Lombardi gambled his entire reputation as a successful coach. In sports, it's not what you did in the past, it's "What have you done lately?" Had the quarterback sneak failed, Lombardi would have been blasted without let-up. The wire story lead in the game probably would have begun something like this:

"GREEN BAY (AP)—Vince Lombardi made a monumental tactical mistake, committing the rock of ages that caused his Green Bay Packers to lose the NFL title to Dallas, 20-17, in the bitter cold of Lambeau Field, here today."

And because Lombardi has been less than cordial to many writers he never would be allowed to forget, publicly, his "rock of ages."

But no one can argue with success. He gambled against the frightening odds and won. He remains a granite-solid man, rather than one who committed a crumbling "rock." Yes, I look toward him in awe.

There are some who tend to minimize the gamble by saying that even if quarterback Bart Starr hadn't scored on the sneak the Packers still would have had time for a field goal. Don't you believe it.

Starr, on the Johnny Carson show the next night, said in retrospect it was apparent the Packers wouldn't have had time to get the field goal unit on the field and into position for a successful try.

As a long-time football official this was evident to me as I viewed the game. Sixteen seconds go *so* fast. And as a whistle-blower my mind visualizes what pressure would have been on the game officials if the quarterback sneak had been short.

The clock is running. It can't be stopped without obvious cause. There is a pile-up, with Starr on the bottom, just short of the goal line. Referee Norm Schachter and his men try to hurry the Dallas tacklers off Starr, who attempts to squirm out of the pile and get his team into position for the field goal.

The Cowboys aren't given to speed in this instance. They take their usual time and Schachter isn't empowered to call them for it. Only if they absolutely refuse to get up can he order the clock to be stopped. Otherwise it must be kept running. The normal procedure in pro games on running plays is to stop the clock only after quarterbacks are tackled during an attempt to get off a pass, the theory being that it's going to take time for his downfield receivers to get back to the huddle.

If Schachter deviates from the normal he is being unfair to Dallas. If he stops the clock Cowboys' coach Tom Landry will have his hide and the Dallas papers the next day will begin something like this:

"DALLAS (AP)—An unprecedented and unforgivable call by the officials gave the Green Bay Packers a chance for a last-second field goal and subsequent . . ."

So Schachter and his crew simply try to expedite the action and the Cowboys, not wanting to stop the clock, cooperate within the legal limits.

The seconds keep ticking away, 10 . . . nine . . . eight . . . seven . . . six. The Green Bay kicking unit is on the field and begins lining up over the ball. Schachter stands over it while he gives Dallas sufficient time to line up on the defense. Five . . . four . . . three.

Now Schachter is about to signal the ball ready for play and a smart Packers' lineman jumps offside and contacts a Cowboy in an effort to stop the clock. The five-yard penalty means nothing in this case. But Schachter can't let the Packers get away with this clear attempt to kill the clock. He'll order it stopped, march off five yards, put the ball down and signal the clock to start immediately. Two . . . one . . . zero . . . the game is over while the Packers are moving back toward the new position of the ball.

Can you imagine the resulting mob scene? It probably would be reported something like this:

"GREEN BAY (AP)—A riot, unlike anything ever witnessed in professional sports in the United States, climaxed the Packers' 20-17 loss to Dallas in the NFL title game here today. It was sheer pandemonium. Fifty thousand fans, who had been cheering their Packers on in subzero weather, warmed up at the conclusion by rushing onto the field and surrounding the officials whose refusal to stop the clock prevented the protesting Packers from getting off a field goal attempt. The police were brushed aside by the onrushing fans. The officials had their clothes torn off, they were brutally beaten and are now in the hospital . . ."

Perhaps my imagination is too vivid. Still, if Starr hadn't reached the goal line I'm certain the finish wouldn't have been without serious incident.

The officials and NFL executives, as well as Packers followers, can be mightily thankful Lombardi's decision to take the mined path to the door proved successful. If it hadn't, more than the coach could have been blown up.

Never was there a more dramatic, unforgettable moment in sports.

10,000 six packs

June 9, 1974

My friend Joe Tait called early Thursday morning, shortly after *The Plain Dealer* had been delivered to his doorstep. Joe, the play-by-play voice of the Indians (and the Cavaliers) had been resting his tonsils following his vivid description of the ugly baseball scene at the Stadium in which the game was forfeited to the Texas Rangers.

When he read my Thursday column, Tait found it necessary to vocalize again. He was unhappy that I put some of the blame on him. This is the paragraph that offended Joe:

"Joe Tait, who is going to get a National Basketball Association referee killed some night with his highly charged criticisms, didn't help on the Indians' play-by-play broadcasts with his repeated huckstering: 'Come out to Beer Night and let's stick it in Billy Martin's ear.'"

Joe argued that I had taken his comment out of context. He said he made the statement only because Martin, the Texas manager, mentioned there would be no problem when the Rangers came to Cleveland because nobody comes to the games here. Tait also said he didn't make the statement repeatedly, just once

I tried to tell Joe that the only words the listeners remembered were "stick it in his ear" and that several listeners told me he had made that statement and similar ones more than once. I hear his broadcasts and right or wrong it was my distinct impression he had said it several times.

That was the point: The impression may not have been the one Joe intended. But that's the inference the listeners got. Thus, Joe, with his high-voltage delivery conceivably helped create an atmosphere that led to the final scene.

Joe came back with, "How about the drawing in Tuesday's *Plain Dealer*, the one that appeared the morning of the game? You had an Indian holding boxing gloves."

That was a mistake, too, I admitted. In retrospect, I felt ill over our contribution to the night's events. If, in the eye of the beholder, that led to any violence, it was terribly wrong. In the aftermath column I accepted our responsibility.

At the time Joe made his comments, he must have thought they were innocuous, just as I thought our cartoon was. Joe and I now agree. We must be ultra careful whenever the problem of crowd control is involved. It was a disturbing lesson.

Yet, while fully accepting whatever blame the public wishes to place on us, I submit the cartoon and Joe's words would have been innocuous and accepted in the spirit of fun—as they were intended—if it hadn't been Beer Night. That's what we didn't take into account. If our contribution was inflammatory, it was only because the fuel was there—the alcohol. Without the fuel, it's impossible to have a fire.

Consider this statistic: 65,000 cups of beer were sold that night, each a can-size, 12-ounce cup, equivalent to more than 10,000 six packs. Of the 25,000 fans there, it would be fair to say half drank little or no beer, either not wishing to stand in the long lines, or not being beer drinkers to start with. Thus, the remaining half averaged four to five beers apiece. In some cases, I saw five fans stand in the beer line, each getting the maximum six cups. That's 30 beers. Some of them drank two cups and the others inhaled nearly 10 apiece. Some adults gave beers to the kids, underaged kids. Rick Passan of our staff saw four teenagers consume 18 cups of beer before the seventh inning.

True, it was only 3.2 beer. But keep pouring that 3.2 into the belly and it builds up to a lot of alcohol, enough to cause a teenager or young adult, full of beer and vigor, to lose his inhibitions.

In these times of runaway inflation, the best buy anywhere for a beer-drinker or a kid seeking a quick high was a bleacher seat on Tuesday night. A fifty-cent ticket entitled a bleacherite to the ten-cent bargain. For a buck he could have five beers. Small wonder the bleachers were quickly sold out. Not even free soup or bread would have caused those long lines. Soon the brew-propelled bleacher fans began to hop into the better seats, roam around the park, disturb the bullpens, jump over the fence and onto the field. The hooliganism was not confined to bleacherites only, but they were in the vast majority.

Our Dan Coughlin, who has more than a passing acquaintance with taverns, reported that many young adults and teenagers had been eagerly looking forward to Beer Night. They weren't baseball fans. They wanted the beer. Thus, in essence, the Indians' management wasn't promoting baseball, it was pushing beer.

The ten-cent beer was the catalyst as well as the fuel that caused the conflagration Tuesday night, nothing else. The contributing factors were there of course, but they were incidental. Never again should the Indians allow six beers to a customer and permit him to come back for more "six packs" as often as his belly permits.

I'm sorry that Indians' chief executive Ted Bonda insists there will be more beer nights. But if the American League does allow them here—and I hope it doesn't—a maximum of two cups is urged. The logistics of establishing such a limit are simple.

Tuesday's disgraceful evening brings to mind another explosive time—the summer of 1940. That was the year of the "Cleveland Cry Babies." (Another column could be written on that incredible season and perhaps some day I will.)

It was the year of the Indians' mutiny against their manager, Oscar Vitt, and eventually became known as the "Vitt Rebellion."

It also was the summer Hitler marched through Europe, and the United States rapidly was heading for Pearl Harbor and World War II. All the unsettling ingredients were there.

The Indians, firmly believing Vitt was an inept leader and manager, were certain they could win the pennant if he were replaced. In June they went to owner Alva Bradley and asked for his dismissal. The first and only such insurrection in baseball history knocked the war stories out of the top headlines. Bradley refused to fire Vitt and the players quickly were labeled "Cry Babies." Wherever they went, they were greeted by signs and symbols of their "infantile" act. Baby buggies were wheeled onto the field, bottles with nipples were brought to the park.

They were battling the Detroit Tigers for the pennant that year and when the Indians got off the train in September for a series in Detroit, 5,000 Tiger fans greeted them in the depot with eggs, tomatoes and other juicy edibles. There were "cry baby" taunts from everywhere. At the ball park baby bottles dangled from the upper deck. And the Indians were pelted with more garbage. All this was duly reported in the Cleveland papers, as well as on sports pages everywhere.

The following week the Tigers came to Cleveland for the final series that would decide the pennant and Tribe fans had been worked up into a Detroit hate. There were 45,000 at the Stadium for the big game. Many brought fruit and vegetables and threw them at the Detroit players. Someone dropped a basket on the head of Birdie Tebbetts as he sat in the Tigers' bullpen. (The fan, incidentally, was arrested and prosecuted.)

Yet, as retaliatory and as angry as some of the fans were inclined to be, the game was played to its conclusion without any other incident or serious interruptions. No one ran onto the field. Mind you, the papers had written all sorts of inflammatory stories. The fans knew all the details. The times were turbulent. We were on the verge of war. The radio voices crackled with descriptions of what had taken place in Detroit.

Yet, despite all these combustible ingredients, in comparison to Tuesday night here the fans' behavior was exemplary. There was no thought of, or need for, protest.

There was one ingredient missing, thank goodness—alcohol. Baseball was the prime attraction –not bargain beer.

Once in a lifetime?

May 1, 1976

It was Thursday night . . . the fifth playoff game between the Cavaliers and the Bullets, deadlocked at two.

You meet your companions for the evening, Buddy Bell and Duane Kuiper, the Indians' two bright young infielders, outside the Coliseum.

"Never saw a basketball game here," says Buddy. "How is it?"

"You're in for an experience."

"How do you mean?"

"You'll see."

We go inside. Most of the sellout crowd already is seated. The noise hits like a sudden wave.

"Don't you wish the Indians had this kind of cheering?"

"We did. Opening Day," says Kuiper.

"You like it?"

"Love it. Makes you want to go."

"This is going to help baseball, too," says Buddy. "You'll see. The enthusiasm will carry over to our club."

You mention the previous Saturday's game. "Nineteen standing ovations for the Cavs. It should go into the *Guinness Book of Records.* Friend of mine who recently had open-heart surgery had a three-day headache after that game. Gave up his ticket for tonight. Couldn't take another."

The noise grows. Mostly whistling and clapping, and clapping. Chanting begins, "GO Cavs." A few stupes, probably new to basketball, have bullhorns, common to hockey but never heard at Cavs' games before.

One fan, with a bullhorn bellowing in his ear, glowers at the blower. You think, "Every goof with a bullhorn should be put in a closet with the horn blowing constantly. Then when he yells, 'Enough,' break it over his head." Bullhorns should be banished from the land, to be used only at sea.

The announcer introduces the Bullets. Cavs' fans boo, mostly good-natured boos.

"Might as well get with it," says Kuiper. He boos, too.

The Cavs are announced. The fans jump up. Standing ovation. Bell and Kuiper are on their feet shouting. Two supposedly sophisticated professional athletes caught in the enthusiasm, the anticipation, the excitement, the frenzy.

"The frenzy," Bill Fitch, the Cavs' coach, is to say later. "You can feel it on the bench."

The din reaches a crescendo of encouragement as the Cavs take positions for the opening tap.

You, the blasé expert, try to fight off the emotions. It's just a game. You must concentrate, think clearly, analyze. Maybe in an isolation chamber. Not in this fury, in this electricity. The fan in front of you tries to read a magazine, *Minnesota Hunting*. Either a flake, or he can't take the excitement.

You think back. Was it like this in 1948, with the Indians? Or in those big years with the Browns? Not precisely. Not the same intensity as in this playoff series. Not as frenetic. Almost, but not quite. Maybe it's the enclosed building, the closeness to the floor, and the players. The familiarity. The smaller squad. The love affair, beginning with the bumbling but adorable infants who never quit no matter how great the odds, to the same grown-up battlers, at last in the playoffs. A love affair between fan and team.

The game begins. The intensity increases, never lets go. Take the greatest prizefight you ever saw, two men of equal strength and skill, pounding each other relentlessly. Take that palm-sweating chase scene in *The French Connection* and expand it for a full 48 minutes. The good guys are behind, they catch up, they go ahead, they fall behind, they catch up. Pulse pounding, fist clenching, teeth grinding.

Only once before can you remember the same apprehension, similar tension on the faces around you. Dick Bosman's no-hitter. You sat in the stands that night. Fans nearby kept muttering. "I can't stand it. I can't stand it." The worry, the doubt, the hope, the deliciousness of approaching glory, the God-awful fret of approaching doom. It was there for Bosman. It's here tonight.

Buddy Bell stares ahead. The spring tan is gone. His face is white.

"Anything wrong?"

"No, I'm wrapped up."

Kuiper's lips are pressed tightly.

The two major leaguers exclaim and applaud a spectacular play. The Cavs have become THEIR team. The fan in front puts down his magazine. He can't read. He can't even fake it.

It is now approaching the final minute. The Cavs lead by one point.

Now they trail by one. Less than one-half minute . . . 20 seconds . . . the Cavs try to find an open man, Dick Snyder passes, the ball is intercepted. Fifteen seconds—the Bullets have the ball and the lead.

Some fans start to leave. It's all over. Beat the crowd. Not this time, pal. You did it once before against the same Bullets. The Cavs were four behind and little time to go. Two quick steals and the Cavs won. It can't happen again, you say, but this time you stay.

You see Bill Fitch on his feet in front of the bench. He's yelling to his men as the Bullets bring the ball down the floor. You think with him, "Foul somebody, grab somebody. Grab a poor foul shooter. Anybody."

He's shouting but his players can't hear above the noise. The seconds drop away . . . precious seconds . . . seconds the Cavs need if they should get the ball again . . . 10 seconds . . . eight . . . Elvin Hayes gets a pass near the Cavs' bench. Campy Russell sees Fitch gesturing. He grabs Hayes . . . Foul . . . Six seconds to go.

Hayes! A great one. He had made nine of his 12 free throws. He had played 46 minutes. More than any other player. Forty-six unrelenting, bruising minutes, up and down, under both boards. If any player had to be fatigued, it would be Hayes. Fatigue . . . concentration-blunting . . . the fine little making and missing.

Hayes faces the hoop . . . he tries to get his rhythm . . . he can't . . . he stops . . . starts his rhythm again . . . and misses . . . But he needs only one and the Bullets can't lose in regulation time . . . And he sets . . . again he tries to regain his rhythm. He shoots, the ball falls off, directly into the hands of a praying Cav. Time-out.

Bill Fitch has his men around him . . . diagramming. He knows the Bullets have only three team fouls. They aren't in a penalty situation. They can waste one foul before the Cavs try to shoot. Fitch thinks ahead. You try to read his mind. He must talk fast. He must be telling his men, "Get the ball inside to Chones, at the key. They'll have to grab him before he tries to shoot. That uses up their fourth foul. But we've got to get it to make them foul right away. Every second counts. Then when we get the ball out again . . . "

In that time-out he has to set up two plays. Anticipate, think ahead, think with the Bullets, think ahead of them.

Time in. The ball goes to Chones at the pivot. Wes Unseld doesn't dare let Chones try to hook toward the basket. Can't foul him in the act of shooting. He grabs Chones. Foul. The Bullets' fourth team foul. Cavs get the ball out of bounds. One second gone . . . five left.

Now comes the second out-of-bounds play Fitch had diagrammed.

Ball should go in to Snyder. He's got the hot hand. If he's not free, get it to Bingo Smith, and go with the same play that beat the Bullets in the final seconds last week on the Bullets' home court.

The Bullets know the strategy too. They come out. Snyder is blanketed. Smith gets the ball with Mike Riorden hounding him. Bingo fakes Mike, shakes him, gets a step ahead . . . doesn't realize . . . hurries his shot . . . maybe figuring to get fouled . . . shoots off his right foot . . . off-balance. No leverage . . . the ball is in the air . . . everybody watches transfixed . . . it's short . . . hits nothing . . . It's over . . . no miracle this time.

Underneath, Jim Cleamons moves toward the ball, grabs, spins it up . . . ball hangs on the rim . . . hangs . . . hangs . . . undecided . . . falls in. Bullets stand around paralyzed . . . fans are stunned. Momentarily they fail to comprehend.

"What happened?"

"Who shot it?"

"Did it count?"

"Did the buzzer sound?"

"What? What? What?"

The Cavs start jumping for joy. They have won, 92-91.

It sinks in . . . 20,000 fans get the message at once . . . Bedlam . . . Pandemonium . . . Buddy Bell is on his feet shouting. Duane Kuiper is shouting . . . A normally conservative attorney is screaming. Later he wonders why he is hoarse.

You think: In 15 seconds the Cavs did three things wrong: lose the ball, foul too late, take a shot that doesn't hit the hoop and they win . . . If Bingo's shot hits the rim or the backboard, it doesn't fall into Cleamons's eager hands and the game is over.

Luck, sure, pure luck. Who says wrongs don't make a right? Three wrongs made a right.

"Unbelievable, fantastic," says Buddy.

"Super game, super, super," says Kuiper.

It's a mob scene on the floor. A fan, the blood completely drained from his face, sits limp in his seat. His wife says, "Promise me you'll never go to another playoff game."

You go down to the dressing room to replay the game with Fitch and the players. Frank Duffy, the Indians' shortstop, joins our group.

"It's nothing," says an enervated Fitch in mustering a grin. "It's like the bottom of the ninth. Your pitcher is throwing a no-hitter and there are two outs. The batter hits you a slow grounder. Before you get that ball and begin your throw, your whole life flashes in front of you."

"Yeah," says Duffy with a shudder. "It's nothing."

You think about Bosman's no-hitter again. This game topped it. In tension, apprehension, in fury, in frenzy, in drama, in unreality, in tempo, in noise, in climax, it topped every sports event you ever had seen.

You say good-bye to Bell and Kuiper and Duffy, who are still caught up in the game, and you go home. You are still perspiring. You take a shower. You go to bed emotionally exhausted. You keep asking yourself, "How much more can you expect from this team. It already has given so much."

Three hours later you finally fall asleep.

Was it fiction . . . ?

April 9, 1975

Everywhere he turned there were microphones. Microphones and photographers and reporters and flashbulbs and TV cameras. The crowd around him swelled and moved as he moved. Not even a head of state could have had more attention.

And the questions from the interviewers . . . over and over he heard them . . . the same ones and silly ones and some attempts at provocation of the first black major league manager. It was enough to make a strong man shout, "Get away, already," and try to head for cover.

But he graciously took it all, handling himself with patience, dignity and intelligence. A top-drawer diplomat, a public relations expert could have taken lessons.

And when Frank Robinson was introduced to the crowd shortly before the first pitch and they cheered him he took off his hat in acknowledgement and waved to them.

And when he came to bat he forgot all the cameras and the microphone and everything but that Yankee pitcher and the little white ball and he concentrated and he hit it. He hit it over the fence. Fiction? Storybook stuff? No, it was real.

And after he ran around the bases and tagged home plate he didn't forget the people, the 56,204 who had cheered his name earlier and who had come to witness his managerial debut on this bitter cold day. He stopped and took off his cap again and waved to the multitude. And even if you were frozen the heart pounded faster and the blood flowed quicker from the thrill.

And his players rushed out to share that moment with him. And who was the first? Gaylord Perry, who had made his rookie days as a manager uncomfortable.

And when the game finally was over and Gaylord Perry had tossed out the final batter it was Robinson who rushed out to put his arm around the winning pitcher.

And all the while the cameras kept grinding, recording it all for history. And when it was over there were the microphones again and more flash bulbs and the reporters and the TV cameras and to the end he handled himself with class and with style.

A magnificent debut. A storybook debut. A virtuoso performance.

Many happy returns, Frank Robinson.

Hayes self-destructs . . . a sad day

December 31, 1978

Woody Hayes fired himself. Just the way General Douglas MacArthur did. When a man becomes bigger than the institution he represents he has to go.

It's a sad moment in football, and particularly in Ohio State football, for Woody made a major contribution to the game. A giant toppled himself.

Even his stoutest admirers—those who came to his defense each time this corner or any other critic related his sideline conduct—were shaken by his actions in the Gator Bowl Friday night. Many of them called to say, "Woody has got to go." This was even before the University made his departure official yesterday.

He left Ohio State no alternative when he threw that punch at a Clemson player. His actions almost precipitated a riot and no university can condone that.

It was only a matter of time when school officials would make the announcement. I thought they would give Woody the opportunity to quit gracefully, although he never took that route previously when it appeared wise. But in retrospect, perhaps the school did handle it in proper though quick action. Keeping him on, even for a few weeks, would have increased the furor caused by the incident. It would have been tantamount to accepting, if not actually approving, his behavior. An apology was necessary immediately. Even considering the outside possibility that Woody might have been provoked, there was absolutely no excuse for his conduct, certainly not from a professor, a representative of an educational institution. An apology wasn't forthcoming from Woody at the conclusion of the game. As usual when he loses or when he acts the fool, he secluded himself.

Moreover if Woody had to go—*and he had to go eventually*—a replacement would have to be named at the earliest.

Even if Woody hadn't punched the Clemson player and were still coaching the Buckeyes today this space would have been devoted to criticism of his strategy. Why a coach of his years and experience wasn't prepared when it came time for the game-tying two-point conversion was beyond me. He had to ask for time-out to decide what to call and then came up with a nothing play.

When I saw all that confusion prior to the conversion I turned from my TV set in disgust. (I didn't even see the slugging until the post-game replay.) That there had been no planning ahead seemed inconceivable.

Woody perhaps had become so emotionally involved in his games, arguing with the officials or getting angry at his players and/or the opposition, it interfered with his coaching and thinking.

Enough of the negative. This is a sad moment. It's sad to see Woody go—a shame really. In Columbus it must be like High Street crumbling. Here the feeling is somewhat the same as when Paul Brown was fired. It leaves a hollow feeling. Even when I have been critical of him I have found much to admire in the man. It was difficult for anyone not to be ambivalent about Woody.

Sad though the moment is, Woody would be angered by sympathy. A strong man, bigger than life, he would reject it. He will go down in history as one of the most successful, most colorful coaches of all time. His achievements far overshadow his emotional lapses. For the most part he has had 28 glorious years and for them he will be remembered and revered.

I'm sure this corner speaks for all Ohio in wishing him well and thanking him for his positive efforts. The players he helped turn into men are his medals.

MacArthur said, "Old soldiers never die, they just fade away." But I don't think this applies to Woody, at least I hope he doesn't fade away. There is too much vitality and competitiveness in the man to permit it. We'll hear from him again.

In fact, if I were a TV network executive I'd sign him quickly as a color commentator.

Happy New Year, Woody, and again, thanks for the memories. The good ones, of which there were plenty.

Puppets at the Olympics

February 19, 1980

LAKE PLACID—It was like watching an experiment in mind control—hypnotized people versus those who were free to think and do as they pleased.

At first, I thought it was my imagination, fed by preconceived ideas, based on what I had heard and read. So I tried to clear my brain and watch as objectively as I could.

The picture remained the same. I was among about 15 puppets in the midst of a free-thinking crowd of 8,000.

For nearly five hours, I sat with a group of Russians at the ice dancing and pairs figure skating at the new Olympic Fieldhouse. My ticket happened to put me among them.

They spoke only Russian; at least I heard no English. Many of them wore mink hats and fur coats that resembled the old raccoon kind the college men of the jazz age wore. They may have been bearskin, though, I didn't know how to ask. Three were women. They wore more luxurious furs.

Most all the men had at least one gold tooth in front. Several had three or four. At today's gold standard, they could be considered capitalists.

They watched the events in relative silence. But, as if on cue, they clapped loudly when Russian skaters came on the ice. It was as though a symphony conductor was in front of them.

They would applaud precisely at the same time, very loudly. And when the event was ended, they applauded in unison. It couldn't have been rehearsed, yet it seemed that way. This is not to say there is anything wrong in applauding your own. That is part of sports. So is being a claque for your favorite.

Still, when the Hungarian pair in ice dancing did a superb number and received a lengthy ovation from the appreciative crowd, not a single Russian applauded. Stone-faced, they sat there, hands in their laps.

In the figure skating, when an exciting American couple, Sheryl Franks and Michael Botticelli, got a standing ovation, the Russians sat there silently.

Unquestionably, some American fans were trying to sway the judges, just as the Russians were when their country was being represented. Yet, the contrast was too great, for the Americans and Canadians and others in the crowd impartially applauded the Russians, too, when they were good. And most of them were very, very good.

Only once was there a negative reaction to the Russian athletes. When Irina Rodnina and Aleksandr Zaitsev, the favored figure skating pair, came onto the ice, one loud-mouth fan yelled, "Go back to Russia." He was immediately shouted down.

The introduction of a Russian figure skating judge was lightly booed, then the cheers drowned them out. That was the only noticeable crowd reaction against the Russians.

The fans may despise what the Soviet leaders are doing in Afghanistan, but they hold no animosity toward the athletes. In good sportsmanship, they wanted these fine skaters to know how much their performances were enjoyed. Media representatives from the various nations equally were carried away by the superb skating. But not the Russians.

It was as if they would be sent to Siberia if they looked pleased except when a Soviet skater was on the ice. Yet, the Russian contingent could have afforded to be magnanimous, to be gracious to the others, for their skaters are much better. Nevertheless, they refused to offer the slightest acknowledgement to any performer except their own.

The Americans in the audience, on the other hand, knowing their applause might possibly influence a judge, clapped without restraint during and after the Rodnina-Zaitsev performance. They were aware of the Rodnina story, no doubt, and it was a human drama that knew no ideological or geographical barriers.

Irina was the exceptional figure skater who had broken with her original partner after winning an Olympic gold. According to rumor, they had been romantically attached. Then Irina learned he was making eyes at the bronze medal winner. She stopped talking to him, and the chill was obvious when they received their gold medals.

She found another partner, Zaitsev, and together they beat her old flame and his new lady. Soon, Aleksandr and Irina married. And now they were after more gold here, not long after the birth of their first child, Sasha.

It was a love story worthy of a movie. And the nonpartisan Americans in the crowd showed their pleasure when the Russians' high score was posted. Nor did the spectators leave when it was over as they could have if they wished to show up the brilliant Russian pair.

They patiently waited while the platform and red carpet were being placed on the ice. As Irina and Aleksandr received their gold medals while the Soviet flag was raised and the band played their national anthem, the crowd stood up and cheered. That's the way it's supposed to be in sports.

Of course, the Russian contingent cheered mightily too, clapping on cue and stopping on cue.

But would they have remained in the arena if an American pair had won, or another free national beat out a Russian pair to prevent a clean sweep? I'm convinced if the Russians hadn't won, they would have silently marched out. In unison, as though under hypnosis. Like puppets.

I still can see Irina joyfully receiving her medal. It was an unforgettable moment in the human drama that is such an integral part of sports. Yet, I still can see her countrymen, brainwashed, applauding only their own. I won't forget that either.

Eric Heiden, the greatest athlete

February 24, 1980

Olympic odyssey . . .

PURE GOLD

As the song goes, we're always chasing rainbows. For the sportswriter the pot of gold at the end of it is the ultimate athlete, the exceptional team. That's our quest, or at least mine.

Like Don Quixote, I went to Lake Placid in search of the perfect

Olympian. Unlike Quixote, I was reluctant to go. I had heard about the bus snafu, the food gouging, the cold on the mountains, the showerless cabin we were to live in. Too many windmills for this timid soul.

Now I'm thrilled beyond measure—and these calloused bones don't thrill easily—that I did go. I saw the super athlete. Eric Heiden. Maybe there have been others as good. Jim Brown. John Havlicek. Perhaps a few others. They don't come to mind quickly. Heiden, I'll never forget.

You had to see his performance in person to appreciate it. Speed skating is *not* a television event.

Picture Jesse Owens winning the 100, 200, and 440 yard dashes, then going out and winning the mile and two-mile runs. It defies comprehension. Super human. Sprinters don't do that. The training makes it impossible. And milers don't sprint for the same reason.

This is also true in speed skating. Except for Heiden. He did both. And won both the sprints and the grueling distance races in record time. Incredible is a mild word for what he accomplished.

The pain barrier of the distance race is tenfold what a football or basketball player must push himself beyond. To overcome it and keep on going for victories and records takes more than is in the heart of most mortals.

The loneliness of the practice takes greater motivation; the time he had to devote to his sport required sacrifices far above those necessary to play the fun games—baseball, basketball, hockey, football.

Those who saw Heiden play hockey say he could have been an outstanding pro. Of course. He also plays tennis well. If he had gone in for any sport, he would excel because he isn't satisfied with mediocrity.

He chose ice skating, he says, "because if you lose you can't blame anybody but yourself. It's just you and a pair of skates."

He wasn't an automatic winner the day he put on those blades. He finished near the bottom in the 1976 Olympics. But he learned that through hard training one moves to higher plateaus. His coach, Dianne Holum, once sent him a note, "Don't be satisfied with second best." He says he never has forgotten it.

In the 1,500 meters I saw him nearly fall when his skate hit a rut. He overcame the slip, put it out of his mind, and went on to finish far ahead of his opponent. The concentration, the inside toughness is seen in only a rare few. I saw it in Eric Heiden. He was worth the trip, worth it a thousand times.

And best of all, perhaps, is that he is such a nice young man. All the pieces are there. Those who know him intimately say he is exactly as he came across to those of us who talked with him for the first time. He refuses to consider himself superior to anybody.

The gum-chewing Eric outwardly is like the boy next door. But there are few like him next door to anybody. There are few like him anywhere.

MIRACLE ON ICE

The United States' spine-tingling unexpected victory over the supposedly invincible Russian team still seems like a dream that one hopes never will go away. It proves that the impossible can happen in sports.

The only expert at Lake Placid who said the Americans had a chance was the Canadian coach, Clare Drake, who also coaches the University of Alberta. He told me he saw something during his game against the Russians that would cause him to bet on the U.S., if he were a gambling man. What it was, he wouldn't say and I didn't believe him. Nobody else thought the U.S. or any other team had a chance. How could amateurs put together for these games beat seasoned veterans who had played together for years and had knocked off teams in the National Hockey League?

Did the Canadian coach see a weakness in the Russian goalie? Or in the Soviets' checking around the net? Or did they pass too much, rather than shoot when they had the chance? He may have seen all of this. But he couldn't know that Jim Craig was going to be so spectacular. The U.S. goalie rose to Olympic heights and that's what caused the remarkable upset. Except for drive and intensity, the Russians outplayed the U.S. But Craig was there to make the stops.

I thought to the very end the Russians would come back. I had seen them do so against Finland and Canada, and it reminded me of an epitaph I had seen on a grave in Boothill Cemetery in Tombstone, Arizona: "Here lies Willie Jones [I don't recall the exact name]. He was shot by a .44. He died quick and sudden." Against the Russian hockey team everybody died quick and sudden. Everybody except the Americans.

At the end, in the final moments, the Russians played as though they knew they were dead. The U.S. made them look that way and no matter how blasé you tried to be about it, you couldn't. Every red, white and blue corpuscle in your body glowed with pride.

Yes, I said it was impossible for the Russians to lose and the young

U.S. team proved it can do the impossible. I heard today that at the deli the Maven was taking the Russians and spotting the U.S. two goals. If I had known that, I would have picked the U.S.

AND THE TEARS

While glorying in the accomplishments of Heiden and the U.S. hockey team, it is impossible to forget those who were victims of the pressures and expectations. Beth Heiden was one of those victims.

She did well, winning bronze, making her one of the three best in the world. But it wasn't good enough for the media, who wanted her to win a gold the way her brother did. "The hell with you writers" are words I won't forget. She said them with a nervous laugh, but they came from within her and the hurt showed. So did the tears that followed. There will be a scar on Beth the rest of her life, for she is not as tough as Eric. And it isn't fair. She didn't deserve it.

And then there were the tears shed by Stacey Smith of Cleveland Heights, following a low score in the ice dancing. She had omitted part of her routine. After all those countless hours of practice, unexplainably she skipped one set. The pressure, the extreme brutal pressure of performing before the largest crowd of her life, undoubtedly caused it. It got to more experienced performers than Stacey. You can practice forever, but you practice alone, not before 8,000 critics who are paying $67 each and millions who are watching on TV.

Afterward she said, "I was skating on automatic pilot. I don't know how it happened. It was a foolish error." And her eyes bubbled up as she said this.

Had the "automatic pilot" in her brain not been faulty, Stacy and her partner, John Summers, probably would have finished seventh. Instead they finished ninth. Still, it was in the top ten, which will give the U.S. an extra spot in the World competition. This was Stacey's goal. Although she is through with Olympic skating, she wanted to help other U.S. skaters. She did, which should help ease the pain of her error.

The Beths and the Staceys are as much a story of the Olympics as are the gold medalists. Maybe more. They are the human story. The winners, in a sense, are superhuman.

TV SHOW

I heard one British writer say, "This is the second worst event I ever covered. The first was World War II." Funny thing, I never saw him at any of the sites. Whenever I saw him, he was watching the games on TV in the pressroom or at the bar in press headquarters. Maybe that's how he covered the war, too.

TV doesn't do justice to the hockey, the speed skating, or the figure skating. You've got to be there to get the full picture and the excitement and the flavor.

On the other hand, it's a waste of time to go out to the slopes to see the ski events, and bobsled, and the luge. You climb up Whiteface Mountain—which became Brownface as the warm weather set in—and you stand along the ski run for a quick look at the skiers as they slalom by. Or you can post yourself at the finish line and see them come in but nothing else.

One writer said, as though he had discovered gold, "I found a spot where I could see 40 seconds of the race." Forty seconds out of a minute and a half. You saw it much better at home.

FELLOWSHIP

I tried to get a reading from the athletes after President Carter announced he would ask the U.S. not to participate in the summer Olympics in Moscow and that his request was irrevocable. The general feeling of the U.S. athletes was they were sorry for those who had trained so hard "but you've got to go along with the president."

A Russian writer, through an interpreter, told me, "We'll be in Los Angeles for the 1984 Olympics even if you don't come to Moscow."

Ty Danco, the Clevelander on the U.S. luge team, said, "We can't talk much with the Russian athletes because of the language barrier, but we get along well with them here in the Olympic Village. I traded a U.S. warmup suit for a Russian suit with Vera Zuzulia of the Soviet luge team. She's only five-two, but she outweighs me, so it fit."

If only the heads of nations would trade good will that readily.

GOOD SKATE

A crowd pleaser in the figure skating was Scott Hamilton of Bowling Green. He was the U.S. flag bearer in the opening ceremonies, and Jim McKay said he had had cystic fibrosis as a child. If so, that would be a fantastic story, to overcome this debilitating disease.

I checked it out. He didn't have cystic fibrosis. He did have Schwackman's Disease, a paralysis of the intestines, which prevented him from absorbing food properly. As a consequence, his body was being robbed nutritionally and his growth was stunted.

Although smaller than the other skaters, he outperformed most of them, finishing a surprising fifth. He is remarkably acrobatic, and he got more applause from the crowd than all the other skaters except the winner, Robin Cousins. Scott would be a hit in a pro ice show.

"Skating," he said, "was my therapy. The best medicine."

The cure has been spectacular.

BUS(T)

It's too bad there had to be a transportation snafu at Lake Placid, for all the other arrangements made by the Olympic committee were excellent. Actually a brilliant job. But the bus snafu canceled the plusses.

By the time I got to Lake Placid, the bus crisis was over. In fact, there was an overkill. Wherever you turned there was a bus, and the fumes were so heavy you could smell them as Heiden skated to his medals. One Lake Placid resident, perhaps straining in her worry, said, "the pollution from the buses will kill the fish in our streams."

"What would you rather have," she was asked, "trout or your new ice arenas?"

"You can't eat an ice house," she said.

PLAY THAT AGAIN?

Absolute truth. Overheard on the bus heading for the slalom event:

Husband: "I wish we had our piano here."

Wife: "Why?"

Husband: "Because our tickets are on top of it."

HIGH FASHION

Reading in advance about the cold weather, I bought a down-filled parka and gloves, insulated socks, thermal underwear, and snowmobile boots. The problem was that after you wore all this clothing up the slope you had to come into the hot pressroom to write. By the time you were through, you were soaked from head to foot. It was impossible to undress before writing, since we roomed a dozen miles from the Olympic Center. And there are plenty of women sportswriters now. They didn't take off their snuggies in the pressroom either.

QUIET PLEASE

Inasmuch as my roomie, Dan Coughlin, wrote a column warning me about his snoring, no doubt you'll want a personal report. Except for one night, he wasn't bad. He snored melodiously, like a lullaby, and he put me to sleep. But that one night, oh my. He was coming down with a cold, and he sounded like Niagara Falls all night. As violent a snoring performance as I ever heard, and I've heard some great ones. I would strike a medal for him except that when I needed a pen to take notes, he gave me one that wrote in indelible ink. For that, I've got to give him something else.

ONWARD AND UPWARD

All in all, the Winter Olympics was an adventure never to be forgotten, even the discomfort. And the Heidens and the hockey team made it rewarding far beyond one's greatest expectations.

And now that I have my parka, gloves, boots, and insulated underwear, I'm ready for spring training.

Were you at Joe's party?

April 20, 1980

The Stadium, Opening Day, Joe Charboneau's Day, from all over the ball park . . . Before the game, in the Cleveland dugout the players are loose, kidding each other about whose picture will be the ugliest on the scoreboard screen . . . Rookie Charboneau has a constant grin . . . Nervous grin? . . . Players are introduced . . . Fans cheer most of the players . . . Boo Victor Cruz . . . Gary Alexander laughs, "I'm not going out. They'll kill me." . . . He goes out . . . Fans are kind . . . Andre Thornton, on crutches, stands in runway . . . Fans cheer his name . . . Decides to come out to acknowledge cheers . . . Gets huge ovation . . . Jerry Dybzinski, the kid from Cleveland, has head down while national anthem is sung . . . Seems to be overcome . . . Admits it . . . "To be out there in this uniform," he said. "A moment I dreamed about every time I came to this ball park."

FIRST INNING—Left field bleachers . . . Crowded even before first pitch . . . Young adults . . . Saturday Night Fever disco crowd . . . Sunbathers . . . shirts off . . . Almost as many gals as guys . . . Picnic time . . . One fan comes in with full keg of beer . . . How was he able to get it through the turnstiles? . . . One section cheers, "I-N-D-I-A-N-S" . . . just like at a high school game . . . Indians run onto field . . . About 30 guys stand up and shout, "Super Joe, Super Joe, Super Joe," as Charboneau takes his place in left field . . . Super Joe doesn't hear . . . Fans have radios all over the bleachers . . . The voices of Herb Score and Nev Chandler tell 'em how it looks from the press box . . . First batter, Alfredo Griffin, grounds out to Veryzer . . . Loud shout in unison, "AWRIGHT." . . . Veryzer goes in hole for Rick Bosetti's grounder, makes good play but throws wild to first . . . Bosetti takes second . . . Scoreboard flashes "error" . . . "Error?" screams a fan. "The scorer must be blind." . . . "The error was given because the bad throw allowed Bosetti to reach second," another fan explains . . . "Oh yeah." . . . Three outs . . . Fan wearing shorts only, very brief ones, stands up, faces crowd and shouts, "Indian Fever, Indian Fever, oh, oh, oh, oh." . . . Fans repeat, "Indian Fever, Indian Fever, oh, oh, oh, oh."

Bottom of first Cliff Johnson up . . . Fan points to forehead and yells, "Hit me right here." . . . Johnson flies out to end inning . . . Fan boos.

SECOND INNING—Move to right field bleachers, below the drummer boy . . . So crowded now some fans sit on upper ledge . . . Fans are allowed to move into grandstand but most of them stay where the fun is . . . Teacher at Normandy High complains, "We came here on a bus from Parma. It had four times capacity. People on each other's shoulders. On one sudden stop people tumbled all over. Don't you think RTA should have known better and had more buses?" . . . Jorge Orta strikes out, "Swing and a miss," says fan, emulating Herb Score . . . Charboneau walks . . . Fans cheer mightily . . . He is out stealing . . . Not a single boo . . . "A buck and half for these seats," says a fan. "Best bargain in town."

THIRD INNING—Lower right field grandstand, next to bleachers . . . Some empty seats . . . Different crowd . . . Girl scouts . . . Boy scouts . . . Groups of youngsters . . . Toronto scores a run on two singles and a double play . . . No comment . . . General disinterest . . . Move to seat near left field foul line in lower grandstand for bottom of the third . . . Much more interest here . . . Veryzer beats out hit . . . Scoreboard shows two Indians slapping hands . . . "Look at that," says a delighted child to his father . . . Fans begin rhythmic clapping . . . Rick Manning ends inning with double play grounder . . . Fans boo.

FOURTH INNING—Upper deck, high, above Indians' bullpen . . . Helicopter view . . . "Do you think Dibby (Dybzinski) will play?" asks a fan in his 20s . . . "Hope so," says his pal . . . Foul ball goes into stands near home plate . . . "If one comes here," says a small boy to his mother,

"I'll catch it," . . . "I know you will," she says . . . No way a ball could reach their seats . . . Blue Jays go out one-two-three.

FIFTH INNING—Walk to lower boxes . . . long lines at concession stands . . . Beer business is booming . . . Fan says, "This is a crappy game." . . . Find seat near Indians' dugout . . . Fan nearby says to companion, "Bet he doesn't get a hit." . . . "For how much?" . . . "Fifty to twenty-five." . . . "Okay."

Blue Jay doubles to left . . . "Charboneau should have had it," says the loser. "Pay up," says the winner . . . Woman asks, "Wonder what happened to the kids. You think they're in the bathroom this long?" . . . Toronto fails to score . . . Move toward a seat along third base . . . See Dan Coughlin in best seat in the house, second row of boxes, just to right of screen . . . "This is the life," says Dan . . . Last year he was in press box on opening day, covering the Indians for these pages . . . Got tired of the traveling and asked to be relieved . . . "Now I can enjoy the game," he says . . . Next to him is Doug Dieken, Browns' tackle . . . Both are dressed better than usual, like big sports, befitting box seat customers . . . "Whatever the crowd is," says Dan, "add eight more. We ate in the Stadium Club and nobody took our tickets." Find seat behind Toronto dugout, 20 rows back . . . Fans keep walking up and down the aisles, interrupting the view . . . Toilet time . . . Fans with poor seats move in and fill those that are momentarily empty . . . Jorge Orta singles . . . Big cheer . . . Charboneau doubles to center . . . standing ovation . . . Ron Hassey up . . . Girl about 15 asks, "Can he hit?" . . . Her girl friend replies, "He's a good RBI man." . . . Count goes to ball three-no strikes . . . "Hope he takes the next pitch," says a man. "Load the bases." . . . Hassey hits the 3-0 count for a double . . . Two runs score . . . "Now that's smart baseball," says the man. "Garcia [the manager] was wise to let him hit." . . . Hassey moves to third on a sacrifice and scores on a fly . . . Indians lead, 3-1 . . . A fan returns to seat . . . "We're winning? How did we score the three runs? Damn. I go out for one hot dog and I miss all the excitement."

SIXTH INNING—Lower grandstand, near left field foul line . . . Family crowd . . . "When are they going to announce the attendance?" somebody asks. "Must be at least 60,000." . . . "Bet you a beer it's over 60,000. What a crowd," says another . . . Waits retires the Blue Jays easily . . . Move to upper left field stands . . . Another helicopter view, but perfect to see Charboneau's line drive . . . Shoots off his bat . . . Toronto fielder hustles back . . . Will it clear his glove? . . . It does . . . The rookie has done it . . . An opening day homer . . . Another standing ovation . . . In the excitement fan spills full cup of beer on fans in front of him . . . Not one dirty look or complaint . . . "I was getting pretty hot anyway," said one of the doused fans . . . Father says to son, "I told you Charboneau was going to hit one out today."

SEVENTH INNING—Lower grandstand, left field corner . . . Joe Charboneau country . . . Everybody stands as Joe trots to his position . . . He turns toward stands, gives fans a big smile and tips his cap . . . Usher who had retrieved the homer gives ball to Joe . . . Again, big smile . . . He sticks ball in back pocket . . . Fan worries, "What if he falls on it? He'll get hurt." . . . Fans begin chant, "Super Joe, Super Joe, Super Joe." . . . He turns toward them and his lips form, "Thanks." . . . They keep cheering; he keeps turning to thank them . . . A father sits down. "I left my four kids off before the game. Told them I'd meet them in Section 40 in the seventh inning. I didn't think anybody would be sitting here now. Never thought the crowd would be this big. Can't find 'em." . . . Bottom of the seventh . . . Move to bleachers again . . . everybody sings with Rocco Scotti, "Take Me Out To The Ball Game." . . . Fans are now going into the bleachers for more sun . . . Plenty of beer . . . Saturday Night Fever again, in the afternoon . . . "Great game, huh," says a fan, slapping has pal on the back." . . . "Dynamite," says the slapee . . . Tall man with open shirt, carried away, says, "We came here to have a helluva time. Great excuse for a party. A whole city party." . . . Fan with a beard asks, "Did you see two little blond kids? Took 'em to the game and lost 'em." . . . Charboneau gets his third hit, a single to left with two on to give the Indians a 5-1 lead . . . Crowd stands and shouts together, "Super Joe. Super Joe. Super Joe." . . . Older fan nearby, drinking from a whiskey bottle containing a liquid that looks like red furniture polish yells to the cheerers, "Have a drink on me." . . . He throws them the bottle . . . They look at it and throw it back.

EIGHTH INNING—Press box time . . . On the way fans are talking about Charboneau . . . "Joltin' Joe." One shouts. "We've got our own DiMaggio." . . . "What a day. What a game," shouts another . . . Very quiet in the press box . . . No place to get Indian Fever . . . No place to get any flavor . . . But good view . . . Balor Moore sends Duane Kuiper sprawling with inside pitch . . . Kuiper makes a comment to the pitcher, who motions him to come on to the mound . . . Kuiper starts . . . Everybody rushes out . . . Charboneau grabs Kuiper and pulls him back . . . From press box it's obvious nobody, except maybe Kuiper, wants to fight . . . Wonder what it looked like from the bleachers? . . . Mike Hargrove hits long fly to right . . . Perfect view from press box

. . . Right fielder has the ball in his glove and drops it. Over the fence, three-run homer . . . No comment from the writers . . . Left the bleachers too soon.

NINTH INNING—Bald-headed fan with heavy belly gets on top of Toronto dugout and leads cheers as Waits retires the Blue Jays . . . He is joined by a fan with equal-sized belly . . . They dance . . . Others join them and dance . . . Indian Fever . . . Game is over but fans won't leave . . . They yell, "We want Joe. We want Joe." . . . Charboneau comes back out, tips his cap . . . Many continue to remain in the stands . . . Father who returned to pick up his four children says, "Haven't found them yet. But I'm not worried. What a game. Glad I had to come back. But if you see four kids tell them I'll be near the Indians' clubhouse door." . . . Huge crowd gathers at clubhouse door. "We're waiting to see Charboneau," one explains . . . Super Joe is inside surrounded by reporters . . . He won't leave for hours . . . This is his moment . . . His day . . . An usher says, "Maybe this kid will turn into another Rocky Colavito."

The last Dieken-Kuiper show

November 29, 1981

You had to be there to feel the warmth and enjoy the fun—the laughs that always come from the Doug Dieken-Duane Kuiper Show.

The is the kind of party it was:

Tom Gorman, the former National League umpire who now works for the league as a supervisor, flew in from New York to tell, in his unique way, the rib-tickling stories about his days of calling balls and strikes. When Gorman saw the beneficiaries of the evening—"God's special children," those with damaged brains who smiled constantly yet must rely on others for life itself—and he saw the professional athletes who showed their love for these special ones, the hardened umpire refused to even take money for his plane fare.

"On behalf of the American and National league umpires you soon will receive $1,000," he said to Mrs. Dorothy Gauchat, the angel who is the heart of Our Lady of the Wayside, the heavenly place in Avon that takes care of these youngsters.

"As soon as I get back to New York, you'll receive a check," he added.

"The other umpires don't know it yet, but it won't be hard to sell them. I promise it to you."

This piece is not being written as a fundraiser for Our Lady of the Wayside or to get you to buy tickets for next year's Sports Night, the best there is anywhere. The tickets are gone almost immediately after the announcement is made and if Wagner's Party Center in Westlake could accommodate thousands instead of 600, the affair would be oversold just as quickly.

It's being reported once again to pass along some of the heart and the chuckles provided by the caring athletes in our community. Also because this one, in a sense, was a farewell to Kuiper, done with laughter, yet with a feeling of sadness and loss. This courageous, community-minded athlete who has been visiting the children at Wayside for years, no longer will be wearing a Cleveland Indians' uniform.

Jerry Dybzinski, the Indians' shortstop, was a surprise guest. "What are you doing here?" asked General Manager Phil Seghi in astonishment. "I thought you were playing ball in Santo Domingo."

"I just got in last night," said Jerry, sporting a Pancho Villa mustache. "I wanted to come home to be with my family." Upon his arrival, he immediately called Herb Score, the master of ceremonies and organizer of the Wayside sports banquet, and asked if he could attend.

Mike Hargrove, the Indians' first baseman, was a first-time guest. He had just been named the Indians' Man of the Year, a signal honor, for it was the second successive season he received this coveted award. "I was pleased," he quipped. "But I wasn't sure if I got it because I had a good year or because everybody else had a lousy one."

Hargrove, also growing a mustache, obviously was touched by the youngsters from the Wayside and the work of Mrs. Gauchat. He said, "I plan on becoming much more involved with the Waysde, if it's all right with you."

Robert E. Jackson, the huge Buster Brown lookalike who is having an outstanding season as a Browns' offensive guard, also was at his first Wayside banquet. He, too, asked, "Would you mind if I come out often?"

His teammate, running back Mike Pruitt, is a regular at the Wayside and at the banquet. He told the audience, "It's a coincidence that every time I come to this dinner we win our next game. We'll beat the Bengals in spite of Doug Dieken."

Joe Charboneau, there with his wife and mother, may have had trouble on the field but he revealed no sophomore jinx as a comedian. He was an enjoyable surprise.

Incidentally, he says he feels great following his recent back surgery, swims daily, does other exercises and even has been playing catch with a football.

Joe had brought along some gifts, an hour-glass for Hargrove to time himself as he gets into the batter's box, hair spray for Kuiper to protect his locks against the winds in San Francisco's Candlestick Park, and for Dieken a "framed photo of Doug taken at halftime." It was a picture of a hound dog wearing a huge muzzle.

"It takes Hargrove longer to go to bat than it did for him to have four children," quipped Charboneau. "The only thing Dieken can't hold is an audience."

Spotting Seghi and Gabe Paul at a nearby table, Joe said, "I bought two dogs, a bulldog and an Airedale. I named one Gabe and the other Phil. But I had to get rid of them. They kept trading bones with all the neighbors."

Even Father Thomas L. Weber, of the Ascension of Our Lord Church, revealed a sense of humor and drew spontaneous applause, a rarity for a pre-meal benediction.

He said, "Father in Heaven, on this eve of Thanksgiving . . . we are especially thankful for the extraordinary dedication of a remarkable woman (Dorothy Gauchat) . . . Continue to bless all that she does . . .

"Lord, we also ask you to bless a special young man who is leaving our community and whom we will miss. We thank you for the example of Duane Kuiper and for all the compassionate things he has done . . . We ask you to give him many more good years in baseball and that during those years may he hit at least *one* home run.

"Finally, we know you are the God who parted the Red Sea . . . the God of miracles. And so we ask you if somehow you could work out a wild card spot for the Browns . . ."

And then came the Dieken-Kuiper show, the dessert all guests had been awaiting. Dieken is quicker on his feet as a stand-up comic than he is as a blocker on the football field, and he's adept there, too, as his Pro Bowl stature attests. Bob Hope, Henny Youngman, and Rodney Dangerfield could use writers with his talent.

Although he works in the anonymity of the football trenches, he may become the most unforgettable athlete this town ever has known because of his wit and warmth toward the less fortunate.

During a slide presentation at the Wayside dinner, he moved from the speaker's table into the audience and watched it with one of the mongoloid children on his lap. To be at the Wayside affair Dieken cancelled an appearance that would have netted him $400. He has been selling $100 raffle tickets for a house, the proceeds to go to the Wayside, bulldozing his teammates and even writers to buy them. He even paid for a quarter-page ad in the Wayside dinner program. Of course, it was typical Dieken, reading:

"SALUTE TO DUANE KUIPER, Baseball's FIRST Designated Fielder . . . Your friend, Doug Dieken."

Herb Score, the MC, had a problem: Which one to put on first, Dieken or Kuiper? Dear friends though they are, at this banquet, where they needle everybody, they aim especially at each other.

"This year," said Score, "because Kuip is leaving and this may be the final Dieken-Kuiper Show, we're going to give them the last word." He then introduced the Browns' offensive tackle.

"All your sympathy and mercy are going to be with Kuiper tonight," said Dieken. "You're going to laugh at his stuff and not mine. I know when I'm licked. He's a great guy. Thanks for having me." He walked away from the microphone as the startled audience watched him in disbelief. Then, with a big grin he stepped back to the podium, said, "However . . . ," and the one-liners began, a few of which follow:

"I'm surprised to see Gabe Paul and Phil Seghi here. I heard they had traded in their Cadillacs for Pintos.

"Hargrove is in the right business. How would you like to be his patient if he were a dentist going through all those motions each time he looked in your mouth?

"Herb Score, I got one of your bubble gum cards—at an antique sale.

"I see Hal Lebovitz. He's the reason *The Plain Dealer* doesn't dare charge more than 15 cents.

"Mike Pruitt and I agree on most everything. We both eat at Lawson's, we both bank at National City. I asked Brian Sipe why he didn't give him the ball more often. He said, 'Every time I try to hand it to him, he's so surprised he gives the fair catch signal.'

"Things really change after a few losses. Lawson's called Monday. They want Pruitt and me to bring back the meat cooler.

"Jim Mueller (radio and TV broadcaster, who was in the audience) has been busy. He's the new director at Bruce Drennan School of Broadcasting.

"I'm happy that Charboneau's operation was a success. They opened his back and removed Manager Dave Garcia's shoe.

"I should have known we were going to have a bad season. I was sitting next to Robert E. Jackson on the bus to one of our games. He couldn't read the street signs without moving his lips. I found out later he majored in remedial reading.

"I'm really going to miss Kuiper. His power alleys are to the right and left side of the pitcher's mound.

"Kuip was traded to San Francisco for a pitcher and a hair dresser to be named later.

"I kid him about not hitting home runs, and he kids me about holding. But I could stop holding."

On a completely serious note, Dieken concluded, "I'm truly sorry to see him go. People with his class don't come around often. We're lucky to have had him as long as we did. I'm a Kuiper fan because of the person he is."

Then it was Kuiper's turn. He had spent hours on his script, aware at the outset it was impossible to top Dieken. "When I see only Charboneau laughing, I know I'm in trouble," he said.

Commencing seriously, he said, "I originally asked for a no-trade clause in my contract and didn't get it. I wish I had."

Then came the barbs and getting even time:

"The whole deal isn't completed yet. Marvin Miller, head of the Players Association, called me to ask if I had read the fine print in my contract. It reads, 'If a player loves the town he's leaving and if he loves the team he's leaving and if he loves the people of the town he is leaving, he has the option to trade the president and general manager of that club anywhere he so wishes.'

"Gabe Paul, I am sending you to Iran. We aren't asking for anything in return. Phil Seghi is going to the retirement community of Sun City in exchange for an old person to be named later.

"I want to say a special hello to Mike Pruitt. This is a man with a BIG problem. He's a running back for the Cleveland Browns. That's like being a windshield wiper on a submarine.

"Poor Mike has a better chance of getting his number called in the Ohio Lottery.

"It's good to see Joe Charboneau here tonight. He and his wife, Cindy, are now the proud parents of a two-month-old daughter, Dannon. Already she drinks milk through her nose.

"Turns out Joe really had a disc problem, the unsold copies of the record, 'Go, Go, Super Joe.'

"Mike Hargrove has meant a lot to the team. They still may be in sixth place, but now they lead the league in number of hours played per game.

"I must say this for Mike. He added a lot to my career—about 50 feet more that I had to cover between first and second.

"And now let's make Doug Dieken feel at home. Would you please throw your dinner napkins to the ground and move your chairs back 10 yards.

"In case you don't recognize him, he's the one sitting in his chair on all fours.

"Doug is under a lot of pressure. The IRS called him. They want him to list all his holdings.

"Last season Doug finished second behind punter Ray Guy of Oakland in 'hang time.'

"Dieken will do anything to get a TV or radio commercial. He volunteered to do one for Ohio Bell. He thought their slogan was, 'Reach out and clutch someone.'"

Tom Gorman followed, relating his funny experiences with Leo Durocher, Yogi Berra, and others, but he's coming back in January to speak at the annual SMACO dinner, so you'll hear or read his anecdotes at another time.

On the way out Kuiper promised he will be back at the Wayside dinner next year. He vowed not to lose his heart in San Francisco.

"Cleveland will remain my home," he said, "and somehow, some way, some day, in some capacity, I'll be back with the Indians."

As Herb Score said, "I've been here since 1955. Of all the players that have come and gone, there never has been a better person with the Indians than Duane Kuiper."

God willing, see you at the Wayside next year, Kuip and Doug and Herb and the two Mikes and Joe and Robert E. and you and you.

And Kuip, the best way to muzzle Dieken, even slightly, is to hit that home run Father Weber prayed for. All of us are rooting.

Here's how Jordan got so wide open

May 8, 1989

The same question is being asked over and over: How could the Cavs allow Michael Jordan to get the inbound pass?

This was with three seconds to go and the Cavs ahead, 100-99, and the Bulls, after calling a timeout, would be inbounding the ball at midcourt.

The phone rang the instant I got home after the game. Calls came from former coaches, others who have followed the game. "Didn't they know Jordan was going to get the ball? How could they let him get so free?"

One longtime Cavs' fan wondered why Lenny Wilkens didn't have all his big players on the floor and why wasn't one of his big men covering the inbounder?

All good questions.

Lenny had only two big men in there, Brad Daugherty and Larry Nance.

I would have covered the inbound passer, Brad Sellers, with my biggest guy. Make it as tough as possible for him to throw a direct pass.

Lenny decided otherwise. He left inbounder Sellers uncovered, preferring to play five men against the four on the floor.

With five on four, one player could rove and pick up somebody, help in hounding Jordan. That makes sense, although I'd rather not make it so easy on the inbounder.

Everybody in the Coliseum knew the Bulls would try to get the ball to Jordan. The problem is: it's virtually impossible to deny Jordan the ball. The man is so elusive he could get out of the most foolproof trap a Houdini could devise.

What the Cavs had to do was to make him eat the ball for at least three seconds. I've run the tape of those last three seconds a dozen times in slow motion. Here's how Jordan came wide open:

Only two Bulls played deep, beyond the free-throw line, Jordan and Bill Cartright. The others got out of there, pulling their guards with them along the baseline. Cartright was closest to the inbounder, with Jordan about five steps to Cartright's right. The Cavs apparently figured the first pass would go to Cartright, for Larry Nance fronted him, his back to the inbounder.

Craig Ehlo was on Jordan. Daugherty was a few steps off Cartright, ready to help out on a switch.

Then Cartright ran toward Jordan and cut to the basket. Jordan broke toward the ball on a simple cross pattern. Daugherty stayed with Cartright. Nance moved in Jordan's direction, but his back was to the ball. He didn't see the passer, but he saw Jordan coming to him and tried to push him back. Jordan danced around the push and got clear. Sellers tossed him the ball.

When Ehlo saw Jordan go toward the ball, he hurried after him. As he reached Jordan, he overran him and slipped slightly. He had been playing on a tender ankle and had injured it again just three seconds earlier when he scored the go-ahead point on a perfectly executed give-and-go inbounds play.

That slight opening was all Jordan needed. He cut toward the free-throw circle and let fly as Ehlo recovered and jumped toward the ball. Too late. Nobody underneath came up to challenge Jordan. Why? Ask them. The ball went in just as the buzzer went off.

And that was it. The Cavs' season was over. I felt as though my stomach had been disemboweled. I'm sure the 20,300 fans felt the same, let down, sick, teased, and just plain lousy.

And then I thought about the game. It was a fantastic game. Tension every second, a memorable sports event. Somebody has to lose and sadly for us, it was the Cavs.

And I thought about Jordan. The Cavs got beat by the world's greatest basketball player. It probably wouldn't have made any difference if one of the Cavs' big players had come up and challenged Jordan on that shot. Just six seconds earlier he went toward the hoop, and Tree Rollins reached high in the air. Huge Tree, with a wingspan matching the Terminal Tower. Jordan jumped above the tower, remained suspended in the air, and scored.

But the sad truth is that the Cavs, hard as they played, also beat themselves. In the fourth quarter, after taking a decent lead, they stopped taking the game to the Bulls. Four times in that period they allowed the Bulls to get tap-in rebounds. When that happens, the big guys are standing and looking, not boxing out. Tree and Daugherty did not have their best games yesterday.

And then there were the turnovers. Time after time the Cavs wasted shooting opportunities with bad passes, a three-second violation, and being too slow after loose balls. The Bulls converted 18 Cavs' turnovers into 16 points.

And then there was that awful halfcourt, stand-around offense. If it hadn't been for Ehlo, his hustle, and his shooting, it would have been a runaway for the Bulls. He alone almost squeaked out a victory for the Cavs. I'll never understand why Daugherty doesn't shoot from out. He's a good shot and nobody guards him outside. But he won't shoot. Of course, the coach should tell him.

For some reason Ron Harper also was bashful. He hesitated so many times when he was open, then when he decided to shoot he was covered. And the penetration, except for Mark Price and Ehlo, was zilch.

Oh well, it's over. There's much to do if the Cavs are to improve next year. They gave us a good show. But next season, please, not another tease.

Only Belle knows the real truth

July 25, 1994

The man has three sons, ages 10 through 16, all sports-minded.

"What should I tell them?" he asked, almost plaintively.

About what?

"The corked bat."

You serious?

"Very"

What's the problem?

"Well, it appears as though Albert Belle used one, but Indians fans seem to make light of it and so do my kids. I'm not saying Albert was guilty. Although cork was found in his bat, his case has yet to be heard. Still he's being treated almost like a hero. There's a strange message here being sent to my kids. What do I say to them?"

What if one of your boys came home with a high grade on an exam and a few days later the teacher called to say your son had cheated?

"I certainly wouldn't applaud my son for cheating. I'd let him know how disappointed I was in him and would try to make sure it never happened again."

Isn't it similar to using a corked bat? It's cheating, it's dishonest.

I agree. But the boys read pieces that rationalize it: About how other players do cheating things, so how can they think unkindly of one of our players when he's caught?"

C'mon. If we accepted that logic there would be no law and order. As it is, we're heading in that direction and we just can't look the other way and let it continue.

"You must agree, though, that corking a bat is not a major crime. It's not like robbing a bank."

True, and neither is the penalty. If you rob a bank you go to jail. If you cork a bat you get a suspension. It's wrong. That's the message you must get across to your kids.

"Then there are those who argue that cheating is part of baseball's mystique—its lore. It's been happening since the game became a professional sport. There always have been incidents of illegal pitches—emery balls, spitters. Bats with metal inside, bats with cork. Fields being slanted to change the course of bunts. Signals stolen from the scoreboard. Isn't it the nature of the sport?"

Baseball lends itself to trickery more than any other sport, because of the equipment. You can't do tricks with a football, basketball or soccer ball that you can with a baseball or a bat. Sign stealing isn't in the same category as bat corking because the opponents easily can change their signs and make the sign stealers look silly. There are other tricks you haven't even mentioned, like having lower pitching mounds in the bullpen of the visiting team. Because so much money is involved in winning, or in getting a high batting average, or in hitting more home runs, teams and players constantly are looking for that edge.

"Sounds as though you're condoning it."

Absolutely not. Just explaining the obvious. The rules forbid doctoring the ball and bat. The penalties are spelled out. But the rule book doesn't mention other forms of trickery except to give the umpires authority to handle any cases of unsportsmanlike conduct that become apparent to them.

"That's another argument I hear from those who say the umpires keep letting all this illegal stuff go—like the spitter. So they, in effect, are putting their stamp of approval on it."

That's just more rationalizing hogwash. Umpires don't have X-ray eyes. They can't look inside bats. And if a pitcher wants to throw a spitter it's almost impossible to catch him. Many years ago Mike Garcia, a Cleveland pitcher, was accused of throwing a spitter. I asked him if he did. "Watch me and see if I do," he said. That day Ted Williams accused

Mike of throwing him spitters. I never saw him do it. Years later he told me how he did it. Immediately after he released a pitch he would spit into his glove. Everybody, including me, was watching the flight of the pitch. We never saw the spit.

"You're saying, in effect, there's so much cheating because it's so difficult to be caught."

Bingo. But it's no less wrong. Baseball really is a game involving the honor system. Like when a teacher gives a test, leaves the room and trusts the kids not to cheat. Baseball doesn't have a police force except to watch the players off the field so they don't become involved with gamblers. Because the players are on their honor they ought to be more honorable.

"Apparently they aren't. So what's the answer?"

The cheating will continue. Look, I've done things wrong in my youth I'm sorry about and wish I hadn't. They still bother me. I don't know if Belle is guilty or not. Only he knows. If he is, he'll have to live with his conscience the rest of his life.

"Ah-ha. That's what I should tell my kids."

Correct. Be an exemplary parent yourself. Teach them right from wrong and if they do wrong they'll know it. Cheating is a big burden to carry. Better to be honest—always.

"Thanks for the conversation. The best answer for my kids would be for Belle to be found innocent. I hope he is."

THE GAME

Outwitting sign stealers is constant battle

January 23, 1958

Bob Feller's fast ball traveled at the rate of approximately 100 miles per hour, which means that in less than one-half second it rocketed from Bob's arm to Jim Hegan's glove.

Furthermore Bob's manner of delivery, with his foot kicked up high, made it difficult for the hitter to pick up the ball until it was almost on top of him. And some of them admitted they never saw it at all.

Yet Hegan never had any trouble catching Bob, not even in Mr. Robert's prime.

Jim explains this: "I knew what was coming. The hitters didn't."

As the Indians' catcher, Jim is the team's quarterback. He calls the signals.

All clubs use the same signals, reveals Jim. "When I show the pitcher one finger I'm asking for his fast ball. Two fingers indicate the curve and three fingers mean a slider." By wiggling his fingers he asks for the change-up and a clenched first signifies the knuckleball.

Obviously if Hegan's signs could be seen by the opposition the pitcher's advantage over the hitter would be nullified. So Jim must hide them carefully. He places his fingers high up against his thigh, and because he has such long legs coaches along first and third find it impossible to see them, no matter how hard they try.

Yankee catcher Yogi Berra, in contrast, is at a disadvantage. His short legs often permit a runner on first to see his signal. When a runner gets to second Berra is more careful, but apparently not until he reads this—if he does—will he realize his fingers often are visible from first base.

Not only does Hegan call the type of pitch, he also gives the location. He may do this by motioning up, down, in or out, with his bare hand, or he may quickly flash a target with his glove.

And he is forever attempting to foil the sign-stealers.

To make it as difficult as possible for the thieves, Jim always flashes three signs before each pitch. In sequence, he may rapidly show the pitcher one finger, then two, then three.

In this case, if the battery had decided in advance that the second signal was the official one, the pitcher would know he was to throw a curve.

In the next inning, perhaps, the third signal would be the official one. Sometimes the official sign is determined by the number of outs. With no outs, for example, the wanted pitch would be given on the first sign. After one out the second sign becomes official. After two outs only the third sign would be regarded.

If this sounds complicated—it is. And when Hegan rapidly flashed the signs at us by way of illustration, it seemed extremely difficult to select the correct one, and we were much closer to him than 60 feet.

"It's not hard to do after a little practice," Hegan assured us. "We don't get crossed up very often."

Feller crossed him up more than any pitcher he ever caught, Hegan discloses. It may have been because he often blinked nervously when he first came up. "I remember once in Boston in '47, I called for a curve," the catcher recalls, "and Bob threw his fast ball. I waited until the last split second for it to break. The ball hit me right here." Hegan pointed to his wrist, adding, "It's lucky for me that by '47 his fast ball and slackened up a little."

Instead of having a broken wrist his was only black and blue for a week.

Teams have employed all sorts of sign-stealing devices. "We were sure that Detroit and Boston were getting our signals for a while but we didn't know how," Jim reveals.

"In Boston we suspect somebody in the center field bleachers must have been using binoculars. When a pitcher has real good stuff and the hitters get a good toe-hold and stay right up there with a solid swing we know something's wrong. We keep switching our signs on every pitch, using the same basic signs but we change the code.

"Just a couple of years ago in Boston during a game Lemon was pitching, we were so positive the Red Sox were getting the signs somehow, I told Bob to call the pitches simply by the position in which he held his glove. The Red Sox immediately stopped hitting."

The Tigers, Hegan later discovered, employed binoculars to steal the Tribe's signs, particularly in 1940 when Detroit beat out Cleveland for the title. "When Al Benton joined us in 1949 he admitted he was the one who sat in the Tigers' bullpen in center field and picked off our signs through binoculars. Another pitcher out there, by shifting his position, would telegraph the sign back to the hitter."

Not until Chico Carrasquel and Jim Busby joined the Indians in '56 did Hegan learn that the White Sox , too, had been stealing Tribe signs successfully.

"They did it from their scoreboard," he discloses. "They'd get the sign through powerful glasses and then relay it to the batter simply by blinking Sherman Lollar's number, which is "10." When they flickered the "1" it meant a fast ball was coming. If the "0" flickered it meant the curve. None of us ever thought to study the board that carefully but after we found out we were on the alert. They don't try that method against us any more."

The Indians have been accused of stealing signs via the scoreboard during pennant-winning '48. In fact, some ex-Indians have so confessed, but Hegan refuses to comment.

"I will say this," he offers. "Boudreau, Keltner and Gordon really could rack the pitchers when they knew what was coming. They were great at stealing signs for each other from second base. It's easy to see the catcher's signal from second. After all, he must make it visible to his second baseman and shortstop so they can anticipate which way to break when the ball is hit.

So if a runner's out there he sees it, too.

"Often when the catcher walks out to talk to the pitcher there's a man on second base and we want to change our signs so they can't be stolen. Occasionally I'll tell the pitcher verbally what the next two or three pitches should be and then I'll go back behind the plate and give a fake sign."

Hegan says he's never gone to the mound to ask a pitcher where he's going to eat dinner or to crack a joke. "I go out there either to slow him up, or to switch our signs or, if a newcomer comes in to pinch-hit, to ask the pitcher if he knows what his weakness is."

Some pitchers tip off their pitches. "We always suspected Tommy Henrich was able to tell what Feller was going to throw," reveals Hegan. "Mel Harder was able to call Mel Parnell's pitches. Red Kress has had good luck calling Whitey Ford's pitches from the first base coaching box."

But for the most part the hitters have to guess. "And they usually try to outguess the catcher not the pitcher," according to Jim.

"Some catchers follow a pattern in calling signals. The studious hitters catch on to those patterns eventually. I'm not the pattern type. I study the hitter, watch his stance and I try to discover as quickly as possible which pitches are working best for my pitcher on that given day.

"But the real secret of callin 'em, as I see it, is to mix 'em up. Sometimes I may use a pattern for the first three innings just to fool the hitters in the late innings."

All the Indians' top pitchers will tell you they have Hegan to thank for much of their success. "He gives you so much confidence when you look at him crouching back there," says Herb Score. "If he wants me to throw a curve on a three-two pitch I don't hesitate. I say to myself, 'If he thinks I can do it I guess I can.'"

A pitcher, of course, has the right to pitch his own game. "After all," says Hegan, "the final responsibility is his. He can shake off a pitch at any time."

Often however, when a pitcher appears to be shaking off a sign he does this merely to confuse the hitter. "Score may shake off a sign," says Hegan, "and come right back with the pitch I originally called for."

For the past six years, Lemon has never second-guessed Hegan. "Once he called for a curve and I shook him off," relates Lemon. "I wanted a slider and the batter hit it for a home run. After that Hegan called all the pitches."

"Wynn has shaken off Hegan's signals more than any other pitcher he's ever caught. "Early devised a set of switches," Jim reveals. "If he held his glove in a certain position before I gave the sign, it meant that if I called for the fast ball he would throw the curve, and vice versa. He had another switch after I gave the sign. In this way the hitter found it almost impossible to steal pitches from him."

Hegan is sure now that Wynn will continue the same switches with the White Sox. "But knowing them won't help us unless we can see what the catcher is calling," he adds.

Virtually the only time Wynn shook off Hegan was when the catcher called for a fast ball with the count in the hitter's favor.

"When Early is behind it seems he just hates to give in to the hitter," explains Hegan. "That's all right, except the hitters are starting to get wise. They know if the count is against Early they're not going to get a fast ball."

Except for one short, unhappy period in his career, Hegan has been the Indians' quarterback. In August of 1947 Lou Boudreau, the manager, told Hegan, "I'll call the signals from shortstop. Watch my glove for the signs and relay them to the pitcher." Boudreau told no one else on the team that he had taken over, not even the pitchers. But he did tell the sportswriters, whom he swore to secrecy until the end of the season.

Even Al Lopez, the Tribe's second-string catcher, didn't know. Lopez remembers, "Once I substituted for Jim and in the fifth inning Boudreau called 'Time.'

"He said to me, 'I called for a fast ball and Lemon threw a curve. How come?'

"You called for a fast ball?' I asked. "Since when are you calling the signals?'

"Lou then told me, 'I've called every pitch for the past month.'"

The story of Boudreau's master-minding broke publicly at the end of the season and it cut Hegan deeply. To this day it bothers him.

"I didn't appreciate it. I'll admit it bothered me and I said so to reporters afterward. It was the most unpleasant period of my baseball life. Many times I'd call a pitch, the pitcher would shake me off and I'd have to go out to the mound and say, 'The man says throw it.'

"It's the manager's prerogative to call the pitches. But I don't think he should call every one. It takes all initiative away from the catcher and makes nothing but a messenger boy out of him.

Aware that Hegan was perturbed, Boudreau called Jim into his office at the start of '48.

"Let's forget what happened," the manager told Hegan. "You call all the signs from now on."

That year the Indians won the pennant.

Are you friend or foe?

June 30, 1966

Perplexed people are pondering, "What's wrong with the Indians?" Sympathetic souls are saying, "Too bad about the Indians." Frustrated fans are fuming, "Same old Indians, always folding at this time of the year."

So many citizens sound bitter. Our baseball writer, Russell Schneider, is one. He picked the Indians to win and he seems to take each loss as a personal slap in the face.

Too many of us—and this is common among young baseball writers, for I went through this agonizing period—wear our baseball hearts on our sleeves.

You are pulling so eagerly for the team to win that each loss leaves you terribly let down. In this emotional climate it's not easy to remain objective, to remember the boys on the field are human beings who breathe and think and forget to think, even as you and I. They have their ups and downs, even as you and I.

What's wrong with the team? The pitching has become terribly thin. It was predicted in this corner a few weeks ago that the Indians were headed for deep trouble. Sam McDowell's sore arm was too much of a burden to overcome. Take Juan Marichal away from the Giants, or Sandy Koufax from the Dodgers or Denny McLain from the Tigers and you'll have floundering clubs.

In addition to the pitching problems the Indians have run into a mental block. Almost everything is a state of mind. We can't turn off our thoughts. Get involved in an auto collision and you drive cautiously for at least the next two weeks. Have a bad time on the second nine holes, as Palmer did in the National Open, and the bogey man stays with you next time you play that round.

Winning is a frame of mind and so is losing. When you're losing one mistake causes you to say, "Oh-o, here we go again," and you make another.

Momentum is developed, in either direction. In baseball only great pitching can halt a losing momentum, for it takes 1-0 victories to overcome mistakes. We need a healthy Sam McDowell.

The reports are encouraging on Sam. Yet for the record I can't subscribe to Birdie Tebbetts' method of rehabilitating him. I can't see the use of a pitcher three successive days in a relief as a method of strengthening a sore arm. Nor do I agree with his use of other starters in relief. But, being human, I, too, could be wrong. Honest, although I sit in judgment I'm rooting for Tebbetts. I'd much rather he proves to be right.

The Indians will start winning again. It's inevitable. With their personnel they should finish third. That's better than seven other teams.

And don't say, "They always fold at this time." It's not true. Usually the foldup comes later. Since the present pattern is different, it's just possible this team will rebound with a bang on July 4th.

Meanwhile the Indians are their own worst enemies. What they desperately need now is friends. Can they count on you?

Should rain decide score?

June 13, 1968

The trouble with writing this column today is that it may be classified by some as "sour grapes."

Believe me, it isn't. I'm not writing it because the Indians have been prevented from winning two games this season by the weather, the latest Tuesday night.

I'm writing this because I don't think the weather should beat any team. I would feel just as strongly about it if the Tigers had been hit in the head twice by the rain.

Baseball is a nine-inning game. The rules should insist that each game be played the full distance. It's the only, sensible, fair way. It's fair for everybody.

Baseball took a big step last year. It decided a game shouldn't be allowed to continue after 1 A.M. After that the clock became a burden on the fans, the players and the listener at home. So a 1 A.M. curfew was established. At that point the game is suspended and is continued the next time the two teams meet.

Suspended, but eventually played to its conclusion—that's the way it should be.

But, if a game is rained out after five innings, it's all over.

Now tell me, baseball brains, is that consistent?

Let's have ALL games played to their full conclusion. Let's not have one rule for rain, another for clocks. If a game is halted by rain make it a suspended game, too, and finish it off at the earliest opportunity.

The present five-inning rule no longer has any reason for being in the book. All it does is create problems, build up frustrations, and always is unfair to one team and the umpires.

It puts the umps in an unnecessary hot spot. How long should they wait for the rain to stop? Forty-five minutes? The team behind yells, "Not enough." An hour and a half? The team ahead shouts, "Too long." Should they allow play to continue in the rain? In the mud? Should they wear radar under their hats? Once it rains, the umpires can't win.

Then there's the stalling and, conversely, the hurrying. The team that's ahead, as the clouds and the fifth inning approach, suddenly goes to work as though a time study is being made. No longer does the pitcher peer in for the signal as if to convince his draft board he has poor eyesight. Almost as soon as he gets the call from the catcher, he's ready to throw.

Meanwhile, the team behind gives a beautiful demonstration in slow motion, hoping the rain will beat the inning.

But now, the fifth inning is over and the downpour hasn't arrived. Suddenly, the action reverses, just as if someone had pushed a button. The team ahead begins to stall, while the other club starts moving in double time as the dark clouds approach.

This "beat the rain" may be a game of sorts, but it's not baseball. Instead it's a farce comedy, worthy of the Hanna boards.

Baseball is the only game that can be legally complete before its normal regulation period. Basketball and football MUST go all the way. The winner of a race isn't the man in front when the rains come. But in baseball that's what happens, silly though it is.

Indians' general manager Gabe Paul long has been an advocate of playing every league game to the full nine innings or more. He now has some backers and they intend to bring it up again at the winter meetings. Lately, baseball has made several progressive moves. Let's add this one to it.

Or else put a dome on every ball park.

What's a George?

August 21, 1969

Most everybody has a gripe about a certain rule in one sport or another.

Take our cousin, George. Please. He pitched in the PD Class A League once upon a time. And he even threw batting practice for the Indians until he low-bridged Bob Feller, after which he was told, "Don't call us. We'll call you."

Well, George has this thing about the "Infield Fly" rule. For several years he has been beefing mightily to us about it. Apparently, he has no other problems, for this "abomination," as he calls it, seems to consume him night and day.

In case you need a refresher on the rule, here it is: "An infield fly is a fair fly ball which can be caught by an infielder with ordinary effort, when first and second, or first, second and third, are occupied, before two are out." The batter who hits such a fly is out the instant the umpire declares "infield fly" and the other runners can advance at their own peril.

The purpose of the rule is to prevent an infielder from purposely allowing a fly ball to drop and turning it into a double play.

George says it's crazy to call a batter out if the infielder muffs the fly ball, or fails to catch it. He says, "Baseball is a game of hitting and fielding. Why penalize the hitter if the fielder doesn't do his job?"

At first we tried to ignore George.

We mentioned the rule has been in the book since 1890, so it has withstood the test of time.

"But that doesn't make it right," he said.

We have tried to talk to him about the weather and girls and such, but he always comes back to the infield fly. And now, finally, he has made his point. We think he's got something.

George's way would be this: The umpire should call "infield fly." But if the ball isn't caught, the batter would be awarded first base, the same as he would on a base on balls.

"That way there is no gift out," he says. "The ball has to be caught."

By George, he's right.

The George rule makes the fielder do what he's supposed to do, namely, catch the ball. It eliminates the basic weakness of the present rule, which forces the umpire to make a judgment that sometimes boomerangs. There have been cases where one umpire called "infield fly" and the other three umps disagreed. There have been instances where the wind got the ball after the "infield fly" call and carried it to the outfield. There have been cases where one umpire called "infield fly," and the base runners didn't hear him, causing ridiculous confusion.

Under the George rule, an error in judgment by the umpire wouldn't be costly. If the ball is caught, the batter is out. If it isn't, all the runners, including the batter, get at least one base. If they want to try for more, they do so at their own risk. "Now that's baseball," says George. "None of this phony 'out' stuff if a ball isn't caught."

Maybe it's because he's completely exhausted us, but we can't find a single reason to disagree. We called Charley Segar in New York, head of the rules committee, and told him about George and the infield fly.

"That rule has been in the books since 1890," he said.

"But that doesn't mean it's right," we said. "Don't make any hasty judgment. Think about it."

He promised he would. And it he doesn't, he's sure to hear from George because we'll transfer the calls. And if he can make Charley see the light some day, an infield fly may be called a "George."

Who's at fault?

January 27, 1972

If I were coaching basketball today I'm afraid I'd have to teach my kids karate—in self- defense.

I saw the Minnesota-Ohio State basketbrawl on TV, Tuesday night, and it was the most frightening, the most brutal of its kind I had ever seen. It rivaled much of the violence we see on the tube and at the movies today, which might be telling us something.

At first I looked upon it as an isolated incident. Then I remembered it was the fourth time a fight erupted during a televised college basketball game this season.

That's four too many and Tuesday's sickening scene at Minnesota should serve as the one which will cause coaches and college presidents to pause for some sober reflection and constructive action.

Almost invariably when a court incident flares out of control it's because at least one of the coaches failed in his responsibility as a teacher. He permitted the importance of the game itself to get out of perspective. He forgot he was a teacher, coaching boys to play a game, not to fight a crusade.

If I were a college president, or a high school principal I would try to get the films of last Saturday's Ohio University-Miami game and Tuesday's Minnesota-Ohio State game and show them to my coach. In turn I would have him show them to the players.

Both games were of major importance to the teams involved. Not only did the Miami-Ohio U. contest have a MAC championship flavor, there was a strong rivalry involved.

Ohio U. was favored. The game was on its home court. Miami outplayed its hosts. It was a frustrating afternoon for the Bobcats and their fans as they suffered their first MAC loss.

Yet the behavior of the players and spectators was exemplary. As I watched that game I was more impressed by the respect the players showed for each other than the fine basketball they displayed. It was a real credit to the coaches, and especially to Jimmy Snyder, the Ohio U. coach, for it was his team that was taking an unexpected drubbing.

I had heard he was a great coach, but always a gentleman and his players certainly reflected it. If they happened to commit a rather severe foul they appeared genuinely sorry and went out of their way to shake the opponent's hand or give him an apologetic pat.

Never did they make faces about the officiating. They accepted their own misplays, rather than try to blame them on the whistle-blowers as some alibi ikes are prone to do.

Now for a showing of the Minnesota-Ohio State game: I saw the final 13 minutes of it and it was evident that a tinder box was developing. Crowd control was poor. Fans were throwing objects onto the floor even though they had been warned by the referees. Not once did the host coach or a school official make an effort to cool the crowd.

With eight minutes remaining the score was tied. Then Ohio State began to edge ahead. Minnesota commenced to commit fouls of desperation and when these were called the players made faces and gestures to let the crowd think they were innocent. The Buckeyes made the free throws and increased the lead, causing more fouls by the frustrated Gophers. Not once did the coach call a time out to tell his men to quit playing the officials and start playing basketball again.

From my vantage point I thought the officials did an excellent job. Aware the temperature was getting hotter, they were on top of every play and rushed between players whenever they saw a dirty look.

Throughout, I got the distinct impression that the new Minnesota coach had built his team to an unbelievable high, that it was vital to win this game at all costs. Minnesota had been down for so long in basketball and now, having tasted some success, he wanted to continue to savor it and only a victory over Ohio State would satisfy his appetite and the community's. That's the impression I got, right or wrong.

At any rate, with 36 seconds remaining Luke Witte was in the clear for an easy basket and the Ohio State center was clobbered unnecessarily hard by the Gophers' Clyde Turner. The officials immediately disqualified Turner for the flagrant foul.

Moments later came the unforgettable violence.

Minnesota, having lost the game, decided to win the war. A horrible deplorable hollow victory, with perhaps the worst casualty list in college history. It was inexcusable.

If I have not mentioned the Ohio State coach in this piece it's because Fred Taylor's record is clear. He has been a great winner and a gracious loser and always a gentleman. If Minnesota has a rebuttal I'd like to hear it.

Wayne Duke, the Big Ten commissioner, was at the game. He is conducting a thorough investigation. Soon he will crack down—I hope. If nothing else, I suggest he makes the guilty parties view the Ohio U. game films.

It would teach them how to play the game. That's all it is, gentlemen—a game.

How important is fear?

September 22, 1974

"Fear," said Al Davis. "It's the only thing a football player responds to. It's the one thing that makes him go."

Al Davis is the managing partner of the Oakland Raiders. He's the aggressive, hard-boiled little guy who once coached the Raiders and, through fear, forced the National Football League to join up with the infant American Football League.

Our conversation took place in a plush Miami Beach hotel lobby prior to a Super Bowl game. He's highly articulate and he doesn't look as tough as he really is. But he talks straight and he talks strong, and we talked until almost four that morning, on the fascinating subject of fear in football, a subject he brought up.

The fear, said Davis, had to be implanted in the player by the coach and the front office.

"You've got to make the man afraid," he said. "You've got to make him so afraid of what you'll do to him if he doesn't produce that he'll be more afraid of not producing than he is of the guy on the other side of the line."

Playing the angel's advocate I mentioned that Blanton Collier was quite the opposite, a gentleman, who rarely shouted, who was a fine teacher and brilliant analyzer and yet with his own comparatively soft manner he was highly successful. Also that Art Modell, above him, was a paternal owner and the two, together, appeared to obtain results.

"So far," cautioned Davis. "But if a coach or an owner is soft in football sooner or later the player will take advantage of him. You've got to drive him constantly, always keep him afraid—afraid of being yelled at or fined, or of losing his job."

"Then you don't agree with the policy preached by some that you can achieve more by a pat on the back than by a swat?"

"Not in football," he said quickly.

I have thought of this conversation often. I thought of it when I heard some players say, "We really didn't appreciate Blanton Collier until he was gone." More than one has admitted to me he took advantage of Collier's decency.

I thought of it during the recent strike, when virtually Paul Brown's entire Cincinnati team reported to camp while the Browns, after reporting, walked out. I remembered how the players had been afraid of Brown when I covered the beat. I remembered a lecture he gave them prior to a game in Los Angeles, a lecture so biting, so threatening that when they went onto the field they set a record in penalties and won the game by a whopping score. Strong men, such as Lou Saban, now a successful coach himself, were deathly afraid of Paul Brown's bite. I remembered, too, that when Brown seemed to become afraid of some of his players—a sudden and unexplainable change in character—he lost his team and, soon after, his job. I remembered that afterward he told a friend he had made a mistake and when he got another chance with the Bengals he became a tough martinet again.

I remembered that Al Davis conversation when I read Steve Jacobson's profile of a "ruthless Sid Gillman," carried a few weeks ago on these pages and I think of it now because the Browns will play Gillman's Houston Oilers today.

Gillman said he doesn't care what they think of him personally, as long as it produces results. So far it has. The Oilers, in the cellar last year, had a good exhibition season and they won their opening league game last Sunday.

Off the field and away from football Gillman is a charming man. But once he walks onto the field he is a driver. His drills can be killers. He's relentless, like an Army officer driving his men for battle.

Said Steve Kiner, a linebacker, "There are people here who hate Gillman's guts. I kind of like him. A lot of people don't. He's not interested in that."

Said Don Pastorini, the quarterback who will miss today's game because of a pulled hamstring, "I've heard the Dallas Cowboys have a lot of animosity and they win. Other clubs have bitching and they win. We always had great togetherness on this team. Maybe we were too friendly."

One unidentified player admitted he feared reprisals from Gillman. There it was again—fear.

I remembered Al Davis' voice, "How do you think Vince Lombardi turned the Packers around? He did it with fear."

"He's right," admits Forrest Gregg, who is now the Browns' offensive line coach. "Really, the players as a whole are more motivated by fear than by love of the game or love for their coach. Not that a coach can't achieve love and respect. But he's got to start out with instilling fear. We were afraid of him.

"Lombardi was a tough man, hard. The first thing he did at Green Bay was to scare the heck out of everybody. How did he do it? Vocally and verbally more than anything else. He was a fiery guy. The one thing he wanted was an all-out effort by everybody.

"Football players as a whole need to be driven. If you came onto the field and ran a play at half-speed he'd scream at you. Nobody likes to be embarrassed or ridiculed in front of others. That's what he would do. He'd yell, 'You couldn't block my sister,' or 'He's stuffing you in your tracks? What kind of man are you to let him do that?'

"He had that fierce look and that growling voice to go with it, constantly demanding, never letting up.

"The players really want to know what's expected of them and they got his message: 100 percent effort, 100 percent performance. He wouldn't accept anything less.

"Some resented it at first. Some couldn't take the abuse. They didn't stay. That was all right with Lombardi. He didn't want the men who couldn't take it. He wanted those who were tough enough mentally to handle it. The mental side of football is just as important as the physical. If you couldn't take what he dished out and folded there, you'd fold in the game.

"He believed in constant pressure. He manufactured it. Pressure though fear of him. There was never an instant on the practice field that you didn't feel it. The only time he let up was the day of the game."

The initial fear of Lombardi remained, but respect and love also grew. "When you realized this man is trying to make me better than I would be if left to my own devices you came to appreciate his effort. You appreciated it when you saw the results," said Gregg, who is now trying to coach the offensive line in the same manner.

"It's the only way I know," he said. "If you're soft they'll take advantage of you. That's human nature." Al Davis, it was remembered, used almost the identical words.

Gregg, who is neither gruff nor grumpy, chuckled when I mentioned, "Then Henry Jordan was telling the absolute truth when he said, 'Lombardi treats us all the same—like dogs.'"

"Yes," he said, "and that's the important thing—to treat everybody the same. Bart Starr got the same treatment Jordan did. If a guy is tough, a driver, all you ask is that he doesn't play favorites. Lombardi never was unfair. He was rough on everybody. You respect that and you respond."

Today comes another test of fear. How much have Gillman's Oilers improved because of it? How much fear do the Browns have of being publicly humiliated by the lowly Oilers if not by their own coaches and front office? We'll see today.

Is baseball such a simple game?

May 4, 1980

Almost everybody—men and women—has played baseball or some variation of it (notably slow pitch softball) at one time or another. The enchantment of the game is that it is so simple.

The basic rules have been unchanged since 1900. Yet, simple as it seems, the game occasionally proves more confusing than complicated ones.

Each day I get numerous questions involving basic plays, such as fair or foul balls and strikes. Inasmuch as the sandlot season is about to open and because the Major League season already is underway, here's a refresher quiz for all of you who think you know this simple game:

FAIR OR FOUL?

1—A batted ball bounces in foul territory between home and first base, hits a pebble before passing first and rolls toward the pitcher's mound where it is fielded in fair territory. The umpire calls it foul. RIGHT or WRONG?

2—A batted ball hits behind the plate, spins and rolls forward and settles on the plate. Umpire calls it foul. RIGHT or WRONG?

3—Batter, running to first, is hit by his own batted ball. He has one leg on the fair side of the foul line, but the ball hits the other leg, which is in foul territory. Umpire calls it a fair ball and calls the runner out. RIGHT or WRONG?

4—Batted ball hits the pitcher's mound and rebounds into foul territory between first and third. Umpire calls it a fair ball. RIGHT or WRONG?

5—Batted ball bounces directly over the third base bag and lands in foul territory behind

it. Umpire calls it a foul ball. RIGHT or WRONG?

6—Left fielder, while standing in fair territory, reaches across to catch the ball on the foul side of the line. He fumbles the ball and it lands in fair territory. Umpire calls it a fair ball. RIGHT or WRONG?

7—Left fielder, while standing in foul territory, reaches across and touches fly ball in fair territory. It drops in fair territory. Umpire calls it a foul ball. RIGHT or WRONG?

8—A batted ball hits the left field foul pole and bounces directly into foul territory, not passing the pole. The umpire calls it a foul ball. RIGHT or WRONG?

9—Batted ball hits the batter's leg while he is standing in the batter's box and rolls into fair territory. Umpire calls it a fair ball. RIGHT or WRONG?

10—Line drive zooms over third base in fair territory, then lands foul. Umpire calls it a fair ball. RIGHT or WRONG?

The answers:

In EACH of the above plays the umpire was WRONG. Here's the definition of a fair ball: One that "settles on fair ground between home and first base, OR that is on or over fair territory when bounding to the outfield past first or third base, OR that touches first or third base, OR that first falls on fair territory on or beyond first or third base, OR that, while on or over fair territory, touches the person of an umpire or player.

"Note: A fair fly ball shall be judged according to the relative position of the foul line, not whether the fielder is in fair or foul territory at the time he touches it."

Conversely, all other batted balls are foul. A key word in the definition is "settles." On all calls between the plate and the base it makes no difference where the ball first hits. It must be judged according to where it finally comes to rest.

Also remember these three things: A pebble is part of the natural ground, just as the grass is. Home plate is in fair territory, as are all the other bases, and so are the foul lines. The foul pole is merely an extension of the foul line. The foul lines really should be called "Fair Lines" and the pole the "Fair Pole."

OUT OR SAFE?

1—Batter gets a hit, over runs first base, turns left (toward the infield) and immediately heads back to first, but he is tagged before he gets there. Umpire calls the runner out. RIGHT or WRONG?

2—Manning is on second. Harrah flies deep to right. Manning goes to third and tags it, then thinking the ball was caught, retreats to second. But the ball is not caught and now Manning and Harrah both are standing on second base. Ball is thrown to the second baseman, who tags Manning. Harrah then races back to first safely. Umpire calls Manning out. RIGHT or WRONG?

3—Manning grounds to short. The throw and Manning reach first base exactly at the same instant. The umpire calls Manning out. RIGHT or WRONG?

4—Manning beats out a single, but instead of tagging first base, his foot lands squarely on the foot of the first baseman, which is also on the base. The first baseman then tags Manning. Umpire calls him out. RIGHT or WRONG?

5—Manning grounds to the right of the first baseman who makes a great stop. With the ball securely in his glove he reaches toward the bag with his bare hand and tags it before Manning gets there. Umpire calls Manning safe. RIGHT or WRONG?

6—Manning, the first batter, triples. Harrah lifts a high pop toward third. The pop fly hits Manning while he is standing directly on the base. Umpire calls Manning safe. RIGHT or WRONG?

7—Same play, except that Manning is now playing softball. Umpire calls Manning out. RIGHT or WRONG?

8—Manning on second. Harrah flies to left. The ball pops out of the left fielder's glove and Manning then races to third. However, the left fielder catches the ball before it hits the ground and throws to second base where an appeal is made that Manning left before the catch. Umpire calls Manning out. RIGHT or WRONG?

The answers:

Again, in *each* case the umpire was WRONG. (Did you think I'd pull that on you twice?)

Play 1—A runner can turn either way after passing first base, just so he doesn't make a break for second.

Play 2—When two men occupy the same base the lead runner is entitled to it. If Harrah had been tagged while both runners were on the base he would have been out. But he wasn't.

Play 3—The ball must reach first base *before* the runner gets there.

Play 4—When a defensive player has his foot on the base, that foot becomes *part* of the base. So when Manning stepped on the foot it was the same as stepping on the base.

Play 5—When the first baseman holds the ball securely he may tag the base with *any* part of his body.

Play 6—In baseball the base is *not* an island of safety, except when the infield fly rule is in effect. When a batted ball hits a baserunner *on* or *off* the base, he is out.

Play 7—In softball Manning would have been safe because in softball the base IS an island of safety.

Play 8—The runner can leave his base the instant a fly is touched. He doesn't have to wait until the actual catch.

INFIELD FLY

1—Runners on first and third, no outs. Batter hits an infield fly which is dropped. Umpire calls the batter out. RIGHT or WRONG?

2—Bases loaded, one out. Batter hits fly to deep short. Shortstop can handle it easily and umpire signals infield fly, but left fielder calls for it and then fails to make the catch and all the runners run to the next base. Umpire calls the batter safe. RIGHT or WRONG?

3—Bases loaded, no outs. Batter hits a high fly toward first base. Umpire calls infield fly. Wind carries the ball into foul territory where first baseman drops it. Umpire calls batter out. RIGHT or WRONG?

4—Bases loaded, no outs. Batter hits infield fly. Runner from second is hit by the fly while a step off the bag. Umpire calls batter out and also the runner on second. RIGHT or WRONG?

The answers:

The umpire was wrong on each play, *except* No. 4. In substance, here is the infield fly rule: When there are fewer than two outs and there are runners on first *and* second, or the bases are loaded, any FAIR fly ball that in the judgment of the umpire can be caught with ordinary effort by an infielder shall immediately be called an infield fly and the batter is out. The other runners can advance at their own risk.

Play 1—This was *not* an infield fly because there was a runner on first base only. The batter was *not* automatically out.

Play 2—This was an infield fly even though it was caught by an outfielder. Therefore the batter was automatically out.

Play 3—The infield fly rule is in effect only on *fair* balls. It is understood that when the umpire calls "infield fly" he means "infield fly if fair." This play was merely a foul ball.

Play 4—Since runners move off the bases at their own peril, the runner was out when hit by the fly while off his base. And the batter was out because of the infield fly. The ump was correct in calling it a double play.

BALLS AND STRIKES

1—High blooper pitch crosses batter's strike zone over the plate and lands on rear of home plate. Umpire calls it a ball. RIGHT or WRONG?

2—Count on batter is three-and-two. He goes into a deep crouch. Pitch is over the plate above his shoulder, but would have been below his armpits on his normal stance. Umpire calls it strike three. RIGHT or WRONG?

3—Batter stands deep in batter's box. Pitch crosses home plate above knee level but passes batter below his knees. Umpire calls it a strike. RIGHT or WRONG?

4—Pitch bounces on home plate. Batter swings and misses it. Umpire calls it a ball. RIGHT or WRONG?

5—Batter steps on plate as he fouls a pitch outside the strike zone. Umpire calls it a strike. RIGHT or WRONG?

The answers:

The ump was right on the first three plays and wrong on the last two.

In baseball, the strike zone is the area above home plate in the space between the batter's armpits and the top of his knees when he assumes a *normal* stance. In slow pitch softball it's the space between the batter's highest shoulder and his knees.

In play 1 the pitch hit the plate instead of passing over it. Therefore it's a ball. In play 2 the ump correctly made the call according to the batter's *normal* stance, *not* the crouch. In Play 3 the ump properly made the call according to where the ball crossed the plate, not where it passed the batter.

The ump was wrong on play 4 because the batter swung at the pitch. A pitch that hits the ground is not dead. On play 5 (a tricky one) the ump should have called the batter *out* for hitting the pitch while he was out of the batter's box.

SCORING OF RUNS

1—One out, Manning on third, Harrah on second. Hargrove flies deep to center. Manning scores after the catch and Harrah goes to third. But an appeal is made that Harrah left second too soon and the umpire calls him out for the third out. Does Manning's run count? YES or NO?

2—Bases loaded; one out. Batter grounds to first baseman who steps on the bag and then throws to second for the double play. Runner from third scores before the double play is completed. Does the run count? YES or NO?

3—Bases loaded, two outs. Veryzer hits safely to center, but Kuiper, who was on first, falls down halfway to second, injures his leg and is tagged out. The two runners ahead of him score before he is tagged. Do their runs count? YES or NO?

4—Bases loaded, two outs. Thornton hits grand slam over the fence. He fails to touch first and is called out on the appeal which comes after all the runners have tagged home. Do any of the runs count? YES or NO?

5—Two outs, Manning is on third. The pitcher is very slow in his delivery and Manning steals home before the pitch is made. After it is delivered Harrah grounds out to the first baseman. Does the run count? YES or NO?

The answers:

On the first two plays the runs count. On Plays 3, 4 and 5 they don't.

Here's the rule: No run can score on a play in which the third out is a forceout or on the batter before he reaches first base. One Play 1, the run scored before the appeal and Harrah's out was *not* a force. On Play 2, the first baseman eliminated the force at second when he tagged first base. Since the run scored before the third out it counts.

On Play 3, Kuiper was *forced* to reach second and since he never got there, no runs count. On Play 4, Thornton was put out before touching first base. No runs count. On Play 5, Manning's run doesn't count because the batter was put out before reaching first base and the play starts when the pitcher takes his position, not when the ball is hit.

Now how did you score? If you were correct on all 32 you hit a homer. Or you should be an umpire.

If you missed no more than two you got a triple, four a double and five a single. If you missed more than that you made an out.

Well, is baseball as simple as you thought?

Phenom of the future–the Big A

March 30, 1976

Write down the name Angelo LoGrande and put it with your war bonds and savings stamps. Three years from now, when you go to your strongbox again, you'll see the name and you won't have to say, "Who's that?"

Immediately you'll recognize Angelo LoGrande as the Indians' budding star, the slugger who's going to be among the great ones, As sure as I'm putting this on paper Angelo, known here as the "Big A," is going to make it big. I mean *big*.

I had heard about this 18-year-old ever since coming to camp weeks ago, about how his chest was so large he couldn't fit into any of the regular uniforms and finally an outsized shirt which once belonged to the Milwaukee Brewers was obtained to cover his expansive chest. Also about how he hit prodigious home runs, over the fence and onto the street.

Gomer Hodge, the ex-Indian now managing in the minors for the Tribe, said, "He's close to being a super man."

Harry Dorish, the minor league pitching coach, said, "He hits the ball so far it's a $5 cab ride to get there."

Sounds like the Paul Bunyan of baseball. Had to go over to the minor league complex and check out those tall tales.

The Brewers' uniform stood out among all those belonging to Tribe farms. The Big A would have stood out regardless, at 6-3 and 217 pounds and that broad super structure of a chest.

Admittedly, a wind was blowing out, but even this couldn't account for the distance he hit those balls.

Nobody else came close and there are several other big kids there. He didn't hit the balls over the fence and into the street. He hit them *beyond* the street, far beyond it.

At first the outfielders stood near the fence. Then they moved into the street. They kept going back, and back, and back. Still the balls sailed over their heads. Unbelievable.

If anything, Hodge and Dorish had understated the case.

"Angelo LoGrande," said Tom McCraw, now serving as batting coach in the Tribe's minor league system, "is *some* kind of ball player." In baseball parlance, this is the ultimate compliment.

They don't talk about the possibility that he might make the majors. It's just a matter of how soon. When Boog Powell retires, the Indians now have two who can replace him—Glen Tufts (whom we wrote about Sunday) and LoGrande. Chances are both will be in the lineup together, one being forced to move to left field. That should make "some kind" of power lineup, as McCraw would say.

Figure on it no more than three years from now, barring injury, of course.

LoGrande is quite a story already, forgetting about the home runs. Like Joe DiMaggio, he is a fisherman's son. Unlike Joe DiMaggio, Angelo was such a brilliant high school football player he was given, in writing, a four-year, full-ride scholarship to Notre Dame. Ever since he was 15, this son of Sicilian parents had dreamt of playing for the Fighting Irish. He also dreamt of playing major league baseball, causing a conflict difficult to resolve when both opportunities developed last winter.

It was because of the football offer that the Indians got him. When the Indians' minor league officials were making their list for the high school draft, general manager Phil Seghi happened to walk in just as LoGrande's card was placed on the desk.

Seghi picked it up, studied it, and said, "Draft him."

But he's got a full scholarship to Notre Dame," the general manager was told. "That's worth at least $20,000, He'll surely take it. That's what everybody figures."

"Well, draft for your needs first, than take this kid," said Seghi.

The Indians passed him by the first day. Luckily, so did all the other clubs. LoGrande, back in Sehome High School in Bellingham, Wash., was waiting for word. He thought he would be drafted early. He was sick when he was ignored. Next day the Indians drafted him in the 17th round.

Now came the time for the decision, the choice that would determine his future—the rest of this life.

He sat on a bench at the minor leaguer compound and talked about it, about how he became involved in both sports, about his parents, his great love for them, and about the advice they gave him.

He is polite and articulate, a 3.00 student in high school. In facial features he resembles Johnny Berardino, a former Cleveland infielder who later made it in films and TV and changed his name to Beradino. (You can see him regularly on "General Hospital.")

Angelo's father, Michael, is a commercial fisherman. The two fished together near their home, San Pedro, Calif. That was the crew, just the two. They began to fish up north, near Bellingham, Wash., for salmon. When he wasn't fishing, Angelo played sandlot ball, from Little League up.

"One day the baseball coach at Bellingham High said he wanted to watch me play," recalled Angelo. "I don't know how he even knew I played ball. Somehow he had heard. At that time I did some pitching. The coach worked me out. I was just 13 going into the ninth grade. The coach told my dad I had a great future. He asked them to enroll me at Bellingham High. He said I could live with him when my parents went back home after the fishing season.

"I lived with the coach for two years and then my parents moved to Bellingham. I never had played football. The football coach asked me to come out. Guess he liked my size. Even at 13 I was big and strong, maybe from the fishing. I made it as a regular linebacker on defense and fullback on offense in my freshman year. Next year I was shifted to quarterback on offense.

He was a triple option quarterback, doing the passing and most of the running. The college football coaches began to trail him in droves. After the high school baseball season, rather short because of the weather, he would play American Legion ball and fish. As soon as his games ended he would head for the dock. From 6 P.M. until 5 the next morning he would fish. Every night.

"My dad bought me a boat when I was 15," he said, "and we would go out separately, but he'd stay close. He gave me 10% of my catch. I made about $2,500 a summer. After I had my own boat my mom always went out with my dad. She didn't want him to be alone. The first time I went out in the new boat the weather was rough. I had a super night, caught about $6,000 worth of salmon. My dad suddenly began to run full board toward me, even though I radioed I was okay. They didn't believe it because the stern was so low in the water. They thought I was sinking. It was low because it was full of fish.

"When my mom saw the load, she actually passed out from happiness. We paid off half the boat on my catch."

In his senior year Angelo got the call he dreamed about. Notre Dame invited him to South Bend. Ara Parseghian personally took him around the campus. It was all his, for four full years, the coach told him.

Now the baseball scouts began to come around, too. Almost every club. "They asked me if I would choose baseball over football," he said. "I never led them to believe I wouldn't.

"I guess they didn't believe. That first day of the draft, when I wasn't chosen, was a real hurt. People called all day to say how sorry they were.

"The next day, when Cleveland finally drafted me 17th, I didn't know what to think. My mind really was messed up. Maybe I wasn't as good a ball player as everybody thought."

He had expected to be drafted within the first five rounds and to be offered at least $15,000. The Indians offered $8,000, an exceptional sum for the 17th round.

"Money never has been a big deal to me," said Angelo, "but I wanted the respect. Seventeenth round had no respect."

He asked his mom and dad what he should do.

"I love my parents," he said.

"And I really love the way they always trusted my thinking. My mom said. "It's your decision, your life. Do what you think best."

"My father never says much. You can tell what he's thinking by the way he looks. He said, 'You know what I want.' He didn't like to watch me play football because he was afraid I'd get hurt, although he did go to the big games. He rarely missed a baseball game.

"I went for a long walk by myself. Two hours. I weighed both sports, the future in each. I thought I'd have a better chance in pro baseball than in pro football. I finally signed with Cleveland. And I'm not sorry. Everything's been super so far."

Angelo LoGrande never has been to Cleveland. He asked if the fishing in Lake Erie is good. Some day in the near future he'll find out. He may even hit a ball into the lake.

"Can't miss" kids easy to find in spring

March 13, 1989

When I told the fellow I was heading for Tucson today to check out the Indians' spring training, he said, "So you're gonna find us another Big A, heh, heh, heh."

Readers often give me that stitcher, "Whatever happened to the Big A?" and then they laugh.

The Big A . . . Angelo LoGrande.

I consider myself somewhat of a talent scout. After all, wasn't I once a birddog for the Red Sox, whose recommendations achieved more than average success?

I force my modest self to mention this only when the laughter about Angelo LoGrande gets too loud.

At Tucson, the major leaguers are quartered at Hi Corbett Field. Along the wall, at the right-field foul line, is a door. It leads conveniently into the minor league camp.

I spend as much time with the minors as I do with the big Indians. I like to see these hungry kids, the ones making far less than those of us who carry lunch pails. Each one has visions of crossing to the other side of the fence and striking gold. The minor league side of the wall is the land of dreams.

It was on a walk through that door in the wall, in the spring of 1975, I think, I discovered Angelo LoGrande. I saw a ball come sailing from the main minor league diamond. It kept rising and rising. It traveled across a road and landed at the base of the big league fence. At first I thought it was a bird. Nobody could hit a ball that far.

Then I saw another. And another. I ran in the direction these rockets were coming from and saw this 18-year-old hunk, swinging easily in batting practice and propelling the pitches out of sight.

Who was this Paul Bunyan, this Natural?

We talked. This 6-foot-4, 210-pounder of pure muscle came from Bellingham, Wash., a fishing town off the Pacific Coast. He was the star quarterback on his high school team, so good he was offered a full four-year scholarship to Notre Dame. He also was the first baseman on the baseball team, but because there was so much spring rain in Bellingham he had only played in 15 high school games. As a result, he didn't get much notice from the scouts and those who expressed an interest were certain he'd choose Notre Dame. Why waste a draft choice on him?

The Indians did, in a very late round, then offered him a decent bonus. To their surprise he signed, figuring if he didn't make it the Notre Dame offer still would be available.

Good story. It became even better when he said his father had come here from Italy and was a fisherman. Ah, I envisioned another Joe DiMaggio, for that, too, had been the background of the Yankee great.

I labeled him, "Can't Miss," dubbed him the "Big A" and wrote how he would be the first to hit a ball into the bleachers and maybe even into Lake Erie. It was played eight columns across the main sports page under a big black "Can't Miss—New Joe DiMaggio" headline.

I followed the Big A's progress in the minors and kept writing about him. He did well at the start. Raw power, longest homers ever seen in this park and that one. His RBIs mounted.

Five years later he was in Triple A, struggling because of a knee he had badly injured when he slipped off his fishing boat two winters earlier. By then he had a wife and twin sons. He decided to stick with fishing as a full time career.

"The bad knee did him in. He couldn't run and he couldn't move around first base," Bob Quinn, the Indians' farm director then and now general manager of the New York Yankees, told me yesterday when I called to ask if he had heard from the Big A recently.

But I'm not going to say anything about that bad knee. Go ahead and laugh about my "Can't Miss" call and all those homers the Big A was going to hit into the Stadium bleachers and maybe into Lake Erie.

The best major league scouts are happy if out of every 10 kids they sign three make it to the bigs. Want to remain humble? Be a scout.

It is so easy to see a kid and fall in love with him only to have an injury or his work habits break your heart. Or what you see sometimes is just a mirage. Take the case of Rudy Regalado, who had such a sizzling spring in 1954 he was dubbed by an imaginative writer, "Rudy the Red Hot Rapper."

Al Lopez, the manager, called us in. "I know you've got to write about this kid and I'm not suggesting you stop. But for your private information he has too many holes in his game, in the field and at bat. This is just a spring fluke. He'll never be more than a utility player at best."

Lopez was right. He was a brilliant field manager but his greatest skill was as a judge of talent. I never have seen anyone as good.

That's the one area in which I have yet to make up my mind concerning Doc Edwards. He has many fine leadership qualities. But how good is he in evaluating talent? Already he has said that when the time comes to pick the Indians' shortstop there will be a meeting of the scouts who are paid for that skill and their input will go a long way in deciding between Paul Zuvella and Jay Bell. I'm not keen on that. If I'm the manager it's going to be my judgment. My job is on the line, not theirs. If the scouts are wrong, they won't get fired. I will.

Fortunately sportswriters don't get canned when a Big A flunks. So you'll hear from me in Tucson.

And by the way, the Big A really didn't flunk. Quinn tells me he bought his first fishing boat with his bonus money, now owns five and financially he has made it to the bigs.

NFL admits error, what can be done?

September 27, 1978

The National Football League officially has admitted it.

"We were wrong," Art McNally, supervisor of NFL officials, told me yesterday. "There was no contact by a Browns' player. The whistle should not have been blown."

The play he referred to, of course, was the kickoff that opened the overtime in the Steelers-Browns game last Sunday. Larry Anderson of the Steelers took the kickoff and during his run he went down seemingly untouched. Referee Fred Wyant, trailing the play, blew his whistle. Anderson got up, continued to run and was hit by Gary Parris of the Browns. As he started to go down he fumbled the ball and Ricky Feacher of the Browns recovered on about the 20-yard line, within easy field goal range of Don Cockroft's toe.

Inasmuch as the whistle had killed the play moments before, the fumble was disregarded. The Steelers kept the ball and marched down the field for the sudden victory touchdown.

So many fans have asked, "What is the league going to do about it?"

By rule they can't do anything about the call. A whistle, right or wrong, kills the play. They simply can try to improve their mechanics to prevent it from occurring in the future.

According to McNally, Wyant, behind the play, saw Anderson trip as he made a cut. He was quite sure it was the shoe of a Browns' player that caused it.

McNally and his staff at NFL headquarters spent several hours the past two days looking at all the films. They obtained Pittsburgh's film, the TV tapes and three different views taken by NFL camera crews.

"At first," said McNally, "we weren't positive. We didn't know who the foot belonged to. The players involved, on both sides, wore white shoes and their stockings were white up to the calves. But after looking at all the films we now are absolutely certain. It was a Steelers' player's foot. Not a player on the defensive team [the Browns]."

Unfortunately, during the rapid action, Wyant was sure the white shoe belonged to a Browns' player.

The reaction of the fans—many of them dropped into the office or wrote us—was, "See, this would have been a perfect case for the use of TV replay to call the play."

I wish it were that simple. It would be truly a wonderful world of sports if all officiating mistakes could be corrected.

But let's look at it practically. McNally and his staff had to spend many hours before they were 100 percent sure the officials were wrong. Would the fans wait that long while a positive judgment was being made? Would they even wait quietly for 10 minutes? And if there was no positive proof, it wouldn't be fair to reverse an official, for it's conceivable he could have been right.

Secondly, what about the rule that makes the ball dead when a whistle is blown? That rule has been in the books for a century on all levels of football, because it's the only rule that's fair to both sides. Otherwise it would have been changed during the evolution of the game.

On the play Sunday, some Steelers perhaps could say in all honestly that they heard the whistle and, therefore, they stopped moving and as a result weren't in the neighborhood to recover Feacher's fumble. Some of them, no doubt, stopped blocking when the whistle was blown. If even one of them did, it would be unfair to allow the play to continue.

"All we can do now," said McNally, who knows every time an official makes such a crucial error it hurts the league, "is to see what we can do to prevent it in the future. Our men were in perfect position on that play. I can't fault their mechanics. And I can see why Wyant, from his position, got the wrong man in the shoe.

"We're going to make an adjustment to get one of the men in front of the play to key on the ball.

"And for next season we are thinking about suggesting that both teams can't wear the same color shoes and that the stockings will have to be colored all the way down."

All the officials in the NFL will be sent a critique on the controversial play. They get them on all plays, but this one will be emphasized.

The officials are put under a greater microscope by the NFL front office each week than they are by the fans and players. Each year some are released. One mistake, of course, doesn't result in a pink slip. If it did, there would be no officials. There isn't one alive who hasn't made mistakes. There isn't one who breathes who never blew a whistle he wished he hadn't.

"We are not offering any alibis or excuses regarding Sunday's call," McNally said. "White shoes or not. We blew it."

McNally doesn't exclude the possibility of using video tapes to correct officiating errors at some future date. "As you know we conducted the experiment in seven pre-season games," he said, "and we soon will put together our data and present it to the owners. It's up to them. If they want video replays to change the officiating calls, they can tell us to do so and we will."

"But how could video reverse a whistle that shouldn't have been blown?" he was asked. "What about the rule?"

"I really don't see how it could," he said.

One heated fan suggested that when there is a serious question about a play, the man upstairs should say, 'Take the play over."

Would that have been fair to the Browns, Sunday? On the next kickoff the Steelers could have returned the ball much deeper. It would have been an advantage to them, not to the Browns. No, the present rule seems the most equitable to everybody.

"But there's got to be a way to correct such an obvious mistake," said the fan. "If this keeps the Browns out of the playoffs, the league should give them their share of the playoff money."

He told me he would try to think of a way to rectify an official's error. I'm waiting breathlessly. I know many patients who wish their doctors hadn't made mistakes. They have to live, or die, with those human errors. Happily in sports it isn't fatal. To some, it only seems that way.

Whatever happened to basketball?

February 1, 1981

By 10 A.M. yesterday morning the parking lot was one-third full and the cars kept streaming in. Soon almost 10,000 fans were in the Coliseum seats to see the 20 top basketball players in the world practice tossing a ball into a hoop. That was it, not much more.

Yet, it was worth the gasoline and the long trip to the Coliseum. These were the NBA's best who will meet this afternoon in the annual All-Star Game before 20,000 and national television.

It proved once again this is basketball country. Give the fans something worth seeing and they'll be there. Jack McMahon, assistant coach for the Philadelphia 76ers who is here to aid Billy Cunningham, coach of the East squad of All Stars, said, "You had it here a few years ago. You could get it back. I remember when you drew 17,000 to 20,000 every night."

An NBA official looked up at the stands yesterday morning. He was obviously impressed. "You have twice as many here to see the workout as they had last year at Landover (Md.)."

So let's not have any more of that baloney about moving the franchise, Ted Stepien, or anybody else. Improve the product and open the doors. The fans will stream in.

A strong case could be made that basketball players are the best all-around athletes in any sport. They must have the most stamina. They must be strong, agile, and resilient.

One of my all-time favorite athletes is John Havlicek. He could play any sport. The two athletes I currently favor above all others are Julius Erving and Larry Bird. They are in the Havlicek mold, constantly moving, excellent passers, tough under the boards, and completely unselfish. I put Magic Johnson in this category, too, but he happens to be sidelined at present.

Basketball is an art form and these men are true artists. That's why I got up early, too, yesterday to watch them work out. And this is not to minimize the talent of Marques Johnson, Kareem Abdul-Jabbar, Artis Gilmore, and the other All-Stars. We have our preferences. Mine is the Bird, the Doctor, and the Magic Man.

* * *

Most of the eyes yesterday were on Julius Erving, the Doctor. They wanted to see some of his spectacular dunks and he obliged to the oohs and ahhs of the crowd. He can suspend himself in the air and make some unexpected move that seems to defy the manner in which the human skeleton is put together as well as the laws of gravity.

Coach Cunningham called his East squad together for a brief meeting. There was no time for any in-depth coaching. He gave them two simple plays, both involving screens around men posted on either side of the foul lane.

They were almost identical to the double-pivot employed 50 and more years ago.

"So what else is new?" observed Marlo Termini, once a high school basketball star here and later a fine coach who now is working for Ted Stepien's organization.

What else is new? Not the basic plays or the uniforms or baskets, but almost everything else.

Before the All-Stars came onto the floor yesterday, two youngsters entertained the crowd. These tots dribbled and somehow managed to push the ball toward the basket and occasionally into it, even from the foul line. Turned out they were Julius Erving's sons, Cleo, 8, and Julius Jr., 6. Already, each is called "Doctor" by his friends. Cleo said his dad gave him a basketball "a long time ago." Joe Castiglione, sports commentator for WJKW-Channel 8, was standing nearby, marveling at the skill of the "baby Doctors."

"Those kids epitomize the evolution of basketball," said a grayhead.

"What do you mean?" asked Joe.

"Did you ever take a two-handed shot?"

"No," admitted Joe, who is 33.

"Years ago," said the grayhead, "everybody shot two-handed. They had to."

"I'm a history buff," said Joe. "I'd like to hear."

Okay, Joe. You asked for it.

THE BALL

The kids today wouldn't believe the old basketballs. They were made of heavy panels of leather, with a bladder inside, and laced closed by leather thongs. Rarely was the ball completely round, for it was hand-sewn. When you tried to dribble, the bounce wasn't always true, especially if the lacings hit the floor.

Few players could palm the ball and to do it they would have to grip the lacings.

But the biggest difference was that the ball was much bigger and that's why the kids couldn't do what you see Erving's sons doing today. Until 1934 the ball was 32 inches in circumference. That year it was cut one inch. Three years later the legal minimum was dropped another 1½ inches. In 1937 the laceless balls were made legal. The molded ball, as we know it today, with thin strips of leather glued to the inner rubber, became official in 1949–50. They are easy to manufacture, and inexpensive models can be purchased at most discount stores. Now almost every family has one.

Years back a school would buy two new balls for the entire season. Now they bring them out in a shopping basket. The more one practices, the better one shoots.

Nobody in the old neighborhood had a ball. A bushel basket would be nailed to a garage or a lamppost and the kids would shoot at it with a softball or a large sock, stuffed with cloth. You couldn't dribble, just pass and shoot.

And when you did have a real, live basketball you had to shoot it with two hands because you couldn't control it with one. And even with two hands baskets were hard to make because the ball was so big.

Remember this, Joe. The size of the basket hasn't changed. It always has been 18 inches in diameter. But the diameter of the ball has shrunk to about 9½ inches, meaning two balls now almost can fit into the hoop, where once it was tough enough to get one to roll in. Scores of 15-14 were not uncommon.

Then came the laceless, smaller ball, and the scores began to shoot up. In fact, the shot heard round the world came from right here in Cleveland and made basketball what it is today. The one-handed shot.

Did you ever hear of Hank Luisetti, Joe?

"Vaguely," he said.

THE JUMP SHOT

Hank Luisetti played for Stanford University in the mid-1930s, just after the ball was cut to its present size. Until then, when a player tried a one-handed shot his coach was certain to say, "Stop goofing around." But when Luisetti shot one-handed, his innovative coach, John Bunn, was enthusiastic.

It wasn't the same jump shot everybody throws up today. It was a one-handed push shot, and Luisetti was accurate with it.

During the 1936-37 season Stanford came to Cleveland to play Western Reserve University at the gym on Adelbert Road. Reserve was a basketball power in those days, playing and beating the best, but Stanford romped, 67-27. Luisetti, himself, outscored the entire Reserve team.

Bunn agreed to bring his Stanford team back to Cleveland the following year, and Max Rosenblum, head of the clothing establishment bearing his name and a long-time backer of basketball in our town, put up the guarantee for a college doubleheader at the Public Hall to be played on New Year's Day, 1938.

Stanford was to oppose Reserve again, and Duquesne was to meet CCNY, the New York basketball power coached by Nat Holman.

Chick Davies, the Duquesne coach, thought he had an exceptional team and could gain national recognition by beating Stanford, so he called up Roy Clifford, Reserve's coach, and suggested, "How about switching opponents? You play CCNY and we'll play Stanford."

Clifford was delighted. Opposing Luisetti once was enough.

Nearly 10,000 jammed into Public Hall. In the first game Reserve scored a major upset, beating CCNY 40-35 in overtime. Then Clifford sat back and enjoyed himself as Stanford beat Duquesne, 92-27, an unprecedented score. Luisetti made 50 of those points, a new high for college basketball. The feat was headlined on sports pages everywhere.

From then on coaches encouraged the one-hand shot, which eventually became the impossible-to-block jumper we see today, mostly because the smaller, molded ball is so easy to handle.

THE PLAYERS

On the floor, Artis Gilmore, the Chicago Bulls' 7-2 center, as a gag held the ball in one hand—he did it so easily, the ball seemed smaller than it actually is—reached toward the basket, feet flat on the floor, and extended his arm. The ball touched the rim. The fans loved it.

Doctor J. tried it. Being six-eight, he was somewhat short. But with a little leap he effortlessly stuffed the ball. His hands, too, are large. He handles the basketball almost as though it were a softball. And he's not unique. Even teenagers on the playgrounds can grab the ball one-handed.

Let's go back into the time machine again, Joe. A six-footer was considered a giant. Invariably he was the center. If there was a kid in high school six-five or more, he was looked upon as a freak. Usually, too, he was poorly coordinated.

Gradually, the kids began to get bigger. Give credit to medical science, the pediatricians who prescribed the proper baby food. Smart coaches began to work with the big kids, get them to skip rope, and soon they became as coordinated as their smaller peers.

And black youngsters began to play the game. The New York Rens and the Harlem Globetrotters set the example. Black athletes because of heredity—an outgrowth of survival of the fittest, say anthropologists—were able to jump higher and run faster and today they dominate the game which is now bigger and better than ever.

In fact, it isn't fair to compare this game to basketball as it was. The old Celtics—Nat Holman, Dutch Dehnert, Nat Hickey, Joe Lapchick, Davey Banks, Carl Husta, Pete Barry, and Pat Herlighy—were the greatest in their time. They would be killed by any modern-day giants. Today it's an entirely different game, different ball, even different rules.

THE RULES

It wasn't until 1932 that the 10-second rule went into the books. Until then players could dribble in the backcourt to their heart's content. In 1936, when the six-footers began to crowd under the basket, the three-second rule was put into effect. In 1937 the center jump after every basket was eliminated.

Then the three-second lane was enlarged so that the Wilt Chamberlains had to move farther away from the hoop.

To the grayhead whose basketball experience extended more than 50 years most of the changes in the game have been for the better.

"What do you think the future will bring?" asked Joe.

Let's step into the time machine again and move it forward.

Ironically, suggested the grayhead, in one respect the game will have to take a step backward. The ball will have to be made larger again. And as the players get taller and their hands and arms continue to grow longer, it's going to become necessary to raise the basket a foot or two.

Years from now, Joe, you'll be standing here and telling some 33-

year-old about the days when the ball was smaller and the basket was ten feet high. And about how you saw Julius Erving and Larry Bird and all the other greats on this very court and about how the present-day player is even better than they were.

Laughing on the inside

December 27, 1981

During a recent Monday Night Football game, a couple of yellow flags were thrown and the officials went into a huddle.

Said Howard Cosell, in his authoritarian manner, "I don't like this uncertainty. It's not good for the game."

"You're wrong, Howard," said Frank Gifford. "Better to take their time and make the correct call. To the extent that is humanly possible, they want to make sure they have it right."

The knowledgeable Gifford is one of the few friends officials have. Admittedly, I'm another. Having been down there in that seething cauldron, where everybody is your enemy, I have a strong feeling for the men in the striped shirts.

Of course, the officials don't expect sympathy or a kind word. They must have a built-in mechanism that allows them to cope with this thankless job. It's called a sense of humor, the ability to see the comedy, even dark comedy, in the pressure situations that constantly arise.

Otherwise, they couldn't do it, not even for the money. It wouldn't be worth the ulcers. And the money happens to be good when you reach the National Football League. A first-year man gets $325 a game. With 16 games a season, plus some exhibitions, that helps meet the family budget. If an official can last 11 years in the pressure cooker, he gets $800 a game. Then there is $2,000 for a playoff assignment and $3,000 for the ultimate, the Super Bowl.

So the money isn't exactly incidental when, and if, the NFL beckons an official. But until then, he must run up and down fields in the lowest leagues, often in abominable weather, for pay that barely covers travel expenses and the cost of cleaning the uniform. He must pass tests, go to meetings and take all sorts of abuse from people who never read a rules book and think they can see better from the stands or sidelines than the man who is right on top of the play.

Still, for those of us who have been through it, there is no adventure that compares to officiating. Every time you pack your bag, you're going into the unknown, you're being tested. And the worst snakepit is the NFL, where millions of dollars are at stake every week. You've got to be able to take it and smile while the snakes keep hissing at you.

Bob Rice, Shaker Heights High teacher and track coach, is now in his 13th season as an NFL official. He remembers the first game more vividly than the one he worked last week. It was Oakland at Cincinnati in 1969.

The Bengals' coach was Paul Brown, which seemed to be a break for Rice. When Brown coached the Cleveland Browns, his sons went to Shaker. Young Mike Brown had been the varsity quarterback and Rice helped coach him.

"Oakland lined up to kick a field goal," recalls Rice. "As the back judge, I got under the goal posts to see if it was good. It was and I gave the signal for the three points for Oakland. Then I went to my position on the sidelines for the kickoff, right in front of the Cincinnati bench.

"Paul Brown said to me, 'Hey, that was close, wasn't it?'

"I said, 'Yes. It was just in.'

"Paul said, 'You know, Bob, there are 22 players out there and 30,000 fans in the stands and you are the only one who thought it was good.'"

Rice remembers smiling inwardly and saying to himself, "Hey, welcome to the NFL."

Gordon McCarter, a Lyndhurst neighbor of Rice and now in his 15th season as an NFL official, recalls a game he was refereeing in New Orleans. The hapless Saints had been playing rather well that Sunday but two successive unsportsmanlike-conduct penalties put them back on their 1-yard line. The calls angered the crowd in the Superdome, where the noise echoes and re-echoes and makes play-calling impossible.

When the extreme sound continued, McCarter asked the Saints' defensive captain, Joe Federspiel, to hold up his hands and ask for quiet. It didn't help.

"I finally said to him," recalls McCarter, "'Joe, have all the players on your team hold up their hands.'

"He said, 'We'll try, but in this town they don't like us any better than they like you.'"

* * *

McCarter remembers another tense situation that drew a funny line: "We were working a game in Chicago between the Bears and Packers, an old rivalry. It was when Dick Butkus was captain of the Bears. The Packers were leading, 20-14, in the last two minutes and had the ball. The Packers stayed on the ground to eat up the time and Butkus kept calling timeouts. He called Timeout No. 1. Timeout No. 2. Timeout No. 3. Unfortunately for the Bears, the Packers made a first down, so they continued to maintain possession.

"With 27 seconds to go," recalls McCarter, "Butkus tackled the ball carrier, jumped to his feet and yelled, 'Timeout.'

"I said, 'I'm sorry, Dick, you can't have it. You already have used up your three timeouts.'

"He said, 'Then charge me one for next week.'"

Bill Kingzett, Brush High athletic director who had to give up officiating in the NFL after a severe leg injury slowed him down, remembers a hilarious moment during a Browns game at the Stadium. The league had sent out a directive ordering a crackdown on all players who encroached on the neutral zone.

"Even if they had a hangnail beyond the ball, we were ordered to call it," says Kingzett. "Flags were flying all afternoon. Our head linesman caught Turkey Jones encroaching three times.

"Turkey became so upset that, during a timeout, he drew a line along the field. He said, 'You're not going to catch me again on the next play. I'm gonna stay behind this line.'

"As soon as we saw it, we had to stifle our laughs. The line he drew was a cockeyed curve. If we hadn't told him, he'd have been offsides again."

On the field, the officials are permitted a smile, but no open laughter. Norm Schachter, a top referee in the NFL for 22 years, relates this incident in his latest book, *Close Calls*:

"Once I laughed during a timeout. I was talking to Joe Connell, my umpire, and he told me something that happened at home. It had nothing to do with football. Did I catch hell.

"'We're knocking our teeth out and you think it's funny,'" growled Sam Huff, the middle linebacker for the Giants.

"Soon after that game, we received a communication from the league office that the officials were not to stand together. And not to laugh on the field. Save the laughs for the ride home."

But you can laugh openly without penalty while reading the book. Known for his keen sense of humor, Schachter, retired superintendent of the Los Angeles City Schools and author of several texts on English grammar, recently put away his whistle. But he still serves as an NFL observer, rates the men on the field, edits the rules book and makes up the tests the officials receive regularly from the league.

If you need a belated Christmas present for a sports fan, I heartily recommend his *Close Calls*. After reading it, the fan is certain to have a new perspective about officials and the game itself. Also an inside look at some of the personalities. And through it all are chuckles.

A few quickies: Schachter wears contact lenses. Between the halves of a Giants-Rams game, a telegram was delivered to him in the officials' room. It read, "Saw the first half. Time for a new prescription." It was signed by his ophthalmologist.

On his way to and from games the passenger seated next to him in the plane invariably engaged him in conversation. Many times, when Schachter said he was a football official, his neighbor would begin to tell him about bad calls, the bets he had lost because of lousy officiating, etc.

"Now," says Schachter, "I say, 'I'm an undertaker.' There is silence the rest of the way."

Once, Schachter was knocked down during a play. A player asked him, "What happened?"

"I must have been hit from the blind side," the referee replied.

"Yeah," said the player. "Right between the eyes."

After a New York Jets loss, Weeb Ewbank, then the Jets' coach, knocked on the officials' door and asked to see Schachter. "He's taking a shower," Weeb was told. Schachter had heard Weeb's voice, so he continued to stay in the shower, hoping to outlast the coach.

After waiting 20 minutes, Weeb shouted, "Schachter, you can stay in there forever and you'll never wash off the smell of your last call."

Schachter lists several truisms for officials. Among them:

- If the fans and players don't know who worked the game, you did a great job.
- You're only as good as your last call.
- Any official who hasn't made a mistake hasn't worked many games.

- Don't waste time second-guessing yourself. There will be millions doing it for you.
- You have to be perfect in your first game and get better from then on.
- Sometimes, it's better to be lucky than good—but not in the long run.
- It's comforting to know you have a mother and father when the coaches tell you differently.

Be forewarned that some of the language in the book is X rated. Occasionally, the mouthings of players and coaches take a blue turn. Schachter remembers the first time he was cussed. More than coincidentally, it was the first time he worked in the NFL.

The startled Schachter went over to Norm Duncan, the crew's back judge who had been in the game for years. "How about this swearing," he asked Duncan. "Do I have to take it? Or do I just let it go?"

"Don't pay any attention to it," replied Duncan. "They don't mean anything. It's just like saying, 'Have a nice day.'"

A few plays later, Duncan called a foul for illegal use of hands and then threw his flag high a second time. "Fifteen yards for unsportsmanlike conduct," screamed Duncan. "No. 44 called me a bleep-bleep."

"I thought that was like saying, 'Have a nice day,'" said Schachter.

"This was different," said Duncan. "It was personal."

Schachter has chapters about the coaches, his all-time favorites being George Halas, Vince Lombardi, John Madden, Paul Brown, Tom Landry and Don Shula. He has enormous respect for them.

Most coaches, Schachter laughingly points out, continually plead, "I don't want any breaks. Just give me my fair advantage." They mean, of course, they want the edge, every close one called his way.

Once, Schachter thought he heard Halas, the longtime Chicago Bears owner-coach, call him an S.O.B. "Were you talking to me?" asked the referee.

"No," replied the quick-thinking Halas. "I was talking to the ball."

A constant screamer was Madden, who led Oakland to Super Bowls. But the officials say they enjoyed him, just as listeners now enjoy his commentary on CBS telecasts. After a game, no matter how hot he seemed during the previous 60 minutes, he usually had a pleasant word for the officials.

Rice, like Schachter, says, "You had to like the guy. During one game he was giving it to our head linesman, Burl Toler. At that time, Burl was one of the few black officials in the NFL. Burl turned to him and said, 'Get off my back, John, or I'll move next door to you.'"

Madden broke up with laughter. He got off Toler's back.

Rice has the all-time classic officiating anecdote. He was working a Cleveland-Pittsburgh game at the Stadium on a Saturday night. You know how hotly contested Browns-Steelers games are. He called pass interference against the Browns near the goal line. The penalty led to a Steelers' touchdown and he was roundly booed. Rice's 9-year-old son, Robert, was at the game, along with other members of the family.

"When I got home," Rice recalls, "I tried to explain to my son that the hometown fans root for their team and get upset when calls are made against one of their players. I said, 'I hope it doesn't bother you to hear the people call your daddy names.'

"My rat-fink son said, 'It didn't bother me, dad, because you blew the call.'"

Luckily for the rat-fink, Rice has the ability to laugh, even at himself. Inwardly, of course.

Is the Maven ravin'?

September 9, 1982

The deli is not a place for Browns' fans these days, unless you want double indigestion. For Ta-Ta-Ta, who loves the Browns, everything he eats has been repeating thrice.

Ta-Ta-Ta, so named because he is generally singing to himself and the words to every melody always include "ta-ta-ta," sat in the corner, sad and quiet, munching on his breakfast consisting of a heel of rye bread, with cream cheese, a little jelly and a dill pickle. He was trying not to listen to the Maven but that would be like not hearing thunder two feet away.

"Ha-ha-ha, look at Ta-Ta-Ta," said the Maven who considers himself the greatest oracle on sports since Adam covered himself with a leaf. "In May he bet me a breakfast that the Indians would finish over .500. He knows he's a loser and I'm gonna order a full course, plus side orders of potato pancakes and kniches. And a Bermuda onion with my bagel and lox."

Ta-Ta-Ta turned white, biting deeper into his heel while trying to feign disinterest.

The Maven laughed louder, almost uncontrollably, which is his way of showing compassion. "Poor Ta-Ta-Ta. Now he can't stand me talking about the Browns. Can I help it if people come from far and near to hear me analyze pro football? They know I was the only one in the world to be exactly right last year. I said the Browns wouldn't win six games. They won five."

"The people are coming back to the deli," said Tire Kicker, "because you're not spitting as much. Not since you had the swollen jaw from that bad tooth."

"Keep my personal life out of this," roared the Maven as a bagel bit shot four tables away. "I don't spit. I haven't spit for a year and a half. I chew more slowly. And you, don't write about my spitting or I won't give you the scoop on the Browns."

Ta-Ta-Ta began to hum, "The sounds of silence, ta-ta-ta, I should live so long."

He stopped humming and almost choked on his heel when the Maven said, "If the Browns get lucky they'll win six games this year. That's my expert diagnosis."

"You mean the unbeaten exhibition season didn't impress you?" asked Tire Kicker, who appraises used cars by kicking their tires.

"No, a thousand times no," shouted the Maven. "When the other teams used their regular quarterbacks they had plenty of time to pass and the receivers were wide open, just like last season. Out of 28 teams, the Browns were 27th in pass defense. They did nothing in the draft to make it better."

"Are you forgetting they now have Cousineau and Chip Banks?" asked Odd Stanley, a bookie who sometimes makes his own line and has declared bankruptcy four times.

"I forget nothing," bellowed the Maven. "My mind is a computer. Maybe Cousineau and Banks are good linebackers. That's meaningless, because every team claims it has fine linebackers. Linebackers and tight ends are the cheapest commodity in football. In the fifth round you could get good ones. The Browns still have no pass rush and no defensive back. The game now is passing. The San Francisco 49ers proved that. They listened to me and hardly ran the ball. They won the

Super Bowl through the air."

"You mean you told their coach, Bill Walsh, what to do?" asked Tire Kicker in awe.

"He must have read my quotes last year," said the Maven in dead earnest. "DeBartolo, who owns the club, lives in Youngstown. He must have seen it in the *Plain Dealer* and showed it to Walsh. He couldn't be that smart himself. He also listened to me on defense by getting a great defensive end and three new backs.

"To continue," continued the Maven, as if anyone could stop him, "I want to make my point clear. The name of the game is pass and sack. I don't see where the Browns have improved their sacks."

"So what are your predictions, Maven?" asked this intrepid writer. "Let's make some bets again. You still owe me, but I'm wiping the slate clean because you were so right last year. And besides you never pay."

"What do you mean I never pay?" yelled the Maven. "When do I lose? All right. Here goes: The Browns' record will be 6-10 or worse. I'll bet 15 sodas to your 10 on that."

"I'll take that bet, too," said Odd Stanley.

"With you, Odd, I don't bet sodas. Make it corned beef, which is more valuable than money. I also will make the same 15-to-10 sodas bet the Browns will finish in last place, even though I think that Houston's coach, Biles, has ruined his team."

"Maven, you're ravin.' They should put you away. I'll take those bets. They're outrageous."

"Ha, you thought I was outrageous last year, but I was right. I also will give you five sodas even that the Rams will knock off the 49ers in their division, then get beat by Dallas for the conference title for five more sodas. And then Dallas will lose to Cincinnati or Pittsburgh in the Super Bowl for another five. Those two will fight it out for first place in our division. The Steelers are my comeback team for this year."

"Not the Browns?" pleaded Ta-Ta-Ta.

"Definitely not the Browns!" screamed the Maven.

Ta-Ta-Ta scraped up the crumbs of his heel, put them in his picket and headed for the door, humming, "Say it isn't so, ta-ta-ta."

Why must pitchers be babied?

August 25, 1986

Athletes are bigger, faster and stronger today. Nobody disagrees. Medical science and nutrition has done that. Records for speed, strength, agility and endurance keep falling.

Why, then, are today's pitchers babied? In size most of them tower over the stars of yesteryear.

But what do managers say to them? Pat Corrales being no exception: "Just give me six quality innings."

Makes me want to regurgitate.

Six quality innings and then often they're gone. Every pitch is counted. Once a pitcher has thrown 100, look out. The poor fellow's arm may fall off.

I don't blame the pitchers. I blame the managers and coaches and front-office geniuses. Some years ago they decided to count pitches. Even in the minors. Gave them something to do. Another unnecessary statistic.

Effectiveness didn't matter. Nor did it matter if the pitcher still had fine velocity and good stuff. What's the count? One hundred twenty pitches. He had to be tired. Get him out of there.

As a consequence, when the kid gets to the majors he's still a six-inning pitcher.

Ridiculous.

Back when athletes didn't have such fine medical upbringing, when their parents didn't have the vitamins and food formulas for their kids, when strengthening programs were unknown, there was a fellow named Iron Man McGinnity, who pitched almost every day. He was two-thirds of the entire staff. He wasn't unique. There were numerous iron men in those "weaker," unscientific days.

On August 28, 1926, Emil (Dutch) Levsen pitched the first game of a double-header against the Boston Red Sox and beat them, 6-1. Manager Tris Speaker said, "How would you like to pitch the second game?"

"Fine," said Levsen, and he beat them 4-1. Can you imagine a manager even daring to think that way today? Levsen would have been out of there by the seventh inning of the first game if he had thrown 130 pitches.

On May 1, 1920, when men comparatively were shallow and callow fellows, the Brooklyn Dodgers and Boston Braves played to a 26-inning, 1-1 tie. The starters, Joe Oeschger and Leon Cadore, were still in there when the umpires called the game because of darkness. Nobody counted the pitches. If that game were played today there probably would have been a minimum of a half-dozen giants on the mound for each team.

Poor Bob Feller. Rarely did he pitch a game in which he threw fewer than 175 pitches because the hitters fouled off plenty and he walked so many. Yet, he usually finished his starts. In 1946 he pitched 36 complete games. In between he warmed up every day. That was his style. He lasted 20 years.

"Today, with the counted pitches," says Bob, "I'd never have a complete game."

When Early Wynn pitched and Manager Kerby Ferrell went to the mound to take him out in the seventh, Early would glare as if to say, "What are you doing here?" and Kerby would slink back to the dugout. Today pitchers are told, "You threw 100 pitches," and they gladly give up the ball.

I think it's high time the baseball minds readjusted their brains and realized how asinine their pitcher coddling and counting is. Especially the Indians. I can understand taking out a starter when you have an excellent bullpen. Until 1954 Manager Al Lopez rarely replaced his starters. But when he developed Ray Narleski and Don Mossi in 1954, he took out Lemon, Wynn, Feller and Garcia in the eighth or ninth. Not because they had thrown too many pitches. He never counted them. They were removed only because he had those exceptional arms in the pen.

The Indians don't have a bullpen. I don't care how many pitches Phil Niekro or Tom Candiotti or Ken Schrom have thrown, or if they haven't had six quality innings. They're better than anything in the bullpen and I shudder when they are removed. Remember Friday when Schrom was pulled? Goodbye lead. Ditto Saturday when Candiotti left. I even shuddered again yesterday when Niekro departed. Frank Wills pulled it through, but not before a hairy moment.

Six quality innings, bah. The last I heard, a baseball game goes nine innings. Where's the quality for the final three?

If I ran the Indians I would throw away all the counters in the minor-league system. The arm is bone and muscle. It gets stronger when it's worked. Until he finally was admitted into the majors, Satchel Paige pitched almost every day of his baseball life, winter and summer, all over the world. He was still unhittable when he finally was allowed into the majors. To make a living he had to pitch every day. Now we've spoiled 'em. Pitchers get a half million bucks for a few quality innings.

I hope young Greg Swindell isn't babied. He's a big, strong kid who seems to throw effortlessly. He threw a lot of innings in college and it would be ludicrous to wean him downward, to the silly "six quality innings."

I was surprised to note he pitches without a windup. There is no wasted motion. On the other hand, his simple delivery has no deception and doesn't throw fear into the batter the way Bob Feller and Herb Score did when each lifted his front foot high in the air, reared way back and whipped a fast ball out of the blue.

Swindell doesn't have the Feller or Score velocity, either. He throws a heavy ball, similar to Mike Garcia's, one that breaks bats. He also is supposed to have much better control. He didn't show it in his debut, undoubtedly because of his excitement and lack of sleep, both blurring his concentration.

Still, from what I saw in those few innings last Thursday he has a better arm than most of the Indians' pitchers. Let him stay up here and grow. For more than six innings. Stop counting.

Change in sports is inevitable

January 3, 2000

Just thinking . . . about then, now and . . .

BIGGEST CHANGE IN SPORTS IN THE PAST CENTURY: The size of the players. When I played college basketball, I was the center because I was 6 foot 3 (I've shrunk since I got married). Now, 6-footers are sent home. When I officiated high school football I was by far the tallest, heaviest guy on the field. Now every high school lineman outweighs me. When I walk among the Cavs I feel as though I'm in Muir Woods in California looking up at the redwoods.

PREDICTION: Thanks to the constant advances in pediatric medicine and nutrition, within 20 years most college and pro basketballers will be over 6-9 and some teams will start five 7-footers. In football most linemen will weigh over 350 pounds and run the 40 in under five seconds.

PREDICTION: Because athletes continue to grow bigger, stronger and faster virtually all records will continue to be broken—the home run mark, yards gained in football, the track and swimming marks, etc. But a few will remain for another century. Joe DiMaggio's 56-game hitting streak, Cal Ripken's consecutive game mark, Wilt Chamberlain's 100-point game, Mount Union's 54-game winning streak.

BIGGEST EQUIPMENT CHANGE: The size of the basketball, which shrank two inches in circumference in the past century. Ditto: the football, once pumpkin shaped and now more like a cigar. The shrinkages changed both games immeasurably, basketball to the dunk and shot, football to the pass.

PREDICTION: The basketball eventually will have to increase in size. As athletes have grown, so have their hands and already the ball has become pea-size to many.

PUREST SPORT: Baseball. It was so well conceived it has gone through a century with virtually no rules changes. The other major sports are nothing like they were 100 years ago.

RESOLUTION: To force myself to continue to jog until, well, until . . .

SUREST PREDICTION: The Indians will win their division.

PREDICTION: The Browns won't, the Cavs yes, if Z is healthy, no way if he isn't.

SECOND SUREST PREDICTION: The Yankees will win their division.

RESOLUTION: To continue writing as long as my publishers accept this stuff, which is as long as you're willing to keep reading it. Keeps me thinking young and getting to know interesting characters . . .

My bride just asked, "Who are the most unforgettable, most unusual sports characters you every met?"

Almost without thinking: Bill Veeck, Satchel Paige, Frank Lane, Bob Feller. Could write a book about each. (In fact, I did about Satch.) . . .

Quick recollection of Veeck: In 1948, offered to drive him to a speech in southern Ohio, hoping our conversation would make a column. Picked him up at the Stadium. He promptly fell asleep. Woke him when we got there. He made his usual comic speech, shook hands with everybody, got back in the car, said, "Leave me off at the Theatrical Grill (a downtown watering hole)."

Fell fast asleep again. Woke him up at the Grill, where, fully refreshed, he spent the night talking with the folks at the bar. I didn't have a word for a column . . .

Quick story about "Trader" Lane, the Indians general manager in the late 1950s who swapped players and managers as though they were baseball cards:

He always carried what appeared to be a half-dozen newspapers under his arm. In spring training, he had just announced one of his deals and an onlooker happened to question the intelligence of it.

Lane exploded, threw his hands in the air and his newspapers went flying. He rushed to pick them up before anyone could help him. Turned out most of them were girlie magazines he had hidden like a schoolboy, inside his papers.

A Feller quickie: In his playing days he loved practical jokes and would buy out novelty stores that sold plastic ice cubes with flies encased, etc., which he would drop into his drinking glass at restaurants to embarrass the waitresses.

His prize prank occurred in Tigers Stadium, Detroit, where the clubhouse had a freezer filled with ice cream sandwiches—bars of vanilla ice cream inside Nabisco wafers. Feller took a bar of Ivory Soap, put two wafers around it, wrapped it in proper foil and put it in the freezer.

Eventually Satchel Paige came along for an ice cream fix and, you guessed it, happened to take the Feller-prepared bar.

Now, Satch had ruined his teeth during all his years of barnstorming throughout the western world, eating poor food and not visiting dentists. Eventually he needed a full set of false teeth, uppers and lowers. Whoever made them did a poor job. They were so loose they clicked when he talked.

He took one strong bite of the "ice cream bar" and when he opened his mouth his choppers were gone. Stuck in the soap. Funniest sight in all my years on the beat.

PREDICTION: Charlie Manuel is no Casey Stengel—now there was another character worth knowing—but he'll add spice to our coverage of the baseball scene.

RESOLUTION: To do everything possible to push Mel Harder's election into the Hall of Fame when the Veterans Committee votes Feb. 29.

RESOLUTION: To remember to try to enjoy each day to the fullest.

RESOLUTION: Not to overwrite. So enough for today.

PEOPLE

Mr. Robert, Master Herbie

May 2, 1955

Bob Feller walked into the clubhouse. He had just pitched a one-hitter, the 12th of his career, to beat the Red Sox 2-0.

Asked to evaluate his performance the great Mr. Robert said, "It was good as any game I ever pitched." Yes, this included his three no-hitters, his fabulous strikeout feats. "I only faced 29 men," he explained.

A 21-year-old pitcher sat in front of his locker thinking, "This is gonna be great . . . me coming on after *that* performance."

Feller thought about it, too. "It's going to be a tough act for the kid to follow," he said.

"Just go out and tell him to do better," grinned Jim Hegan seated nearby.

The kid went out, struck out the first three men on 10 pitched balls, struck out the side again in the second inning and again in the third. Nine strikeouts in three innings. Nine more to go and he would have tied the mark set by Feller himself, back in 1938.

The kid didn't make it. He finished with 16 and the Indians won, 2-1, to take a doubleheader, putting them in first place. Herb Score had followed a tough act with an amazing one of his own.

In straight comparisons, Feller's job had to be rated a shade better. But from the long range view Score's performance is the more important. Feller, at best, has only a few more years to play. Score is but 21.

Sam Mele, a Red Sox hitter, judged Score to be the "fastest pitcher I have faced in the majors." Said Mele, "He's just a little faster than Bob Turley and he has a much better curve."

Manager Al Lopez, mighty pleased that his pitching has been able to carry the club during this horrible hitting slump, insisted to unbelieving Boston writers that Score wasn't his fastest yesterday.

"I've seen him faster this spring," said Lopez, "and so will you. The more confidence he gets the harder he'll fire. Now he still has a tendency to aim the ball."

And how did these two great performances affect his pitching plans? Lopez was asked.

"It sets up our pitching," declared the elated manager. "We've always been a pitching club and now to have a kid like Score is like finding a diamond to add to the greatest collection in the world."

Master Herbie saw the first five innings of Mr. Robert's masterpiece. Then he went into the clubhouse and tried to sleep on the trainer's table. "It wasn't exactly a sleep," he said later. "I was concerned. Last two times I'd been knocked out of the box. I wanted to do well enough for them to keep me up here."

Feller saw only the middle innings of Score's strikeout story. He had his youngsters at the game and he wanted them home in time for dinner. He left in the seventh. That was his plane that buzzed over the Stadium.

Yes, Feller knew he had a no-hitter going until Sammy White singled to kill it in the seventh. "I tried to throw him a fast ball but it sailed. He reached out and nubbed it," said Feller later, not at all unhappy about losing his fourth no-hitter. "If it's in the books for me to pitch another no-hitter I'll do it," he said philosophically.

Mr. Robert credited his control for the excellent performance. "And when I didn't get the ball where I wanted to I was lucky enough to have good stuff," he added. In all, there were only three hard hit balls off Feller: two line drives and a long fly which Ralph Kiner caught.

Feller was particularly gratified, he explained, because he had worked so hard since April 17, when he made his first start and was knocked out of the box.

"I stayed late at the park each day, I did more running than regularly, I did more calisthenics to strengthen my back muscles and I tried to perfect every pitch I have.

"It paid off," he concluded.

Score also was aware that he might be approaching a record. "I knew I had an awful lot of strikeouts," he revealed later. "But I wasn't counting 'em. I'll tell you the best out of the game was Kiner's catch of Sammy White's drive." It prevented a home run.

In the first inning Score surprised himself. After whiffing the top three hitters he came to the bench and said, "Where did I come up with that curve ball?"

Actually he came up with it during the week. Mel Harder worked several hours with Score in an effort to gain curve-ball control for the rookie.

"In the first innings I had a good fast ball and a great curve," said Herb. "Later the curve wasn't as good and neither was my fast ball. I'm just glad I got by."

Yes, he had done better. Last summer he fanned 17 against Minneapolis. He whiffed 16 in seven innings against St. Paul. In high school he often fanned 22 and 23.

"But this," he said, pleased with himself, "is the big leagues."

Piersall fractures me

January 24, 1958

Behind the plate Jim Hegan is a very serious soul but when Jimmy Piersall steps up to bat the Indians' catcher breaks up.

"I can see him laughing behind the mask," reveals Herb Score.

"Piersall fractures me," confesses Hegan. "He's actually singing every time he comes up the plate. All the while he's up there he's either singing or jabbering. He sings popular stuff and he hasn't got a bad voice, either."

Between notes he'll turn to Hegan and say, "How's my favorite catcher today. Please give me a good pitch." Or he'll be singing melodiously, reveals Hegan, and suddenly jump away from an inside pitch. "He'll hit a blue note and say, 'Jim tell that pitcher out there to be careful. Tell him I've got five kids.'"

Piersall carries out this song and chatter "to relieve his tensions," according to Hegan. The Red Sox outfielder, it must be remembered, is the author of *Fear Strikes Out,* which he wrote after recovering from a mental breakdown.

In general the hitters are sociable when they come up to bat. "It's usually 'Hello, how's the wife and kids,' or some such remark," says Hegan. "And then it's all business. I'm not very talkative myself, so if they want conversation they have to provide it."

In marked contrast is Yogi Berra. "He's always talking behind the plate," discloses Hegan. "He's even talking while the pitcher is about to deliver the ball. I'm sure he does it purposely, trying to distract the batter. Most of the hitters pay no attention to him but I've heard some turn around and say, 'Shut up.'"

Berra also talks when he comes to the plate. Hegan relates, "Yogi will say, 'Boy its hot. I'm beat. I don't see how I'm going to catch a doubleheader today.' Then, boom he hits one out of the park. I tell Yogi, 'Don't tell me your troubles. Tell 'em to Stengel.'"

Hegan calls Berra the one hitter he has found with absolutely no weakness. Says Hegan, "You fool him once or twice and you say to yourself, 'Now we've got him.' Next time you call for the same pitch he hits it over the fence. If he has a weakness we've never found it. We throw him bad pitches and he hits 'em. I'm beginning to think the best place to pitch Yogi is right over the plate."

The most quiet hitter was Joe DiMaggio. "He was quieter than I am," observes Jim. The veteran Tribe catcher calls DiMaggio "the toughest hitter I've ever seen with men on."

Comparing DiMaggio with Williams Hegan mentions, "Joe was more dangerous in a scoring situation because Ted will take a base on balls with men on, even if the pitches are just a fraction off the plate. DiMaggio never would. He was the best curve ball hitter I ever saw."

From Hegan's observation post, which is only a few feet behind the hitters, "Williams has the greatest power of concentration I've ever seen. First time he comes up he'll say hello and then he'll be oblivious of everything but the pitcher. He twists so hard on the handle of the bat that I wouldn't be surprised to see him squeeze it into sawdust some day."

The Indians, says Hegan, have found Williams to be a much better hitter since he came back from Korea than he was before. "We used to be able to fool him often," explains Hegan. "We can't seem to be able to get him out any more."

As for Williams, he says the Indians do him a favor when they don't catch Hegan. He pays the Tribe veteran this compliment: "When Jim isn't behind the plate it's worth an extra base hit to me."

Hegan classifies Mickey Mantle as the most powerful hitter ever to step in front of him and he explains why Mickey's batting average is now so high:

"When he first came up he had a glaring weakness: he'd chase the high fast ball. Now he lays off and makes the pitcher come to him. I'd say that now he doesn't swing at half as many bad pitches as he used to."

And now that Mantle has a higher average, insists Hegan, he gets more breaks from the umpires. He explains, "When a hitter gets a reputation for having a good eye, the umpire figures, 'Well, if he let that pitch go it must be a ball.' Pitchers lose lots of strikes to Williams. It works in reverse on the poor hitters."

Hegan squawks to the umpires only when he believes he has a legitimate beef and this is more often than the fans realize.

"The umpire will take a lot from a catcher as long as he stays in his crouch and keeps looking at the pitcher—and doesn't swear. If you turn around and complain, they won't take very much. They don't like to be shown up."

Hegan says it is generally accepted among the players that Ed Runge, a relative newcomer, is the best umpire in the American League. Runge gets Jim's vote not only for his excellent judgment but also for his temperament.

"There are other umpires with very good judgment," explains Hegan, "but they have a chip on their shoulders. You can't question them at all. Runge will listen—up to a point. He'll admit it when he blows one. If umpires only realized it's no sin to admit they could be wrong, they'd have less trouble. You are not inclined to argue with someone who admits to being human."

However, the best umpire during Hegan's 13 years behind the plate was a martinet, the late Bill McGowan.

"When McGowan wanted to bear down," recalls Hegan, "he was the greatest. But if a catcher complained to him the next five pitches might be right over the plate and he'd call them balls. He was especially rough on rookies."

Hegan remembers an incident which occurred in Detroit. After Jim registered a few complaints McGowan said, "I thought you were supposed to be a great catcher."

Hegan retaliated with, "I thought you were supposed to be a great umpire."

"I am," replied McGowan.

There has been much talk about the shrinking strike zone but Hegan hasn't noticed any contraction during his career.

"It's all judgment," he observes. "Some umpires call a high strike and others will give you the low pitch. It depends how they stand behind the plate. Runge and Larry Napp crouch and they'll give the pitcher a strike if he gets the ball just above the knees. Cal Hubbard (now the supervisor of umpires) was so big he was a high-ball umpire. Bill Summers is short, but he doesn't squat so he's better on high pitches than low ones."

Nine innings are a long time to stand in front of an umpire without some conversation and Hegan admits, "We do talk once in a while. Charley Berry is talking all during the game even if you don't answer him. He talks about football, basketball, baseball—any subject."

Once in a while, after a hitter argues strenuously about a pitch the conscience-stricken umpire will eventually turn to Hegan and ask, "Did I miss it?"

"If I think he did," says Hegan, "I won't say so directly. I'll say, 'Well, it might have got the outside corner.'"

And the hitters, too, question Hegan after they argue about a pitch. "If I disagree with the umpire, I'll wait until he's out of earshot before I tell the hitter," confesses Hegan.

On occasions when Hegan quarrels with the man in blue, the hitters speak up and say, "C'mon, Jim, you know that was a bad pitch."

"That gripes me," Hegan admits. "I tell them off. They're just trying to butter up the umpire."

Hegan realizes, "When I argue for a strike I know the umpire isn't going to change his decision. I'm just hoping he'll give us the next one."

Evidence that the umpires hold Hegan in high esteem is that he has been thumbed out only twice during his 13 years. Once really doesn't count because it was in an exhibition against the Giants last spring at Wichita Falls, Texas, when he thought he was safe at first but the umpire (Shag Crawford of the National League) disagreed. "I argued and when I went back to the bench I yelled something I shouldn't have and I deserved to get thrown out," Jim relates.

The only official heave-ho came last summer in Chicago. Hegan had started the game, but was removed for a pinch-hitter. When Umpire Joe Paparella called a strike against Rocky Colavito on a pitch that was very low, Hegan yelled from the bench, "Hey Joe, the ball nearly hit the ground."

Paparella turned toward the bench and gave Hegan the thumb. "I didn't hear what you said," the umpire later told Hegan, "but once a man is taken out of a game he's not allowed to say anything.

"You won't get fined," Paparella promised Hegan. "I turned in a good report on you. But if you do get fined, I'll pay it."

Paul Warfield: Cleveland's prize rookie

December 1965

If he read his press clippings (and who doesn't?) Paul Warfield indeed opened this football season with more pressure on him than any rookie in Cleveland Browns history. For a starter, his coach, Blanton Collier, announced, "This boy has more potential than any other football player I've ever seen." Further, a Cleveland sportswriter predicted, "Warfield will make you forget Lavelli and Speedie."

Dante Lavelli and Mac Speedie. From 1946 through the early 1950s, as the Browns piled up championships, Lavelli and Speedie caught Otto Graham's passes with such skill fans considered them incomparable. Warfield as good as Lavelli and Speedie. Ridiculous.

Ridiculous in the summer, perhaps, but not today. Warfield hasn't made the fans forget Speedie and Lavelli, but he clearly could. The six-foot, 186-pound speedster already has established himself as one of the National Football League's outstanding receivers and, says one scout: "If he had Graham throwing to him, the football field would become nightmare alley for the guys trying to cover him."

The man so heavily praised speaks softly, modestly and politely. Aware of all the compliments Warfield says, "I've learned to take the kind words and the criticism in stride. My main goal is to satisfy myself and the only way I can do that is to strive for improvement."

The Browns made Warfield their No. 1 draft choice after only a relatively brief inspection of his play at Ohio State. Though he didn't miss a game during his three varsity years, made *Time*'s All-America team in 1963, was All-Big Ten two seasons and was chosen for several post-season All-Star games, the Browns basically drafted him on the basis of his *high school* performance.

At Ohio State, Warfield's special talents, many experts insist, were wasted. Under coach Woody Hayes the Buckeyes play a possession game. When Paul was there they did little passing and they didn't open up their running to fit his breakaway style. Says one Big Ten scout, "Woody doesn't like a back who ducks and darts all over the place. He isn't interested in the home-run hitter who can go 90 yards on one play. He wants the back who puts his head down and heads straight for the goal line on an off-tackle play. Warfield isn't big enough to run over people."

The Browns' director of player personnel, Paul Bixler, who saw Warfield play exactly three times, once in each of his three varsity years, says, "In those games he didn't have a chance to do anything outstanding, but I could see the opposition was scared to death of him. They always seemed afraid he'd break away and go for the long one. Several times he got behind the defense but he rarely was thrown the ball. I did like the way he covered his man on defense. I put him down in our book as a possible defensive back.

"Usually, we can check a boy out pretty well in spring practice, but even here we were stopped on Paul. Each spring he went out for track. We did know this: He was a helluva athlete—an outstanding one in all sports, including baseball, which he played back home on the sandlots every summer. But except for the fact he was a good centerfielder, we didn't know he could catch a ball. We had been told he dropped his share of footballs. But in one game I saw he only touched the ball three times."

Dub Jones, once a great pro back who now coaches the Browns' ends, recalls how it was decided to put Paul at the top of the Browns' list. "A year ago last summer at Hiram, a man from Warren visited our camp and sat around talking with us after the workout," says Jones. "He gave us such a brilliant picture of the boy we couldn't get it out of our minds. All the coaches were present during the conversation. It stood to reason if he had it in high school, he'd still have it."

Before training camp, coach Collier hadn't decided whether to play Warfield on defense or offense. The defense definitely needed bolstering, and Warfield had all the skills required of a good defender. "But when we took one look at his moves in camp," says Bixler, "there was only one answer—the answer to a real need. He was our flanker, period."

Says Jones: "He's the type of boy, from the instant you look at him, see him run, catch a ball, see him fake, see his instincts, you don't have to be a genius to realize you have a natural on your hands. You say to yourself, if he has the other qualities it takes to be a good receiver, you've got a star in front of you."

The "other qualities," according to Jones, are toughness to take punishment, and the intelligence to cope with various coverages thrown at him. Warfield seems to have them.

Mostly, Warfield excels because of reflexes and speed. In a game against Dallas, a hookshake pass pattern was called. Warfield, the left flanker, is supposed to hook, then fake to shake his man and grab the pass. When Paul realized his defender wasn't fooled by the fake, he changed direction and raced away. Quarterback Frank Ryan saw this, decided the receiver had shifted his direction permanently, and threw deep. But the rookie, figuring Ryan would expect him to be in the area originally plotted, cut back.

Warfield looked over his shoulder, saw where the ball was heading, reversed himself again, and caught up with it for a touchdown.

Warfield has been timed doing 10 yards in 9.6 seconds, but other equally fast dash men have failed as receivers.

"You have to be quick to go along with your speed," says Jones. "And this boy has it."

In track, Warfield also excelled in the broad jump and was a top Olympic prospect before he decided to enter pro football. His best leap was 26 feet, 2 inches. In the U.S.-Russian meet at Palo Alto a few years ago, he finished third.

Occasionally, in going after a pass, he employs his broad-jumping ability. "Truthfully," he says, however, "I've got to cut down on the jumping unless I'm going up in the air for a high one. When I leap I lose speed and timing. Another thing, sometimes I move too fast for my own good. In a recent game, I faced my guard squarely, then took too many steps before I got moving and fell down. I've got a long way to go in this game."

So far, he's found the pro game more enjoyable than the college game—and not because his talents have been put to better use. "Surprisingly," he explains, "it's more relaxed than college ball. At Ohio State the coaches try to fire you up. Here, they don't. They don't want you to get too emotionally charged. Instead, they try to get us ready, mentally and physically. They want us to look forward to the game—to have fun. And it is fun."

Warfield began his football career at the First Street Grammar School in Warren, Ohio. The school system had a touch-football league for the youngsters. Paul, weighing 72 pounds, began as a quarterback, but when his teammates discovered he couldn't throw long, they moved him to end, where he was highly successful.

Yet, when he advanced to junior high, he didn't try out for the team his first two years. "I weighed only 95 pounds and my mother was afraid they'd run over me," he recalls. "She said nothing doing. So I stayed away and delivered newspapers."

Paul had an ally in his dad, a long-time employee at Republic Steel in Warren. The city is a football hotbed, and at the factory the chief fall topic of conversation always is the Warren High team. Papa Warfield, who once played guard for a high school in Tennessee, dreamed of the day he might brag about his son playing for a high school.

Paul and papa worked on mama, and finally she consented when the boy's weight reached 130. He was a ninth grader then. With no previous experience at tackle football, he made the team. From there he moved to the high school and did so well, 67 college offers awaited him at graduation time. He chose Ohio State, because in high school he had been a runner and the Buckeyes were a running team. "Also, two Ohio State grads from Warren, Dr. Clyde Muter and Dr. Joseph Logan, sold me on the school," he says.

Though he didn't have the opportunity to run wild for the Buckeyes, he established the reputation among the coaching staff as "never having played a bad game." Both the Browns and the Buffalo Bills of the American Football League made him their No. 1 draft choice. The offers from both were substantially the same: a two-year contract at $15,000 per season, plus a $5,000 bonus.

"Believe me," says Warfield, "I had difficulty studying during the two weeks after the draft. If I signed, I wouldn't be able to go out for track. I'd have to give up my dreams of the Olympics and I had some thoughts about a pro baseball career."

Finally he said yes to the Browns. "I had followed them as long as I can remember," he explains. "Every summer I went to Hiram to watch them work out. You might say I had a favorite player—Jim Brown. So I had a feeling for that team. Besides, I wanted to play in the area where I plan to live after my football days are over."

Paul is settled in Cleveland with the Warren girl he married a week before the opening game. In the opener he didn't catch a pass. Naturally, he received an unmerciful ribbing from his teammates.

They have had a few opportunities to rib him since.

Is there a greater coach than Collier?

January 2, 1966

Green Bay, Wisc.—The one thing you notice about Blanton Collier when you're traveling with the Browns is that you really don't notice him. He appears lost in the crowd.

This was exactly the opposite with Paul Brown. He was The Man. When he got off a plane all eyes were on him. Not that he blew any horns. It was just that he was PAUL Brown, the supreme boss of the team. He naturally commanded attention.

When the Browns landed here yesterday the buzzing was "Where's Jim Brown?" and "There's Lou Groza" and "Which one is Gary Collins?" and "Isn't Frank Ryan getting gray?"

No one inquired about Collier except the reporters there on assignment, seeking to interview him. Hidden inconspicuously among all the giants, he wasn't easy to locate.

If Blanton were coaching the Bears I'm convinced he'd have walked home with the division title. The Bears have better personnel than the Browns. The raw truth is that many clubs have more player talent than the Browns. The Browns have one superstar, of course, in Jim Brown, but there are at least two clubs in the Eastern Division with more overall ability.

In other words, I think the Browns won because of Collier. He's a superior coach; he makes the difference and he doesn't care the slightest that he was ignored by the voters.

"He's sincere in the part he wants to play," says defensive end Paul Wiggin. "They could go on making others Coach of the Year from here to eternity and it wouldn't bother Blanton. He just wants to go on winning championships."

If the Browns were to vote he'd be Coach of the Year, unanimously.

I have never seen a man more dedicated to his job. It's impossible for any human to work more diligently than Blanton. If you're a boss and you hire someone who concentrates on his work from the moment he arises until he falls asleep late at night you've got an unusual employee. If, in addition, he is highly intelligent and able, you have a prize. Collier is a prize. One in a million.

I doubt if there is a man alive who knows more football than Blanton. But more important: he is an outstanding teacher. Patiently, through countless hours of movie viewing and deep thinking, he has analyzed every facet of the game. He knows each step in the offensive lineman's charge, every movement of the quarterback, the ball carrier and the blockers and he has an equally keen knowledge of every defensive position.

He has broken down every single action and then teaches them, step by step, until the whole, correct motion is developed.

Talk with the Browns and they'll agree there are several men on the club who couldn't have played pro ball if it hadn't been for Collier. If they provide the heart, the determination, he'll teach them how to play.

The pedagogical Collier is a firm believer in cybernetics, which sees the brain as a complex electronic device. The proper information is stored in it, the right button is pressed, and it responds correctly.

In the case of Frank Ryan, the coach has worked with the quarterback, a second-stringer until he got here, trying to perfect every single motion, from taking the snap to dropping back in the pocket, to planting his feet for the pass, to viewing his receivers, to concentrating on his targets, to cocking his arm, to the ideal release of the ball.

It's now all stored in Ryan's brain. Today the job will be to press the right button, to trigger the mechanism. This is true also of all 40 members of the team. Some can trigger their own. Others will need help. Collier will talk with each man individually, hoping he can say the right word to every one.

Last year when it came time to prepare for the title game against the Colts he said to his men, "Give this game your undivided attention, your complete concentration for two weeks and I promise you we'll win." What did he do during those two weeks? Set up new plays? Devise unusual strategy?

No. He minutely reviewed every single fundamental, going over the most elementary items. The refresher course proved successful as the Browns routed the Colts.

Again for today's game, Collier repeated the review. Regardless of the outcome the Browns are going into the game fully confident they're ready. Says Jim Brown, "I feel satisfied where we're at. We have reached the point we want to be in readiness."

Collier is the antithesis of Vince Lombardi, his coaching rival today. Lombardi is outwardly strong, of the bulldog type, a driver. He'll probably chastise a player who hasn't put out. Collier never would publicly hurt anyone. He's a warm, sensitive man.

"He never likes to be called the fatherly type," says Dick Modzelewski, "but I think he is."

Some say if he has a fault it's being too soft in a game that requires fire and brimstone but Modzelewski refutes this. "You'll be surprised," he reveals. "This is an inspirational man. He's not the type of coach that jumps up and down on stools or raises the devil. Blanton makes a few calm statements and to me this does the most good. He's the teacher-type, easy to play for. We're all adult and he chews you out in his own intellectual way. He knows how to get the best out of every player."

There was the case last summer of the young player who broke a training rule which would have caused him to be thrown off any other team. Collier, knowing the player's background, feared the boy would turn into a bum if he were cut. Collier had a fatherly talk with him and gave the boy a second chance. So far it's working out. The boy helped the Browns win a big game this year.

To the suggestion that Collier might be too easy, Jim Brown bristles. He replies, almost angrily. "How can you say that when he's successful?

"He's definitely not weak, or too soft. Not so anybody would take advantage of him. His sensitivity appeals to me. I respond better to that man than to a rough individual. You have a tendency not to ever want to let him down.

"You never want to hurt Blanton. So he has a grip on you when you sleep. Other coaches have you only on the field.

"The greatest thing about Blanton is that he knows how to utilize his forces. He gets more from individuals because he understands their talents and takes advantage of them. Paul (Brown) tried to teach everybody to do the same thing exactly the same way. We're not all made the same. Blanton recognizes this and takes advantage of it."

It was 24 hours after the Browns had beaten the Colts last year. Jim Brown, still tired and bruised, was relaxing on the couch in his living room. Suddenly he jumped up. "I want to send a telegram to Mrs. Collier," he said.

He composed his message, went to the phone and read it: "Congratulations. I can imagine how happy and proud you are. Without Blanton's knowledge and integrity as a man we never would have made it."

Should the Browns retire Lou Groza?

November 27, 1966

People are more cruel than anybody.

When Lou Groza, who had been written off by many, came back to kick the Browns to victory in the first Dallas game he was the hero. Letters came in praising The Toe.

"Let's have another day for him," several readers suggested.

After the Thanksgiving loss to Dallas the first letter we received was a blast at Groza. The old man ought to quit. Consign him to the ash heap.

Sure, why not? Forget about the many, many clutch games won for us by his golden toe. It isn't even "But what has he done for us lately?" because lately he helped us win some big ones. With our forgetful fans it's, "What did you do for us today?"

If the answer is, "Nothing," the cruel reaction is "Get rid of him." This is what I heard in our own office. It's what I heard all over town.

To those who have reacted this way I say, "You're wrong—dead wrong." I suggest you're letting your emotions overcome your thinking. We lost: Lou missed three field goals; Dallas kicked four. Ergo, it was Groza's fault. Consequently he's got to go. If this is your logic, I say it's false. I believe it would be a mistake to say farewell to Groza.

And I don't say this because of sentimental reasons. I still consider him among the finest kickers now in uniform. He's still much too good to be kissed off.

If you think Groza lost that game, you don't know your football. The Browns lost because they didn't dirty the seat of Don Meredith's pants. Not even once. Meredith rested back there as if in a rocking chair and pin-pointed the passes because the defense allowed him to do so. Sure, there were injuries and the rushers were handicapped. But that's part of the game.

The plain fact is that Meredith could have relaxed behind his line, read a 900-page novel without interruption and then after closing the book he could have flipped the ball to a waiting receiver.

How different it was in the first meeting between the two clubs. Meredith was upended play after play. He hurriedly threw four interceptions. He lost his composure.

But with time on his hands Thursday, he drew more confident as the game progressed. With this confidence the Cowboys gained momentum—and victory.

Groza merely was the handy scapegoat—a scapegoat in more ways than one.

His teammates know this. This has been a strange year for Lou. He's been the victim of circumstances not of his own making. Yet, you won't hear him offer a single excuse.

Kicking field goals, if you have the ability, is a matter of timing, pure and simple. The timing involves three people: the center, the ball holder and the kicker.

First Groza lost his veteran holder. Bobby Franklin was claimed by Atlanta and Jim Ninowski took over the job. No two people have the identical actions. No two holders place the ball down exactly the same or with the same speed. Lou, after years of kicking a Franklin-held ball, had to readjust to Ninowski.

Here's what one of Lou's teammates told me:

"At the beginning of the year John Morrow was having trouble centering the ball on kicks. You saw how many were off target. The ball holder calls 'set' and within the count of one-thousand-one the ball is snapped. Lou starts moving at the one-thousand-one. If the snap is high and the holder has to bring it down, Lou can't stop his movement. He's just a little off.

"Finally Morrow got back into the groove on his snaps. And then he was hurt. Monte Clark had to take over. He centers the ball a little slower than Morrow. Lou had to adjust to that. Then Monte hurt his arm, tore the bicep muscle, and this made a snap even slower. A new job, a bad arm—it's lucky he was able to center at all.

"Lou had to start moving on the count, but the ball was getting there a fraction too late. He had to hurry his movements. That's why I believe Dallas had time to block the last kick."

But if you talk with Lou he won't comment on this. "I don't like to make excuses. I'm not going to make 'em."

"All right then, hypothetically," I asked, "what if a center is high or slow. How does it affect the kicker?"

"Well, he doesn't have as much time to look at his target," Lou replied.

He added quickly, "Now I'm not saying this happened. Don't put words in my mouth. I'm not passing the buck. The place-kicking is my responsibility. Whatever happens I have to live with it."

Lou knows he's being sharply criticized around town. Being a big man in character as well as in stature he takes it as a pro. "Anytime you're in this business," he says, "you have to accept it. You take the good with the bad. You simply try to prevent the bad from happening."

Lou isn't kicking footballs for money. He has a thriving insurance business and other investments. He's the one man who is playing the game for fun—not for cash. No one will have to hold any benefits for him. He wants not tears or sympathy, certainly not from me.

He doesn't want to hang around if he doesn't have it. He's an honest man. He would be the first to admit he was over the hill. In 1961, when he hurt his back, he retired. After the back healed the Browns asked him to return. Right now this honest man still thinks he can kick with the best.

"There's nothing wrong with my leg per se," he declares. "If there is anything, it's that I've developed a hook. Those I've missed have gone wide to the left. I don't know how it came about. Maybe I'm pressing a little. Ordinarily you don't think about kicking; you do it naturally. When something goes wrong you press and your rhythm isn't natural."

What went wrong, says a Browns' veteran, was the timing—the snaps from center. When something upsets a golf pro's timing a hook or a slice results.

"If anything was wrong with my leg," suggests Lou, "I wouldn't be able to kick for distance. "I've had a better field goal percentage from beyond the 40 than on the shorter ones."

As of now he has no desire to retire. "I feel good," he adds. "I intend to go on as long as they'll have me."

But Lou is beginning to wonder if his bosses want him. "When you've had a bad year at 42," he observes, "and you read you're not included in the Browns' plans for next year you wonder if the writer knows something, or if he's just surmising.

"And when the club brings in other kickers for trials it makes me wonder what kind of confidence they have in me. From what I see, and what I read, they've almost written me off. I hope it isn't true. But I can see their point. I'm 42 and I am having a bad year."

Lou has beaten off competition before. The Browns drafted place-kickers. Lou outkicked them and they sent the challengers away.

"I don't mind more competition," he says. "Bring 'em on. I think I still can kick with the best."

What if the Browns release him? Would he sign on with another club?

"I don't know," he reflected. "I've had all my fun with the Browns. I wouldn't sign with anybody just to hang on. I don't need the money. I wouldn't do it for dollars.

"But I don't think I'm at the end of the rope. The only reason I might go elsewhere would be to prove a point."

The point: That his detractors are wrong, that his leg is still young, that all other things being equal, at 42, he remains the Golden Toe. As it must to all men the end, some day, will come for Lou. But I submit the time is not now.

He was 42 when he kicked the three field goals to beat Dallas just a month ago. Have you forgotten so soon?

Little boy lost

March 25, 1973

Tuscon, Ariz.—He is sixteen years old and lost.

Large, frightened eyes stare from his round, childlike, ebony face. His head recently had been shaved and the hair is just beginning to grow back.

Pedro Guerrero is the baby here, the youngest player in the Indians' system. He's lonely and bewildered.

He speaks no English. He fails to comprehend even a friendly hello. This is the first time he has ever been away from his home, San Pedro Demarcoris, of the Dominican Republic.

Everything he sees here—except a bat and a ball—is foreign to Pedro. Only when he is facing a pitcher does he feel relatively comfortable and even that has been a jolt.

The first day of batting practice each hitter was given five swings. Pedro dug in against veteran Vince Colbert.

Colbert jammed him on three successive pitches. Pedro hit each one on his fists, spraying the ball to right field, although trying to pull.

Without explanation he walked out of the batter's box, refusing the remaining two pitches.

That night he told his roomie, ex-major leaguer Marcelino Lopez, he never saw pitches like those before, that he never had to hit to the opposite field that way and that he quit because his hands hurt.

"Never, as long as I live, will I forget that," Lopez reported Pedro as saying.

Lopez was assigned as Pedro's roomie—baby-sitter, guardian, mouthpiece—because he came out of his native Cuba at the same age to make the majors. That was 14 years ago.

"Pedro came here with a big suitcase," said Lopez. "It was empty except for one pair of pants and a blue shirt. No underwear. No baseball equipment. He didn't even know what a supporter was."

Pedro had received $66 for initial expense money. Lopez took him on a shopping spree: underwear, socks, two shirts, baseball shoes, and other necessary equipment. Only $17 remained. A sympathetic and more affluent rookie gave him two pairs of pants.

"Pedro said it was the most money he ever spent in his life," said Lopez.

The boy was shivering. The weather has been cold here. "Buy him a sweater," said farm director Bob Quinn.

From Quinn and minor-league coach Joe Azcue, who acted as interpreter, the Pedro Guerrero story was pieced together.

He started playing ball, Little League variety, at age eight, as most kids do in the Dominican Republic.

At eleven, Pedro had to quit school to go to work; his family desperately needed financial help. He lived in a one-room house, inhabited by ten, including his grandparents, aunts, uncles, two brothers, and a sister. (Now, sleeping with just two roommates, in one motel room, is like living in a palace to him, strange and unsettling.)

As a breadwinner, at eleven, he worked as a cement mixer and wheel-barrow-toter for $2 a day. When he grew a little taller—he is now 5-foot-11 and weighs 164—he graduated to the sugar mills, carrying 200-pound sacks for $3.20 a day. His father, once a sugar-mill employee, is now an invalid, partially paralyzed.

Pedro, meanwhile, continued to play ball, moving up to what is similar to our American Legion League. The program in the Dominican Republic is headed by Pedro Gonzalez, once an Indians' second baseman. Gonzalez, noting the boy's talent, continually encouraged him.

A smooth-fielding, switch-hitting third baseman, the boy led the entire island in hitting, with a .438 average.

"He told me," said Azcue, "that he bats better right-handed, but he also bats left-handed just for practice. He said he was batting for a high average right-handed, then when he went to left-handed another kid caught up to him. So he went back to right-handed again and got way ahead of the other kid. Then he returned left-handed again because he needed the practice."

The Indians' Latin American scout, Reggie Otero, saw Pedro and was impressed with his raw talent. He offered the boy a $2,500 bonus to sign.

Gonzalez begged the boy to wait, telling him he was too young, that he would continue to improve and that the money would come when he was more mature and in a better position to handle himself in the United States.

But $2,500 was more than anyone in his family ever had seen. His parents signed for him.

The other day, Quinn took Pedro to the Federal Building here to get his social-security number. "Now we can pay your bonus," he told the boy through Azcue. "Ask him how much he wants us to send home and in whose name to write the check. The rest he'll put into an account here and tell him I want an accounting for every cent he spends. We've got to take care of our baby."

Azcue conveyed the message.

"He is so, how do you say, frightened," said Azcue. "The other day we brought out the rubber pants for sliding practice. All of a sudden Pedro disappeared. I found him hiding in the lavatory. He never saw sliding pants before. He got scared."

Nor did the Indians' baby know how to slide. In the attempt he sprained his wrist and was taken to the hospital for X-rays, another bewildering experience.

"You have to put yourself in his shoes," suggested Azcue, "to know what he's going through. I went through it myself, although I was a little older when I left Cuba and I didn't come from as hard a home life as he did. But in a couple of years he'll be talking English good and he'll be all right. He's a good kid, just a baby with talent."

"Ask him about his family. Ask him if he's lonely," the interviewer suggested.

Azcue relayed the question.

The boy tried to reply. He couldn't. Huge tears rolled down his cheeks.

Azcue took the boy in his arms and hugged him tightly.

Will the talent bloom?

March 2, 1975

The dispatches from Tucson, so far, have scarcely mentioned George Hendrick. This is good—and expected. The Indians' center fielder seldom talks baseball with reporters. He hates interviews worse than rattlesnakes. And he has yet to cause any problems.

This is not to say that he will. He never does cause waves in spring training.

Yet, when the season does begin he'll be a big story. Will he continue to be George, the brilliant player one day, or one week, and an apparent malingerer the next? Under Frank Robinson will Lonesome George bloom into the full flower of his God given talent? How will Robinson handle him if he falls into the previous Hendrick pattern, one which can be so frustrating to a manger?

Unquestionably, George will be a challenge for his new boss. He would be a challenge to any manager, not merely a rookie pilot.

Shortly before Larry Doby was notified he wouldn't be back with the Indians, a notice he anticipated, we asked him about Lonesome George. Doby had been relatively close to him. As batting instructor and outfield tutor, his eye continually fell on Hendrick.

"Is George's talent worth waiting for?" we asked Doby. (Our opinion, expressed several times in this space, is a strong affirmative.)

"Definitely," said Larry.

"Can he be handled?"

"Sure," confidently replied the man who had experienced plenty of knocks himself when he became the first black player in the American League. "It's not that difficult. But he does require understanding. With George, you can't get on him right after he makes a mistake. You have to wait a couple of days and then say, 'George, you should have caught that ball.' Or 'George, do you think you ran as fast as you could? What if the first baseman had dropped the ball?'"

"But why should you have to do that with a big leaguer, a guy who's getting a big salary?"

"Because," replied Doby, "no two players are alike. Everyone must be handled differently. George is overly sensitive. He's 24 and a father, but he's really not mature. In many ways he's just a kid himself. Like kids often do, he over-reacts. You have to have patience with him. He's worth it."

Dave Duncan may know Hendrick even better than Doby does. They were together at Oakland. They came to the Indians together in the Ray Fosse deal. Duncan saw Hendrick emerge from the A's farms.

And Duncan, no longer being a member of the Indians because he was just traded to the Baltimore Orioles, is now in an ideal position to make an objective, unbiased analysis of the puzzlement of George Hendrick.

"He has a difficult time handling any type of pressure," said Duncan when we put the puzzlement to him. "George wants to be George. If a manager looks at George and says, 'He can do everything in the world' and then expects him to do it every day, he'll be disappointed.

"George doesn't want to have to answer for his failures," continued the catcher. "He recognizes them, but he doesn't want to have to answer to the writers or the manager. All super stars go through this period. Everybody else looks at them as potential super stars but the player himself has yet to gain that required self-confidence.

"It's got to happen progressively, for the fear of failure, the fear of being told about your shortcomings, can cause you to end up being a failure."

Duncan and Doby both agree that Hendrick is still immature. Duncan puts it this way: "Not only is he young in actual age, he is probably younger than his years. It's going to take time for him to get it all together.

"Hopefully the new manager and his coaches can create an atmosphere that will take the pressure off George until he's ready to respond to it."

This will require some doing, for the highly sensitive outfielder is easily offended. Possibly an insecure upbringing has made him so vulnerable. Apparently he reacts to discipline and criticism by turning away from it, by turning away from his managers and writers who must provide it, and he retreats into his own private world.

Ken Aspromonte wasn't the first manager Hendrick turned away from. Duncan reveals that at Oakland Hendrick was at odds with Dick Williams. Insiders say that as a consequence Williams readily agreed to the trade that sent George to Cleveland.

"I can understand why George became upset," said Duncan. "There were a lot of frustrations on the A's. Many players would be brought up from the minors for a week, then sent down, then up, then down. Joe Rudi was one. Hendrick was another.

"He got mad at Williams. But it wasn't Williams. It was Charley Finley who was pulling the strings. Rudi could see it and he could handle it. Most of us could. George, instead, got mad at the manager."

Aspromonte alienated Hendrick innocently enough. That is, he didn't know he was doing it. The manager, going through stages of maturity himself, was trying to shake up the whole team. It happened early last season, after the Indians blew a 5-1 lead in the ninth inning in Fenway Park. Admittedly, it was a difficult loss to accept, but a less emotional manager would have taken it in stride, or at least would have waited until the next day to allow himself to cool off and collect his thoughts before lecturing his charges.

But Aspromonte, who by his own admission was still trying to acquire patience and control his temper at that time, locked the clubhouse door after the defeat and ripped into his players, spanking the whole team vocally.

Among the things he said, according to one player, was, "Don't any of you guys ask me for any time off, not even if you have to go to your mother's funeral." Ken vehemently denies making such a statement, but several players say his language could have been interpreted as having that meaning. In the manager's mind, he simply was using strong words, not literal ones, to emphasize the point that he wanted total dedication.

Whatever, the year before the grandmother who raised George had died and he was given time off to go home. To George, the manager's words were meant personally, if not for the whole team, and he felt angered and insulted. He was positive the manager would realize the impact of his statement and would apologize. Next day a practice was called and George arrived fully expecting a retraction. Aspromonte, unaware of the interpretation, said nothing more.

From that moment on Hendrick shunned the manager. There was no communication. The outfielder even kept his bat with him in the dugout so he wouldn't have to pass Aspromonte on the way to the bat rack. Kid stuff, of course. But this is what Duncan meant about establishing the proper atmosphere while the enigmatic Hendrick matures.

It will require remarkable patience, perhaps even more than Frank Robinson has. The new pilot says he looks on Hendrick as just one of 25 players. There will be no special privileges. Fine. But there must be special understanding for each individual and maybe just a little more for the man-child Hendrick.

Perhaps with George it's best to maintain a sense of humor, as well as understanding. Late last summer my wife and I saw him at a behind-the-fence Stadium party. I said, "Hello George," and stuck out my hand. His face froze and he gave me a limp paw as he looked in the other direction.

"And this is my wife," I added, ignoring the extended cold fish. He turned to her, positively beaming. He have her a warm hello, a charming smile and a vigorous handshake.

I thought it was funny. Inwardly, George may have been laughing, too. He had scored some points against a sportswriter.

The most amusing and possibly the most revealing anecdote about this man-child comes from Dino Lucarelli, long-time Indians' public relations director who has just given up the post to accept a position with Art Modell's Stadium Corp. The incident previously was reported here but it bears repeating.

Because it was Dino's job to occasionally force interviews on George, the outfielder didn't always appreciate the public relations director. Once Dino passed George and his three-year-old son, Brian, outside the locker room.

"Hello George," said Dino.

No reply.

"Hello Brian," said Dino.

No reply.

George turned to his son and said, "Didn't I always tell you to say hello to people?"

A doctor's diary?

January 29, 1978

We can't let Dr. Victor Ippolito walk away from the position he has held a record 32 years as team physician for the Browns without picking his brains. There's so much about the Browns stored in them—and in his files.

Happily, Vic isn't going to quit cold turkey Browns' owner Art Modell has asked him to stay on as a consultant. So an association Vic began with football at age 13, as a halfback at Roosevelt Junior High, won't be snapped entirely. From Roosevelt, Vic went to Cleveland Heights, where he became an all-scholastic. Then to Western Reserve University and more football glory.

Therefore he was uniquely suited for the post as team physician when the Browns were born in 1946.

In those 32 years he personally examined every player who signed a Browns' contract. He was their father-confessor in time of trouble. He prescribed for all their aches and pains. From now on, Dr. John Bergfeld, head of sports medicine at the Cleveland Clinic, will have that responsibility.

"A man has to know when to quit," said Vic. "I'm 65. I had a coronary five years ago. It can get awfully cold at the Stadium in December. And because of the increased responsibility a team doctor now has—with so many clubs being sued by the players—the paper work has increased enormously. It's time to turn it over to a younger man. I'll miss the close association with football because it's been such an enjoyable part of my life."

To get him started, we asked Vic to talk about some of the players. Who was the strongest one?

"The strongest who ever lived has to be Jim Brown," he said without hesitation. "Do you realize he missed only one quarter in nine years of hard play?" He repeated for emphasis, "Just one quarter. And even then he didn't want to say out. It was in New York, against the Giants in the late 1950s. He had a cerebral concussion. He was dazed. I made him stay out for a quarter, until I could see he was okay. Then I permitted him to go back in.

"When they talk about O.J. Simpson, and compare him to Jim Brown, the durability of Jim far overshadows Simpson, great as O.J. is. Simpson was out most of the past season. Compare that to the one quarter I forced Jim to stay out.

"To show you the kind of competitor Jim was and how perfectly he kept his body in condition let me tell you about this one incident that stays in my mind. It was in his second-last season with the Browns. He was having some personal problems so he scarcely had been in camp. There was a scrimmage schedule for Saturday afternoon at Hiram, a Touchdown Club affair. Jim's personal matters were over at 11 A.M. He drove to Hiram. The scrimmage started at 2 P.M. He put on a uniform, scrimmaged for an hour and gave an outstanding performance.

"I personally never heard him complain. He never even went into the trainer's room until the last few years he was with us and then for only minor treatment. He could have played for at least two more years after he quit.

"One time I was positive he had a fractured toe. I said, 'Let's x-ray.' He said, 'What will the x-ray show?' 'It might show a break,' I said. He said, 'So what's the use of taking it, I'm gonna play.'

"In another game in New York, the Giants keyed on him constantly, as all clubs did. Sam Huff and the others zeroed in on him, play after play. After the game his face looked like a prize fighter who had no defense. Battered and bruised. Like he had stood n his corner and was constantly hit. Besides, his elbow was terribly swollen. The worst I ever saw. I wanted him to come back home and check into the hospital for x-rays. But he had a speaking date in New York, at a press luncheon, the next day. He stayed over that Monday. The next day he was back at practice and never said a word about his awful elbow or the bruises. He never missed a practice and played in every exhibition game.

"No doubt he's the greatest player I've ever seen. Think how marvelous it is for a coach to have a player of his caliber that he can rely on every Sunday. The Browns' coaches always knew they had Jim Brown. As mortals go you'd have to call him a superman."

How about Marion Motley, Doc.

"You can't compare athletes from different periods. If they both were out for the team both would be regulars, one at fullback and the other at halfback. You know it was Motley and Bill Willis, two great people and great athletes, who opened the door for the black athlete. Paul Brown brought them in and they were so good and so classy they forced the owners to appreciate what the black athlete could do and they began to look for more Willises and Motleys."

The doctor's face lit up at another recollection. "Otto Graham," he said. "He's got to be one of my all-time favorites. One time we were playing San Francisco. Big game. Early 1950s. A San Francisco player, Art Michalik I believe, gave him a forearm, right in the face, after Otto had stepped out of bounds. The inside of Otto's mouth was all torn. It took me the entire time between halves to sew him up. About 20 stitches as I remember. He left the locker room. I didn't expect him to play. I followed after I cleaned up. Lo and behold, Otto was in the game. He won it for us.

"Near the end of the game Michalik was hit. I guess our guys wanted to teach him a lesson. In those days the home team physician took care of both clubs. I had to sew his face up. He said, 'Doc, tell the Browns

I didn't mean to hurt Otto. I didn't know he out of bounds.' I believed him. That was the game, incidentally, that caused Paul Brown to come up with the football face guard."

How about some of the other players, Doc?

"It's really unfair to single them out. There were so many in 32 years, so many great ones, the Lavellis, the Grozas, the Speedies, the Bob Gains, where do you start? Where do you stop?

"Abe Gibron . . . His mother came from Michigan to see me as a patient. Out of Abe's pay check a certain amount always went to his mother. He was a great player and a kind man.

"Mike McCormack . . . during the exhibition season he developed a torn cartilage. Had to have surgery. Three weeks after the surgery the season started. He said, 'I'm the team captain. I'm going to play.' It's rare, almost impossible, for a player to play football three weeks after knee surgery. Mike McCormack did.

"Gene Hickerson . . . I'm positive he played the last four years with a torn cartilage. He refused to have it x-rayed. Remember our championship game in 1964 against the Colts? Gene was living at the Commodore Hotel. He had a viral infection. I went to his room to see him. Temperature of 105. He played the entire game against the Colts. Great player, Hickerson.

"Dick Schafrath . . . Always respected him. You know his normal weight was only 212. He knew at 212 he couldn't play pro ball. He was one of the first pros who started to work with weights. Built himself to 245. He did it himself at great sacrifice. Now we provide all sorts of fancy machines, the Nautilus and others, for the players. We didn't have them then. Dick had to go out and find the weights."

Doc, aren't there some players who aren't so stoic, who constantly complain about aches and pains?

"Remember George Young," he said. "Fine defensive end. Before every game he became terribly nauseated. Vomited, although he didn't have anything to eat. I'd give him a pill, any kind—aspirin, soda, mint, even a piece of sugar—and he'd be better right away.

"Doug Dieken, our present offensive tackle, could have played in any era. Doug always has something wrong. He's constantly saying, 'This hurts,' or 'That hurts.' But he plays. Greg Pruitt complains, but he goes out and has a fine game. Remember, compared to the size of the men he's playing against he's taking a severe beating. Pound for pound, he's a great athlete. You haven't seen the real Greg Pruitt yet. In the next two years, I predict, you'll see a greater one."

The worst sports injury Ippolito ever saw was Tommy Thompson's dislocated knee. "Happened against the Steelers in Forbes Field. Awful. Had to be reduced immediately. He was through for the season and didn't play much after that.

"Remember when Lenny Ford's jaw was busted. That was a sickening sight. It was wired shut for about six weeks. He couldn't eat. Lost weight. The wires were taken out on a Friday, two days before we were to meet Los Angeles for the NFL championship. Lenny was supposed to watch, not play. His substitute wasn't doing the job. Lenny went in. He was remarkable. Without him we wouldn't have won. I never have seen a greater defensive end. He could play with the best today.

So many stories have been published in recent years about players using drugs, "greenies" to give them a lift, about the use of steroids to make the body bigger, about the use of dope and marijuana. In some cases the team doctors have been sued. The Browns have had virtually no bad publicity of this nature, which must be a tribute to Ippolito's policies and his philosophy.

"I'm absolutely against the use of steroids," he said emphatically. "I'm not so naïve as to think that some players haven't used them secretly, especially since the stories have come out with the Russian athletes, weightlifters for example, who use them to increase their performance. But it's never been proven that they actually do increase performance and there is evidence of harmful side reaction.

"I'm totally against any artificial stimulation. I never have prescribed a steroid or a stimulant to an athlete. I have been against them all my life. Any player who needs a drug to play has no business playing.

"I'm not talking about the vitamins. There's no harm in them. They're not stimulants.

"As for amphetamines (the "greenies" and the "bennies" that supposedly give one a high) in every player's playbook is a page which I sign. It says I'm absolutely against these drugs. We never carry them in our bags. The trainer is not allowed to have them in the training room. I've never seen a player take them on his own, but I'd be a darn fool if I said some of then didn't try them. Not in the early years, but since the 'flower generation' and since what they've read about the Russian athletes. Let me say this right here. The Browns have an exceptional trainer in Leo Murphy. He is with them all the time. He does an outstanding job."

Are any of the players smoking marijuana, Doc?

"I don't know. Not to my knowledge. I'm completely against it. They know it. Whenever you need something artificial it leads to something else. As a doctor, regardless of some of the supportive statements people have made about marijuana, I'm opposed to its use. It may lead to other problems. Who needs that?"

Ippolito remembered that Paul Brown even had a cigarette smoking ban. "He had a rule. No player could smoke in front of him. I was the only person who did. I cut it out. Never smoked again.

"I'm not saying Paul's players didn't smoke. But those who did, couldn't smoke as much because they were around him a good portion of the time. I think all public figures should set a good example for our young people. I'm a doctor. You're a sportswriter. We shouldn't smoke or drink in public. And an athlete, who is being paid to be a public figure, should show even more restraint. Youngsters see the athlete smoke. They think it's all right. It isn't. Smoking is harmful. No question about it."

Doc, you keep mentioning Paul Brown. He must be something special in your mind.

"Well, as a football coach he is. Paul Brown is Paul Brown. He was the great innovator. He started all the things that are now common practice. When he took over the Browns, football wasn't that organized. You remember how it was when we played in high school and college. He organized the sport. He made it what it is today and I'm not trying to take anything away from George Halas and the others when I say that.

"He established a daily schedule. Everything was mapped out, a timetable for each activity. Even the doctor got one. Players who had been on the Browns and then went to other teams would come back and tell me how disorganized the others were in comparison. Then the others began to change—in an effort to catch up. Eventually they did.

"He started the playbooks, the complete testing program, from physicals to IQ. He was the one who had his assistants study the films to grade every player and to pay them accordingly. When it comes to coaches, whether you liked him personally or not, you've got to put his name right up there at the top."

In 32 years, Ippolito has seen many changes in the game. He talked about some.

"Of course the players today are much bigger and faster and quicker. That makes a big difference in how the game is played. Bill Willis was a 190-pound defensive lineman. Now they're all 250 or more. And all of them are well-conditioned. Now each team has its training center open the year-around. The players know they must stay in shape if they want to play. Because of the size and strength of the men and the better equipment the hitting is much harder than it ever was.

"Another change is the paper work. For the doctor it has become voluminous. I never have had a malpractice suit with the Browns but that's because our owners and coaches have been so far-sighted and so cooperative. Art Modell never questions anything I recommend. The player's health is paramount. The cost is of no consequence. I think the Browns are far ahead of all the other clubs because of Art's attitude. We did complete blood tests, electrocardiographs, x-rays of the lungs, sickle cell anemia tests, long before the other clubs did. They have been part of our routine. About six years ago the players in the league got together and asked for a minimum standard physical to be established. We had been giving one for years, far above the minimum."

So that players can't come back at a future date with a complaint about how they were handled medically, Dr. Ippolito writes everything down, or talks it into a Dictaphone for his secretary to transcribe. He took out Brian Sipe's folder. It was the size of a large novel. Even the smallest hangnail, and its treatment, is covered. Incidentally, at Ippolito's request, Sipe was just examined in San Diego by Dr. Paul Woodward, team physician for the Chargers. The report: "Brian apparently is making excellent recovery. (He was out half of last season with a shoulder fracture.) No pain, X-rays show the fracture to be well healed."

During each game Ippolito records every injury, a virtual diary of all the action. The report is sent to the coaches, to Modell and a copy goes in the player's folder.

He produced the "diary" of the Browns' final game, against Seattle, in the Kingdome. The day before the game, Saturday, 23 players had various portions of their anatomy thoroughly checked by the doctor. The coaches were advised that Larry Poole should not be allowed to play because of a bad sprain.

Next day there were pre-game examinations for six of those 23.

As the game began the injuries were listed. At half-time Greg Pruitt required five silk sutures to close a laceration on his chin. In the beginning of the fourth quarter Pruitt "on a run was twisted back and had a mild sprain of the right knee. He came out and did not return because previously he had a slight pain in the neck (noted in the Saturday report). Because of the pain in his neck and now his knee, it was thought best to keep him out the rest of the game."

The diary revealed that Doug Dieken's "great toe, bursa, was injected with 3 cc of Barbocain," a pain-killer in the nature of Novocain.

"Doctor," we asked, "you say you're against drugs. Isn't this in the nature of a drug? It hides the pain."

"Glad you asked," he replied. "Let's say a fellow has a sore finger and I don't think he can injure himself further. Will I inject him? I will. If I think he can injure himself more by playing he won't play. If just a little injection will permit him to overcome the pain and not hurt himself further, yes, I'll do it. Now, I would not advise this for high schools or colleges.

"All pros must realize that team doctors are exactly that. We want to keep the players healthy, and we want what's best for them—and the team. I'm sure the players feel that way about me. Otherwise I wouldn't have been here for 32 years."

Ippolito was asked about his worst experiences.

"There were two," he replied immediately. "The first was the championship game in Green Bay in 1965. We stayed in a small town outside Green Bay the night before. Then came a snowstorm. The team bus got caught in it. It took hours to get to the Stadium. We lost the championship in that bus. No question about it. I saw players come apart on that ride.

"The other bad one was also a cold day, the most bitter cold I can remember. It was the championship game in Minnesota in 1969. Some of our players had severe frostbite that day."

And the great moments?

"Our first game in the National Football League was unforgettable. We had won four straight championships in the All-America Conference, but everybody scoffed at that. Now we were going to play with the big boys. That was in 1950. We opened against Greasy Neale's outstanding Philadelphia Eagles and beat them 35-10. That opened everybody's eyes.

"The second exceptional moment was our last game that season against the Los Angeles Rams for the championship. I can still see Lou Groza's field goal sailing through the goal posts in the closing seconds to beat them, 30-28.

"A third unforgettable game was our victory over the Baltimore Colts to win the championship in 1964. John Unitas was supposed to pick us apart. We didn't belong on the same field, the experts said. Our preparation for that game was almost perfection. We won, 27-0.

"But to be honest, almost every game has been great to me, every moment. The men I've met are unforgettable. It's been wonderful. If all I had to do was simply be on the sidelines between 1 P.M. and 4 P.M every Sunday, I'd still be around."

He finally has hung up his Browns' stethoscope. They'll miss him.

Would you bet on Paige's age?

December 10, 1978

So Satchel Paige finally has disclosed his age. From Orlando, Florida, where Satch was attending the baseball meetings this week, came the headline, "Satch reveals his age." He says he is now 72 and that's official.

Hope he didn't put any money on it because he'd lose. He lost once before and it cost him. Well it should have.

Ages do have a way of changing, though. Like Luke Easter's. I covered the Indians when Luke played here and whenever I asked his age he'd laugh and say, "I'm a lot younger than you."

We'll, turns out he isn't. Luke suddenly gained a number of years when he became eligible for his baseball pension. He didn't mind showing his birth certificate to get in on the payoff.

Even women, you know, suddenly become honest, when it becomes time to get their Social Security checks.

How old am I? Luke wouldn't want me to tell.

But back to Satch's age. Maybe he gained a couple of years for the same reason. I happen to qualify as an expert on the subject but I'm glad he never asked me to vouch for him with the Social Security folks. Wouldn't want to blow his cover. Not that I could really. I wouldn't swear to anything about Satch.

Well, that's not exactly true. I'd swear that he was one of the greatest pitchers the game has ever known. And I'd swear he's the most interesting, most unforgettable sports personality I've ever met.

I got to know Satch so well by default, you might say. Back in 1948, that glorious year when the Indians won the pennant in a playoff game and then captured the World Series, Bill Veeck, in a surprise move, signed the legendary Satchel early in July. Veeck was highly criticized for bringing in the old timer. *The Sporting News,* baseball's "bible," blasted him editorially, calling it a showboat stunt just to sell tickets, something Veeck was not beyond. In fact, he delighted in agreeing Satch was old.

Satch proved Veeck a genius. His success on the mound forced *The Sporting News* to retract and the fans filled ball parks everywhere, not only to see the old man perform, but to marvel at his brilliance. The better he pitched, the older Veeck said he was.

Satch unquestionably was hot copy and Nat Howard, the editor of *The Cleveland News,* wisely contracted with him, through Veeck, to run his life story. Ed McAuley, baseball writer for the *News,* was supposed to ghost it, but he had so much to handle covering the Indians and doing a daily column that the added chore was impossible.

One day Howard came by the sports department and said, "Go see Paige. His life story is your assignment."

Before my mouth could close, he walked away.

The Indians were in Washington, playing the Senators. Satch didn't know me. I didn't know him. As an umpire I had worked some games in the Negro League at League Park and the Stadium in which he had pitched during his days with the Kansas City Monarchs and other teams. And I never had given him any trouble so he wouldn't remember me. Almost every pitch was a strike. Easiest pitcher to umpire for in the whole wide world.

I remembered some of his pre-game stunts. To draw fans the teams had to put on a pre-game show the way the Harlem Globetrotters do now. Satch would stick two bats between home plate, about six inches apart and throw the ball right through them. Or he'd knock a cigar out of a teammate's mouth. Uncanny control. Those windups, the hesitation pitch, meant nothing. His "Bee Ball" was his pitch, because as he later told me, "It be where I want it to be." It "be" all right—straight and fast.

But back to Satch's age. I grabbed a plane for Washington to introduce myself and hoped he would open up about his life. On the way to Hopkins Airport, I saw the billboards, "Read the Satchel Paige Story, starting Monday in The Cleveland News." And I hadn't even said hello to the man.

At the Shoreham Hotel in Washington, I knocked on Satch's door. Larry Doby, his roomie, answered. We were friends. I explained my mission. He wasn't encouraging.

"Satch isn't here," he said. "But be careful. He carries a gun."

Larry wasn't kidding and he obviously wasn't partial to that pistol. Fact is, it scared him.

Seems that Satch took to carrying the protection years ago, when he was barnstorming and got paid a wad of bills at each stop. It became a part of him.

I finally went to Griffith Stadium and waited for Satch there. The Indians were to play the Senators in a night game. Eventually he showed up. That was to be the problem. Satch has little conception of time or place or space. He missed a few planes—"birds," he called them—and Manager Lou Boudreau fined him a couple of times. In exasperation Lou finally gave him a schedule and said, "If I ever catch you without it, there will be an automatic fine."

Satch always had an excuse. "I knew it would be a late game," or "My feet told me it was going to rain." When he played for the Kansas City Monarchs, I learned later, the owner of the team paid a man to stay with Satch and to make certain he showed up.

Oh yes, back to his age. He was stretched out on Lefty Weisman's trainer's table. Naked. No fat. Long and lean. Body didn't look old. Couldn't see any wear and tear. Life story for the paper? He didn't remember at first. Okay, if we could get together. Tried to make a few appointments. Foolish. He kept owners and presidents waiting. Why would he keep them with me? Finally discovered he would show up at two places eventually—the trainer's room in the clubhouse or his room at the Majestic Hotel on E. 55th Street near Quincy. At those spots I would wait for his stories and his wisdom.

And stories there were. About his childhood days in Mobile; how he realized his great control by throwing rocks at tin cans; that he got the name "Satchel" because he carried satchels at the railroad depot for a dime each and how to make more dimes, he strung ropes all over his body and attached the satchels to them, making him look like a "satchel tree"; about his barnstorming days, and a memorable confrontation against Josh Gibson, the fabulous Babe Ruth of the Negro League, maybe even better, some say.

Once Satch and Josh had been battery-mates with the Pittsburgh Crawfords. Then Satch moved on to the Monarchs and Josh to the Homestead Grays.

Satch and Josh were sunning on the beach in Puerto Rico where they were playing winter ball and Josh said to him, "Some day my whole family is going to be in the stands and all your friends, too. You'll be pitching and I'll come up with the bases drunk (loaded). I'm going to drive the ball and you clear out to left field."

Satch said, "We'll see."

In February, 1942, the Monarchs met the Grays in Pittsburgh, in a playoff. Gibson's family was there. So were Satch's Pittsburgh pals. The Monarchs were leading, 6-3, in the last inning. When the first Gray batter got a hit Satch called out to his manager, Frank Duncan, and said, "I'm going to walk the next two."

"But that'll bring up Gibson," said the astonished Duncan.

"Right," said Satch and explained about the Puerto Rico promise. "Got to show the man," said Satch.

When the bases were "drunk" Satch called in his outfielders and ordered all his teammates to sit down.

"Me and you," he said to Josh.

Josh Gibson struck out. Satch said it took hours to clear the straw hats off the field.

Oh yes, his age. His philosophy had the wisdom of a thousand years. He always walked slowly, especially to the mound. "Why hurry into trouble?" he would say. Or "Never look back, somebody may be following you." "Eat nothing but fried foods," was another Satchelism designed to explain his longevity. All these rules for longer life, about 10 of them, eventually became so famous Dwight Eisenhower, when he was president, had them printed up and placed on the wall of his office in the White House.

That fried food bit was one of Satch's funnies, I hasten to add, should you intend to take his rules seriously. Satch had eaten plenty of fried food in his time and his stomach did much complaining. Rumbled a lot. Once he stood on the mound, staring at Catcher Jim Hegan's signals, yet refusing to pitch.

Hegan, whom Paige called "Big Catch"—he rarely knew anybody's true name—came out to the mound and said, "I went through all your pitches, Satch. What's up?"

"I got gas," said Satch. A bicarbonate was rushed to the mound. He emitted a thunderous belch and continued to pitch fluidly.

"My arm can pitch 100 years," he told me. "But I might have to get my stomach upholstered in five or six."

He kept his arm in shape through his own magic, always carrying a heating lamp and a massage machine in his personal satchel. Also he would stand in the shower and let the hot water hit his shoulder. He could pitch every day, as he did on barnstorming trips in which the fans were guaranteed to see him work at least three innings. That was the marvel of it. No matter how old or young he was his arm had done enough pitching for 10 men.

Satch enjoyed the speculation about his age—and Veeck's reflections on it—up to a point. He was between marriages in 1948 and he didn't want the girls to think he was *that* old.

His former wife had told reporters the Bible in the home of Satchel's mother revealed he was born July 28, 1905. That would have made him 43 when he was with the Indians. But Satch's mother told writers the Bible showed him to be 44.

"It's the same Bible," said Satch, "and even it doesn't have it clear. My mom had 11 children and she never could keep track."

Satch was told he could straighten everybody out in his life story.

He pulled out his draft card. It showed his birthdate to be Sept. 18, 1908. That would have made him not quite 40.

"Is that right?"

"I don't know," he said. "I gave them a number. Close, maybe."

He tried to figure it out. "I was 17 when I started pitching for the Chattanooga Black Lookouts. That was in 1927. Let's see. That would make me 38."

"But what about all these people who say you pitched long before that, even in 1915?"

"Tell you what," said Satch. "Anybody who can prove I pitched before 1927 gets $500."

The offer was made in the *News,* in bold headlines.

From then on Satch couldn't take a step without someone bothering him for clues. They would knock on his hotel door. They would accost him everywhere. They looked in his eyes. "Clear. No spots."

They checked his skin. "Like a baby's."

They studied his hair. Not a gray one.

All sorts of attempts were made to claim the money. Each proved to be without foundation. Finally a Clevelander went through a newspaper library in Chattanooga and discovered a box score. A "Satchel" was listed as the pitcher. The date, 1926. He obtained a Photostat and brought it back to Cleveland.

"Maybe," admitted Satch, "that was me. The only man who would know is Alex Herman. He got my mom's permission to take me out of Mobile to Chattanooga. If he says it's me, I've got to pay."

Alex Herman, head of the Unity Burial Association, in Mobile, confirmed it. I still have the fascinating letter, telling about those early days.

When Satch was shown Herman's reply, he said, "Must have slept out a year."

When it came time to pay, Satch had the "shorts" and I didn't have the heart to nag him. Veeck paid the $500 and gladly. Satch had been a gold strike for him.

If Satch was 17 in 1926 he would be 69 today. Or maybe he has just turned 70, depending on his true birthdate.

Somewhere since that payoff he lost some sleep. At least two years. Maybe it was all that fried food.

Whatever, the man's a marvel and I hope he can add on real years for a long, long time. And 20 years from now, whatever he says his age is, believe, believe. But don't bet on it.

How did he turn out this way?

January 21, 1979

The game was about to begin. The large gym was packed, beyond capacity it seemed. The players were being announced. First the Cathedral Latin starters. Then the St. Joseph High players.

"Clark Kellogg, center, All American," boomed the voice from the loudspeakers.

How unnecessary, you thought. How unfair, how out-of-line to put such added pressure on this 17-year-old before these screaming fans. Not even in a pro game would one player be spotlighted, singled out, in this circus-like manner. How could this youth, any youth, handle it? How could he live up to the buildup before every critical eye in that gym?

Clark Kellogg did.

He played full throttle for the entire 32 minutes, never loafing, displaying skills beyond belief for one in his teens. At six-eight, he handled the ball like a point guard, dribbling, passing. Unselfish, he fed teammates with quick wrists and uncanny peripheral vision. He leaped for rebounds, made jump shots, took on Latin's best player personally in a second-half man-to-man and smothered him with perfect defensive footwork.

You thought back. In more than 40 years of watching high school players, being one yourself, coaching them and refereeing them, had you seen anyone better?

The answer came without hesitation. Not from this area. Clark

Kellogg is the best high schooler you ever have seen in Greater Cleveland.

"Why confine it to Greater Cleveland?" asked Ray Dieringer, coach of Cleveland State University, who was just one of the many college coaches in the audience. (Joe Hall, for example, had come up from Kentucky to see Kellogg that night and waited until long after the game was ended to talk with him about enrolling there.)

Well, maybe Jerry Lucas was on a par when he played at Middletown High. Or maybe John Havlicek. Maybe. It's that close and Kellogg is that good—good enough to be mentioned with the likes of Lucas and Havlicek in their school days.

"And just as good as he is as a player," said the admiring Dieringer, "he's just that good a student and as a person. And that's why every coach in the country is drooling to get him."

How did Clark Kellogg Jr. get that way? What has made him so special? And where does he go from here? For answers you visit his parents, about whom he always speaks so highly, to whom he always gives credit.

The Kelloggs live in a small, modest, six-room home in East Cleveland, just a block behind Shaw Field. The house, recently painted, is well-kept, neat.

Inside it is the same, neat and clean.

Clark Kellogg Sr. and his wife, Mattie, are home. It isn't often they're home together these days. Clark is a Cleveland policeman, working on the robbery squad. When he isn't on duty, he works part-time as a security guard at Women's Hospital. And when he isn't on either job, he's watching his kids play.

Mattie works afternoons and evenings, 30 hours a week, at St. Luke's Hospital as a ward secretary in pediatrics. She decided to go back to work only after their five children became old enough to handle the chores.

The extra work for both parents is necessary to keep the refrigerator stocked—"We have an open door policy on it; the children and their friends can go into it any time and two days' supplies here could feed another family for two weeks," says Mattie—and to send the children to parochial school and pay all the other bills.

The Kelloggs are Protestant, yet Clark Jr.—whom they call by his middle name "Cliff" because they don't want him going through life being a "Junior"—and his brother Eric, 16, go to St. Joseph, a Catholic school. Eldest daughter Joy, 15, attends Villa Angela and they hope their other two daughters, Robin, 13, and Leigh, 9, eventually will go there too.

The two boys and Joy take public transportation to their schools when it would be much simpler for them to walk to nearby Shaw High.

"We thought they could get a better education at the parochial schools," explains Mattie. "Cliff (remember, that's Clark Jr.) and Eric have partial scholarships, which help, but we have full tuition for Joy."

That may change soon, for Joy, like her brothers, is an outstanding basketball player and the star of the Villa Angela team.

The Kellogg parents are a handsome couple. Clark, 40, is a muscular six-four and Mattie is a highly attractive five-ten. Clark's dad, a former boxer, is six-seven.

All the children have inherited height. After Clark Jr.'s six-eight, comes Eric's six-six, Joy's five-ten, and Robin's five-eight. Nine-year-old Leigh is rapidly catching up.

The Kelloggs were teenage sweethearts, going together since they first met at Addison Junior High. Clark was 14 then and Mattie 13. The romance continued through East High, where Clark and his brothers, Eugene and Shelby, were top athletes. Clark was all-scholastic in basketball and football and threw the shot in track. After an eight-year courtship, during which Clark tried college, Mattie finally said, "yes."

She speaks softly, slowly, and thoughtfully. Obviously a gentle woman, her great strength of character and love for her husband and children are so tangible they can be felt.

"I gave Clark five healthy children," she says. "He gave them their athletic ability."

"Not true," says Clark. "She won a lot of bowling trophies."

She doesn't worry when her husband puts on his police uniform, not even when she reads about the fatalities in the department.

"When we were first married, he had a job as a machine operator in a factory," she recalls. "He hated it. He was tough to live with. When he joined the police force, there was a remarkable change in his personality. He's happy and that makes me happy."

Clark enjoyed his police work more when he was in the juvenile unit—now disbanded by the city as an economy move—where he helped organize Police Athletic League teams for the kids.

That's where Clark Jr. got his start.

"I never pushed him," says the father. "When he showed interest, I helped him. I played in The Plain Dealer Class A League and he'd come along and sit on the sidelines. We had a police team that played high school faculties and he'd ask to go with me. Then I had a PAL football team at E. 105th and St. Clair. He was about ten and the youngest player. Played end. Both ways. He could tackle and he could catch the ball. I thought football might be his game. At the same time he was wrestling at the YMCA and won the state title in the 95-pound class. About then he began to shoot a few baskets at the Y. But he didn't seem to care for it that much. He could have gone to Columbus with the Y basketball team, but he turned it down to wrestle."

And then it happened. Pop put a basketball hoop in the backyard and from then on the game consumed his son's free time.

"All the children in the neighborhood came," relates Mattie. "Soon we had to limit the number. It bothered me. The stray balls broke windows, we never could grow any grass, and every week we would have to buy him, and then later Eric, a new pair of tennis shoes. Every week, almost without fail. Clark had to add concrete to make the court larger.

"Much as all this disturbed me, we would say to each other, 'At least we know where our children are. We know what they're doing.' We say the same thing now when all their friends come here to visit and play records and empty our refrigerator."

Of course, the father got into some of the backyard games, and so did Uncle Shelby and others of their generation. "I'd play one-on-one occasionally with Cliff," Clark Sr. admits.

"He did much more than that," adds Mattie with a smile. "His father emphasized the importance of ball handling, the way guards do. That's why he can do it now."

"Well," picks up Pop reluctantly, "Cliff already was tall for his age. Tall and spindly. In my day a big guy would get the rebound, throw it out, run down the court, and wait for the others to bring up the ball. The big guy usually isn't well rounded, not a complete part of the team. I wanted Cliff to have the ability to take the ball the full length of the court himself, if necessary."

Although delighted with Cliff's success, both parents obviously are somewhat in awe of the remarkable way he has developed as an athlete, scholar and person.

"He gives us the credit," says Mattie, "but that's not it. I give him the credit. He always has been an unusually good child. Never a problem. He always listened. He's the type you can talk to. He disciplined himself and still does.

"If he has homework and the other children are here listening to records, he'll go up to his room and study. It's no secret how he got four A's and one B on his last card. He works at it.

"He has his own weight program to build up his strength. His dad emphasized the importance of that and Uncle Shelby bought him a bench and weights and showed him how to use them. The weights are in the basement, and Cliff has his own schedule to keep his muscles toned."

"He is a boy who sets his goals and keeps them," observes Clark Sr. "He stopped football after one year because he decided he was more physically equipped to play basketball, being tall. It made no difference to me, just as long as whatever he did was in earnest.

"The other children aren't like Cliff. Eric (who, at 16, is a sophomore at St. Joseph and a starter on the varsity) doesn't work as hard, not even at basketball. But I can just see his interest beginning to change. He's getting more involved. Eric has a mind of his own, an individual. No one can push him. He goes along at his own pace.

"But Clark, he has to be the best at whatever he does. When he painted houses one summer, he took pride in becoming the best trimmer. He loves to excel."

He has excelled to such an extent that many see a great future for him in the National Basketball Association and at times he has envisioned himself playing for big pay.

"At one point," says Mattie, "pro ball was his main goal. But it has changed. Now it's to go to college and be a successful person. Pro basketball isn't out. But no longer is it the bottom line. His eyes have been broadened by other things in which he could be successful."

Adds Clark Sr., "Pro ball is limited. You've got to have everything going for you to make it. I've emphasized that."

Last summer the young athlete worked as an apprentice for the Novak Insurance Agency and he quickly realized the possibilities open to him in the business world. Next July, at 18, he intends to have his license as an insurance agent.

The next step is to go to college and to prepare himself. "I've told all my children," says Clark Sr., "that I'm an example of the value of a college education. I went to Indiana and then to Kent State. But I never finished. Now I tell them I'm working two jobs and I'm still on the short end. Maybe it would have been different if I had finished college. A degree is no guarantee, but it helps."

Thus, college always has been one of Clark's goals and now he's the goal of more than 100 colleges.

In the Kellogg home there are boxes filled to the brim with letters from basketball coaches from every major school in the United States.

"They come in every day," says Mattie. "Some we haven't even opened yet. I try to look at all the letters and report to him. We talk, Cliff, his dad, and I. But it will be his decision. He told us what schools he is interested in."

He already has visited four of the many to which he has been invited: Ohio State, Michigan, Notre Dame, and Kentucky. By NCAA rule he is allowed to accept only two more invitations. However, he and his dad have made some private visits to some campuses at their own expense to help cement the decision.

"Unless there's a great change, he'll go to one of the four schools he already has seen," reveals Clark Sr. "The coaches keep sending literature and calling and saying, 'We don't want to bother you, we're just staying in touch.'"

"He thought about going to a west coast school," says Mattie, "but we sort of swayed him away. I'm not too keen on having my child go too far. Yes, all my children will listen to me."

(For what it's worth, after listening to the parents, your radar tells you Clark Kellogg next fall will be playing at Ohio State. Just a feeling, no solid clues.)

The entire family is close. Pop, mom, and the five children often sit around the table at night for give-and-take-discussions. "Everybody gets a lick in," says Mattie. After a game often as many as 20 relatives and friends will come back to the Kellogg home to discuss the action. Mattie, who rarely has seen one this season because she works evenings, gets her play-by-play from them.

Pop goes to all the games, stands in a corner of the gym with his policeman pal, Al Kirkwood, and they watch silently, even when they dislike an officiating decision. Pop never second-guesses the coach.

Mattie worries about her son's sensitivity. Like her, he is gentle. He is vulnerable, too, and exposes himself to possible hurt.

Yet, with all the adulation, especially from his peers, he has been able to maintain a low-key profile. He doesn't consider himself a big deal.

"Would it be tough to be Clark Kellogg?" Mattie asks herself thoughtfully. "Not for him. He is always patient. He goes out of his way for people. He goes to St. Joe's gym every Saturday morning to work with the kids.

"And he is so trusting. Clark, tell about the time he was robbed."

"He was about ten. We gave him 50 cents and sent him to Lawson's for milk and bread. On his way, two boys stopped him. They said, 'You got any money?' Cliff said, 'Yeah,' and showed them the 50 cents. They took it and ran.

"Cliff came back crying. But he was so alert that he was able to give me a perfect description of both boys. He and I went out in the car, and we found them. They were from another neighborhood. They had gone to a small shop and spent the 50 cents for four chicken wings. I took the wings away and scolded them. Cliff's eyes were as big as saucers.

"Now, if it had been Eric, he would have told the boys it was none of their business whether he had any money. He's not that trusting. Cliff is, but at the same time, he's sharp."

Clark's sensitivity was especially evident to Mattie a week ago, after the St. Joseph team went to Toledo Scott for a game and lost. He fouled out in that one.

When the team returned, some brainless rooters took their disappointment out on the St. Joe coach's car, smashing windows and slashing tires. That upset Cliff. Also, during the game, the Toledo players baited him. After the victory one said, "We poured milk on Corn Flakes (Kellogg) and ate them all up."

"I thought guys on an undefeated team would have more class," said young Kellogg later. His dad and Uncle Shelby and Al Kirkwood, who were at the game, sat up most of the night with him, talking it over.

Mattie waited until the next evening. "I'm the buffer," she says. "I had my private talk with Cliff. His dad is more emotional, more involved. I don't rant and rave. I just try to boost his morale, remind him there are other games and that he'll play those boys again somewhere. It's only a game, and I tell him, 'You know what you can do.'"

Adds Mattie, "Sometimes, I find it hard to believe myself that he is so good. I really don't know how he turned out to be so thoughtful and kind."

One clue is on the mantle in the Kellogg living room. In the center of dozens of young Clark's trophies is a framed, handwritten poem. On Mother's Day he wrote:

Though we may not show it, day in and day out,
Mother, you are someone we can hardly do without.

You wash our clothes and fix our meals each and every day,
And all the things you do for us are in a caring way.
You punish us when we're wrong and praise us when we're right,
And you make the sacrifices of working a job at night,
Once in a while you frown and sometimes you may whine,
But this is part of raising kids, and, Ma, you're doing fine.
For all these reasons and because we had no dough,
Mother dear, we love you and we wanted you to know.

Playing tennis to stay alive

June 25, 1981

Only the name of the husband and wife have been changed. Let's call them Bill and Sally.

Tennis is keeping Bill alive.

"If he were to stop," says Sally, "that would be the end."

I first met Bill a dozen years ago. A lithe, handsome man, he was a tennis champ, one of the finest players in the area. Best of all he was a gentleman, always a pleasure to play with and to watch.

Sally was not interested in tennis. He wanted her companionship on the court, so he cajoled her, worked with her, and eventually she began to enjoy it.

Bill's nephew, Barry Belkin, was born with a paralysis, requiring a brace on his leg. When the brace was removed, Bill took him out to the tennis courts and taught Barry the fundamentals. Through Bill's efforts, Barry's coordination improved and the limp virtually disappeared. Barry developed into a competitive player and became a tennis instructor in his free time.

Bill won many tennis tournaments. Then he seemed to drop out of sight. This week I found out why.

About seven years ago Bill's memory began to waver. During a tennis match, he would forget the score. "If we were going out," says Sally, "he would ask, 'Where?' I would tell him. A few moments later he would ask me again. His driving got bad. He didn't seem to know where to turn. I thought he was preoccupied. I accused him of not listening."

Then his checkbook became unbalanced. A builder and apartment manager, he always had been meticulous with figures. Now he was paying Higbee's bills to May Company. He paid some bills twice.

In restaurants he would leave a $10 tip where normally $1 would have been sufficient and vice versa.

"It got progressively worse," says Sally, and she feared he had had a stroke.

Five and a half years ago, when Bill was 56, the doctors finally diagnosed the problem. He had Alzheimer's Disease.

In medical circles this ailment, discovered in 1906 by Alois Alzheimer, a German neurologist, often is known as the "waste basket disease" for its symptoms are similar to several neurological disorders. Only by eliminating the others can the doctor finger it as Alzheimer's and even then the ultimate diagnosis can't be made until an autopsy reveals an entanglement of the nerve endings in the brain.

It is estimated that as many as 1.5 million American adults have Alzheimer's, an irreversible disease, cause unknown. Nor is there a known treatment or cure. Alzheimer's is terminal.

So far . . .

Sally is a fighter and loves her husband dearly. She is not giving up.

She knows one thing. The more active Bill is, the "longer he can keep going." Victims of Alzheimer's are unable to concentrate. They can't read. They have no attention span. They sleep a lot. Sometimes they appear in a stupor. Gradually their bodies deteriorate until they become susceptible to pneumonia and other ailments. They lose the ability to breathe.

But Bill remains in good physical condition. He has lasted much longer than predicted, and that he has not deteriorated physically is more than a minor miracle.

Sally credits tennis exclusively.

For a while, Bill was able to remain in his foursome. But after a few years he forgot how to serve. He no longer could play an actual game.

Then Sally and Barry took over. They began to hit balls with him. Barry even sought an evening job so he could volley with his uncle whenever the weather was nice.

I saw Barry and Bill spend an hour on the court the other day. They kept hitting back and forth, chasing balls. Barry now displays the patience his uncle once had with him. Bill looks great, runs hard, swings hard, and, if you didn't know, you would think he is a mentally alert, healthy adult taking a workout.

At first, after Bill's illness was diagnosed, Sally cried every time she heard his name. She felt helpless, trapped. Their children were married and living out of town.

Because Alzheimer's is considered a disease that requires custodial assistance, rather than nursing care, it isn't covered by medical insurance. She ran the business as long as she could and now has to work part-time as a secretary to pay the bills.

She sought others to lean on for their advice and experience. Except for the doctors, she discovered there was no organization pushing for research or seeking any form of help for victims of the disease.

She knew this was a fight against time to try to save Bill. Through Dr. Joseph Foley at University Hospital she obtained the names of others who had loved ones stricken by Alzheimer's. What began with a meeting of three people has grown into an Association, of which she is president, with offices on Warrensville Road. Now there is a nationally combined effort to help others, to push for research.

She knows that when she comes home after work Bill is comparatively bright on the days he has played tennis with Barry. On other days he is "fuzzy." During a month's vacation she was able to play tennis with Bill every day. He was more alert. He showed less regression.

Sally is certain physical activity would be a boon to anyone with Alzheimer's, just as it is with her Bill.

She wonders if there are others like Barry who would be willing to spend time with Alzheimer victims, walk, exercise, or rally with them, even play music or read to them, anything to keep them from vegetating, from fading out.

Meanwhile, research goes on in the slim hope that the cause and the cure will be discovered.

And, meanwhile, her Bill "is in a holding pattern," playing tennis every possible day.

What's behind a big leaguer?

April 4, 1982

Little did Ben Bando dream 36 years ago that when his son, Sal, began to play catch with him that it was the beginning of the wonderful world of baseball for his family.

Today Ben wears one of Sal's three World Series rings and his wife, Angela, has a World Series pin on a beautiful charm bracelet Sal gave her. Sal earned these when he was captain of the World Champion Oakland A's.

Ben and Angela followed him from his tot days, from Little League, through high school, college and the majors. They never missed a sandlot game. It's something for one son to make the majors. Now they are following their other son.

Ben and Angela Bando, married 42 years, returned to their home in Solon today after spending spring training in Tucson. Each day they sat in the stands in Hi Corbett Field, coming into the park when practice began and leaving when the exhibition game ended. They always brought a bag of fruit for their lunch. They watched all the Indians, for they know most of them personally, but mainly they watched their youngest son, Chris, 26, the team's rookie catcher.

Sometimes Angela would leave a little early to prepare dinner for Chris, his roomie Jerry Dybzinski, Von Hayes and others who might drop into the apartment the elder Bandos had rented for the spring. The dinner, of course, would be spaghetti. She brought the pasta, which she made, from home, because the stuff in the stores is too rich in starch. She must have brought bushels.

Angela always has seen to it that Chris and Sal have had good meals, which to her means "the high-protein kind" of pasta and fruit, plenty of fruit.

Sal and Chris are strong and sturdy. The stomach is one building block in making a major leaguer. Some of the others are inherited and must be nurtured. The Bando boys always had a natural competitiveness and desire to play, which their parents fostered and never turned off.

How?

"By being so understanding and supportive and never pushy," says Chris.

"My father without a doubt has been the biggest influence in my life and Sal is right behind. My mother is a special woman. You won't find another like her in this world, except my sister. It's like I had two fathers and two mothers.

"I was never short on attention and love. It was a marvelous environment in which to grow up."

Sal, who retired as an active player last season and is assistant to the general manager of the Milwaukee Brewers in addition to owning a successful investment company and a country club in that city, makes almost the identical comment. Except that since he is the eldest, he credits his parents exclusively.

Parents can learn from the Bando family example, especially Little League parents.

Ben and Angela grew up around old Central High. Their families were large, and had a total of 10 brothers and sisters, and they were very poor. Ben played softball, an infielder in fast and slow pitch. Angela, an admitted tomboy, played softball and basketball.

They met one Sunday morning coming out of St. Bridges Church, at E. 22nd St. and Scovill Ave. One of Angela's sisters had known one of Ben's brothers, setting up the introduction. They began to date and were married within the year.

They would have had a large family, too, except for the loss of four children through miscarriages. Sal was born when they had been married four years. His sister, Victoria, arrived 11 years later and Chris was born the following year.

Ben is a carpenter, working for himself mostly. He was in the Air Force when Sal was born and Angela had to give up the apartment they had rented for $20 a month to live with her parents.

When Ben got out of the service he used his carpenter skills to build a home in Shaker. Before it was finished he received an offer for it, so he built another in Warrensville Heights and that's where Sal grew up and played high school ball. Later he sold that house and built the one in Solon where the Bandos, including bachelor Chris, live. Their daughter, Victoria Ansberry, married and with two sons, lives on the next street.

Sal, the father of three boys, has a big house in Milwaukee. When the Indians open there Tuesday, Chris will stay with him.

Sal, broad shouldered and round in face, resembles his mother. Chris is a younger edition of his dad. I haven't met Victoria. All of them say she is pretty.

"We live for our children," says Angela. "What else is there in life? They have been very good to us."

Sal sends his parents a check every week. They never asked for it although Ben admits, "It helps out. It helps us make these trips."

Chris is equally thoughtful. Now that he has a major league salary he not only helps out at home, "he is sponsoring the Go team that gave him his start on the Cleveland sandlots," mentions his dad. This summer it will be called "Go Bando." Chris is delighted his parents spent the spring in Tucson. "This is the greatest time of their lives," he said. "They love it. I hope they can follow me here another 10 years."

Being self-employed allows Ben to take off every spring. The Bandos have done this ever since Sal entered Arizona State University.

There was a time both boys worked for Ben. "Let's say they were helpers," he says with a laugh. "When they played sandlot ball they worked a few hours on my jobs just to make a couple of bucks. But by 1 P.M. they were gone, playing ball somewhere." And the instant Ben was able to put away his tools he and Angela went to watch them.

"I think we saw every Little League and sandlot game Sal and Chris played," says Angela. "We spent more time in Gordon Park freezing on cold nights than we did at home."

Ben insists he never forced sports on his sons, never asked them to play. "As soon as Sal was old enough to throw a ball he'd say, 'C'mon dad, let's play catch.' I didn't teach him. I just played with him and let him do what came naturally."

"But you did one thing," Angela reminded him. "You never said no. You never said you were too tired."

Ben laughed. "But I was glad when Chris came along Sal was there to play with him. I was running out of energy."

"And you did another thing," said Angela. "You always encouraged them. You always had a kind word. You always complimented them. You never said anything about their mistakes. Sal cried when he lost. You always made him feel better."

"Well, we made a good team," said Ben. "I earned the money, you fed them and drove them to the games and we were always there when they needed us. You spent as much time in Suburban Hospital when Sal got hurt as I did at work."

Sal and Chris agree that their dad to this day has a low-key, encouraging manner and they are certain this has been important in their success.

"But don't think they weren't disciplinarians," says Chris. "They made us stay in line. I still remember when my mom washed my mouth with soap when I said a bad word."

Sal says that although he always thought his dad was laid back and just a calm spectator he learned otherwise many years later. "I came back one winter to visit the family and Chris was playing in a CYO basketball game. I sat in the stands with my dad and couldn't believe how he kept yelling at the referees. 'You weren't that way when I played,' I said. He said, 'Yes, I was.'"

Both boys always thought their mother went along just to be there, but was afraid to look, fearing they might be hurt.

"But I found out she watches everything," said Chris. "She was at one of our high school games and I was playing short. I made a high throw and she yelled 'Oh,' and fell back in her chair. A few innings later I made another high throw and she did it again."

Carefully as she watched she couldn't avoid a foul ball one afternoon in Phoenix Stadium. She and Ben were there to see Sal play for Arizona State. "She was sitting right next to our dugout and the hitter sliced a foul against her leg," remembers Sal. "It swelled up and she had a black and blue mark for six months."

Angela shrugs off the incident, something she can't do when she remembers the scares Sal and Chris gave her.

The Bandos began going to Arizona when Sal got a scholarship there, thanks to Rick Liskovec, the coach of the Go team in the Connie Mack League. Liskovec, a Clevelander, teaches math at Arizona State and he recommended him for the grant. They continued their trips when Sal went to camp there with Oakland. They always took Chris and Victoria along, enrolling the children in school in Arizona during the visit. One semester Chris was able to play high school ball there in the winter and then play for Solon in the spring.

"On one of our first trips," remembers mama, "we went sightseeing and almost lost Chris. We drove up Camelback Mountain (outside of Phoenix). We went as high as we could go with the car. That left a slight incline to the top. Chris climbed up. When he started to come down his momentum caused his little legs to go fast and he couldn't stop. He was heading right for the edge of the cliff."

"My wife jumped in front of him just in time," said Ben, picking up the frightening moment. "If he hadn't run into her he would have gone over the ledge."

Then there was the time when Sal was 14 and the doctors suspected he had cancer. He was rushed to Babies and Children's Hospital for tests. "I was in orbit that weekend," said Angela. Fortunately, the symptoms were the result of an iodine shortage and the problem never recurred.

And then there was the night at the Stadium when Sal came here with his Oakland A's to play the Indians.

"Dennis Higgins was pitching for Cleveland," Sal remembers. "He accidentally hit me in the face with a pitch. I went down. My parents were in the stands. They didn't know if I was dead or alive. I was carried into the clubhouse. My dad rushed inside while my mom waited by the door. He told her I was going to be okay, which he really didn't know at the time. Then my parents rushed me to the hospital. It turned out that nothing was broken. Just a badly swollen face."

"Let's not talk about that," said his mother. "It's a good thing he decided not to play football. He broke his collarbone twice when he was the quarterback at Warrensville High. Chris played football his first two years at Solon. Sal told him to concentrate on baseball. I'm glad he did. Coming from Sal, he listens. When I say something, he says, 'When did you become a coach.'"

"I may say it," admits Chris, "but she knows I listen. It's true I do respect everything Sal says, too. He's been there."

It was Sal that turned his young brother into a switch-hitter.

"I followed him around," Chris remembers. "I was batboy on his sandlot teams and I even made a couple of trips with him in the minors and was the batboy. He said I should try to switch hit right from the start. He said it would be easier for me to make it that way."

Even now the brothers phone each other every week. Sal does for Chris what his dad once did for him—and still does for Chris—provide constant encouragement.

"Chris thought he should have been brought right up after his good year in Triple A," mentions Sal. "I pointed out the times I had to be patient."

Sal says he knew his brother would be a big leaguer the instant he saw him behind the plate at Arizona State. That was in his junior year. Until then he had been an infielder. But when all the catchers graduated the coach asked Chris to try the position. "He had all the actions," remembers Sal. "I knew he had the determination. The way he handled himself as a catcher I felt he'd make it."

While his dad and mom gave Chris support, it was Sal who provided the motivation. "He always wrestled and kidded with me, always challenging me," says Chris. "It made me always want to beat him—in anything. I couldn't wait until I grew up to beat him in something. We would play one-on-one in basketball and we'd push each other around and neither of us would give an inch. Finally, I did beat him some.

"We play a lot of racquetball. He once said, 'If you ever beat me I'll quit.' When I was about 18 and he came to town with the A's we went to the Cleveland Athletic Club for a game. I went diving for everything. I beat him. He said, 'Aw, the court is too small.' Yeah, he still plays and I beat him once in a while.

"Sal wanted to play for the Indians. They thought his legs were too thick and refused to draft him. I think one reason the Indians drafted me is that they saw what they missed in Sal. Because of him I got something he wanted."

Sal gets a kick out of his brother's desire to surpass him. "I keep letting him know he has a long way to go," he says. Then he throws out another motivator. "To this day—he's 26 and I'm 38—I can outrun him. He won't race me. He knows better. Tell him that."

Sal was advised his brother stole two bases this spring. "The pitchers probably weren't looking," he said. "Tell him I stole 20 one year."

The needling is part of the closeness. Sal has had many baseball thrills, but the two moments that immediately come to mind are the games in which he faced his brother. The first was a spring exhibition when the Oakland A's played Arizona State. Chris was the third baseman and Sal grounded to him.

"You can't hit one past me," kidded Chris.

"Then there was the moment that had to be unique in baseball," Sal recalls. "The timing was unbelievable. It was last August, the last time I played in Cleveland, the last time I ever will play there. That day they had called up Chris. He played and I played. Finally, we were in the big leagues together. After the game, when everybody else had left, we stayed on the field and talked."

He was wrong. Not everybody had left. In the stands were Ben and Angela Bando—also savoring the moment.

Who is Lou Boudreau?

July 17, 1983

Lou Boudreau will be at the Stadium tomorrow night, brought here by the Cleveland Baseball Federation for its annual Sandlot Night.

Lou's visit commemorates the 35th anniversary of the 1948 season, when the Indians won the pennant in a playoff game against the Red Sox and then went on to win the World Series.

Prior to the Indians-White Sox game tomorrow Boudreau will receive a plaque.

Lou Boudreau . . .

If you're 40 or younger you probably never saw him play. Oh, what you missed. Many of today's teen-agers and young adults may not even know the name.

But in the 1940s he was a household name in Cleveland.

In recent years we have had few heroes in Indians' uniforms. In Boudreau's day there were many. He was the tops, No. 1, the Boy Manager. Player-manager.

Every kid in town mimicked his strange stance, resembling a question mark. He was the exceptional athlete who, despite bad ankles and lack of speed, always seemed to position himself perfectly, the flawless, graceful shortstop and the clutch hitter.

A leader by example, his performance was an inspiration to his teammates. When he hung up his glove and remained a manager some of that quality was absent and after stints as manager at Boston and Kansas City he left the field permanently.

He was clean cut, personable and more handsome than most movie stars. The whole town took to Lou. Women went ga-ga over him.

The town, in fact, once even rebelled against Bell Veeck, a hero, too, in favor of Lou. Veeck, the incomparable promoter, purchased a poorly run franchise in June, 1946, and as much as he admired Boudreau the player, he had less passion for him as a manager.

Prior to the 1948 season he wanted to trade Boudreau and bring in another manager. I was writing then for *The Cleveland News* and we concocted the Boudreau Ballot, giving the fans the opportunity to tell Veeck whether or not they wanted a new manager. They certainly told him. It was almost unanimous.

Veeck walked the streets telling the fans he would bow to their wisdom, although the suspicion remains he kept Lou because the deal he was contemplating fell through.

And Lou, being the fiery competitor he was, reached unbelievable heights that year, as if every corpuscle was seeking to show Veeck he was wrong.

Fans who were there never will forget Sunday, Aug. 8, 1948. That year the American League saw a pennant race worthy of a Hollywood script. On that Sunday, as it was through most of the season, four teams were breathing on each other. The Indians, Yankees and Philadelphia Athletics were separated by two percentage points for first place and the Red Sox were a mere 1½ games behind. As was true often that season—the Indians broke all attendance records—the Stadium approached capacity as the Indians battled the Yankees in a doubleheader.

Boudreau was out of the lineup, wrapped like a mummy, one of the few games he missed. His painful ankles were taped. He couldn't walk without a hobble. His right thumb was bandaged, too sore to hold a bat.

In the seventh inning of the first game the Yankees were leading, 6-4, but the Indians loaded the bases. Thurman Tucker, a left-handed hitter, was the next batter. In came Joe Page, the Yankees' great relief pitcher.

Out of the dugout appeared the gritty Boudreau. He limped to the plate with a bat in hand.

When the dramatic announcement came through, "Boudreau batting for Tucker," there was a moment of disbelief. Then cheers—cheers for the manager's courage. Next, the entire crowd seemed to hold its collective breath.

Lou came through, singling home two runs. The stadium rocked the way it does now during a giant fireworks display. Only longer.

The inspired Indians went on to win that game, and swept the doubleheader.

When they finally won the flag in Fenway Park in the historic first playoff game in American League history, Veeck, on his wooden leg, rushed onto the field to congratulate the manager he didn't want. After he finally got through the crowd, Lou asked him with a smile, perhaps an impish one, "Is there something you wanted to say, Bill?"

"Yes," said Bill. "Thanks. Just thanks."

Yesterday was Lou Boudreau's birthday. He turned 66.

In Chicago the present generation knows him much better than its

Cleveland peers. He is the radio voice of the Chicago Cubs. For 25 years he has been a play-by-play analyst for the Cubs on radio and TV.

He will fly to Cleveland this afternoon after broadcasting the Cubs series against the Dodgers in Los Angeles. Before the game he will be honored. Moments later he will hurry to the airport. He must be at the mike when the Cubs play in Chicago Tuesday afternoon.

I talked with Lou yesterday, via telephone to Los Angeles.

Lou wears bifocals. "To read the commercials," he said.

His arthritic ankles still pain him. So do his knees, a result of the many blows he took while turning double plays. The legs keep him from participating in Old Timers Games and also away from golf. At the recent Old Timers Game, prior to the All-Star Game in Chicago, Lou had to confine his physical activity to coaching.

"I may have surgery to remove a bone chip from my right knee," he said. "I think then I may be able to play golf."

He and his wife, Della, live outside of Chicago, in Harvey, Ill., where Lou was a high school basketball star and was recruited by the University of Illinois.

They have 10 grandchildren.

One son, Jimmy, 22, has just begun a pro baseball career, pitching for Salinas, a Cubs' farm in the California State League. "He is a relief pitcher," said Lou, adding proudly, "with a 2.50 earned run average. He pitched for Arizona State University in the College World Series."

Lou's eldest son, Lou Jr., who spent much of his youth in Cleveland, lives in Phoenix and works for an advertising company.

Lou's two daughters, Barbara and Sharon, still have strong sports ties. Barbara married a University of Illinois football player, Paul Golaszewski. They live in Frankfort, Ill. Sharon married Denny McLain, the former Cy Young winner, whose off-the-field exploits often overshadowed his exceptional pitching performances for the Detroit Tigers. They live in Florida, where McLain is in the second mortgage business.

That marriage, once rocky, is back in the groove. "Denny has squared away," said Lou. "Age has mellowed him as it has all of us."

The years of performing on radio and TV are revealed in Lou's speech. His diction is excellent, his voice vibrant. Still youthful, in fact.

"I suppose I do second guess once in a while from the booth," he said, "Well, it's not really a second guess. I try to explain the manager's options in advance, whether he might bunt, steal or hit-and-run. After he decides which I try to explain his reasoning.

"From the booth it's a lot easier to manage because you have second and third hindsight."

Much as he enjoys the broadcast booth, he'd still prefer to be on the field, "where the action is."

"The first year or two was horrible," he admitted. "I wanted to be in uniform. I still would if it were ever possible. But nobody has approached me, so I don't think it is."

If he did manage again he'd minimize the "lefthand hitter vs. righthand pitcher stuff. I've seen it overdone," he said. "Yes, I overdid it, too, when I managed."

But if he had to relive his life he wouldn't change the scenario. "I enjoyed being a playing manager. But I still have one question in my mind. Would I accept managing again at the age of 24? I enjoyed it at that time, but looking back it was quite young.

"I had only been in the majors myself for four years when I became manager in 1942 and it took me away from the guys I had been buddies with. I couldn't pal around with one or two because the others would think I was playing favorites.

"I was lucky. I had great coaches. I enjoyed their company and their input. But they were much older. Still, every time I ask myself that question—would I accept the job again at 24?—I have to answer 'yes.' It was a challenge I couldn't turn down."

Nor would he rather be playing today than when he did, even though his salary would be at least 10 times greater now.

"The players don't have as much fun," he said. "They don't enjoy the game nearly as much." Since he still travels with them, sees them on and off the field, his is an expert opinion.

"Now it's more business than baseball," he added. "The players get multi-year contracts and high salaries. They have security. It has to change the perspective of many of them. In my day, a two-year contract was a rarity.

"And now if a club wants to make a trade it needs a lawyer to examine the contract written up by the player's agent.

"Also, traveling by train helped bring the players closer. The quick plane trips take away from that. The camaraderie is gone."

That triggered Lou's memory of 1948. "No club ever had the camaraderie that one did. The makeup, the chemistry was there. There were no jealousies, no cliques.

"There were characters all right. Satchel Paige, for one. But everybody genuinely liked each other. We all were friends. At times they even called me up at 1:30 in the morning to talk baseball. Can you imagine that happening today?

"I remember almost every moment I was in Cleveland. They couldn't have been more satisfying. The city was good to me, in warm memories and friends. But 1948, with that race, that playoff game and the World Championship, how can you top that for one season?

"And for one game, the biggest, best and most important has to be that playoff in Fenway Park."

It also has to be as fine a one-man show as ever has been put on in a clutch game.

"We were tense going in," he remembers. Lou homered to give the Indians a 1-0 lead. "That relaxed us. Then Kenny Keltner hit a three-run homer and I made an important defensive play on Ted Williams to cut off a rally," he said (which reminded me, it was Boudreau who devised the highly publicized Williams shift, crowding the right side of the infield and daring him to hit to left, away from his power).

"Then I got another homer in the sixth inning." He also got two singles and walked for a perfect day as he provided leadership by example.

It was then, after the 8-3 victory, that Veeck said, "Thanks."

A few years ago a flood hit Lou's recreation room in Harvey, destroying many of his mementoes. There were so many, his entry into the Hall of Fame being the climax. The legend on the plaque he will receive from the CBF at home plate tomorrow night covers some of those highlights.

It's our town's attempt to say, "Thanks" again.

Another Cleveland baseball hero, Vic Wertz, died last week. He came here after Boudreau left and helped the Indians win their last pennant, 1954. They lost the World Series to the Giants in four games.

But the Indians would have won the first game—it's conceivable that would have changed the outcome—if Willie Mays hadn't made an unbelievable catch of Wertz' drive to the deep dead center of the Polo Grounds with runners on first and second. In any other park it would have been over the fence.

Wertz' death and the recollection of that smash brought this letter from an acquaintance who asks to be identified as "Uncle Looie."

"While millions saw the great over-the-shoulder catch Willie Mays made, only a few servicemen in the Pacific back in 1944 saw Vic Wertz hit a ball even farther.

"Vic, along with Clarence Campbell of the Indians, played on the 494th Bomb Group. The Marines on nearby Peleliu also had a team. So we hopped into a Higgens boat and went over to Peleliu to cheer our boys. I, of course, made a few wagers with the Marines.

"The Marine pitcher looked like Eddie Lopat (the Yankee pitcher who was an Indians' killer) against our squad. That is, until Vic got hold of one that seemed as though it was going to clear the island and land in the Pacific.

"While Wertz was literally walking around the bases that ball struck a coral reef and instead of bouncing around crazily, came back straight on the fly into the center fielder's glove. He threw it to the catcher who tagged Vic out just as he was about to touch home plate.

"Vic couldn't believe it. Neither could we. We all went back to Angaur, stunned and broke.

"Honestly, Hal, that ball would have cleared any park anywhere."

Perhaps, for Vic, it was the portent of things to come.

Boudreau . . . Wertz . . . May the present generation soon have honest-to-gosh Indians' heroes to remember, too.

Why did Sudden Sam go wrong?

September 18, 1983

He should be in the Hall of Fame today. He had the talent. Instead he drank himself out of baseball and into oblivion.

Does the name Sam McDowell ring a bell? Sudden Sam?

I had heard McDowell, who won 20 games for the Indians in 1970, was in town to give the keynote speech to the Ohio Association of Alcohol and Drug Abuse Counselors. I remembered a Sunday morning perhaps 15 years ago. The phone rang. It was Sam. He was in jail in a nearby suburb. Could I help?

What happened? Oh, he had been drinking and caused a disturbance the night before. I made a few phone calls.

It was far worse than he had described. The drunk had beaten up his pretty wife, his high school sweetheart. Still, the judge would be understanding if I vouched for Sam and his wife agreed to drop the charges.

I told Sam, "You blankety-blank. If I help you this time you've got to promise you'll never touch that girl again."

"I promise," he said.

He lied.

I hadn't seen Sam since he left baseball. I wanted to talk to him, ask questions. How? Why? Perhaps his answers might offer insight to those of us who see athletes today risking ruin with drink and dope.

He was wearing a sweater bearing the monogram "SS."

"Now it stands for 'Sometimes Sudden,'" he said with a pleasant laugh, personable as always when he was sober. I never saw him drunk. Only heard about it.

His six-five frame now carried 45 pounds over his 218 playing weight.

"I'm just starting to diet," he said apologetically.

Soon he will be 41. He was gone in his prime.

"When did you stop being an alcoholic?"

"I didn't," he said. "An alcoholic never stops. I was one before I took my first drink only I didn't know it. I haven't had a drink in over three years. I'm still an alcoholic."

I always thought his problem was that he thought he was too smart. Nobody in the majors could throw faster than Sudden Sam. He was overpowering and had an explosive curve. Instead, too often, he would try to outsmart them. Fool them with soft stuff. He did the hitters a favor and exasperated his manager.

"That," he said when I mentioned it, "is part of an alcoholic's personality. If you give an alcoholic, a child or an adult, a personality test it's amazing the picture always is so similar.

"I had all the traits: Show off. You're the big shot. Mr. Cool. Defiant of authority. Difficulty finishing anything. A loner.

"Drugs or alcoholism, they're both diseases of escapism. The only difference is that one is solid and the other is liquid."

There's another difference, although perhaps there shouldn't be: There isn't the same stigma on an alcohol abuser, especially an athlete. Had there been, Sam never would have remained in the majors 10 years. He would have been suspended or barred.

He was arrested eight times for drunk driving, also for assaults. Sometimes he was a comic drunk, more often a mean one. Once, during spring training in Tucson, he started a hotel fire.

"All of them were fixed in one way or the other," he said. "I was a con man. I talked my way out of them, just as I lied to you. Then your family lies to protect you. I made liars out of my wife and my parents.

"Only by the grace of God I didn't kill my wife—or get killed. I got so obnoxious in one bar I started a riot. The owner pulled a gun and cocked the trigger. I was so drunk I pulled the gun out of his hand.

"I was an ass. There is no way I should be alive today."

Sam said he got started for the same reason "kids or adults get started. I wanted to be wanted, to be accepted."

He said when he came up as a rookie in 1963 nobody associated with him "because that's how most rookies were treated then."

Then he had a good outing in Chicago and veteran pitchers Barry Latman and Gary Bell invited him to dinner. Latman ordered a premeal daiquiri and Bell a beer.

"I wanted to be like them," said Sam. "I ordered a daiquiri, then a beer."

It was like feeding honey to a bee. "They weren't alcoholics," he said. "They had no problem. I did although I didn't know it."

By 1965 he was "getting blitzed" after every game he pitched. The next day he would come to the park, work out "then get blitzed again." The following two days he wouldn't touch alcohol, conning himself into thinking he'd be sharp again when he pitched.

He had so much natural talent he initially won 17 games employing that routine. He had other good years. But not as good as they should have been. The escapades began to surface. During the 1969 season Gabe Paul asked him to see a psychiatrist. "Do it as a favor to me," Gabe put it.

"But I didn't quit then," said Sam. "I had to do it my way. After I stopped going to him I quit."

He stayed off the stuff in 1970 and won 20 games. When he won his 20th, ironically, they toasted him with champagne in the clubhouse. Even the owner, Vernon Stouffer, came down to lift a glass with him. That was all Sam needed. He was off again.

Sam never had another outstanding year. Soon the Indians traded him to San Francisco for Frank Duffy and Gaylord Perry. It is more than mere coincidence that the carefully conditioned Perry is still pitching and Sam has been long gone from the majors.

"I didn't quit baseball," said Sam. "I was thrown out."

He sold insurance, making as much as he did in his best baseball years—$70,000 annually—continuing to con himself that he had no problem. "An alcoholic truly doesn't believe it. I was the know-it-all who could solve the world's problems. How could I have any of my own?"

But by 1979, his marriage on the rocks and "the inner pain more devastating than any I had ever known," he began to admit to himself that yes, maybe, he was an alcoholic. He went into a rehabilitation center. He apparently also joined Alcoholics Anonymous but won't admit it "because it's supposed to be anonymous."

Now he attempts to help others with alcohol and drug abuse problems. He has formed his own counseling service, works with five major league baseball teams and two NFL teams.

He says most of his work is done at 2 and 3 A.M. "There is nothing more beautiful than to see a kid on the verge of suicide, then eight months later have the sparkle of life return to his eyes and laugh again."

As Sam talked I wondered, is this still a con? Am I being taken in again?

"I like to think I've changed," he said. "I choose to believe I'm honest. I suppose you think I make a lot of money out of this. Much of the work with kids is free. I have a built-in credibility with them because I'm an ex-athlete and the pay-back is seeing them come back to life.

"I make less than half what I made at insurance. I live alone in an apartment. And I don't expect anything from you. My marriage ended in divorce, although we're still good friends. Thank God our son and daughter turned out well.

"I can't deal with what might have been if I weren't an alcoholic. I'm one and am trying to deal with it and help others, if I can. That's all."

LOOKING BACK

’48 season wrapped up in one game

January 20, 1958

[*This ran in a series of articles about the 1948 Indians.*]

Quick now: Whose hit clinched the 1954 pennant for the Indians?

Everyone to whom we have posed this question replies, “Dale Mitchell.”

Wrong: The answer happens to be Jim Hegan.

The Indians were at Briggs Stadium on a rainy Saturday afternoon late in September. They needed but one game to win the pennant and, going into the seventh inning, they were trailing, 2-0.

With a runner on base, Dale Mitchell was sent up to pinch-hit against Steve Gromek. He hit a two-run homer, tying the score. Hegan then stepped to the plate and smacked the very next Gromek pitch into the left field seats. The Indians won, 3-2.

Hegan’s teammates congratulated him. But none of them had seen the historic blow, they confessed later. They had been too busy excitedly pounding the beaming Mitchell.

That’s been the story of Hegan’s life with the bat. He hasn’t made much noise with it and, when he did, everyone was looking elsewhere.

And the merest fraction robbed him of what undoubtedly would have been the biggest hit of his life—a grand slam World Series homer.

The near miss came in the opener of the ’54 Series against the Giants. The bases were filled in the eighth inning and Hegan was at bat facing Marv Grissom.

“I figured on his screwball and he threw me one just right. When I hit it, I knew it was going,” Hegan recalls. But there was a strong wind blowing in from left at the Polo Grounds. Would it be powerful enough to hold the ball back? The answer came when the ball settled into Monte Irvin’s glove in deep left.

"Monte told me later," Hegan reveals, "that the ball just missed the upper-deck overhanging scoreboard by a fraction of an inch. He never thought it would clear."

The Indians lost that opener in the 10th inning, 5-2, and the Giants went on to sweep the Series in four games. Had Hegan's blow gone all the way could it have been the spark the Indians needed?

"I don't know," says Hegan honestly. "I do know there was a letdown after we won the pennant in Detroit. After that, if you'll remember, we had a tough time in winning enough games to set our record of 111 victories.

"We just didn't play good ball after we clinched it. It was the only slump we had all season and it carried into the World Series. I've heard many people say Willie May's catch in the second game took the starch out of us, but I can't say one play did it."

The starch was already gone.

What a contrast between 1954 and 1948!

"None of us with this club in '48 ever will forget that season—and it was all wrapped up in one game," summarizes the Indians' catcher.

That one contest was the playoff game in Fenway Park between the Indians and the Red Sox—the only playoff game in the history of the American League.

"That game was the most tense, most exciting single event in my life," is the way Hegan describes it.

On the final day of the regular season, a Sunday, Hal Newhouser of the Tigers beat the Indians' Bob Feller, 7-1. On the same day, the Red Sox, who had been deadlocked for second place with the Yankees, beat the New Yorkers, 10-5.

The standings now read: 96 victories and 58 losses for both the Indians and Red Sox.

"We had a meeting right after the Tigers beat us," Hegan reveals. "Lou Boudreau (the manager) asked us who should pitch the playoff. 'It's your money,' he told us, 'so you decide.'

"He started to go around the room asking opinions but Joe Gordon spoke up. Joe said, 'You've made the choices all year, Lou. I say we should go along with whatever you say.' Everybody agreed."

Boudreau had Bob Lemon, Gene Bearden and Feller available, for the latter had pitched only three innings in the loss to Newhouser. Lemon already had won 23 and his last start had been Friday. Bearden had won his 19th Saturday.

Lemon seemed the logical choice. He had the most rest, the greatest success that season against the Red Sox and he was right-handed. Fenway Park favors right-handed pitchers.

Nevertheless, when the players turned the decision back to Boudreau, he named his southpaw. He told the squad, "All right. My choice is Bearden. Now I want this kept secret. I don't want the Red Sox or the reporters to know."

"It's lucky that I don't have any trouble sleeping any time anywhere," says Hegan. "I went to bed early on the train to Boston and I slept. I guess some of the others couldn't, but those that stayed up didn't bother me."

The next day at Fenway, Hegan recalls, "Everybody kept asking me, 'Who's pitching?' I kept answering, 'One of the three.' Thinking back I've often wondered if anything actually was gained by keeping it a secret.

"We were just as curious about the Red Sox pitcher. We thought it would be Mel Parnell. To our surprise, we heard it was going to be Denny Galehouse. When we learned that, it was the first time we began to think, 'We're gonna win this thing.' Realizing one of the Red Sox' ace pitchers wasn't going to start was the jab that built up our confidence."

Hegan discloses that the Indians heard later from some of the Red Sox players that Joe McCarthy, the Boston pilot, had made the rounds of his regular starters, asking which was ready, and when he received a negative response from all of them, he had to choose Galehouse. "He got the job by elimination," says Jim. "Besides, Galehouse did pitch great in relief against us once early in the season."

It's a matter of history that Bearden, with only one day's rest, beat the Red Sox on five hits, 8-3. Kenny Keltner hit a three-run homer, a double and a single and Boudreau sparked his men with two homers and two singles.

"As soon as the last out was made," remembers Hegan, "Keltner, Boudreau, Gordon, Eddie Robinson and I charged Bearden. We grabbed his cap, rumpled his hair and hugged him and then the guys from our dugout came out and carried Gene off the field on their shoulders. Without him, we'd never have won."

That night, there was a celebration at the Kenmore Hotel. "I spent the evening avoiding being doused by champagne. Fortunately, I was agile enough," grins Jim in recollection. To this day, Jim never has touched anything stronger than milk.

"We missed some of the fun because Clare and I were staying in

Lynn (a suburb of Boston where Jim was born), and we left early." The "fun" included a couple of champagne-inspired brawls.

"You've got to remember," says Jim in explanation, "that except for Joe Gordon, this was the first pennant for all of us. You can't blame the boys for living it up."

Two days later the World Series began at Braves' Field. Boudreau held a clubhouse meeting. He talked about the party of the night before. "You had that one coming," he said. "But from now on the training rules are in effect. We're back to business."

But the Indians still couldn't realize they were in the World Series. Hegan discloses, "The playoff game took the edge off. Until we got shellacked in the fifth game, it seemed as though we were still playing out the regular season."

Bob Feller pitched the opener and lost it, 1-0. In that one came the much-publicized, much-disputed pickoff play.

Hegan gives his catcher's eye view of it. "Phil Masi (a pinch-runner) was on second base with one out in the eighth inning. We had purposely passed Eddie Stanky and Tommy Holmes was up.

"From shortstop, Boudreau gave the signal for the pickoff, by putting his gloved hand over his knee. I squatted down and gave a sign and Feller went into his stretch. The moment Feller turned and looked directly toward me, Boudreau was able to see the back of his head and both Bob and Lou began to count to themselves, one-thousand-one, one-thousand-two, one-thousand-three. On the count of two, Boudreau was there.

"From where I sat, the ball beat Masi by plenty and Boudreau had him but Umpire Bill Stewart called him safe. He comes from Massachusetts, too, and we've talked about it since. He still claims he called it right and I still think we had Masi."

Hegan, of course, had one advantage over Stewart. He knew the play was coming. Stewart didn't.

Bob Lemon beat the Braves the next day, 4-1, and the Series came to Cleveland. Gene Bearden took the first game here, 2-0, and the next day Steve Gromek bested Johnny Sain, 2-1.

Now it was Feller's turn again—his turn to realize one of his lifetime goals: a World Series victory. But Feller didn't have it that day.

Hegan did his best for his batterymate, but fate simply refused to allow him to be a batting hero. In the fourth inning, the tribe trailed, 4-2, and Jim blasted a three-run homer. Boudreau admitted later, "I was going to take Feller out for a pinch-hitter, but Jim's homer kept him in." But not very long, for the Braves continued to rap Mr. Robert and won, 11-5, before 86,288, the biggest crowd in World Series history.

"That was the game that made us suddenly award of our situation," relates Hegan. "We were so sure we were going to win that game that none of us had packed for the trip back to Boston. I remember we were living off Lee Road at the time, and I had to send my mother-in-law home for my shaving kit. We grabbed a train at the Terminal and she met me at the East Cleveland station with my kit—and also World Series tickets for my relatives in Boston."

Hegan played a key role in the sixth—and final—game. The Indians were ahead, 4-3, going into the bottom of the ninth and the lead-off hitter worked Bearden, who had relieved Lemon, for a walk. Sibby Sisti, considered a good bunter, came in to pinch-hit for pitcher Warren Spahn.

"He tried to sacrifice," recalls Hegan, "and he popped up in front of the plate. They say all baseballs look the same but that ball was the prettiest I ever saw. I jumped up to get it, but Sisti stopped dead in front of me. I'm still convinced he was trying to block me. I managed to get around him and grab the ball."

He then threw to first to complete the double play. The next hitter, Holmes, flied to Bob Kennedy.

"When Bob caught the ball, he jumped up and down like a little boy," grins Hegan in recollection. The Indians mobbed Bearden. Again they carried him off the field.

"On the train ride home," recalls Hegan, "Larry Doby and I spent most of the time singing. Johnny Berardino got up to make a speech. His chair collapsed and he fell smack in his steak and gravy. Will Harridge (the president of the American League) came into the diner for breakfast, took one look at the mess and hurried out.

"The car was in such a shambles and so stained with champagne that the railroad officials complained. Bill Veeck told them, 'Don't worry, I'll buy you a new car.'"

At the Terminal, the team was met by such a crowd that Clare Hegan couldn't get through to her husband. "They put all the players in autos and we paraded through Cleveland," remembers Jim. "There were hundreds of thousands lined along the sidewalks.

"Clare finally made her way to 80th and Euclid. As we went by I saw her wave at me."

And then there was Satchel Paige

January 22, 1958

Bob Feller . . . Bob Lemon . . . Mike Garcia . . . Mel Harder . . . Herb Score . . . Allie Reynolds . . . Hal Newhouser . . . Gene Bearden . . . Satchel Paige . . .

Jim Hegan caught all these headliners and many, many more pitchers whose names occasionally were found in agate type at the bottom of the box scores.

One of these lesser lights remains in his memory. He was a tell skeleton of a pitcher named Russ Christopher whose courage in relief helped the Indians win the 1948 pennant.

"Christopher was dying. You didn't have to be a doctor to see it," relates Hegan today. "When he took his uniform off, you wondered what kept him alive. He was wasting away and his skin was yellow. He had a bad heart and the doctors had told him not to pitch, but he figured since he didn't have long to live, he might as well die pitching."

Every time Hegan signaled for a pitch he felt a tug at his heart. "It killed me to see him use up what little strength he had," Hegan explains. "Once he got hit on the arm by a line drive and I asked him if he wanted to test it with a few practice throws. He grinned that sweet, sad grin of his and said, 'No, Jim, I can't afford to waste any.'"

Christopher was hospitalized shortly after the '48 season. He never pitched again and he died in 1954.

Hegan caught Reynolds at the start of the "Big Chief's" career and Newhouser when "Prince Hal" was "at the end of his rope," as the Tribe catcher puts it.

"I'm glad I got to know Newhouser," continues Hegan. "When he was with the Tigers, we wanted to beat him more than we did anybody in the league. He was like an arrogant, temperamental prima donna on the mount. If somebody hit a homer off him, he'd throw his glove in the air or stomp around.

"We heard through the baseball grapevine that he wasn't too well liked by his teammates, either."

Then Newhouser joined the Indians in 1954 and Hegan found him to be "a real guy." The veteran catcher reveals, "He was a lot of fun in the clubhouse, an agitator, needling anybody and everybody, but all in fun. We enjoyed his presence.

"I think what happened to Hal is that he mellowed. I've seen it happen to others as the years go along. During Bob Feller's early years, he stayed off by himself and was all business. Maybe it was because he was shy. Later on, he became a regular fellow, one of the clubhouse comedians, and one of the most popular men on the team."

When Reynolds was with the Indians "he was a pumper," according the Hegan's description. "He was like Ray Narleski is now, the type that rears back and fires. After he went to the Yanks, he developed a slider and his curve improved."

Hegan gives the chief reason for Reynolds' success with the Yanks: "He had a better team behind him."

There were some critics who questioned Reynolds' courage when he pitched for the Indians. This doubt stemmed from an incident during a Tribe-Yankee game in 1946, when Reynolds slid hard into Joe Gordon, who was covering second base. Gordon became pugnacious and Reynolds backed off and returned to the dugout.

"Reynolds always had guts," says Hegan. "He didn't acquire it with the Yanks; players don't change inside overnight. He always had it. He was smart enough to realize if he took a punch and hurt his hand he'd be losing his bread and butter."

Because the pitches of so many greats popped into his glove, Hegan was asked to classify them:

THE FASTEST: "Feller and Score. I'm often asked to choose between them. I can't because there was a span of 10 years between the time Bob was at his fastest and Score came up. Only a pitching meter can tell. Bob's fast ball once was timed at 98.6 miles an hour. I hope someone gets around to timing Herbie.

"There is a big difference in fast balls," Hegan disclosed. "Even though Feller was faster than Lemon or Garcia, his ball was easier to catch because it was lighter. Feller, Wynn and Score throw their fast ball high. It moves up. Lemon's sinks as much as a foot sometimes and Garcia's bears in and down on a right-hand hitter. When they come down, they feel much heavier. Must be the pull of gravity. A high fast ball is a home run pitch—when the hitter can connect. That's why there were so many homers hit off Wynn."

THE BEST CURVE: "Feller's was the biggest and Harder's and Lemon's snapped the most, and anybody who tells you a curve is an optical illusion never put on a catcher's mitt."

THE BEST SLIDER: "Lemon's. It's so good that often the hitter will turn to me and say, 'Wow! That was some curve'"

Fans undoubtedly will be happy to learn that even some hitters can't distinguish between the two pitches. But there is a major difference. "A curve," explains Hegan, "is thrown with a loose wrist in order to make it snap. It has a lot of spin, and as it breaks away from the hitter, it also drops. When we were kids, we called it an 'out drop.' The slider is thrown with a stiff wrist and has very little spin. To the hitter, it looks like a fast ball, only it suddenly slides away—toward the outside corner, the pitcher hopes. But Lemon's slider not only slides, it sinks the way his fast ball does. That's what makes it so great."

MOST CONSISTENTLY GOOD PITCHER: "Early Wynn. Even when he doesn't have good stuff, he throws his pitches with so many different speeds he keeps the hitter off-stride. In all the years he was with us, he very seldom was shellacked. He had the fewest bed days. When Wynn was on the mound, we always knew we'd be in the game."

BEST TEMPERAMENT: "Feller and Lemon. They both realized they were great pitchers and would win their share of games as well as have their bad days. They could shake off a defeat quickly. Garcia has an easy-going nature, too. Score is conscientious and gets mad at himself when he does something wrong. We're fortunate here that we never had a pitcher who got mad at his teammates when they made errors behind him."

HARDEST LOSER: "That's easy, Wynn. He'll break up the clubhouse after a tough defeat. It takes him a day to get over it."

BEST CONTROL: "That's easy, too. Satchel Paige. Control is what made him so great. In spring training, he would drop a ball in the outfield, measure off 60 feet and pitch to me, using the ball he had dropped for a plate. In 50 pitches, maybe three or four wouldn't be perfect strikes."

Hegan has one big regret. "I'm sorry I didn't get to catch Satch when he was younger. He must have been blazing fast. Even when I caught him—when he was 40 or 50 or whatever age he was—he was fast. He had an easy, deceptive motion like Don Mossi's, but the ball was on top of the hitter before he realized it."

The Indians enjoyed Satch's presence, according to Hegan. "He was what we needed in '48. He made us relax by the way he acted, and he had a way of saying things that made us laugh. He had a fine sense of humor."

Hegan doubts if Satch ever did learn his name. "He always called me 'Big Catch,'" Hegan relates. "He didn't know anybody's name except Bill Veeck's, and he called him 'Beck.'

"Once I threw the ball back to Satch extra hard and he yelled 'Time' and called me over. 'Hey, Big Catch,' he said, 'you ain't the pitcher. I am.'"

Hegan recalls another incident. "You remember how Satch took his sign? He'd step on the rubber, lean way over toward me and stare at the signal with his great big eyes. This particular time I gave him a sign for a fast ball. He stared and stared and finally stepped off. Then he got back on the rubber and I signaled for a curve. He stepped off again.

"He only had two pitches even though he claimed to have a dipsy-do and other crazy ones. I went out to the mound and said, 'So what's the story, Satch. I called everything you've got.'

"'I got gas, Big Catch,' he said. Then he gave a big belch. 'I'm okay now,' he said. And he was."

"Satch constantly complained of stomach trouble," recalls Hegan. He'd say, 'I got the miseries,' and it was easy to see why.

"On one plane trip, he ate three dinners, and when the hostess asked him if he wanted another, he said, 'No. It ain't that I'm full, I'm just tired of eating.'"

Do you remember wonderful 1954?

July 18, 1965

The Old-Timers are here today . . . 1954 . . . old-timers? . . . That wasn't so long ago.

What a season, '54! . . . It was delightful traveling with the Indians that year . . . until the World Series . . . We hardly lost . . . Even when we were far behind in the ninth, somehow, in some way, we'd win . . . A Hank Majeski or a Dave Pope or a Sam Dente would come off the bench to provide the unexpected slam.

In spring training, that year, there were so many problems . . . who'd play first? for example . . . we even tried Rocky Nelson . . . Big smiling Luke Easter, the sausage man, was around, but his old legs were like the sausage he sold . . . In spring training, we were in some small town playing an exhibition against the Giants . . . The dugout was crowded . . . Luke got a chair for Manager Al Lopez so the Senor could sit outside the dugout and study the game. "How thoughtful," said Al. "Thanks." . . . With the manager out of the dugout Luke was able to sit in it—and take a nap. Luke had to do his napping elsewhere soon after that . . . Deciding he was too old, Lopez sent him back to the minors.

That spring Lopez took one look at two rookies, Ray Narleski and Don Mossi. The latter had been just fair in the minors . . . The other was a stubborn young man . . . The manager said immediately, "I've found my relief pitchers." . . . An old man named Hal Newhouser, tall and blond, and with a crooked left arm, was given a tryout . . . He made good on his final appearance . . . So Newhouser and Feller, those great rivals, finally were on the same team.

Then there was Rudy the Red Hot Rapper . . . Regalado had limited speed and only a fair glove . . . Yet how could we ignore this rookie . . . In every exhibition game he got hits and hits and hits . . . Besides he was fielding spectacularly . . . Lopez refused to go overboard on Rudy, but his spring impact helped us win the pennant, in an odd sort of way.

As I said, we were having trouble finding a first baseman—and Lopez wanted to get Rudy into the lineup. The hitting had bogged down and maybe—just maybe—Rudy might be for real . . . The manager prevailed upon Al Rosen to shift from third to first base, a move that was severely criticized . . . Rudy went to third . . . Almost immediately, in Detroit, he pulled a muscle . . . His big chance—and he pulled it . . . But while Rosen was at first a runner crashed into him, fracturing his forefinger. . . Now the Indians had nobody to play first . . . Bill Glynn played there for a while, got three homers in one game in Detroit, just missing four in a row . . . But Lopez wanted a more consistent power hitter . . . He finally gave outfielder Vic Wertz the first baseman's mitt and this move won the pennant . . . Vic, obtained from the Tigers, was a blaster that year.

Rosen went back to third and he played out the season with his index finger pointing skyward . . . He was voted onto the All-Star Game, but didn't think he'd be able to play . . . Casey Stengel, the manager, said, "You tell me." . . . Just before the game Rosen said, "Put me in." . . . Also before the game Al went up to Ted Williams and asked for some batting help to cure his slump . . . In the game Rosen was the big hitter . . . The American League won, 11-9, in one of the most exciting All-Star Games ever played . . . Bobby Avila and Larry Doby also were batting stars, although the game actually was won by a bloop by Nellie Fox . . . After the game Williams came up to Rosen and said, "Give me some batting tips."

There were other injuries . . . Avila won the batting championship despite a broken finger . . . When the team was in Washington the

Mexican Embassy threw a party for Beto . . . He was a big man in his country then and he's an even bigger one now . . . The batting championship he won in '54 added to his political credentials.

George Strickland, sliding into third, in Yankee Stadium, was hit in the face by the throw . . . His jaw was fractured, had to be wired shut . . . Poor George could take only liquids, lost weight, became weak and sat out while Sam (Win Plenty With) Dente filled in super-star fashion . . . All along Sam was saying the Indians had to win the pennant because his wife needed a mink cape . . . When the Indians won, she got it.

And back to Strickland, there remains the indelible picture of him, sprawled out and stunned just beyond third base after the throw fractured his jaw . . . Yet, half-conscious and in pain he groped blindly with his hand for the third base bag . . . "What courage!" we in the press box exclaimed . . . Revealed George later, "I was only feeling around for my teeth. A bridge was knocked out."

And in Boston one night, after a tough game, some smart guy in the Kenmore Lounge made a crack about the Indians . . . Despite his finger, Rosen challenged the loudmouth to go out in the parking lot behind the hotel . . . They went, the heckler taking along a friend . . . Rosen and his adversary took off their coats, squared off . . . Rosen decked him with one punch . . . The friend ran away.

What pitching we had that year! . . . Lemon and Wynn, 23-game winners . . . Garcia 19 . . . Mike wanted that 20th terribly . . . It meant a bonus . . . On his try for the 20th he was getting bounced . . . Lopez wanted to keep him in so he could get it . . . Hank Greenberg, the general manager, called down, "Tell Mike not to worry. He'll get the bonus regardless." . . . Feller was 13-3 . . . Art Houtteman, picked up from the Tigers, won 15 . . . and then there were Mossi and Narleski.

The big day was Sept. 12 . . . A doubleheader with the Yanks who refused to be shaken off . . . They won 103 games that year and still lost the pennant—thanks to Sept 12th . . . The Stadium held a record crowd . . . Would the Tribe choke in the clutch? . . . Not with Lemon and Wynn pitching . . . We took two, Casey barred the clubhouse, dressed rapidly and lost himself in the huge crowd that left the park . . . despite all the people, a sad and lonely figure as he walked back to the hotel . . . Probably the only day in his life he didn't want to talk.

Ironically, the desire to break the victory record could have cost us the World Series . . . To win 111 games meant the big hitters had to play, despite their ailments . . . Going into the World Series, Rosen, Doby and Wertz were heavily bandaged . . . Strickland, of course, was still in a weakened condition . . . Even so, the Indians should have won the first two games in the Polo Grounds against the Giants . . . There was one fly ball, hit by Hegan, with the bases loaded, that just missed the scoreboard in deep left center . . . another inch and it would have been a grand slam . . . Later Dusty Rhodes hit one slightly more than 250 feet down the right field line for the homer that won the game . . . and there was Wertz' blast caught by Willie Mays . . . So it went . . . but forget the sad ending . . . It was really anti-climax.

A wonderful season . . . made so by some wonderful guys . . . Welcome back Old-Timers . . . 1954 Indians . . . Welcome back 1954 All-Stars . . . Welcome back Old-Timers.

Old-Timers!

Was he really a bonehead?

July 10, 1977

If you were at the Indians' game June 29th you can tell your children's children that you saw baseball history being made.

At least I think you can.

To the best of my research never before in the majors did two teams walk off the field, go into the clubhouse assuming the game had been won and then have to be ordered back to finish the game.

A quick refresher: The Indians were playing the Orioles in the second game of a twi-night twin bill. It was the bottom of the ninth, two outs. The Indians had runners on first and third. They trailed, 3-2. Paul Dade grounded to the Birds' second baseman who bobbled the ball, then threw wild to first. The umps allowed both runners to score and the Indians raced off the field thinking they had won, 4-3.

Earl Weaver, the Orioles' manager, collared the umps as they left for their dressing room and pointed out that, by rule, the runners were allowed only two bases from where they were *at the time of the pitch,* since Dade had not yet reached first when the throw was made. This meant only one run could score, not two.

By golly, realized the umps, Weaver was right. Embarrassed, but impartial, they had to send messengers to the Indians' clubhouse to tell Manager Jeff Torborg to get his men back on the field. Weaver brought his Birds back out, too, and they won in the tenth, 5-3.

Many fans already had left the park, thinking they had seen the Indians win. Others who listened to the radio turned it off when they heard Joe Tait shout, "The Indians win." They didn't discover otherwise until the next day.

I have checked everywhere possible . . . in the record books . . . with long-time major league officials . . . with umpires who have retired. None can recall a similar incident. They can't even remember anybody talking about such a situation—where the teams were called back onto the field the same night to finish a game that appeared to have been decided.

My cousin George, whose teachers always said he knew more baseball history than American history, asked, "How about the Merkle bonehead play?"

The Merkle case was different. Unique, too. Baseball filberts remember the name and they mention "bonehead," but by now most of them have forgotten the specifics except that it involved failure to touch a base.

Perhaps no player ever received the rough treatment he did from newspapers and fans. The word "bonehead" remained with him—haunted him—the rest of his life.

Yet, he was strictly a victim of an unusual set of circumstances. A thorough review reveals the rap was undeserved.

Fred Merkle, a native of Toledo, Ohio, was only 19 when he wrote his name indelibly into the "goat" book of baseball. He was a teenage member of John McGraw's great New York Giants' team of 1908.

On the afternoon of September 8th they were playing their chief rivals for the National League flag, the Chicago Cubs. Over 22,000 fans jammed the old Polo Grounds stands and flowed onto the field.

The plate umpire that day was Hank O'Dea, an old pitcher who had begun his umpiring career in the National League back in the 1880s, when only one umpire worked a game. O'Dea was tough. He had survived numerous battles and had earned the respect of the players. His partner that afternoon, on the bases, was Bob Emslie.

Going into the bottom of the ninth the score was 1-1. Merkle came up with two outs and Moose McCormick on first. He sent a long single to left, sending McCormick to third. Merkle said later he was confident he could have made it into a double, but with two outs and a runner on third, he didn't want to risk it. If he had, the Merkle "bonehead" play never would have occurred.

The next hitter, Al Bridewell, singled over second base. McCormick scored with the apparent winning run. Merkle ran halfway to second, turned around and broke for the clubhouse as the jubilant fans began to swarm toward the infield.

Stupid? A bonehead?

Not at all. This had been the custom. In the many thousands of games up to that day, players routinely ran off the field on such plays. They didn't bother to tag the next base once the winning run was in. It was understood the game was won. Get off before the crowd came on.

Unhappily for Merkle, Johnny Evers was playing second base for the Cubs. (You've heard of him, the middle man in the celebrated Tinker to Evers to Chance double play combination.) Evers was a stickler for the rules.

He called for the ball. It came in toward second and Joe Tinker got it. The Giants' first base coach, Joe McGinnity, the famous "Iron Man" pitcher, saw what was about to happen. He ran to second, wrestled with Tinker for the ball and threw it into the stands. Evers shouted to his bench for another ball, and someone threw him one. He stepped on second and insisted that Merkle be called out.

Emslie said he wasn't watching Merkle. He didn't see him fail to touch second. But O'Dea had seen it all and he told Emslie what had happened.

At this point it is necessary to go back three weeks. O'Dea had been umpiring a game between the Cubs and Pittsburgh. The situation was identical, bottom of the ninth, runners on first and third, two outs. Warren Gill, who was on first, did exactly what Merkle was to do three weeks later. On the game-winning single he ran off the field. Evers, the rules stickler, screamed that the book insisted the next base had to be touched.

The umpire ignored him. Evers continued to shout. The umpire majestically walked off the field. Guess who the ump was? Hank O'Dea.

That night O'Dea took out his rules book and went over and over it. By the book Evers was right. There were no loopholes. O'Dea decided that if the play ever came up again the next base would have to be tagged . . . or else.

Merkle became the victim of the "or else." If the umpire hadn't been O'Dea, if the second baseman hadn't been Evers, Fred Merkle would not have had to go through life with the "bonehead" tag.

O'Dea told Emslie that Merkle hadn't touched second and therefore should be called out. Emslie did so. O'Dea then nullified the winning run. The score remained 1-1.

In his report written that night to National League president Harry C. Pulliam, O'Dea described exactly what occurred and added, "The People ran on the Field. I did not ask to have the Field cleared as it was too dark to continue play."

The Giants protested the decision. They wanted a 2-1 victory, claiming the appeal wasn't legitimate. The Cubs protested, too. They wanted a victory by forfeit, arguing that the Giants were responsible for crowd control and should have continued the game.

A meeting of the board of directors of the National League was called.

Sample testimony:

MR. EBBETS (a director): "Why did you declare Merkle out?

MR. EMSLIE: "Because he failed to touch second base and the ball was there and McGinnity was there and interfered with it, that is why."

The directors, after a lengthy consultation, ruled the game a tie. Because of that tie the Giants and Cubs *both* finished the season deadlocked for first place. A playoff became necessary. The Cubs won, 4-2.

Had the Giants won, the Merkle play would have been quickly forgotten, an interesting anecdote and nothing more.

But to the city of New York, with its huge population and many papers and writers, it became a catastrophe. They didn't let up on poor Merkle. Short stories were written about the play. One yarn had McGraw bringing Merkle back to the Polo Grounds in the dead of night to touch second so that at the hearing he honestly could say, "I did touch it."

Seven years after the play Haywood Broun interviewed Merkle and asked him, "Do you get any fun out of baseball?"

Merkle replied, "No, I wouldn't call it fun. I have too rough a time out there. The worst thing is I can't do things other players do without attracting attention. Little slips that would be excused in other players are burned into me by the crowds."

Despite the goat horns he managed to survive in the majors for 18 years, revealing his ability and character.

But even long after he retired the name Merkle brought a snicker. "Oh you're the guy . . . " they would say to him.

Fred Merkle, many years later, became a part-time scout and birddog for the Indians, working out of his home in Daytona Beach. He saw a big kid in Lacoochee, Florida and recommended him to the Indians. He was the scout who signed Jim (Mudcat) Grant.

Mudcat remembers, "He said to me, 'I don't know if I should recommend you or not. My name could work against you. I'm supposed to be a bonehead, you know.'

"I said, 'What do you mean?'

"He said, 'Nothing.'"

Merkle never told him the story.

"He was anything but a bonehead," said Grant. "He was one of the nicest men I ever met. He always was at my side, ready to help me."

Merkle died in 1956, just before Grant made it to the majors.

"I understood he was supposed to get a bonus if the Indians called me up," Mudcat recalled. "I went to Frank Lane (the Indians' general manager) and asked him to give it to his wife. I understood the Indians did."

"Merkle deserved to get something out of baseball. He sure gave it a lot."

Including his name.

Nice guys finish last?

August 9, 1977

It was a gray day, but it didn't dare rain on the parade of three of the finest gentlemen ever to put on baseball uniforms.

It was their day . . . the greatest day of their lives, they said—Al Lopez, Joe Sewell and Ernie Banks—as they entered the hallowed Hall of Fame.

Commissioner Bowie Kuhn may have been exaggerating slightly but not much in his introductory remarks when he said, "This is the greatest day we have in baseball, better than the World Series and the All-Star Game."

For Sewell, Lopez and Banks it was—they said so, emotionally and humbly. And the sun did come out to greet them, to chase away the rain and shine upon three of the nicest guys ever put on this earth. If there were a Hall of Fame for niceness alone, these three would be charter members. Who said nice guys finish last?

Before they received their plaques, three others were honored posthumously—Martin Dihigo and John Henry (Pop) Lloyd of the Negro Leagues and Amos Rusie, the National League Pitching Star of the late 1800s.

Then little Joey Sewell, once 5-6 and now shrunk to about 5-4, but at age 78 more spry than many youngsters, said it for the three who were there to be honored.

"It's nice to be here—in person," Sewell told the huge crowd that overflowed the well-kept grounds behind the Hall of Fame building. "I'm thankful you selected me while I have the faculties to enjoy everything, to be able to move around and see the scenery."

Move around? Joe spent more time signing autographs and talking to fans than anyone we've ever seen here in Cooperstown.

At 78 he still works every day for a dairy in Tuscaloosa, Ala.

Thirty-two of his relatives were in the crowd, including his brother Luke, a fine catcher who joined the Indians after Joe did and who now lives in Akron.

In Joe's backyard at home, Luke told us, there's a huge oak tree and each time Joe has a grandchild, he carves the name of the new baby on it. The list now has grown to 13.

Joe didn't tell the crowd about his first year in the majors. It was 1920. He had been a shortstop that spring for the University of Alabama, which won the college championship. The Indians signed him for their New Orleans Pelicans farm team and he helped them win the championship. Late in the Indians' season, shortstop Ray Chapman was hit on the head by a pitched ball. The blow killed him. Sewell, the young shortstop, was rushed to Cleveland. Nervous and frightened at first, he soon settled down and helped the Indians win the pennant and World Series.

That made three titles in a row for young Sewell, that memorable year of 1920—the most memorable to him prior to 1977.

His teammate, Bill Wamby, the second baseman on that world championship team, came here from Cleveland to see Joey honored. Wamby, who made the only unassisted triple play in World Series history, said, "The guys kidded Joey. They said I made the triple play alone because I didn't dare throw the ball to him. They told Joey I was afraid he'd drop it." Wamby, 85 himself, quickly added, "Of course that's a joke. Joey was a good fielder."

But as a hitter, one who rarely struck out, Sewell gained his greatest fame. In each of two seasons he struck out only four times, a record that probably never will be broken. As Commissioner Kuhn said, "That's as often as some hitters strike out in one day."

"I still can hit a bottle cap with a broomstick," Sewell told us, adding proudly, "I only wear glasses now for reading the small type."

He fanned only 114 times in over 7,000 times at bat and batted .312 during his lifetime. In 1923, for the Indians, he hit .353 and knocked in 109 runs, a prodigious feat for a giant, let alone a player as tiny as Sewell.

In a glass case in the Hall of Fame is his contract, showing he made only $6,000 for that achievement.

"Now," he told us, "it probably would be worth a couple of hundred thousand dollars."

Perhaps that's why, in his acceptance speech Monday, he thought it necessary to say, "I would like to see the greed, selfishness and hate that seems to exist today eliminated from the game.

"It's been a great game. I hope we can keep it that way."

Lopez, the most successful manager in the entire history of both the Cleveland Indians and the Chicago White Sox, had written a speech, but he became too emotional to deliver the prepared text.

His voice broke. The tremors of emotion were difficult for him to control at first and in typical Lopez fashion he asked his family, his former coaches and his friends to stand up and share the tribute to him.

He noted that he played for only six managers in his long major league career—one which saw him break the mark for catching the most games. He named the managers: Wilbert Robinson, Casey Stengel, Max Carey, Bill McKechnie, Frankie Frisch and Lou Boudreau.

"All of them," he noted, "are in the Hall of Fame today. I had great teachers."

Lopez mainly wanted a message taken back to the fans in Indianapolis—his first minor league managerial job—Cleveland and Chicago, the three cities where he piloted teams. To the writers from those cities he said from the podium, "Thank them for being so nice to me."

Then he thanked everybody "for the proudest and happiest moment of my life," his voice cracking with deep emotion to the end.

The big hero Monday, the main man, the one most of the crowd came to see was Ernie Banks. Bus-loads and plane-loads of fans came from Chicago to pay tribute to "Mr. Cub" . . . the power hitter who retired just five years ago.

(Stan Musial, who came here for the ceremonies, revealed he was bumped from his plane reservation by Banks' followers.)

And if Sewell and Lopez are nice guys, Banks is the epitome of the label. Rarely has anyone ever seen him angry.

When he was notified of the election into the Hall of Fame—he is only the eighth to make it the first time he became eligible—he called Eddie Matthews, whom he beat out for the honor, and told him how sorry he was that Eddie didn't make it, too.

Banks is known in Chicago as "Mr. Sunshine" because of his ideal temperament, and the sun did come out as he stepped to the microphone.

He said, "We have sunshine, fresh air and we have a team behind us."

His arms swept across the Hall of Famers who had been inducted in previous years and were seated on the platform behind him. "Let's play two," said the 45-year old Ernie, who loved to play the game so much he looked forward to doubleheaders while other players griped.

His remarks were similar to Lopez's. He thanked everybody, especially the late Philip K. Wrigley, who owned the Cubs. "My career and honor belong to him."

Ernie still works for the Cubs, heading their group sales program in an exceptional manner.

It was an exciting show for the many thousands of visitors—and a sad one. Also on the platform, in wheelchairs, were Red Ruffing, who made the difficult journey here from his home in Beachwood; Cal Hubbard, the only man to be in both the Football and Baseball Halls and now suffering from dizzy spells and emphysema; Richard Marquard, the old pitcher; and Roy Campanella, paralyzed by an auto accident.

It was sad to see these Hall of Famers, these former physical giants, now so terribly confined. Hubbard and Marquard struggled to rise when their names were called. Ruffing and Campy merely waved. But all four brought back memories of their greatness.

Perhaps Bowie Kuhn was right—perhaps the Hall of Fame induction is baseball's greatest day.

You had to be there to feel the drama of it, to be touched by it. Try to make it next year.

"This is my first visit to Cooperstown," Joe Sewell said at the conclusion of his speech. "I'll be back."

Their moment of glory

August 21, 1977

You go to Cooperstown to see the Baseball Hall of Fame induction ceremonies and you leave with pictures that linger in the mind.

Coming out of a sneak preview of a movie the other night a man said, "I saw you at Cooperstown."

"Was it worth the trip? Was it better than this movie?" I asked.

"I'll never forget it," he said, "It was everything I dreamed it would be."

Cooperstown itself is a quaint, peaceful town of 2,500. The Hall of Fame Museum is the main attraction, although there are two other museums in the town where James Fenimore Cooper, the writer of those famous stories of the pioneers and Indians in that beautiful Mohawk Valley country, was born.

The Hall of Fame has memorabilia to stir every baseball fan, old and young. Even a non-fan becomes impressed during a tour of the building. And no one can walk through the marble area where the busts of the enshrined players are on display, along with the respective records of their feats, without gaining a feeling of awe.

The induction ceremonies, too, are indeed impressive.

Yet, what you remember most at this very minute are the lingering images of the old-timers, the baseball immortals who already had been voted into the Hall of Fame and who came back to sit on the platform during last week's ceremony.

Many of them come back every year for this return to glory and it is sad to see how mortal they are.

They gather each year during the first week in August to see some of their old baseball pals, to bat around stories about the game they played so well. But they go there each year mostly to be remembered.

They begin to arrive Saturday night, 36 hours before the induction, and they are put up at the Otesaga Hotel. The hotel resembles an old southern mansion and its veranda faces the clear blue Otesaga River. There are rocking chairs on the veranda and you can look at the peaceful river as you rock and rock and relax in your reveries.

The hotel is a summer vacation spot for old folks mostly and the Hall of Famers often are mistaken for the guests, and vice versa. A doddering man with silvery white hair constantly was besieged for autographs. He was just a visitor, anxious to obtain autographs himself.

The autograph seekers . . . don't knock them. You walk into the Otesaga and you wish you had a baseball, or a program or just a piece of paper and a pencil for the signatures of these men whose busts you had admired in the Hall of Fame building.

You, who said you'd never ask for an autograph, soon find yourself crowding around these old heroes . . . making their day and yours.

There's Freddie Lindstrom, somebody says. You remember picking him for your team when you were a kid and played the spin-baseball game. Lindstrom, who made the New York Giants as a kid, himself.

"You were 19 when you joined the Giants, weren't you, Fred?"

"No, 18," responds the old third baseman who batted a lifetime .313.

"How old are you now?"

"Seventy-one."

"You look marvelous."

"Thanks," he says, as he signs your card.

As you walk away, a friend says, "You know, Fred now wears a pacemaker."

A very old man comes up and recognizes you. "Hello, Hal."

You look blank, make some embarrassed small talk trying to hide your ignorance and walk away.

"Who was that?" you ask Al Lopez, who is there to be inducted into the Hall.

"Fred Lieb."

My God. Fred Lieb. He's 91 and he remembered you. You hadn't seen this exceptional writer in 20 years. He had written dozens of books on baseball and for years had been a top writer for baseball's bible, *The Sporting News*. His latest book just arrived in your office last week, *Baseball, As I Have Known It*, and it has been acclaimed by reviewers. At 91.

He, along with Damon Runyon, Grantland Rice, Ring Lardner and other great sportswriters already are in the Hall of Fame, in a special section for baseball scribes. Fred should be in there twice. The second time when, if ever, he retires.

You rush up to him. "I didn't recognize you, Fred. Sorry."

"I didn't think you did," he said. "I'm getting older. You're not." Sweet man.

There's Joey Sewell. You recognize him. He hasn't changed. He, along with Lopez and Ernie Banks, are the 1977 inductees. He looks the same as he did when he was a batting coach for the Indians in spring training. Seventy-eight, he says he is. Spry. Still works at a dairy in Tuscaloosa, Alabama, every day.

"Hey, you're from Cleveland," he says. He calls over to his wife and daughters, "Here's a fellow from Cleveland.

"Great city," he shouts for everyone to hear. "Cleveland was great to me."

Cal Hubbard's son and wife wheel the old umpire across the room, toward the elevator. This former giant of a man who is the only one ever to be inducted into both the baseball and football Halls of Fame, appears pathetically shrunken as he sits in his wheel chair.

"I'll get out of this thing," says the old umpire, always the fighter. "I keep getting dizzy. Must be my ears. I'm gonna see a doctor." He has emphysema, along with other physical problems and nearly died after recent surgery.

Pauline Ruffing wheels her husband, Red, through the lobby. She drove him here from Beachwood, Ohio. Red, too, was once a giant of a man. She handles him with love and care and strength and she stops the wheelchair so he can sign the baseballs thrust at him and enjoy the recognition. Red has had a couple of strokes and can't move without his Pauline.

Two others are in wheelchairs . . . Roy Campanella, paralyzed years ago in an auto accident but never without a smile . . . and Rube Marquard, born in Cleveland back in 1889. In 1912 he won 19 straight games for the Giants, a record that still remains. Both Campy and Rube sign happily, the adulation momentarily making them forget their incapacity.

Three Pinkerton detectives swoop in. They ask some of the autograph hounds to leave. You learn that those told to exit came in with boxes of baseballs and were in the business of getting the signatures for future sales. There's a boom in baseball memorabilia, you're advised, and a baseball with the signatures of Hall of Famers commands a big price.

Jocko Conlan, the old bantam-rooster umpire from the National League sees you and gives the "safe" sign as his hello. (He repeated the gesture when introduced to the crowd at the Hall of Fame ceremonies.)

"I don't go in for this appeal stuff on the half-swing," he says, referring to the new baseball rule which permits a catcher to appeal to a base umpire when a "ball" is called on a checked swing.

"When they used to yell 'Half swing' at me," Jocko says, "I'd say, 'Okay, I'll call a half-swing on you this inning and another half-swing on you next time you come to bat.'"

Jocko, who had several highly publicized run-ins with Leo Durocher, including a famous shin-kicking affair, still can't stand Leo. "No good," he says at the mention of his name.

"Are you reading the sports books that come out now?" he asks. "The filthy language. Awful. That language belonged in the clubhouse, not in books for kids to read."

Jocko now uses a hearing aid. "Wish I had it while I was umpiring," he says with an impish grin. "I could have turned it off."

In a corner is another old-timer with a hearing aid. Stanley Coveleski, who pitched the Indians to the pennant in 1920 and who won three World Series games for Cleveland that year.

"I'm from Cleveland. I talked to you on the phone a few years ago," you say by way of introduction.

"You want to talk?" he asks eagerly. Most of the old-timers, many who were reticent with reporters in their baseball days, appear anxious to talk now. A smart author, Don Honig, takes advantage of this. He sits next to Coveleski and turns on his tape recorder. Honig is getting taped interviews with all the old-timers here. They'll be in his next book.

"How old are you now, Stan?"

"Eighty-seven," he says. "I still drive my own car. I go fishing every day." He lives in South Bend, Indiana, and when he goes fishing he sits there and nobody knows him. Here he is Stan Coveleski, Hall of Famer, and he is enjoying each moment as he sits in a corner chair and signs his name.

He appears to be chewing tobacco.

"Yep," he says, "I've been chewing since I was 12. Never stopped. Put in a chew in the morning and keep at it all day. It's kept me alive."

You keep watching him. Never once do you see him spit. Not once the whole afternoon.

Luke Appling saunters by, still a spring in his step. He is now a batting coach for the Atlanta farm teams. Somebody asks him about his remarkable ability to foul off pitches until he got the one he wanted.

"Someone told me," he says proudly, "they had to order two dozen balls a day just for me. In those days the clubs got the baseballs for nothing from the manufacturer. Now they have to pay. If I was still playing they'd probably cut me 'cause I would be costing the team too much."

Burleigh Grimes, the old spitballer, is telling some of his pals, "This game has been good to us. It's time we started putting back into the game what we got out of it." (Later that day he put his words into action by going into the Hall of Fame museum and signing autographs for the thousands who went through the building.)

Another old-timer says, "Hello."

This time you don't fake it. "Could you tell me your name?"

"Lloyd Waner." The famous "Little Poison" of the Pittsburgh Pirates. His brother, Paul Waner, "Big Poison," died some years ago.

"My goodness, Lloyd Waner." Another name from those days when you played spin-baseball with the kids in the neighborhood. "How old are you? What are you doing now?"

"Seventy-two. I don't do much anymore. Just a little gardening. My feet bother me. The legs aren't so good. I left 20 years of them on the ball field."

And what memories he left there. And Coveleski and Hubbard and Lindstrom and Lopez and Grimes and Sewell and Ruffing and Campanella and Conlan . . . and all of them.

---

21 years ago today

May 7, 1978

A story clickety-clacked over the Associated wire that caused the memories to come tumbling back. Pictures returned of a frightening moment and the aftermath . . . the days of anguish that followed.

The Associated Press in New York had asked Til Ferdenzi, an old friend, to do a flashback piece. Til is now manager of sports publicity for the National Broadcasting Company. Before that, for 11 years, he had been the baseball writer for the *New York Journal American*.

On May 7, 1957, exactly 21 years ago today, he was in Cleveland. The Yankees, the team he was covering, were here to play a night game against the Indians.

That was the night a wicked line drive off the bat of Gil McDougald hit Herb Score on the right side of his face, flush against the bones surrounding his right eye. He went down instantly. Blood gushed from his eye and nose.

Until he moved slightly, all of us—fans, players, writers—feared the worst. Was this brilliant young pitcher dead?

Til's story gives his recollections of that near tragic night from his position as a New York writer. He covered Gil McDougald.

I didn't get to see Gil until the next day. I was covering the Indians. More than covering the story that night, I became personally involved.

Perhaps a writer shouldn't. But with Herb it was impossible for me to remain detached. I had seen him from the day he first reported to the Indians for a workout. He was so open, so wholesome, so friendly, so nice and so talented. Herb was of Hall of Fame stature in all respects.

In his first major league season he won 16 games and was named rookie of the year. He followed that by becoming Sophomore of the Year and winning 20. A dozen strikeouts a game were common. At that time the Number One magazine in the nation was *The Saturday Evening Post*. During Herb's second season the editor called me.

Would I be willing to "try" to do a comprehensive profile on Herb for the *Post*? It would be strictly a gamble on my part. If the story wasn't accepted I wouldn't be paid.

Not one cent.

The editor mentioned the assignment previously had been given to three others. I knew that and it frightened me. I had seen them interview Herb, follow him around, one after the other. All of them were nationally known. All of them had signed contracts. All of them had been paid. Yet, the *Post* found none of their manuscripts acceptable. Would I care to try after these three outstanding magazine writers had failed?

I had worked for other magazines. But never before on speculation. Sure pay or no work.

"Let me talk with Herb," I told the editor. "I'll need his cooperation."

"Take it," said Herb. I did.

There was no deadline. Digging for background and anecdotes I got to know Herb's mother and his two sisters and the Brooklyn priest who was his closest friend. At times I virtually lived with Herb.

On May 7, 1957, the *Saturday Evening Post,* containing the Herb Score story, hit the newsstands.

There's an old wives' tale about major magazine pieces being a jinx for an athlete. They get on the cover of a big one and coincidentally something negative happens to them. That night, 15 minutes before gametime, I saw Herb at the Stadium. He was warming up. He paused long enough to yell over, "Good story, Hal."

Twenty minutes later he was in an ambulance, sirens piercing the night, on his way to University Hospital. I followed him.

McDougald was the second Yankee batter. We were still filling out our scorebooks when it happened. The line drive came back so rapidly to the pitcher that he couldn't have seen the ball until it was upon him.

The white blur hit him in the eye and bounced off with such force to third baseman Al Smith that McDougald was an easy out at first base. He would have been an easy out even if he hadn't hesitated briefly when he saw the ball crash into the pitcher.

I was supposed to be covering the game. The hell with the game. From that moment it was forgotten. The stretcher was brought out. Herb was carried off. The noted eye doctor, Dr. Charles I. Thomas, who had written the textbook on ophthalmology and who was a great baseball fan, hurried to University Hospital to examine Herb.

The only bulletin was, "He won't know how much damage there has been to Herb's eye for some time."

Will he see again?

"We don't know yet."

His hospital room was kept completely dark and he wasn't allowed to move. He would have to remain in the dark and immobile for many days. At Herb's request I got to see him for a moment. His eye was covered. His face was swollen. He was a mess.

"Please call my mother," he mumbled. "Tell her not to worry. Tell her I'm in good hands. Tell her everything's going to be all right."

Mrs. Score lived in Lake Worth, Florida. She had raised her three children alone. Her husband had left the family many years before.

The call finally was put through. What words do you use? How can you say it? Somehow you do.

Her anguished reaction remains unforgettable. I think of his mother's words often when I look at Herb.

"Oh, those beautiful baby-blue eyes," she said.

Meanwhile Til Ferdenzi sat in the Stadium press box getting the "no news" bulletins on Score and wondering about the effect of it all on

McDougald. That, he decided, was the human interest story for New York readers.

As I knew Score, Ferdenzi knew McDougald. Like Herb, Gil was class, pure class. As Til describes it perfectly, the accident "was like Sir Lancelot felling Sir Lancelot."

Til, too, decided to ignore the game. He went down to the Yankees' clubhouse, hoping McDougald might come in. Although the rules permit no reporters during the game, Til chanced the wrath of Manager Casey Stengel. He went into the clubhouse. It was empty. He sat down on a stool in a far corner and waited. The clubhouse attendant saw him, apparently assumed he was a Yankee official, said hello and Til nodded back.

Here's Til's recollection: " . . . Finally the game ended and Casey was first through the door. 'No writers in here until we get McDougald out,' Casey snapped at the clubhouse man.

"A stream of Yankees followed. It was not a happy crowd of ball players. They seemed to look straight through me as I sat on the stool, trying to make myself as inconspicuous as possible.

"McDougald entered the room alongside his close friend, Hank Bauer. The infielder sobbed as he came into the privacy of the clubhouse.

"'I'll quit this game if he loses his eye,' McDougald moaned. 'The hell with it. I'm not playing anymore.'

"Stengel, determined to snap McDougald out of his misery, shouted. 'You'll play or I'll fine your butt off.' When that had sunk in, Casey added a postscript. 'You've got a family to support. You'll play . . . '

"McDougald was completely out of control now. Bauer tried to comfort him, but McDougald shrugged him off. 'It doesn't help to say it was just one of those things,' he said to Bauer. 'I know it was an accident. It looked to me like the poor guy couldn't get his glove up in time.'

"Bauer urged his friend to get dressed so they could leave the clubhouse before the writers pounded the door down. I did not approach McDougald. It did not seem like the right time."

I saw McDougald the next day. He, Hank Bauer and Yogi Berra came to University Hospital to see Score. They couldn't get into his room, but Herb was told they were there.

McDougald told me of a phone call he had received. It was from Herb's mother. In all her misery she had thought about Gil.

"She called me at the hotel this morning," he said. "She told me she was sure Herb would be all right. She said any batter could have caused it. She'll never know what a comfort she was. I'm still shook, but she really helped. She said the Lord will take care of both of us."

The Lord has. Although Herb never pitched effectively again, his eyesight eventually became almost completely normal. He doesn't blame the injury for ruining his career. When he tried to pitch again, his stride was different and he injured his arm.

Yet, never once has he complained. His faith and understanding are such he never complains about anything. He is happily married, the announcer for the Indians' games.

McDougald, who pulled himself together after the incident to help the Yankees win several pennants, is now the highly successful owner of a maintenance company in Nutley, New Jersey.

Today, Herb and Gil will be miles apart, but inevitably their thoughts will be zeroing in on the exact day 21 years ago. Happily, the pain is gone for both. Those beautiful baby-blue eyes turned out fine.

What goes into a streak?

July 30, 1978

There is such a difference between Pete Rose, now on a hitting streak, and Joe DiMaggio. Their personalities . . . Joe rarely said much as a player. He speaks more now in one Mr. Coffee commercial then he did in a full week to the New York writers. Not that he was antagonistic or unfriendly. Joe simply was shy and quiet. For writers, Rose is a delight. Friendly and outgoing, he is easy to approach, always ready to talk. Jinxes don't bother him. He tells you he's good. He tells you he'll hit.

Rose is 37. DiMaggio was 26 when he hit successfully in 56 straight games. That was in 1941, the year Rose was born.

In playing style the contrast matches their personalities. Always immaculate and smooth, DiMaggio made each play seem effortless. Rose dirties his uniform quickly with headlong slides, resembles a dead-end kid and plays like one, appearing to do everything the hard way.

Their hitting styles, too, are Fred Astaire vs. John Travolta. Complete opposites. Rose crouches. He is a singles hitter, the Reds' leadoff man. DiMaggio stood straight up and open and had power. He batted fourth, cleanup. Rose bunts often. DiMaggio never did.

But in one aspect of their batting, the sameness is undeniable. DiMaggio stared at the pitcher, never took his eye off the ball. The same with Rose. Watch him. Once in the batter's box, the intensity never leaves him for an instant. The ultimate in concentration, both.

In common, too, is the response to pressure. As with the greatest athletes, in the heat their adrenalin flows, throttle wide open.

The pressure on DiMaggio as he got his base hits day after day, wiping away the former consecutive game hitting records, was no different from the pressure on Pete Rose today. True, there was no TV in DiMaggio's time when he inched his way upward and past Willie Keeler's mark of 44. But the radios and the newspapers made as much of it as we are making of Rose's feat today. Perhaps even more. When the all-time mark is 44—as it was when DiMaggio was chasing it—and you make it, it's a much bigger deal than when you hit 37, 38, 39 and 40 if the all-time high is 56.

Radio stations would interrupt their programs to announce what Joe had done that day. And cool and unperturbed though he seemed outwardly DiMaggio, now 63, admits the pressure grew as he wiped away the marks.

In that streak of 56 games—which meant he hit safely in every game for more than one-third of the season—he got 91 hits, batted .408, hit 15 homers, four triples and 16 doubles. He knocked in 55 runs and scored 56 times himself. And he fanned but seven times, a remarkable low for a power hitter.

Before the streak began the Yanks, an outstanding team, played .500 ball. During his streak, they played at a .759 clip. DiMaggio carried them day after day after day.

In his brilliant career Joe played a total of 1,736 games for the Yankees. He says he has a poor memory. He says 37 years ago is too far back to remember. But he does remember. How could he forget? "Of all the games I played for the Yankees," he says, "I remember best the night my streak was stopped."

It was stopped right here, at Cleveland's Stadium, July 17, 1941.

The streak began on May 15. The day before, against the Indians, Mel Harder had stopped DiMaggio cold in his three at-bats. Between those two hitless days against the Indians he did what no batter in baseball may do again. It started with a single in four tries against Edgar Smith of the White Sox. The next day he got two against Thornton Lee.

By June 10th his string had reached 25, against such greats as Bob Feller, Schoolboy Rowe, Harder—the next time he faced Mel—Dizzy Trout, Hal Newhouser and Lefty Grove.

"The pressure started to build around then," recalls Joe. "I drank an awful lot of coffee." He didn't intend it as a commercial. He always drank plenty of it.

During the streak his favorite bat, a Louisville Slugger, Model D-29 (36 ounces, 36 inches), marked with an indelible green pencil, disappeared. Joe was distraught. Tommy Henrich used the identical model. He offered it to DiMaggio. After a thorough search of the clubhouse failed to produce DiMaggio's bat, he took it and kept his streak alive. But it wasn't his bat.

Next day he got another, one with his name on it, sandpapered the handle to his comfort and with the replacement he passed Hornsby's 33. Now, not only was he nervous, he actually became deeply interested in the streak himself. The challenge . . . There were so many intangibles. It seemed almost impossible. The pitchers . . . so careful . . . the knuckleballers . . .

"It was like trying to climb the highest mountain," he said. "I wanted to see how far I could go."

Except for his favorite bat, Joe wasn't superstitious. But he continued to wear tape on a jammed thumb long after it healed. He wore it throughout the streak.

He was looking for his 37th against Bob Muncrief and the St. Louis Browns. Muncrief stopped Joe easily in his first three at-bats. Muncrief could walk him and it would be all over. Muncrief pitched carefully, very carefully, but the pitches were not purposely awful. DiMaggio singled and kept the streak alive.

"I couldn't walk him," said Muncrief later. "It wouldn't be fair to him or to me. The challenge was there for both of us. He's the greatest I've ever seen."

Two days later DiMaggio again was hitless going into the ninth. He was the fourth man up. Would he get his last chance? A leadoff single by Red Rolfe meant he was still alive. To save him an opportunity, Tommy Henrich asked Manager Joe McCarthy if he could sacrifice bunt to kill off a possible double play. McCarthy said, "Go ahead." Henrich sacrificed successfully. The next batter made an out. Two outs, runner on second, first base open. The strategy cried for a walk to DiMaggio.

Browns manager Luke Sevell decided otherwise. He couldn't stop DiMaggio's streak that way. He told his pitcher, Eldon Auker, not to pass him purposely, but not to give him anything good to hit. DiMaggio doubled.

There was another game against the Philadelphia A's. "McCarthy was very good at trying to help me," recalls Joe. "Johnny Babich was pitching for the A's. He was tough for us. He beat us three times in 1940 and cost us the pennant.

"My first time up he threw three pitches as wide as the catcher could reach. I looked for the hit sign from McCarthy and he gave it to me but the next pitch was even wider.

"I smelled what was happening." Not all pitchers were like Muncrief.

"The next time he went to 3-0 again but the fourth pitch wasn't as far out as he wanted. It was high and away, nowhere near a strike, but I reached for it and slammed it right between his legs for a hit. He went down on his tail and when he got up he looked white as a ghost."

The crowds grew as the streak grew. On June 27, against the A's, Joe made it 40 straight games and interest in world events—war was everywhere—seemed momentarily suspended.

More than 31,000 fans crowded into compact, sweltering Griffith Stadium on June 29 for a Yankee double-header against the Senators. The opening game pitcher was Dutch Leonard, a tough knuckleballer. DiMaggio led off the second inning. The crowd became completely silent. He hit the ball sharply. A fly ball to Doc Cramer in center.

He came up again in the fourth inning. Leonard threw three knucklers that were bad, all balls. The crowd booed each one. Again McCarthy gave Joe the hit sign. The dancing knuckler dipped low. Joe lofted it for an out.

On his third at-bat, Leonard got him to one-and-one and tried a fast ball. The Senators' catcher, Jake Early, said afterward, "I thought the ball was in my glove. I don't know how he hit it."

The ball sailed deep to left center. George Case, fleet as a rabbit, gave chase. Would he catch it? He barely touched the ball and it rolled to the 422-foot sign at the bleacher wall for a double. Joe had tied Sisler, who then said all the same things Tommy Holmes did the other day when Rose equaled his National League mark.

Between games, again his bat—the replacement he had honed and had treated with olive oil and rosin and then burned the mixture to make it sticky—"I had slippery hands," says Joe—disappeared. The bat he had sandpapered to fit comfortably in his hands had been taken from the bat rack. He had to find another. Again Henrich offered him the bat he was using. Joe preferred another, not wishing to break Henrich's.

The first time up he lined out and said, "If it had been my bat it would have been a hit." Next time, another line-out. When he got back to the dugout Henrich begged him, "Try my bat."

"It feels good," said Joe, but he didn't use it and flied out.

In the seventh inning he came up for the fourth time. He said to Henrich, "Okay, give me your stick."

Senators' pitcher Arnold Anderson pitched him so tight on the first pitch Joe almost fell as he leaned back. "He's set up for an off-speed pitch, outside," thought the pitcher.

He thought wrong. Joe swung Henrich's bat and the ball whistled off it for a clean hit to left. He had broken Sisler's record. As the crowd cheered wildly his teammates rushed out of the dugout and joyfully mobbed him.

"That's what I remember best about that moment," says DiMaggio.

He stayed with Henrich's bat.

For a while DiMaggio thought there was only one mark to beat, Sisler's. But some historian discovered that 44 years earlier, before the modern records, Willie Keeler who "hit 'em where they ain't," had run up a string of 44.

On July 1, the fans jammed into Yankee Stadium for a doubleheader against the Red Sox. Even Mayor Fiorello LaGuardia was there. They groaned as he made easy outs in his first two at-bats.

In the fifth he hit a slow bounder toward third. DiMaggio slipped as he started to run. Red Sox third baseman Jim Tabor fielded the ball cleanly, saw he had a play on DiMaggio and threw to first. The throw was wild. What would the official scorer call? Dan Daniel of the *New York World Telegram* had to make a decision. The Yankees came out of the dugout and looked toward the press box.

Daniel hesitated, then raised his arm. A hit. He said later, "I made the call as I saw it because Tabor was lucky to make the play at all. It was a tricky grounder and a hard chance and he had to hurry."

Still, it was a tainted hit, the only one of the string. DiMaggio got Daniel off the hook with a clean single in his next at-bat. He was still chasing Keeler without argument. He needed but one hit in the nightcap to catch him.

There was a question as to whether the second game would be played. Rain clouds had gathered. Joe ended his part in the drama quickly with a single in the first inning. Now the question was: Could five innings be played? The rain played its role in the DiMaggio scenario with perfect timing. It threatened constantly but held off until the fifth inning was completed. With the Yanks ahead, 9-2, a storm descended on Yankee Stadium. The hit was official. Keeler's mark had been equaled.

The next day it was the same Red Sox again and another banner, buzzing crowd. Joe no longer was tense. He had tied the record and the accomplishment took off the pressure. Now he wanted the record for himself exclusively. He was bearing down, but relaxed.

Heber Newsome was pitching for the Red Sox. Joe drove Stan Spence deep to left field for an out. Next time he blasted a certain hit to left center. But the outfield is deep there and the center fielder made an unbelievable stab to rob him of the mark.

The center fielder's name was Dominic DiMaggio, his brother.

No one could rob him the next time. He ripped a home run into the left field seats. He had the record.

A writer noted, "It was the first time we saw a grin on Joe's face during the entire streak. Up to then he had been dead pan."

After the 45th it was a piece of cake for Joe. He wasn't chasing anybody and the hits arrived like the sun . . . day after day after day . . . And with his precious bat, the one that had disappeared.

The day after Joe set the record he received a phone call. It was from Newark, N.J. "I know where your bat is," said the man. "One of the guys pulled it from the bat rack in Washington and took it home for a souvenir. He just wanted to brag that he had your bat."

Joe, trying to control himself, said he wanted it back. The caller said it would be returned if there would be no trouble. "The guy loves you, Joe," he said.

"No trouble," promised Joe. "Just get it back."

The next day, the Fourth of July, it was in the clubhouse when he arrived. Joe tested it. It felt good. He used it from then on . . . 45 . . . 46 . . . 50 . . . 51 . . . 55 . . .

On July 16th the Yankees came to Cleveland Stadium. As always the crowds were big. They were there to urge him on, but wanted to be on hand at the historic moment when Joe would be stopped. That day he got two hits off Al Milnar and one off Joe Karkauskas. He was at 56.

The next night 67,467 were in the Stadium to watch DiMaggio.

Normally, DiMaggio and his roommate Lefty Gomez walked to the Stadium from the Hotel Cleveland. This time, because they were surrounded by kids as they came out, they decided to jump into a nearby taxi. William Kaval, who is now 67 and lives in Parma, was the driver. He recognized DiMaggio instantly. "I never liked the Yankees, Joe, but I like you," he said.

As they reached the Stadium Kaval told him, "Joe, I hope you keep the streak going for 100 games, but I feel you're not going to get a hit tonight. I hope you do, but I don't think you will."

"Well, if I don't, I don't," said Joe as he paid the driver.

After they were out of the cab, the angry Gomez, who felt the taxi driver had jinxed Joe, asked, "How much did you give him?"

"Fifty cents," said Joe. The meter had registered only 20 cents for that short ride.

"You gave the so-and-so a tip after he put the hex on you?" shouted Gomez in disbelief.

Gomez told the story often, making the cab driver the villain.

Several years later, Kaval asked *The Plain Dealer's* Russell Schneider to try to get an autographed ball from DiMaggio. Joe gave it to him.

The Indians pitched Al Smith that night.

"I can remember like it was yesterday," says DiMaggio, "the way Ken Keltner played me at third base, half way to left field and right on the line. I remember, too, it had rained the night before and the ground was soft."

Keltner, who lives in Milwaukee, also remembers, "Joe was the greatest player of my era," he says. "But he never bunted so I never played him close. Sure I played him near the foul line. I'd rather have him hit a single in the hole than a double down the line."

On Joe's first at-bat Keltner stole a hit from him with a remarkable back-handed stab. In the fourth, Joe walked. In the seventh he hit another shot down the line. Hard. It would have handcuffed some third basemen. Keltner made a fine grab and threw him out.

In the eight inning the Yanks, ahead 2-1, loaded the bases, with one out. Jim Bagby Jr. replaced Smith.

Bagby, 62, and now a tool designer at the Lockheed plant near Atlanta, Ga., remembers the hot night.

"I can't recall my exact feelings," he says, "but I know I felt no pressure or nervousness. I certainly wasn't going to lay it in and let him hit it. He'd have to earn it. We were trying to win a game."

He threw three fast balls, only one a strike. On the fourth pitch, a low fast ball, DiMaggio bounced toward Lou Boudreau at short.

"It really wasn't that easy," said Bagby. "Just before the ball got to Lou, it hit something and took a weird bounce." Boudreau reacted quickly, raced into the hole and threw to second to start a double play.

"It wasn't the pitching," admits Bagby, "that stopped Joe. In essence, it took three outstanding fielding plays. In looking back, I'd have to say Keltner deserves the most credit."

"If everyone says they were great plays," says Keltner with a laugh, "well, I'm willing to go along with everybody. But I had no special feeling about stopping Joe. I felt bad because we lost, 4-3. I went in the clubhouse, took a shower and picked up my wife. On the way to the parking lot we suddenly had a police escort. We hopped in the car and away we went.

"The next day I asked the cops why they were there. They said some wild DiMaggio fans were waiting to get me."

Would he have been able to field those balls if the game had been played on the artificial turf now so common in Pete Rose's National League?

"Good question," said Keltner. "No one will ever know."

DiMaggio, as always, remained in the clubhouse long after the game was over. "I felt a little downhearted," he recalls. "Strangely enough, I wanted to keep it going. But I quickly got over it."

The next day he started a new streak. He hit safely in the next 16 games.

* * *

Yankee fans presented Joe with gifts and his teammates bought him a silver cigarette humidor. "But don't buy it at one of your usual wholesale spots," said the wife of pitcher Johnny Murphy.

They bought it at Tiffany's, with a special engraving of Joe swinging a bat. He cherishes it to this day.

He didn't get a bonus from the Yankees for filling the ballpark so often and helping the Yanks win the pennant and World Series. He did expect a raise in 1942.

Instead he was told, "There's a war on. We'll have to cut you $2,500."

They finally offered him his same salary, $37,500. Joe rejected it. Eventually he got a $5,000 raise.

Think what Pete Rose will be making next year. That's another difference between the two. But then you can't get a taxi ride for 20 cents today.

A treasure in the trash

Sunday, January 14, 1979

It was clean-up time in the office. The old boxes, filled with yellowed papers and magazines, had to be thrown away. You thumbed through several. They had little value. Into the wastepaper basket they went, piles upon piles.

One sheet caught your eye. Perhaps it was the silhouette of an Indian in full war bonnet that did it. That glance saved a unique baseball document from the rubbish heap. It proved to be a vital page out of one of the most dramatic chapters in the entire history of baseball. It was the original letter signed by the Indians in 1940, the year of the Cleveland Cry Babies.

On official Cleveland Baseball Company stationery, address League Park, Alva Bradley, president-treasurer; C. C. Slapnicka, vice president; Frank Kohlbecker, business manager; and Oscar Vitt, manager, was handwritten the following:

"We the undersigned publicly declare to withdraw all statements referring to the resignation of Oscar Vitt.

"We feel this action is for the betterment of the Cleveland Baseball Club."

Underneath, 21 of the 25 players on the roster signed their names:

Russ Peters, Joe Dobson, Mike Naymick, Frank Pytlak, Mel Harder, John (better known as Johnny) Allen, Lou Boudreau, Al Smith, John Humphries, Ken Keltner, Bill Zuber, Harry Eisenstat, Sam Hale, Al Milnar, Ben Chapman, Rollie Hemsley, Beau Bell, Ray Mack, Clarence Campbell, Jr., Bob Feller and Hal Trosky.

The others on that unforgettable ill-fated team were Jeff Heath, Ben Chapman, Oscar Grimes and Roy Weatherly. They weren't in the clubhouse when the sheet was passed around after the game on June 16, 1940. Weatherly and Chapman had left early; Heath and Grimes were out with injuries.

The letter was given to *The Plain Dealer* that night. It was reproduced on the sports page the next morning. The retraction was too little and too late. The damage already had been done . . . three days before.

A full book, rather than chapter, could be written about that season. It was the year the Indians lost the pennant by one game and those who played in it, to this day, wonder if the outcome might not have been different if: (a) they had been able to dispose of Oscar Vitt as manager and (b) if they hadn't rebelled against him in the first place.

No one will ever know, for their uprising against the manager was unsuccessful.

Space doesn't permit a full recounting of that season. The memories remain with anyone, fan or player, who lived through it and they came flooding back as those signatures on that handwritten document were reviewed.

Vitt was a talker. The players said he made nasty cracks about them behind their backs and the words eventually found their ears. Once, for example, Bob Feller, who had pitched a no-hitter to open that season and who was perhaps the best pitcher in the league, was being hit hard in Boston and Vitt turned to the players on the bench and was reported to have said, "There's my star out there. How can I win the pennant with him?"

The players thought they could win without Vitt. The disenchantment had begun late in 1939 and carried over into the next season. They were convinced they had the best club in the league, except for the talkative manager.

The discontent grew through May and by early June the veterans were holding secret meetings, plotting ways to have Vitt replaced. Many of the usually calm and level-headed players were in agreement with the more outspoken ones, such as Hemsley, that something had to be done.

In Boston, Hal Trosky confided to Frank Gibbons, baseball writer for *The Cleveland Press*, that the players were considering a meeting with Alva Bradley, the club president, to ask for Vitt's dismissal. Gibbons advised patience, killing the opportunity for a scoop, in the best interest of Cleveland baseball.

On the train back from Boston, the players caucused secretly again and decided immediate action, not patience, was the answer. Because Mel Harder was so low-key, level-headed and highly regarded by the front office, he was asked to serve as spokesman. He agreed, readily.

Harder called Bradley on the morning of June 13. Bradley said his door always was open. Within an hour 12 designated players were in his office on West 3rd St., near St. Clair.

Trosky, one of the ringleaders, wanted to be with the group, but upon arriving in Cleveland he learned of his mother's death and immediately took off for Iowa. He phoned from the airport to tell Bradley, "I'm with the players 100 percent."

They presented Bradley with a petition signed by all the players except four. Roy Weatherly, always the individualist, was totally against it. The veterans refused to get Lou Boudreau and Ray Mack involved. They were considered too young, having come up late in 1938. Harry Eisenstat was in the hospital.

Bradley took the petition, asked questions, told the players he would study the matter. "Keep it quiet, meanwhile," he said. "If it gets out you'll be ridiculed everywhere."

But the secret couldn't be kept. Trosky would have told Gibbons, as he had promised, if he had remained in town. And someone leaked the full story to sports editor Gordon Cobbledick of *The Plain Dealer*. To this day, no one knows which players did it.

Cobby confronted Bradley with his information. The president couldn't deny it. On June 14, *The Plain Dealer* splashed the story. On the same day Paris fell to the Germans. Even so, the "Vitt Rebellion" got the full treatment, an eight-column Page One headline.

Bradley made a decision. The players would not run his club. Vitt remained. Fans cheered him and booed the players.

It was then that Bradley tried to take the heat off the incident by getting the players to sign the retraction, the precious document that almost went into the trash barrel.

Fans scoffed at the contrived retraction, especially those in other cities. Wherever the Indians went they were called "cry babies." Signs greeted them at all ball parks.

The treatment was especially harsh in Detroit, whose Tigers were fighting the Indians for first place. Detroit fans greeted the Indians at the train station with baby carriages. The players were pelted with fruit and eggs. Fans would string baby bottles and dangle them from the railings at the ball park.

And the race itself went down to the final week. The Tigers came to the Stadium for the showdown. Bob Feller started for the Indians. The Tigers countered with an unknown, Floyd Geibell, deciding to save their ace, Schoolboy Rowe, for the next day, since they needed only one more victory.

Cleveland fans, angered over the treatment the Indians had received in Detroit, came prepared to retaliate. They flung garbage at Hank Greenberg, playing left field, as he went after a fly ball. One fan in the upper deck dropped a basket of fruit on the Tigers' bullpen, hitting catcher Birdie Tebbetts squarely on the head. He had to be helped to the dugout.

The umpires threatened the crowd with a forfeit and the game continued. Feller gave up only three hits—and lost, 2-0. A two-run homer by Rudy York just made it past the fair pole into the left field stands. The pressing Indians got six hits, but never with men in scoring positions.

They finished second. Vitt was fired at the end of the season.

Three men who signed the retraction document still live in Cleveland—Milnar, Feller and Eisenstat. Milnar is 65 now, retired one year from his job as a security guard at Fisher Body. The left-hander, who grew up on Cleveland's sandlots and is now a grandfather six times, says he went along with the rebellion reluctantly. "I had my best years under Vitt," said Milnar "My feelings were good toward him. I was young. I felt the same as Roy Weatherly did. But I went along with the other fellows—the team—while he didn't.

"They called me up on the phone about the meeting in Bradley's office and I went. Sure I remember about the cry baby stuff. How could anybody forget?

"All of us were sorry about it afterward, in a way. I remember signing that letter you found."

Bob Feller, now 60 and in the Hall of Fame, was at the Justice Center, in Judge McAllister's court, when he was shown the paper. (He was suing for damages a man who claimed the ex-pitcher had stolen his plane. Final arguments go before the jury on Tuesday.)

Feller welcomed a brief respite from the trial to talk about that season, although his mind remained on the court proceedings.

"Yes, I remember signing that," he said. "It was Alva Bradley's idea. But it didn't work. Vitt's trouble was that he talked too much. It's everybody's trouble, I guess. The man is dead and I don't want to say any more."

He turned to his wife and his attorneys to tell them about the baby carriages that greeted the team and other incidents. It gave them a few needed laughs before returning to trial.

Eisenstat, 63, is now a vice president for Curtiss Industries, handling their national accounts. Last year he underwent double bypass heart surgery and has made an excellent recovery. The former left-hander had joined the Indians the previous season, in a trade with the Tigers for Earl Averill.

"I was very much against the revolt against Vitt," he said. "It's not that I favored the way he handled the players because he did talk out of both sides of his mouth. It simply was that I wasn't in favor of striking out against a manager.

"But I didn't have much to say in the matter because I was in the hospital at the time. I was involved in a collision while covering first base and broke a blood vessel.

"The guys kept filling me in by phone, Hemsley, Trosky, Johnny Allen, Jeff Heath and the others, and I tried to get them to cool it. I was in favor of sitting down with Vitt and talking things over, but I had little influence. Now, after my experience in industry, I know I was right.

"I was strongly in favor of signing the statement you found, but the damage already had been done. I know the whole thing hurt our concentration. I don't know if it lost the pennant for us, but it certainly didn't help. It put us all on edge.

"I'll give you an example, which is pretty funny now. My roommate was Bill Zuber. We were in Detroit, on the 20th floor of the Book-Cadillac Hotel. I got up in the middle of the night to go to the bathroom. I heard Bill talking in his sleep, something like, 'Oh, my arm.'

"His own voice must have woke him up. He saw the window wide open. He looked in my bed and didn't see me. He began to yell, 'Eisie, Eisie,' and ran for the window. He thought I had taken the big leap.

"I ran out of the bathroom and saw him rushing to the window and I yelled, 'Bill, don't jump. It's not worth it.'"

The document that brought back all the memories was placed in safe-keeping. Had other priceless pieces of memorabilia already been tossed in the wastebasket?

Every item was dumped out and examined carefully.

By sheer luck the only valuable one had been salvaged.

Remember the glad/sad season?

April 22, 1979

This is the 25th anniversary of the Indians' team that set an American League record, 111 victories. It's a record the Red Sox thought they were going to beat last season but fell woefully short of—among other things, like the pennant.

It would be a natural to have the '54 team back at the Stadium for a reunion, but none is scheduled. Maybe for their 30th anniversary?

It was a year of marvelous memories, of stars and substitutes coming through, of late rallies for victories, of hardly any losses and of the dismal World Series against the New York Giants, who swept the Indians away in four games.

We saw four of the heroes of that remarkable season during our recent spring training trip to Florida. And we asked each of them to share their recollections.

Three are now with the Yankees: Bob Lemon, their manager; Jim Hegan, their coach who was Lemon's catcher and roommate with the Indians; and Al Rosen, the Yankees' president.

Jim Hegan: "All I can think of is the World Series. Isn't that awful? After winning 111 games you can't remember anything but those four defeats.

"Every time I see Monte Irvin he calls me 'Almost Hero.' He reminds me about the time I came up in the second game, at the Polo Grounds, with the bases loaded and I hit a high fly to left. You remember the distance was short there and the scoreboard stuck out.

"Monte was playing left field and he says he was sure the ball would hit the board for an automatic homer. He says he stood under the board waiting for it to hit. It missed by so little, according to him, you couldn't see any light between the ball and the board. That would have meant four runs. We lost, 3-1.

"I wish I could remember something nice, but I can't. Just that miserable Series."

Bob Lemon: "Why did you have to ruin my day? I still can see Dusty Rhodes' homer in that first game of the World Series. (It came in the 10th inning to end the game. Lemon was the pitcher. Rhodes was up as a pinch hitter.) I still can picture the ball just making it into the stands. (The distance was exactly 260 feet from home plate. It's illegal now for foul lines to be that short.) We left 13 men on base in that game.

"About the rest of the season? Well, it was a lot like our Yankees of last year after we got going. When key men got hurt, like Al Rosen and Bobby Avila, other guys would come like Hank Majeski and Sam Dente, and do the job. It was a team effort. Everybody contributed.

"And then came Rhodes' homer . . . "

Al Rosen: "It was an odd season for me. I'll never forget the day I broke my finger. It was in June. We were playing in Chicago. Jim Rivera was the hitter and Ferris Fain was on first base.

"I had been moved from third base to first to make room for Rudy Regalado. You remember the great spring Rudy had, and Al (Manager Al Lopez) wanted to get him into the lineup, hoping he was still hot.

"Rivera hit the ball toward first and Fain blocked my vision. I didn't see it. The ball hit my right index finger. And that was the beginning of my baseball demise.

"I kept on playing for several days even though it hurt. When it failed to get better, a friend took me to the hospital while we were in Philadelphia. X-rays showed the break. The playing while it was broken had made it worse.

"It couldn't happen today, not with all the medical advice the clubs now have. There's a doctor at every home game. We take every precaution.

"I had a fabulous All-Star game not long afterward, one of those unexplainable days, but I never was the same hitter after that injury and it's the reason I decided to call it a career a few years later. I couldn't stand being mediocre.

"Still, for that one season, my broken finger proved a break for all of us. We had just obtained Vic Wertz from the Orioles. He had been an outfielder, but after I got hurt Lopez put him on first and he was sensational. He hit about 15 homers in half a season. I went back to third when I was able to. (With his painful finger Rosen managed to knock in 102 runs and hit .300, a fine year for most, but disappointing to him; the season before, he had knocked in 145 runs and batted .336.)

"It was a tremendous feeling, playing with a bunch of guys who came through day after day. We became very close. But for me the major memories are of the broken finger and that catch by Willie Mays in that first game of the World Series.

"As I recollect it was the eighth inning and the score was 2-2. Larry Doby and I both got on base to open the inning and the Giants replaced Sal Maglie with Don Liddle. He was a left-hander and Durocher (Giants' manager Leo Durocher) wanted him to face Wertz. You remember what Vic did. He hit it so far to dead center that Larry was almost home and I was nearly at third when Willie Mays caught the ball.

"I couldn't believe it. He caught it with his back to the plate at least 460 feet away. He was so far out after the catch he couldn't double us and you know how quickly he could get rid of the ball. Imagine! A 460-foot blast and we couldn't score. That would have been the ball game.

"Isn't it funny about that season? The memories should have been super, 111 victories, a dream record. But for me, the finger and the Series took off the shine."

Two nights later we had dinner with Al Lopez at his favorite spot, the Spanish Park Restaurant, in Tampa. He had just finished playing in a Celebrity Golf tournament with other former ball players and assorted athletes. In Tampa Al is the Numero Uno celebrity. The main ball park, where the Cincinnati Reds train each spring, is called "Al Lopez Field."

The 1954 season?

Twenty-five years later, he, too, had only one vivid recollection, the World Series.

"Such a disappointment," he said, "After what we had done during the year. If we had opened the Series in Cleveland we would have won it. Wertz's ball would have been way out—all the way to the bleachers. And Rhodes' ball would have been an easy out. As a matter of fact, he wouldn't even have come to bat.

"But what's the use of talking about ifs? We lost in four straight and it was a blow that's hard to erase.

"What got me more than anything is the way Durocher acted afterward. When we lost that fourth game on a Saturday, a lot of the writers came into my office at the Stadium. We talked a little while and then I asked to be excused. I wanted to go over to the Giants' dressing room to congratulate them and Leo. One of the New York writers said it was too late. He said the team had a charter plane, and they were going to celebrate in New York. He said they already had taken off.

"So I didn't go over there. Instead I asked Spud Goldstein, our traveling secretary, to send Leo and Horace Stoneham, the Giants' owner, telegrams of congratulation from me.

"I don't know if he got the message. But all that winter Leo kept telling the New York writers what a bad guy I was for not coming in after that last game.

"During the winter meetings in New York, Dick Young, the columnist for the *Daily News*, asked me about it and I told him what happened.

"He said, 'Leo's making you look like a heel. How come you didn't come in to congratulate him?' I told Dick what happened. He said, 'Would you pose for a picture with Leo now?' I said, 'Sure, anytime.'

"We started to go over to the hotel room where Leo was staying and then Dick said, 'Oh, the hell with it. Leo doesn't deserve the courtesy, not after the way he's been talking."

And that's what has remained in the minds of Hegan, Lemon, Rosen and Lopez about a glory year with an unhappy ending, the glad-sad season of 1954.

Lopez, in fact, wanted to change the subject, to talk about other men and other times, and quickly it became story time in that restaurant in Tampa.

"How's Herb Score doing?" he asked. "I'll never forget the first time we saw him. Hank Greenberg had invited him to the Stadium, Herb was just out of high school, or still a senior.

"Birdie Tebbetts, one of our catchers, was warming Herb up when I came out to say hello. I asked him if he was ready. He signaled to Tebbetts that he was going to cut loose.

"Tebbetts shouted, 'What? You mean you haven't thrown hard yet? I thought I was catching bullets.' Birdie yelled over to Joe Tipton (another Indians' catcher). He said, 'Joe, its time for me to hit. You catch this kid.'

"Herb's first pitch almost hit Tipton between the eyes. The next one hit him on his big toe. We had to call on Jim Hegan to take over.

"What a pitcher Herb would have been if he hadn't got hurt. He was the fastest I ever saw. He had a great curve. Everything. Too bad that his career was cut short by that line drive to his eye (off Gil McDougald's bat in 1957). I think he tried to come back too soon after the injury and the medication he was taking was a factor. His arm never was the same."

Lopez had just seen Ralph Kiner, the ex-Pirates' slugger now in the Hall of Fame, in the golf tournament.

"Kiner told me a funny story," said Lopez. "He said the year he hit 51 homers and knocked in 127 runs he asked for a raise. He had been getting $35,000. Instead, Branch Rickey, the Pirates' general manager, sent him a contract calling for a cut.

"Ralph went to see Ricky and said, 'Didn't you make a mistake? You know I led the league in homers.'

"You know what Rickey told him? 'No it wasn't a mistake. We finished seventh with you. We can finish seventh without you.'"

Which brought the conversation to present-day salaries and how much a Kiner would be worth. Probably a half million, it was agreed. And how about a Ted Williams?

"About a million a year," thought Lopez.

He laughed. "I met Ted at a party several years ago," Lopez said. "He said, 'Al, something has been bothering me for a long time. People tell me that you say I hurt more hitters than I helped.'

"I was sort of embarrassed, but I told him, 'Yes, that's what I believe.'

"'Why?' he asked.

"'Because you'd take two strikes and wait for your pitch. The other guys would copy you and they'd take a third strike and they'd come back to the bench saying, 'It wasn't my pitch.' Some of those guys need four and five strikes.

"Ted didn't know what to say. I saw him again after he became manager of the Washington Senators. He came up and said, 'Al, you know, you were right.'

Now back to 1954, Al . . .

"Did I ever tall you about the time I played for Casey Stengel . . . "

A home run into the bleachers?

February 9, 1982

Like the first robin, a harbinger of spring is this question:

"Did anyone ever hit a home run into the center field bleachers at the Stadium?"

No matter how often we reply, "No. Never, never, never, never," the question annually rears its disbelieving head.

Just when we hoped we had the fans educated, lo and behold, fellow staffer Dwayne Cheeks, writing about the Cleveland Buckeyes, quoted a former player, Willie Grace, as saying the legendary black slugger Josh Gibson did it. Grace told Cheeks, "The most impressive home run I ever saw him hit came at Cleveland Stadium, sometime between 1942 and 1945. He smashed the ball into the center field bleachers. It didn't bounce in there. The home run reached there on the fly . . . a good 500 feet from home plate."

W-e-l-l-l, as Jack Benny used to say. You can imagine the letters and phone calls from readers after they saw that item. "What do you have to say now, smart guy?" was among the nicest comments directed this way.

Here is why I say again: Nobody, but nobody, not even Josh Gibson, has hit a home run on the fly into the bleachers. It never happened. Never, never, never.

Willie Grace, like so many of us in our dotage, is imagining something that didn't occur. I was familiar with the Buckeyes and the players who performed in the Negro Leagues during those unfortunate years before the color line was lifted by professional baseball. But rather than trust my memory or the files, I went to the man whose family has seen every game played at the Stadium, amateur and pro, from the day it opened in 1932 to the present.

The Bossards, the only groundskeepers the Stadium ever has had, have watched every pitch. The grounds crew must be on the field during the game, ready for every emergency.

Says Harold Bossard, 70, "I was at every Buckeyes' game. Wilbur Hayes, owner of the team, would slip me an extra $10 to get things ready the way he wanted. Gibson hit several tremendous home runs at League Park. The longest I recall was one that traveled more than 450 feet into the bleachers in left center. It was a wallop. Maybe Mr. Grace has League Park confused with the Stadium.

"Josh played just a few games at the Stadium and he never hit one into the bleachers. Nobody ever did it. No way.

"But Josh could hit. I remember a game at League Park. The Buckeyes were leading 1-0 and Josh was up. A woman in the stands kept shouting to the pitcher, 'Be careful. Be careful.'

Josh hit the next pitch over the wall in right center, a wallop. The woman yelled, 'I told you to be careful!' Everybody roared, including Josh. I'll never forget that."

Nor will Harold ever forget the time he played against Josh. The groundskeeper in his youth was a minor-league shortstop and Josh's team came barnstorming through the Dakotas. "They played us one day," recalls Harold. "He hit a line drive that came at me so fast I barely saw it. Couldn't get my glove up in time. It hit me on the chest and knocked me down. I had the bruise on my chest for months."

There is little question Gibson, a fine catcher as well as a powerful hitter, would have been a superlative major leaguer. Josh was a contemporary of Satchel Paige's. Paige considers him the greatest hitter ever.

All the evidence I have been able to gather indicates that Satch was just approaching 40 when Bill Veeck signed him to pitch for the Indians in 1948. Satch and Veeck went along with the stories that he was in his 50s or 60s because they made the remarkable pitcher an even greater gate attraction. The only time Satch would deny the Methuselah stories was when they limited his attraction to the opposite sex.

Satch lived up to all his clippings during that wild and wonderful 1948, when the Indians set attendance records and won the World Series. Without Satch's contribution they could not have done it.

Gibson, a few years younger than Satch, came upon poor health and died the year before his old batterymate finally was admitted to the majors. It's a shame they and other fine black ballplayers of their era were denied all those years of glory.

The true testimony to the brilliance of Josh and Satch is that in spite of all the handicaps, the lack of opportunity and publicity, they still managed to make an indelible imprint on the pages of baseball history. Who knows what unforgettable home runs Josh might have hit in the majors?

Nevertheless, in the few games he did play in the Stadium he never hit one into the center field bleachers. Nobody did on the fly. It never happened. Never, never, never.

How could we forget the 50th anniversary?

August 1, 1982

Something was missing at the Stadium yesterday—a ball game.

Either the schedule makers goofed, or the Indians did in not reminding them.

Yesterday was the 50th anniversary of the first major league game played at the Stadium, the ball park that has survived politicians, controversy, thousands of tons of fireworks, rock concerts, grand opera, midget auto races, huge religious meetings, and sports events of all kinds. You name it the stadium has housed it. Four All-Star Games. Even two World Series.

The grand dame still looks good for her age, provides better vision, entry and departure and seats for fans for baseball and football than some of her newer, costly counterparts.

Yes, yesterday there should have been a celebration at the ball park. Former Indians' stars should have been brought back, the way they were on that historic opening, July 31, 1932, when, despite the Great Depression, more than 80,000 saw a tense battle between the Indians and Connie Mack's super team, the Philadelphia Athletics.

In a letter, Kevin Willbond of Perrysburg laments the failure to hold a birthday party for the park he continues to love. To him the Stadium is as much a Cleveland landmark as the Terminal Tower. He raps our town for "Not blowing its own horn and not caring" about this park that has provided us with so many highs and heartbreaks—so many memories which could not have occurred without that big oval on the lakefront.

The Stadium has been an anchor in keeping the Indians from moving elsewhere. The giant crowds when the team is in contention have helped entice prospective buyers whenever the team is on the block. And beyond that it has become the city's hub, where east side and west side come together, second only to the Public Square.

Had there been a game at the Stadium last night only four men who played in that historic one 50 years ago could have been brought back: Mel Harder, Earl Averill, Luke Sewell and Willie Kamm. The least we can do is hear from them today. But first some background on the Stadium that was born long before many of you who are reading these words. Perhaps it will add to your appreciation of the grand lady.

The first suggestion that an athletic field should be built on the lakefront came in the mid 1920s from Floyd A. Rowe, supervisor of health and physical education for the Board of Education. He sought a centrally located field where both east side and west side high schools could play football.

When 300,000 carloads of fill dirt and rubbish were dumped between W. 3rd and E. 9th and a land site began to materialize, the visionaries commenced to think in bigger terms, especially E. S. Barnard, president of the Indians then, who later became president of the American League.

Barnard had taken over the team when its owner, Jimmy Dunn, died and he was trying to sell it for Dunn's widow. He knew it would be more attractive if the Indians could play in a place seating many more than cozy League Park, where a crowd of 26,000 meant fans had to stand behind ropes in the outfield. Barnard did sell to a syndicate of prominent Clevelanders, headed by Alva Bradley, who exerted its not insignificant clout on the city's elected officials to erect the Stadium.

A campaign was begun to sell the voters on a $2.5 million bond issue. The sales pitch, which included the possibility of bringing the 1932 Olympics here—Cleveland eventually lost out to Los Angeles—proved so effective that on Nov. 6, 1928, the voters approved it, 112,338 to 76,975. The fact that 1928 was a time of prosperity helped. The horrible depression was soon to follow, so the vote came not a year too soon.

But if one citizen, Andrew Meyer, had had his way the Stadium would not be here today. On May 29, 1929 he sued the city in an effort to prevent construction. He claimed it could not be built for $2.5 million and he also questioned the city's title to the land. He lost in the lower courts, but didn't quit until the Ohio Supreme Court threw out the suit on April 30, 1930.

(He did prove correct about the cost. The final total was about $3 million and today it would cost more than $100 million to build one of similar size and structure.)

On June 30th, the first bulldozer took its initial bite out of the landfill. An enormous task faced the Osborne Engineering Co., a Cleveland firm which had build Yankee Stadium. In some spots the land was just two feet above the lake, in others it was 40 feet above. Since much of the fill was trash, a foundation had to be established that would hold securely the huge steel, brick and concrete structure which was to rise above it. More than 2,500 pilings were driven into the landfill, some as deep as 65 feet, until they reached solid ground.

The weather cooperated and the work went swiftly. But on Jan. 30, 1930, a strong wind off the lake snapped cables holding a construction tower. The scaffolding collapsed, dropping two workers, Thomas Kelly and John Last, to their death, 120 feet below.

The edifice was completed on July 1, 1931, in a record 370 days. That afternoon it opened for tours and the next day there was an official dedication. It was named Cleveland Municipal Stadium while bands played and a huge choir sang.

It was 115 feet high, the outside circumference was one-half mile, occupying 4½ acres; it contained 4,600 tons of steel, 3.3 million bricks and 70 miles of electric wiring, the largest multi-purpose Stadium in the world with individual seats—and still champion in that respect.

For night events, 250 bulbs, 1,000 watts each, were fixed on the roof. By present standards they were not much better than moonlight. Today 1,300 high-powered bulbs illuminate the Stadium field.

The first event, appropriately, was a world heavyweight championship fight between Max Schmeling of Germany and Young Stribling. The date: July 3, 1931. Schmeling retained his title with a technical knockout in the 15th round as 37,396 watched.

The first baseball game was NOT a major league affair. It was played between Al Koran Shrine and Al Sirat Grotto on July 14, 1931, during the national Shrine convention here.

The first football game was played the night of Sept. 9, an exhibition between the Cleveland Indians of the National Football League and the semi-pro Pennzoils. The Indians won, 10-0, before a crowd of 35,000. John Carroll made the Stadium its home field in 1931 and the first Charity Game saw Cathedral Latin beat Central High, 18-0, for the city title. Significantly, both schools are gone, but the Stadium lives on.

All these events merely were appetizers for the day the Indians, for whom the park actually was built, would play on the lakefront. There was much dickering about the lease, while the Tribe continued to play at League Park. Finally everything was set—for 50 years ago, yesterday.

Bob Gill, who later became the Indians' traveling secretary and is now retired and living in Lakewood, remembers that hectic time. He had been in charge of concessions at the Indians' Toledo farm and he was rushed here to see that the Stadium was properly stocked.

"We had to roll in cases of Coca-Cola ourselves," he recalls. "In those days it was sold in the stands by the bottle. The vendors would carry them in tubs filled with ice. They sold so fast we began to send the kids out with the full cases and threw a few chunks of ice on top. They even sold the wooden cases, because the fans who didn't have seats wanted something to stand on.

"Billy Evans, the general manager, got mad at me because I hadn't provided any Coke for the press box. Who had time?"

The day, a Sunday, was ideal, sunny and pleasant. Fans flocked in from all over Ohio, many by train. There were parades and bands and dignitaries. The Washington Senators' baseball clowns, Nick Altrock and Al Schacht, former major league players who had developed some riotous baseball sketches in pantomime, performed. Many former Cleveland greats went to the mound to take bows. Among them: Paddy Livingston, Chief Zimmer, Elmer Flick, Larry Lajoie, Tris Speaker, Bill Wamby and Cy Young.

Gov. George White pitched the first ball to Mayor Ray T. Miller while Philadelphia's leadoff batter, Max Bishop, stood in the box. The umpire for this ceremonial pageant was no less than the baseball commissioner himself, craggy-faced Judge Kenesaw Mountain Landis, and flanking him were Will Harridge, president of the American League, and John Heydler, the National League president.

Then the Indians ran onto the field. The infield had Eddie Morgan at 1st, Bill Cissell, 2b, Johnny Burnett, ss, Willie Kamm, 3b. Joe Vosmik was in left, Earl Averill in center, Twitchy Dick Porter in right. Luke Sewell was the catcher. Mel Harder, just 22, went to the mound to face the World Champion Athletics, whose lineup contained some of the greatest names in the history of baseball:

Max Bishop 2b, Mule Haas cf, Mickey Cochrane c, Al Simmons rf, Jimmie Foxx 1b, Eric McNair ss, Bing Miller rf, Jimmie Dykes 3b and the remarkable Lefty Grove, pitcher. Bishop stepped into the box again and the game was on.

For seven innings it was scoreless as young Harder matched the veteran Grove. In the eighth, Harder got two strikes on Bishop, then lost him on four balls. Haas sacrificed him to second, Cochrane singled him home and that was it, the only score of the game.

Yet, 80,184 (76,979 paid) fans—the largest crowd in baseball history at the time—went home pleased, according to newspaper accounts.

The Plain Dealer covered the opening on five pages. It had been a tense game, fine plays, exciting to the end when Eddie Morgan flied out deep to the outfield.

Of the 20 players who were in that historic lineup none of the Athletics is alive today and just four from the Indians.

We located Willie Kamm, now 82, in his home in Burlingame, Calif., outside of San Francisco. Willie, a slick third baseman, told us after he left baseball in 1937, he never worked again. He played the stock market and did well. "But lately it's hurt me," he said. "I hope it comes back."

He didn't marry until he was 55, wedding a lady 17 years his junior whom he had gone with 18 years. "We didn't live together the way they do now," he said. "That kind of thing was unheard of." They have a son, 27.

"The thing I remember most about that opening day was the crowd. None of us ever had seen anything like it—or expected to. The day before, we played at League Park to about 10,000 people. The players made a pool on what the crowd would be at the Stadium. Each of us put a buck in and made a guess. The closest anybody came to it was 35,000.

"The game was supposed to start at 3, but it was delayed. We wondered why. Somebody said, 'Take a look out the clubhouse window.' We could see nothing but people. The game was being held up to get them in.

"After the game we just sat around and talked in the clubhouse until everybody was gone. We knew we wouldn't be able to get up those ramps and through the crowd."

He remembers, too, how tough it was to hit at the Stadium "because of the very poor background. I think the first two games we played there were 1-0. Most of them were low scores."

Willie suffered s stroke three years ago and has difficulty getting around. "The other day I found myself lying on the sidewalk," he said. He lives 10 minutes from Candlestick Park and until recently went to the Giants' games with friends.

"There aren't enough good players now for all the teams," he said. "But it's still a great game." And then he added sadly, "I know I've gone to my last one, but I'll keep watching on TV."

Luke Sewell, 81, a widower, lives in Akron. In "fair health," he plays golf occasionally. Luke retired 10 years ago from a foundry and machine shop he ran, and spends time with his six grandchildren and one great-grandchild. His older brother Joe, once an Indians' shortstop, will be visiting him tomorrow after attending the ceremonies today at the Hall of Fame where he is enshrined.

"Sure I remember that opener at the Stadium," said Luke. "Mel pitched a whale of a game. Cochrane broke his bat on the hit that beat us.

"Center field was packed and Grove's overhand pitches came right out of the crowd. You had to crouch down at the plate and raise up just enough when the ball came in so you could see just a piece of it against the green of the center field fence.

"I hit a ball that went into the stands, just six inches on the wrong side of the foul pole. There was a man on base at the time. Six inches the other way and we'd have won the game.

"It was so tough to see the ball while catching that you became like a prize fighter, ducking foul tips. After that opener we complained about the background so they blocked off the middle of the bleachers, but in those days the concrete was so white it hid the ball. I felt dizzy every time I finished catching there."

Luke still loves the game but says, "It's fouled up, just like the world. Maybe my values are distorted, but how can you justify paying a ball player $1 million when the president of the United States gets only $200,000?"

Mel Harder was found heading for a 50th anniversary of his own. He and his wife Sandy had driven 2,000 miles from their home in Sun City, Ariz., to their daughter Penny's home in suburban Chicago, where next week the entire family will gather for Mel and Sandy's golden wedding anniversary. Daughter Gay, who lives in Burton, O., plus five grandchildren, will be among those there to honor them.

Sun City is where the Milwaukee Brewers train each spring and Mel rarely misses a game. Their pitching coach is Cal McLish, who once was tutored by Mel when the latter was pitching coach for the Indians in 1959. Mel also taught such greats as Bob Feller, Bob Lemon, Early Wynn and Mike Garcia.

The 223-game winner was shocked to learn there are only four players still living from that opening game lineup, for he still feels young at 72.

"Each year lately I keep feeling better," he said. He plays golf three times a week in the 113- degree Arizona sun.

He joined the Indians at age 18 and as the youngest on the staff never expected to be given the honor of starting that first game at the

Stadium. "Roger Peckinpaugh was our manager," he remembered. "Wes Ferrell was scheduled to pitch. But he wasn't feeling well. Peck came right to me and said, 'You're it.' It was a big thrill. I was ready. That crowd was something."

He recalled every inning clearly, almost every pitch. "The background helped some. Lefty and I battled for seven innings. In the eighth I had Max Bishop 3 and 2 and I'd swear the next pitch was a strike. But Bishop had the reputation of having a great eye so when he let it go, the umpire, Bill Guthrie I think, called it ball four. Then he scored. I still can see Cochrane's hit that brought him home. Went just past me and just beyond the reach of our second baseman. He was playing over because Cochrane was a left-handed hitter.

"You know I had forgotten this was the date of the Stadium's 50th anniversary. I was thinking of our own."

We caught Earl Averill in his home in Snohomish, Wash., as he was packing up to go to Cooperstown, N.Y., for the Hall of Fame ceremonies. He, too, is a Hall of Famer.

Earl, 80, checked with his wife for the number of grandchildren (18) and great-grandchildren (10) they have. He still drives to Seattle, 40 minutes away, to see major league baseball, despite six pins in his back to correct a congenital condition that forced him out of baseball. "I wear a brace. Tight, too," he said. "Otherwise I'm feeling fine."

He, like Sewell and Kamm, talked about the difficult background that day, "Part of the time I had to shut one eye to see. It helped a little. Moses Grove pitched that day, didn't he?" Told that he got one of the four hits Grove allowed, he said, "I generally sneaked one most every day."

Although the wall at League Park was friendly to Earl's left-handed power, he preferred the Stadium. "Didn't have to hit 'em as high to get 'em out. And besides I liked to field there. The center field fence was 450 feet from the plate. [The present portable fence wasn't erected until 1947.] You'd think you couldn't catch the ball, but if you kept going you got it. I liked that." In that game Earl made a spectacular catch—coming in.

"Say," he asked, "has anybody yet hit a ball into the bleachers? I figure with the lively ball maybe they did."

Nobody has, he was told. Certainly in that respect the lakefront ball park continues to reign supreme.

Happy 50th birthday, Cleveland Stadium. And happy 50th wedding anniversary to the Harders. Many happy returns. Too bad there wasn't a party here yesterday so they could celebrate their golden anniversaries together.

Did he or didn't he?

October 24, 1982

Red Ruffing was there—but nobody asked him.

The World Series just concluded caused every major sports page in the nation to recall that this is the 50th anniversary of the historic 1932 World Series in which Babe Ruth supposedly called his shot, a prodigious home run into the center field bleachers at Wrigley Field, said to be the longest ever hit there.

Through the years numerous stories about that home run have been written, some apparently authenticating Ruth's feat and some debunking it. The stories last week quoted all sides.

The Sporting News, the weekly often referred to as the "Baseball Bible," devoted three pages to THAT home run and came up with a film strip taken by a home movie buff who was sitting in the stands behind home plate. It clearly shows Ruth holding the bat in his left hand and seemingly pointing straight ahead with his right hand.

Let's set the scene:

It is the third game of the World Series. In the first inning Ruth had smacked a three-run homer. In the twilight of his career, 37 years old and now too slow to play right field, he had been moved to left. Yet, even fading, he had hit 41 home runs during the regular season. He was still Mr. Yankee and, therefore, typified The Enemy to all the Cubs' fans. In this Series there was even greater antagonism, especially among the Chicago players whom Ruth, with good reason, had taunted. The papers made much of it.

Now he is at the plate in the fifth inning. The fans boo mightily. From the stands comes a lemon that rolls near his feet. The Cubs' pitcher is Charley Root. The count goes to two balls and two strikes. The account in the Official World Series Records states he purposely took the two strikes.

Now the Babe makes his memorable gesture. Now the pitch. Now the swing. Now the ball flies off the bat deep into the stands.

And now comes the controversy.

Ruth had pointed toward the fence. "If he had," said Root, "I would have knocked him down." Root's widow, to this day, becomes angry whenever it is said that Ruth called the shot.

Cubs' players, of course, backed Root. Burleigh Grimes, a Cubs' pitcher, suggested that Ruth held up two fingers toward their dugout, as if to say, "I've got the big one left."

The Sporting News talked with survivors from that Yankees' team. Joey Sewell, their third baseman, is convinced Babe pointed to the Cubs' bench, not to center. Ben Chapman, the Yankees' right fielder, remains just as positive that although the Babe appeared to be pointing toward center, he actually was pointing to the pitcher and that after Ruth came to the bench he said he didn't call the shot. Instead, he was calling Root everything "I could think of."

And so the controversy has raged to this moment.

But neither *The Sporting News* nor any of the writers who researched that game on this 50th anniversary talked with Charles H. (Red) Ruffing.

Ruffing, a member of the Hall of Fame, has been a Clevelander since 1950 when the Indians brought him here to coach the pitchers. He now lives in Beachwood.

He was the Yankees' ace in 1932 and pitched the opening game of the four-game Series sweep over the Cubs.

A phone call was made to Ruffing. "Did you see Ruth call his shot?"

"I sure did," said Ruffing without hesitation.

The call was followed by a visit to his home and two hours of engrossing baseball nostalgia.

Perhaps researchers didn't phone Red because they may think he can't talk. He had a stroke on his right side 11 years ago that left him speechless. Two years later another stroke paralyzed his entire left side. Miraculously his right side, except for some weakness, recovered. He can talk normally and the grip of the hand that once struck out the greats is firm.

Now 77, he is confined to a wheelchair, but with the help of his wife of 48 years, Pauline, his son Charles Jr. and crutches, he is able to take some steps.

His remaining hair is still red and, despite his condition and the recent loss of an ear due to surgery to remove skin cancer, he looks surprisingly fit. "I eat like a hog and sleep like a log," he said.

His memory remains sharp.

"I don't care what anybody else says," he replied when asked about Ruth's feat. "I was sitting right there. I saw it.

"I was going to pitch the next day if there was a fifth game, so I sat as close as I could to the hitters, at the edge of the bench right by the steps leading to the plate. I had a perfect angle when Ruth came up.

"I saw him point with his fingers. In my mind there was no doubt. He was pointing to center field as if to say he was going to hit one there. All I can tell you is how it looked to me.

"After he trotted around the bases he came into the dugout and sat next to me. I said, 'Babe, what if you had struck out?'

"He said, 'Then I'd have been a jackass.'"

Ruffing said he was called to Hollywood a few years ago where a TV documentary was going to be made on that famous home run. "They had the script all written to show the called shot was a phony. Curt Gowdy, the announcer, was reading from the cue cards. They were surprised when I disagreed. I said, 'Curt, I'd like to ask you something. If Babe didn't point to center, why did all the Cubs go to the top of their dugout and tip their caps to him as he rounded second base?'

"Curt said, 'Let's run the film again.' Sure enough, there they were, tipping their caps and bowing.

"You know what started the whole thing? There was a lot of name-calling in that Series, the worst I ever heard. It was Babe against the whole Cubs' team. During the season our shortstop, Mark Koenig, had been traded to the Cubs and without him they wouldn't have won the pennant. Then they voted him only a half World Series share.

"When Babe heard this he shouted to their bench, 'You cheap S.O.B's.' He never let up and they kept jockeying back at him, calling him an old man. He had the last word with that homer.

"I don't know why Charley Root was so upset. It was no disgrace to have Babe hit a homer off you.

"Once when I pitched for the Red Sox he checked his swing and the ball went like a bullet into the left field bullpen for a homer in Yankee Stadium.

"He was something, the Babe."

"You know how I got from the Red Sox to the Yankees?" said Red, who was an excellent hitter as well as an outstanding pitcher. "I was hitting fungoes before a Yankee game and I hear a voice. 'Hey Ruffing.' It's Miller Huggins, the Yankee manager. He says, 'I hear they want to move you to the outfield. Tell them to go to hell. Next year you'll be a Yankee.'

"'How do you know?' I asked. He said, 'If I don't, who does?'"

The next season Ruffing was traded to the Yanks. He learned later that the concessionaire at Yankee Stadium had loaned the Red Sox owner $75,000 and the deal cancelled the debt.

"When I got to New York," said Ruffing, "Huggins was gone and Bob Shawkey was the manger. He said, 'You are now a Yankee. You will talk Yankee talk. You will eat like a Yankee and dress like a Yankee and you can't go out with the Babe. If you do it will cost you.'"

Red eventually "sneaked out with Babe" on occasion.

"There never will be anybody like him," said Red. "My first roommate was Tony Lazzeri and he told me stories about how Babe and Huggins always clashed because the Babe paid no attention to any rules.

"Once Babe grabbed Huggins, who was about 5-1, and tried to throw him off a train. Another time he reported to the Yankee clubhouse just when the game was to start. Huggins said, 'Babe don't dress. The traveling secretary has a ticket for you to go back to New York.' Ruth called him plenty of names but he returned to New York and was fined $5,000. That didn't stop the Babe. Everything he did, the home runs, the way he ate, drank, lived, was to the hilt. He enjoyed himself.

"Yes, the Babe drank. I remember during prohibition when we left spring training he asked me and Lefty Gomez to carry some bottles of scotch back to New York in our suitcases. When we got there we could hardly lift our arms because the bags were so heavy. Ruth just laughed. He said, 'You ought to be glad you could carry the bottles for old Baby.'"

Ruffing, virtually a non-drinker, and Babe got along fine. The pitcher remembers, "Once he invited me to his house for dinner. His wife made me a steak and Babe had hot dogs. He loved those dogs. Between games of a doubleheader some of the boys who sold hot dogs always came into the clubhouse. They knew they had a sure customer with Babe. He'd eat them as fast as they could slap on the mustard."

The Babe never remembered Red's name. "He didn't know anybody's. Once I was in the hotel lobby and he said, 'Come with me. I've got to go to the hospital to visit the mother of a good friend.' When we got there he waved in my direction and said, 'This is Meathead.' To him everybody was 'Meathead' or 'Pal' or 'Kid.' Once he shook hands with the governor of New York and said, 'Hello Kid.'"

Despite the Babe's irreverence, "he was one of the kindest, nicest guys you ever saw," said Ruffing. "Give you the shirt off his back."

The last time Ruffing saw Ruth was in 1947, shortly before Babe died. Ruffing was ending his career with the White Sox, after losing several years in the service during World War II.

"The Babe was working for Ford Motor Co., showing up at baseball clinics," recalled Ruffing. "He had cancer of the throat and could hardly talk. He didn't recognize me. I said, 'I'm Red Ruffling.' He said. 'Oh yeah. How I used to hit you when you pitched for the Red Sox.'

"Actually he didn't hit me that much. Lou Gehrig was the one I couldn't get out. But Babe was dying and I didn't want to spoil his fun."

Ruffing also was there when Gehrig was dying. The Iron Horse played in 2,130 consecutive games before he succumbed to amyotrophic lateral sclerosis, now known as "Lou Gehrig's disease."

"We saw him wearing away every day," said Ruffing. "It got so he couldn't even hold a match. In spring training that year (1939) we had an exhibition game with Brooklyn. I was standing in the outfield shagging flies. Lou took batting practice and as soon as he finished came out to me and said 'Watch me next time I bat. See if I'm following through.' I watched and said, 'You're just going half way.' He said, 'That's all I wanted to know.' Then next day he went to the Mayo Clinic. He kept playing for a while. He didn't know what he had, but we were told he had only about one year to live.

"I'll tell you how bad he was. The day after I pitched Joe McCarthy, our manager then, told me not to come to the park early. Instead I was to go to Lou's room and help him dress. I said, 'What's wrong?' He said, 'Just help him dress.'

"I did. That day, the first time up he doubled against the left field wall. To the end he was a helluva hitter, for me much tougher than Ruth.

"We had a pitcher named Johnny Allen. One day, he covered first on a ground ball to Lou. Lou gave him an off-balance throw and Johnny stumbled and dropped it. He told me, 'If I ever pitch against the Dutchman, I'm going to knock him down four times in a row.'

"I said, 'Don't Johnny. If you do, you'll get hurt.'

"Next season Johnny was traded to Cleveland and I couldn't wait to see what he'd do when we came to League Park. Sure enough, he knocked Lou down. I don't have to tell you what happened. He hit the next pitch over the laundry across the street from the right field fence.

"Johnny told me later, 'Never again. I should have listened to you.'"

Ruffing, too, is an indelible name in baseball, a 273-game winner. He hit 37 home runs, sharing the mark for pitchers with Bob Lemon. Naturally the Designated Hitter doesn't appeal to him.

"The game has changed in so many ways," he said. "You can't even knock a batter down anymore. All of them stand too far from the plate even though they wear helmets. In our day we'd say, 'You're going down' and down he went. The umps never said a word."

Red's highest salary was $22,000, obtained after a long argument. "Ed Barrow, our general manager, wouldn't give you a nickel. He's say, 'Damn it, you were in the World Series, weren't you?' As if that was supposed to be our raise, and as if I had nothing to do with getting the team there.

"Now the guys make so much in salary, the World Series money is no incentive."

Red has seven World Series rings and his Series record is an exceptional seven victories against two losses. "Some years ago Bob Feller called me up," said Ruffing, "and said he knew a guy who would pay me $1,200 for each ring. My wife said, 'Nothing doing. They go to our three grandchildren.' Of course, the rings are worth much more now. They are solid gold and have diamonds." Two eventually were given to his daughter-in-law to be made into pendants. The others are kept in a bank.

Red has had many big moments in baseball. Once, with the Red Sox, he fanned Ruth, Gehrig and Bob Meusel on 10 pitches, all fast balls. "The extra pitch was a foul tip the catcher couldn't hold," he remembered.

But his biggest thrill came last summer when he watched his 7-year-old grandson, Charles, get the winning hit in a Beachwood Little League game.

"He ran over and hugged me," said the Hall of Fame pitcher. "That feeling beat them all."

Trip to Hall evokes memories

January 15, 1984

My bride, thinking I needed a football fix this week while the National Football League was resting up for the Super Bowl, suggested we drive to Canton to see the Pro Football Hall of Fame. She was just being sweet to me, for she had her fill of football long ago.

Although the Hall is virtually in our backyard and I had been there several times for inductions, I never had taken a tour of the building.

We spent a leisurely and fascinating two hours there. If you, too, want a grid fix, we recommend it. My bride seemed even more curious about everything than I.

I was astonished at the growth of the museum, 51,000 square feet loaded with memorabilia and graphically displaying the past and present, including a movie theater that regularly shows classic games.

There are huge charts showing the all-time passing and running leaders, kept up every week. Unlike the NFL's records, these include performances in the old All-America Conference, which the Browns dominated. Until recently, Otto Graham had the highest rating of all passers. But now Joe Montana, having become eligible by heaving the minimum 1,500 passes, has moved ahead of Graham. Now comes the tough part for Montana—to stay ahead.

Near the entrance is a full-length statue of the legendary Jim Thorpe in action. One of the most interesting exhibits was the evolution of the players' gear, from the 1920s to the present. Those old helmets and shoulder pads were like paper compared to today's engineered equipment.

It's a banquet for nostalgia buffs and it gave me the desire to talk with someone who had been through the NFL's infancy, to tell me the way it was before it became so slick, so sophisticated, so Super-Bowlish. When we returned home I called Ralph Vince and we met for lunch.

Vince, 83, is a senior partner, still very active, with the law firm of Burke, Haber & Berick. He played on the Washington & Jefferson team that pulled a major upset by deadlocking a heralded California team in the 1920 Rose Bowl. Many ex-footballers in town know him well for he coached at St. Ignatius High, John Carroll, University School and even helped out at Baldwin-Wallace. He was one of the founders of the Touchdown Club.

In the pros he played against Thorpe, George Halas, Red Grange, Fats Henry and many others now enshrined in the Hall. He was on Cleveland's first team, the Indians. In those days cities that had baseball teams generally gave their football team the same name.

"Sammy Deutsch, who had a jewelry store downtown, got the first franchise here," he recalled. "That was in 1923. I was coaching at Ignatius then, going to law school at Western Reserve University at night and playing pro ball at the same time. We never practiced.

"We had about 16 players, all from the Midwest, and we gathered on Sunday mornings in a sample room at the Statler Hotel. Our coach was Horse Edwards, an old Notre Damer who came in each Sunday from South Bend. He would diagram about five running plays and a few pass patterns on the blackboard. For defense he'd say, 'Every one of you S.O.B.'s protect your territory.' That was it.

"Then we'd go out to Luna Park or League Park, if it wasn't occupied by the baseball team, and play the game. There was no platooning. All of us played 60 minutes unless injured. I was a 175-pound guard. The regulars got $100 a game. Our star, Doc Elliott, the fullback, probably got a little more. The subs got $25 or $50.

"After each game we would take a quick shower and hurry to the front office to get our money. They'd pay us in $1 and $2 bills. We always were concerned about whether they'd have enough. I marvel now when I read about multi-year pacts for multi-millions, much of it paid in advance."

That 1923 Cleveland team had three victories and three ties. The Canton Bulldogs, being a major attraction, played a schedule twice as long.

"We played a postseason game with the Bulldogs at League Park," recalled Vince. "They were the first pro team to hold daily practices and we were no match for them. They finished the season undefeated. We had a big crowd for that one, about 17,000."

That crowd apparently caused Deutsch to bring the Canton team here and merge it with his Indians and in 1924 the team became the Cleveland Bulldogs. They finished on top again and the next year the franchise went back to Canton. Herb Brandt, who owned a wholesale meat company, took over the Cleveland franchise and kept the name "Bulldogs." So, according to the NFL record book, there were two Bulldogs in 1925, revealing the kind of organization the NFL was then.

Other Vince recollections:

"Thorpe always would put on a kicking exhibition before each game. By 1923, when he was with the Oorang Indians, he wasn't that tough to tackle, but he could punt like hell.

"George Halas, who owned and played for the Chicago Bears, was rough and gruff, from the old school. In the early 1940s, when I officiated in the NFL, I was doing a Cleveland Rams-Bears game. From the sidelines he kept yelling, 'Ralph, don't be a homer. Don't be a homer.' Some years later he asked me to scout the Cleveland Browns for him. And I did.

"Fats Henry, the Bulldogs' great tackle, weighed 220 and was considered huge. But he could move. I saw him make a play I doubt ever has been repeated. A kicker went back to punt and Fats got in there so fast that he snatched the ball before it reached the kicker's toe and ran for a touchdown.

"We played Red Grange in an exhibition at Luna Park. After Red left college, C.C. Pyle, a promoter, took him around the country with a pickup team. Red would make all sorts of moves just to pick up a few yards. He was much better in college.

"Funny what I remember the most clearly. We were playing Rock Island (Ill.) and I had to take a late train because I was coaching at Ignatius. I changed clothes on the train and when I came out of the toilet in my uniform the other passengers thought I was a strange animal. I got to the field just as the teams were lining up for the kickoff. Coach Edwards said, 'You little so-and-so get in there.' And gave me a shove. The whistle blew, the game started and I already was out of breath."

Vince goes to the Hall of Fame every year to renew the juices. We'll be going back, too.

Ah, the memories of Tucson . . .

March 3, 1986

Good old days, warm Tucson.

Forty years ago the Indians brought their bats and balls to Tucson for the first time. And this weekend in Tucson there will be a civic party to celebrate that event.

How the 40 years have flown. It seems only yesterday that as a member of the sports staff of *The Cleveland News* I started to do occasional pieces on the Indians. Three years later, 1950, they became my beat and I made my first trip to Tucson. The recollections could fill pages. Just a few:

In those days everybody arrived by train. It pulled out of the station at Euclid Avenue and East 55th Street and all the players east of Tucson kept boarding it at various stops, the main one being Chicago.

Two days later we got off at Tucson. There were no taxi cabs at the station, unlike today where a chartered bus waits for players everywhere—it's in their agreement—there was nothing. Cabs would come eventually, we were told.

"The hell with it," said Harold "Muddy" Ruel. "Let's go."

Ruel, 57, the slight-built coach who once caught the fabled Walter Johnson fastball, picked up a suitcase that appeared to weigh more than he did and began a brisk forward march to the hotel.

Without a murmur, all the players followed: the stars, including Lou Boudreau, Bob Feller, Joe Gordon, Ken Keltner, Dale Mitchell and Jim Hegan, just to name a few, all carrying huge bags stuffed with clothes to last the entire spring.

The small army walked the half-mile nonstop to the Santa Rita Hotel, and not one gripe. Today's players would kill the traveling secretary who made them walk, let alone pick up a bag.

Tucson: it was just the way I had pictured it through cowboy movies, Cactus, palo verde trees and sand, surrounded by four impressive mountain ranges. It was purple mountain majesty when the sun hit them right. Clear dry air, high sky, no clouds, hot in the sun, cold at night. The lush, emerald green grass cultivated by the Bossard family at the ballpark was like an oasis in the desert.

Today the players can stay wherever they want. The club will give them a room and board allotment, Forty years ago the Santa Rita was the team's headquarters. The players slept there and ate together in the team dining room.

The lone exceptions were the black players, Larry Doby, the first black to play in the American League, and Luke Easter. The most western battle in the Civil War had been fought at Picacho Peak, just outside Tucson. There was still a touch of the South in that cactus cowtown.

One evening the phone in the lobby rang and Spud Goldstein, the traveling secretary, was summoned to reply. (Spud, incidentally, has been invited to Tucson for the celebration this weekend.)

The caller, a woman, told Spud it was a shame the black players had to stay in homes of black citizens and couldn't be with their teammates at the Santa Rita.

"I agree," said Spud.

"Well do something about it," she demanded.

"We're working on it," said Spud.

The caller continued to berate Spud and the Indians for accepting Tucson's color line.

"Honest lady, we're trying to break it," he said. "By the way, what's your name?"

"Mrs. Goldberg," she replied.

"Well, mine is Goldstein," said Spud, "and don't we have troubles enough?"

Tucson country, the home of Cochise and Geronimo, Doc Holliday and Wyatt Earp . . .

Once we dug up some earth and found some arrowheads and broken pottery, an Indian burial ground . . .

And there was breathtaking Sabino Canyon, seen often on movie screens, where we would picnic with the players on an off day.

Every spring a movie was being shot in Tucson. The weather and scenery were ideal; real cowboys were available as extras and the costs were less than in Hollywood. The stars lived in the same hotel as the players. The Santa Rita was a second-rate hotel by today's standards, one of the only two decent ones in Tucson.

Lee Marvin and Charles Bronson were bit players then. Invariably they were there every spring, Marvin at the hotel bar each evening. Herb Score and I drove out into the hills to watch Alan Ladd at work. Ladd stopped the filming to get Herb's autograph.

That grand lady, Helen Hayes, as sweet as could be, sat in the lobby with the players after shooting scenes, in which she played a nun, at a nearby mission. The lovely, red-haired Rhonda Fleming was there one spring. The player who roomed next to her said he couldn't fall asleep. The thought of this beautiful woman so near and yet so far was driving him wild.

Happy anniversary, Tucson. See you soon.

No appreciation for former heroes

July 2, 1990

As we were walking down the runway leading from the Indians' clubhouse to the dugout Saturday evening, Manager John McNamara observed, "Imagine all the great players who walked through here? I think of their footsteps every time I come through this tunnel."

Unfortunately, I doubt if many of his players do.

We entered the dugout just as Kenny Keltner was being introduced at home plate. He was being honored as the Cleveland Baseball Federation's "Man of the Year."

In the dugout only the coaches, McNamara and Brook Jacoby, appeared interested in the proceedings. Jacoby's father had been a ballplayer in the Indians' organization.

One player who shall go unnamed because he obviously is a mental minor, stood near the top step and ridiculed the presentation. "Who's the old coot?" he asked as the stooped, balding Keltner, now 73, graciously accepted the plaque which extolled his feats.

If the mental midget and his blasé teammates would have been listening they would have realized—if they really cared—that Keltner is part of baseball history here. Few, if any on this team could carry his glove.

In his 11 years (1938-1949) as the regular third baseman, Keltner made the All-Star team seven times. Only Bob Feller made it more times—eight. In the 1948 historic playoff game against Boston, he hit a three-run homer in the fourth inning to crack a 1-1 deadlock, allowing the Indians to win the pennant and the subsequent World Series.

His name is even better known to followers of baseball history because it was his glove that halted Joe DiMaggio's consecutive 56-game hitting streak. The smooth fielding Keltner made two remarkable backhand stops to rob DiMaggio of apparent hits.

That was on July 17, 1941, before 67,468 at the same Stadium where he was being honored Saturday night and ignored or laughed at by several of the me-generation players of today.

(That memorable night Keltner required police protection when he left the Stadium. It was feared some fans, unhappy that DiMaggio's streak had ended, might take it out on Keltner. The next day DiMaggio began a new streak that lasted 16 games.)

I mentioned my disgust at the conduct of this particular player to Herb Score. He said, "These guys are different. When I was a kid I knew the names of all the older players. I had baseball cards. I read about them. When I met a former player I looked up to him. I doubt if many of the players today know anything about baseball history. I asked Greg Swindell if he ever heard of Sam McDowell. He said, 'He's some old left-hander, isn't he?'"

I shouldn't have been surprised. Just recently I took Luke Easter's 11-year-old grandson, Ryan, onto the field to meet some players. In several instances, when the legendary Luke's name was mentioned in introduction, it was, "Easter who?"

It became necessary to explain that Luke Easter's homer of 477 feet remains the longest ever hit in the same Stadium in which we now were standing.

Knowing the history of the business you're in isn't essential, but it would seem only natural to be keenly interested in it. It might make a player appreciate the game more than just playing for the paycheck. It might even inspire him to remember he's following large footsteps when he goes down that runway and onto the field.

Ironically, Keltner knows all the current players, even if they don't know him. He lives in Milwaukee and rarely misses a game when the Indians are in town. I wonder how many of the present players will be going to the ballpark after they cash their last check?

I firmly believe that every player starting in the minors first should be sent to Cooperstown to spend a day at the Baseball Hall of Fame. Young baseball writers, too. And I think it would be wise for the Indians to indoctrinate each rookie with a history of the team. We've had great ones here for them to emulate, the Speakers, the Lajoies, the Fellers, the Boudreaus, the Wynns, the Lemons . . . I could fill a full column with names of true stars who wore the uniform with "Cleveland" on the front.

Baseball history is part of the game, part of its enchantment: the comparisons, the tradition, the lore, the stories. It's what has set the game apart from other sports and allowed it to remain hugely popular even as pro football and basketball gain followers. Baseball remains No. 1 as the reading sport. No matter how few fans may be in the stands, the polls always show readership in the Indians to be extremely high.

Recalling Williams' milestone home run

June 24, 1991

Story time . . .

John Henry Williams, son of Ted Williams, the Hall of Fame hitter of the Red Sox, phoned the Indians' front office last week. He is collecting memorabilia of his famous dad, and sought a copy of a photo of a milestone homer his dad remembered.

It was snapped at the Stadium late in the 1953 season after Williams returned from the Korean War.

Williams had been called to war for the second time. He had lost three years of his baseball career in the early 1940s, enlisting in the Army Air Force in World War II. In 1952, he was called again to fly the skies in Korea. Again he served with distinction.

Jerry Coleman, another major leaguer who also was a U.S. flyboy in Korea and now is a broadcaster for San Diego Padres games, goes into raptures every time Williams' name is mentioned.

"He had the keenest eyesight of anybody I've ever knows," said Coleman. "It made him a fantastic pilot, just as it made him a superlative hitter. Do you know that when he returned from Korea and took his first batting practice at Fenway Park, after a couple of pitches he said, 'Something's wrong.'

"He took a few more swings and said, 'Home plate is off,' The grounds crew came out and measured it. Sure enough, it was off. By an inch."

Back to the photo. The Indians, knowing I had covered baseball for the late Cleveland News during the 1950s, asked if I remembered the picture. Williams' son had said it was a photo of his dad's first home run following his return from Korea. "It came off Mike Garcia," young Williams had said.

How could I forget that home run? I can shut my eyes and see the whole incident now.

After Williams hit that homer off Garcia, the next batter, George Kell, stood at the plate to congratulate Williams. The Splendid Splinter, as he was called because he was tall and lean, went right by him.

The next day, buried in my game notes, was this line: "In one respect the war hasn't changed Ted Williams; he still doesn't shake hands after hitting a home run."

That night Williams hit another homer. This time, after he stepped on home plate, he shook hands with Kell and everybody else nearby, including the astonished umpire.

While still shaking hands he looked up at the press box, which then was an open porch hanging above the screen. His super vision sought me out and it didn't require a lip reader to get his message.

He said, "How do you like that, you son of a blank?"

Our photographer snapped his camera at precisely that instant, recording the unique and, in retrospect, funny scene. Maybe that's the picture Williams wants. I hope it has been saved. I'd like to send it along, but not as a peace offering.

Williams generally had running feuds with sports writers. It began when a Boston columnist, Dave Egan, writing under the byline, "The Colonel," used Williams as his whipping boy day after day. No matter how well Williams did, Egan would find something to carp about, often personal. Egan had style, a vivid imagination and the parlay made him highly readable.

The circulation for his paper soared as readers turned to see what nasties the Colonel had about Williams that day. Rival Boston writers, seeking to please their copycat editors, soon began to take off on Williams, too. It became yellow journalism at its worst.

What bothered Williams mostly was that the Colonel never went onto the field or in the clubhouse. He would shoot his unfair darts from the safety of the press box. "I'd like to meet him face-to-face just once," Williams had been heard to say.

So, after Williams had given me his long-distance blast following that homer, I knew I couldn't pull a cowardly Colonel. I had to face him. With trepidation, I went into the visiting clubhouse and directly to Williams' locker.

"Did you mean me?" I asked, attempting to smile in an effort to diffuse his anger.

"You're damn right I did," he fumed. "Boston has the worst writers and Cleveland has the second-worst. Why would you want to write a thing like that?"

We went back and forth, with a few S.O.B's thrown in, but eventually I detected a slight softening. Perhaps it was wishful thinking.

Seven years later, in 1960, his final season, he hit his 500th home run. It happened at the Stadium and J. G. Taylor Spink, editor-publisher of The Sporting News, immediately called me. I was his Cleveland correspondent and he wanted a full-page interview with Williams for the next issue.

Oh, oh. I was dead. I was among the second-worst, right at the top. Never, never would Williams give me the time I needed, if any.

Again I went down to the Red Sox clubhouse. Hesitantly, I told him of Spink's call.

"Meet me at the Stadium tomorrow morning at 10," he said.

At the appointed time he was there. He placed two folding chairs in left field. We talked for an hour. He answered every question. We've had many friendly conversations since. Great guy, Ted Williams.

I've got to find that picture.

A SPORTSWRITER

Anybody want satisfaction?

July 6, 1975

Clubhouses have been no-man's land lately for sportswriters. The Red Sox took off on a writer. Ralph Houk, the Tigers' manager, allegedly became physical with a Baltimore reporter. There were other incidents, too.

I figured maybe the Indians might be thinking I was chicken. Because duties keep me in the office until late. I rarely get to the Stadium in time for the first pitch. Since I'm back at the desk early the next day, I often make a quick getaway at the conclusion of the game.

Besides, if you've seen one clubhouse, you've seen 'em all and I've seen more than my share. There's nothing glamorous about sweaty underwear. Still, the guys undoubtedly figure it's unfair that I can crack them in the paper and they can't crack back at me. So, without crash helmet, I dropped into the Tribe's home-away-from-home the other night.

I stepped into Manager Frank Robinson's office, chatted briefly. He gave me a nod and a not unpleasant smile. I'm entitled to my interpretation. The players in front of their lockers were cordial. But then my old pal John Brohamer came in—and he had fire in his eyes. He doesn't like me. He told me so. I thought he was kidding but he denied it.

He still resents a line I carried early last season. The Hammer isn't Mr. Speed and I wrote that lack of range at second base was a Tribe weakness.

The Hammer is the kind of guy who drives himself beyond his own ability. He made himself a big leaguer through sheer determination. In fact I once wrote a column of praise, comparing him to Eddie Stanky.

But like so many athletes, negative lines remain indelible and the compliments are never remembered or acknowledged. Or maybe the jibes are what he prefers to recall as a motivational tool.

So the Hammer, in his quiet way, gave me a blast the other night.

I'm sure the fact that his latest injury has caused him to lose his position to speedy Duane Kuiper has been eating his insides and he had to take it out on somebody. At least that's my rationale.

I told him my job is to call 'em as I see 'em and I didn't expect him to like my criticism. I would have been amazed if he did.

"But my criticism has nothing to do with my personal feeling for you. I respect you and I like you," I said. I put my hands on his shoulders, friendly like.

"Well, I don't like you," he said.

"If it will make you feel better," I said, jokingly, "why don't you take a swing? It would make a good story."

"Not me," he said. "You've got the pen." He walked away angrily.

I still like him. The Hammer is quite a guy.

The slight confrontation reminded me of a couple of others that occurred in that same clubhouse. Every baseball writer worth his salt has had his share of uncomfortable, if not embarrassing, confrontations. It's the toughest job in the entire newspaper business. You virtually live with the athletes you write about. You see them every day. And don't let them kid you. They read the sports pages. Every word.

The drama critic can pan an actor on the Hanna stage and never have to fear facing the angry thespian. Not so with the sportswriter.

My roughest moment involved Dave Philley, back in 1954. Philley was an outfielder, somewhat of a loner, who rarely said much. I had just written a piece about him, revealing he once had been an amateur boxer—undefeated. He was solid and his biceps bulged.

I was the official scorer that night. Early Wynn was pitching. He had a no-hitter going after seven innings.

I kept saying to myself, "The first hit off him had better be a good one." It was foolish to think that way but I was a relatively new official scorer and this was my first experience with an almost no-hitter.

Philley came up for the Indians in the bottom of the seventh. He hit a shot off the Orioles' first baseman, Dick Kryhoski. It should have been ruled a base hit, but I began to rationalize: A more agile first baseman might have had it. If an Orioles batsman hit one like that I'm not going to call it a hit and spoil the no-hitter. Sure, this was wrong thinking. But that's the way my mind went.

I called it an error.

I could see Philley looking up at the press box, but in the excitement of the remaining innings, I forgot about that call. Wynn meanwhile missed his no-hitter. He eventually gave up a couple of clean hits.

I went down to the clubhouse for the post-game story. As soon as I stepped in the door, there was Philley.

"Who was the official scorer?" he asked. He was on fire.

"I was."

He raised his fists. "Put 'em up," he said. "I want satisfaction."

And I had just written that story about his pugilistic days. Ouch.

I thought some of my friends on the team would step in and tell Philley to cool it.

Instead they jumped in on the fun.

"Hit him, Dave," goaded Bob Lemon, always the chief instigator. "He did you dirt. Hit him."

Others chimed in, big grins revealing their delight.

"I want satisfaction," Philley kept repeating, fists cocked.

I can't recall a more embarrassing moment. What to do? Fight him and get killed in front of everybody or walk away chicken-like?

I finally said, "Dave, if you want satisfaction, let's go outside. I'm not going to fight you in front of these clowns."

He didn't seem to hear. He kept muttering, "I want satisfaction."

At last the other players mercifully had had enough sport and they stepped in.

Toby Cuccinello, an Indians' coach, said, "Hal, that should have been a base hit. Why don't you change your scoring decision?"

"I can't now. It would be as though he forced me to."

But I did change it the next day, realizing I had been unfair to Philley. Satisfaction or not, I didn't want to cheat him.

I have seen Philley many times since that incident. He always has been cordial and rather warm. I don't think he even remembers the confrontation. I've never forgotten it.

I had several hassles with Ted Williams. Once, upon his return from flying duty in Korea, he hit a home run and as usual ignored his teammates' extended hands. I mentioned that in a note.

Next day Williams hit another home run, shook everybody's hand at home plate including the umpire's, then looked up at the press box and it didn't take a lip reader to interpret, "How do you like that, you blankety blank blank."

I went into the clubhouse after the game to let Ted have a whack at me personally. This time it wasn't a scorer's decision. It was a story, one everybody saw, and had to be covered.

He told me off. I can't recall my rebuttal, probably because it was insignificant compared to his language.

But after that, Ted was absolutely beautiful with me. Once he came out to the park two hours early for a private interview. Face the issue, even if it means a belt in the belly, that's the moral to the story, I guess.

Admittedly, sportswriters can become quite irritating. Bobby Avila must have thought I was as nasty as a Mexican bandit for a brief period. Spring training had begun and Bobby, as usual, hadn't reported.

I had read in *The Sporting News* that he was still playing winter ball in Mexico and was hitting about .400.

Late one night he checked into Tucson's Santa Rita Hotel.

After the usual greeting I inquired, "Where have you been?"

He said he had been involved in an auto accident in Mexico and had hurt his leg. He had been waiting for it to heal.

"What about this Avila who has been hitting .400 in the Mexican League?"

"Not me," he said. "That's my brother, Pedro."

I called a Mexican writer and was told it was, in fact, Bobby Avila. There was no Pedro.

I had some fun with a tongue-in-cheek account and the headline read, as I recall, "Not me, Pedro."

The story was picked up on the wires and traveled with us as the Indians and Giants barnstormed northward, toward opening day.

Finally Avila had had enough. He came up to me and said, "What are you, a damn spy?"

I once wrote a critical piece about mild-mannered Dale Mitchell, the Indians' left fielder of the late 40s and mid 50s. Knowing it's necessary to brave the wrath as promptly as possible, I went into the clubhouse early the next day. Dale was sitting in front of his locker, looking as pleasant as always. He saw me, smiled warmly and, with a wave of his hand, invited me over.

"Ah," I thought. "A true big leaguer. He can take it."

"Hal," he said, "do you have a brother?"

"Yes, I do."

"Well," said Dale, still grinning, "the hell with him, too."

That, Mr. Brohamer and friends, is the perfect squelch. It has more impact than a punch in the nose. Besides, my brother is a terrific guy.

What is a sportswriter?

June 30, 1974

One of the glory days of my life came two years ago when I was cited by the National Collegiate Athletic Association as one of the nation's top journalists for reasons still unfathomable to me . . . and no doubt to you.

To receive the award, along with Howard K. Smith, the brilliant TV newscaster, and Clark Mollenhoff, the *Des Moines Register and Tribune*'s Pulitzer Prize-winning political writer, and other truly notable journalists was an honor beyond my fondest dreams. We were invited, all expenses paid, to the elegant Diplomat Hotel in Hollywood, Fla., for a luncheon attended by almost 1,000 and each of us had a moment in the spotlight as our journalistic accomplishments were extolled.

To prove it wasn't a figment of the imagination we received beautiful plaques on which were inscribed our respective successes, heavy in my case with complimentary lies.

Deserving or not, I was so proud. How pleased my dear father would be, I thought.

That night I took the plaque to him. Now in his 80s, he lives in a retirement hotel in Miami. Still aglow from the honor, I told him about the fabulous affair, sparing no details. Then to climax the moment I took the plaque out of its velvet cover and handed it to him.

I waited for the proud look to appear on his face and for the words of praise and joy in his son's achievement.

He studied the plaque at length. Savoring each word, I thought. Finally he looked up. He said, "You know, I don't need much money anymore and I have save d up a few dollars. I'd like to send you to medical school." His 55-year-old son he wanted to go back to college and study medicine.

In my dad's eyes, his other son, the doctor, is a success. His eldest son, the sportswriter, is a failure.

Someone who has an eminently higher regard for sportswriters is Jerry Holtzman. It's sheer coincidence, no doubt, that Holtzman himself happens to be a sportswriter (I wonder how his Jewish father views him?). Jerry, the baseball writer for the *Chicago Sun Times,* holds sportswriters in such esteem that he has just completed a book, three years in the making, about the men who are legends in the profession.

It's called *No Cheering in the Press Box* and will be on the book stalls late next month, published by Holt, Rinehart and Winston. Already it gives indications of being a best seller.

Even before publication eight chapters have been reprinted in magazines, which probably is an Olympic record for books, and it has been selected as the Sports Illustrated Book of the Month for September.

I intend to buy a copy and send it to my dad. Although it's about (ugh) sportswriters he'll be able to identify with the men between the covers. They average 74 years of age; like him many are widowers and living in relative loneliness. All of them are perceptive men who spent their lives entertaining and enlightening readers by writing about others and this is the first time their own in-depth stories are being told.

In truth, Holtzman didn't write the book. It wrote itself. Holtzman was the creator, the inspiration, the vehicle and the editor. As for actual writing, he wrote three introductory paragraphs to each chapter.

What he did was search out the men whose work made their bylines indelible to readers of their era and to those of us who followed. He took his tape recorder to them, asking probing questions, when necessary, and let them talk. Some he visited three times to get their full fascinating stories.

These men, having been great interviewers in their day, knew what their interviewer wanted. And, being lonely, they had a desire to talk. "I felt a strong kinship with all of them," says Holtzman.

John R. Tunis, now 84 and living in Essex, Conn., relished Jerry's visits. Despite all his successes, Tunis, who began writing sports in 1915 and has written 41 sports books highly popular with teenagers and now is almost finished with his 42nd, never had been interviewed before. He was one Holtzman visited three times. "I didn't want to leave him either," says Jerry.

That the book was a labor of love is evidenced by the work Holtzman put into it. Had it been a chore, he never could have finished. Although the book now contains the stories of 18 old sportswriters, Holtzman interviewed 44. He eliminated some of the more prominent interviews in favor of a lesser known individual when the latter's story had more to offer the reader.

In all, he had more than 1,000,000 words on tape. At first he hired a stenographer to transcribe the interviews, but when he found the typist substituted a word or two of her own on occasion, he dismissed her and commenced to type each precious word himself. No one was going to erase or doctor his tapes.

Cutting the 44 interviews to the 18 best was an impossible task, rivaled only by the problem of editing those remaining to proper chapter size. Finally the million words were distilled to a meaty and highly readable 90,000.

"It's not a sports book, really," says the author. "It's a book about people. I've often been asked by young college kids, 'What's it like to be a sportswriter?' That's what motivated me to start the project. After they read the book I think they'll know. It's all new stuff. Not more than two paragraphs in the whole book ever appeared anywhere else before."

Only one of the men in the book, Red Smith, is still writing sports. He's the columnist for the *New York Times*. Holtzman interviewed Jimmy Cannon just before the colorful syndicated columnist died last year. Ford Frick, the retired president of the National League, originally was a brilliant sportswriter and he's in the book.

The interviews took Holtzman all over the United States and even to Europe. He found Paul Gallico living in splendor in a 450-year-old, five-story castle in the south of France, along the Mediterranean. Though Gallico is now 76, he remains familiar to readers, TV watchers and movie goers. His *Snow Goose* won TV Emmy awards and he has a new book coming out, said to be headed for the best seller list, *The Boy Who Invented the Bubble Gun*.

"Gallico lives in true splendor," says Holtzman. "He greeted me in a green jacket, the epitome of the sophisticated cosmopolitan. But the next day when I came back he said, 'See, I'm wearing red and black. That's my old high school colors, DeWitt Clinton (N.Y.) High.'"

Often the writers preferred to talk about their old press box pals, rather than themselves. Red Smith talked about the late Westbrook Pegler and others gave him an insight into the renowned Grantland Rice.

Richard Vidmer, who wrote for the *New York Times* and the *New York Herald-Tribune,* traveled with Rice on the golf circuit.

"Rice was such a good guy, he couldn't be unfriendly to anybody," Vidmer, now 74 and living in Orlando, Fla., told Holtzman. "One evening, about 7, we were sitting in our hotel room after finishing our day's stories and we were having a few drinks. The phone rang, I answered it and the party on the line asked for Granny. He took the phone and I heard him say, 'How are you? Glad to hear from you. How's the kids? Come up and have a drink. The boys will be glad to see you.' Then he turned to us and asked, 'Who's Joe Meagan?'"

Although Holtzman made it a point in the interviews not to concentrate on sport heroes these men covered, priceless anecdotes about Babe Ruth and others are woven into the book. The writer closest to the Babe was Marshall Hunt, who covered baseball for the *New York Daily News*. In reality he covered the Babe, for Colonel Joseph Patterson, owner of the *Daily News,* was aware of the readership appeal the Babe had and he assigned Hunt to follow the slugger the year around, on and off the field. Hunt's stories helped build the *Daily News'* circulation to tops in the nation, where it remains to this day.

Holtzman found Hunt, now 75, living in Olympia, Washington. "He told me about a trip with Ruth to a small town in Minnesota in the dead of winter," related Jerry. "They were on the top floor of a three-story hotel. Earlier in the day the Babe had been given the key to the city. It was snowing and hailing. The hail was pounding against the windows. In the midst of that awful weather the town band came out and stood on the street below the Babe's room to serenade him. Hunt says he'll never forget the sight of the tuba player, his cheeks puffed up, blowing into his instrument in the dead of winter.

"Hunt turned to the Babe and said, 'I hope you realize the significance of this occasion. You're bigger than the president of the United States. They've given you the key to the city. On this terrible day the band is here to play for you. And there's that bald-headed tuba player playing his guts out. It's a tribute few, if any, men ever received. You should appreciate and cherish this moment.'

"The Babe turned to Hunt and said, 'C'mon kid, let's eat.'"

When it was time for Holtzman to say goodbye to Hunt they walked together to the highway. "He pointed the way to the airport," recalls Jerry. "I identified with that man and it was difficult to get into my rented car and take off. Here I was 47 and he was 75. When I did finally say so long, it was like one generation passing the baton to another."

I think my dear dad would understand that. Doctor or sportswriter, in the good name of our parents and our professions we're trying to carry on.

What is a father?

June 19, 1983

(Several readers have requested—no kidding, I have the letters—that I reprint a Father's Day column, run in this space some years ago. They even sent in copies of it. Here it is, freshened with a few additions and deletions.)

A father is the fellow who . . .

Finds it difficult to fall asleep before his son's athletic debut, Little League or varsity. (The son, of course, sleeps soundly.) . . .

Finds it impossible to sleep after his son takes a third strike with the bases loaded. (The son, of course, sleeps soundly.) . . .

Makes a comeback, at age 40, by taking batting practice against his 10-year-old-son. Strikes out. End of comeback . . .

Makes another comeback, at age 50, by playing basketball against his son, one-on-one. Son beats him. Takes on his daughter. She beats him, too. End of comeback . . .

Despite these defeats, can't convince his family he wasn't a great athlete in his youth, but doesn't try too hard . . .

Makes another comeback, at age 55, as a jogger and begs his wife and kids to jog with him. He jogs alone . . .

Takes his kids to Bat Day, Ball Day, Helmet Day, Jersey Day, Jacket Day, Peanut Day when he'd much rather be playing golf or nesting on the veranda. On Beer Night he goes alone . . .

Throws his golf clubs and tennis racquet in anger but chastises his son for slamming his bat to the ground . . .

Tells his kids not to yell at the ump but can't withhold his own voice when his son is called out on a bad pitch . . .

Can't understand how John McEnroe's father tolerates his son's court misconduct, yet when his own children misbehave he takes their part against the teachers and others in authority who try to discipline them . . .

Wonders if he's doing the right thing . . .

Tells the kids he's the boss then turns to his wife and asks, "What should we do?" . . .

Always laughed about girls asking to play Little League, but now that he has a daughter he wants the rules changed so she can join . . .

Tells the guys at work, "You should have seen the home run my daughter hit last night."

Then worries about his daughter being a tomboy, but walks around with a 50-inch chest expansion when she wins a college basketball scholarship and smiles when she starts using perfume . . .

Hates the ride to the Coliseum but never misses a Force game because his kids want to go . . .

Shows photos of his kids to anyone within 100 yards, yet before he had any he laughed at other fathers who did the same . . .

Tells everyone he meets that his grandchild called him "Da-Da" the other day . . .

Runs around the block holding the rear of his kids' two-wheeler while they learn to ride it and then shuts his eyes when he sees them riding with no hands . . .

Grows old fast when his kids get their first driver's license . . .

And then buys them their first car . . .

Wonders if he's doing the right thing . . .

Gives up watching a championship sports event on TV so his kids can watch a cartoon show . . .

Delivers their paper routes when they get sick . . .

Attends his daughter's cheerleading practice . . .

Never watches the game, just that certain cheerleader . . .

Can't fall asleep until the kids come home from their dates and parties . . .

Is tickled when his son has his first date . . .

Enervated though he is after a hard day at work, does his son's chores when the boy comes home tired from football practice . . .

Buys an expensive watch to time his daughter at swimming practice . . .

Doesn't buy himself a suit or new shoes so he'll have enough money for a racquet or better basketball shoes for his kids . . .

Wonders if he's doing the right thing . . .

Tells his wife to cool it when the kids come home dirty after playing outdoors . . .

Merely smiles when she says, "Then you wash their clothing." . . .

Tells his wife, "Don't worry, the boy is young. The bones will heal quickly," and wishes he could believe it . . .

Says to himself, "Why can't my kids be the way I was?" . . .

Wonders how his dad was able to raise such a good son while working night and day to pay the bills.

Forgets he, too, occasionally misbehaved as a kid . . .

Plans vacations with his kids and then keeps yelling at them, "Quit fighting or I'll stop the car and let you off right here." . . .

Wonders why kids have to become teenagers . . .

Wonders if he's doing the right thing . . .

Wonders if his kids ever will experience a winning season for the Indians and wishes they could have experienced the thrill of 1948 . . .

More and more keeps telling them about "the good old days." . . .

Can't understand why his son worships some of today's high-priced athletes, forgetting a player's salary never influenced him when he chose his childhood heroes . . .

Worries about his kids copying peers who smoke and drink . . .

Wonders if that's how marijuana smells . . .

Becomes angry at athletes who take dope, fearing they set a bad example for the kids who seek to emulate them . . .

Enjoys short dresses but abhors them on his daughter . . .

Knocked the constant wearing of jeans by his kids but now owns three pairs himself . . .

Is delighted his daughter resembles his wife . . .

Wonders when the kids will begin to think he has some intelligence . . .

Wonders if the present generation was born tired . . .

Has a beautiful day when his kids enjoy some measure of success . . .

Has a sleepless night when his kids experience failure or disappointment and are unhappy . . .

Wonders if he's doing the right thing . . .

Wishes his son would know his schoolwork as well as he does the major league batting averages, conveniently forgetting that he knew them, too, 15 years ago . . .

Is certain the kids take after his side of the family when they bring home a good report card . . .

Wonders how his kids can stand *that* music . . .

Tells his wife to punish the kids . . .

Tries to make certain his kids get the college education his parents were never able to afford . . .

Barely beats his son at arm wrestling and never accepts the challenge again . . .

Whose macho pride is hurt when his son tells him not to lift heavy things and offers to do it for him but is secretly pleased at his thoughtfulness . . .

Has a sore arm after playing catch with his son . . .

Wishes his daughter didn't have a crush on some of the Browns and Indians . . .

Gets his kids the dog they promised to take care of and ends up walking it and fighting with the neighbors about cleaning up after it . . .

Suddenly feels very old when his son asks to borrow his razor . . .

Thinks all the nagging wasn't in vain when his 22-year-old son finally gets a haircut . . .

Feels the same watching his 30-year-old son play softball as he did when he watched the boy as a Little Leaguer . . .

Feels funny looking up to a son who is six inches taller . . .

Wonders if he's doing the right thing . . .

Thinks his daughter could have done much better but he is the happiest guy at the wedding . . .

Wonders if he'll ever have grandchildren . . .

Tells the son he once urged into sports to switch to bird watching when, at 35, he keeps getting injured playing slow pitch softball . . .

Now thinks he should have advised his son to be a lawyer or an agent . . .

Sometimes wishes it were possible to have grandchildren without having children . . .

Feels so inadequately mortal while his family expects him to be Superman most of the time . . .

Doesn't know the clothes sizes of anybody in his family and always is amazed when they know exactly what size gifts to buy him . . .

Says, "Just what I needed" and then shoves another pair of argyle socks into the crowded drawer . . .

Thinks his kids are spoiling their kids, while he can't do enough for his grandchildren . . .

Never stops being a father . . .

Loves his family more than life itself . . .

Happy father's day.

Browns game stirs emotions

December 28, 1987

The gray-haired fellow embarrassed himself.

He always had tried to be so objective, so unemotional, although not always successful.

"It's not really that important," his bride had said as she saw him tensing up as the Browns-Steelers game approached. "It's just a sports event."

"I know, I know," he said, trying to convince himself.

At this age, the gray-haired fellow knew he should have been blase, totally unaffected. He had seen so many games, thousands.

He had lived through the historic, unforgettable 1948 baseball season, climaxed by the nail-biting Indians-Red Sox playoff game and then the victorious World Series. He had covered every game of the Indians' 111 victories, including the Sunday dramatic double-header sweep over the Yankees in 1954.

He had seen the birth of the Browns, relished their first year in the NFL when Paul Brown's upstarts won the championship on Lou Groza's last-instant field goal. He had seen other Browns' thrillers and championships.

He had been at courtside through the Cavaliers' Miracle at Richfield and had seen the United States Olympic hockey team's dramatic upset of the Russians. These were just a few of so many highlights, thrills and moments that should have made the Browns-Steelers game seem, well, routine.

"Just another game," as my bride had said. After all, the Browns already had made the playoffs.

Strangely, it wasn't. The gray-haired fellow couldn't recall another occasion where he inexplicably had become so uptight, so apprehensive over the outcome, so anxious for the home team to win. It may have happened before, but if so it had faded from his memory. Certainly, he never expected this tension. Not after all he had been through himself on the field and in the press box.

But here it was Saturday morning and he was feeling nervous; there was a funny feeling in his stomach. His heartbeat was up. The adrenaline was pumping. That last feeling he had remembered. It had been there before in big games when he had played, coached and officiated.

But that was eager anticipation. This wasn't. This was anxiety.

He tried to analyze why. The best he could figure was he had developed a special bond with this team. He had gone to the practices. He had seen how much Marty Schottenheimer and his staff had put into every moment. He had seen Art Modell bleed after the loss to the Colts.

He had seen Ozzie Newsome, Hanford Dixon, Cody Risien, Clay Matthews, Eddie Johnson, Bob Golic grow with the team, just to name a few. He had seen them pump iron, play in pain, heal bruises in the freezing water. Good people all. More than good. Class. High class.

He had grown especially fond of Frank Minnifield, whose thighs weren't much bigger than a lineman's forearms, yet who played with the heart of a lion and whom you wanted at your side in a dark alley.

He admired the way Bernie Kosar avoided special favors, refused to take any personal credit, just wanted to be part of his gang, the unheralded men in the offensive line. Class people there, too. And Kevin Mack and Earnest Byner, two sweet guys. Also the special Carl Hairston.

That they cared for each other was seen at Wednesday's practice. It was a ragged workout, another reason to be apprehensive. The Pro Bowl selections had been announced before the players took the field. Seven Browns had made it.

After the workout the gray-haired fellow congratulated Minnifield. The cornerback was less than elated. "I wish they hadn't announced it until after Saturday's game," he said. "This is a distraction. Some guys on this team should have made it and they didn't. I feel for them. It takes away my own happiness. It took away some of our concentration on the field today."

The disappointment throughout the locker room was for Hairston, the elder statesman, the quiet leader having his finest season at 35.

Although Hairston clearly wanted it, he said sincerely, "I have a bigger mission right now—the Central title."

On the other side of the locker room Matthews, the extremely bright and candid linebacker, was saying, "If I said to you I wasn't pleased at being named to the Pro Bowl I'd be lying. But it really doesn't count for that much. The team thing is what gives me true pleasure—to win as a team. There's no feeling like it. The ultimate would be for us to win the Super Bowl."

Then he added, "I know all this sounds trite, cliche stuff, but I'm telling you how I really feel inside."

"You're a sentimental old poop," said his bride when the gray-haired fellow told her about the practice and what was said.

That probably was it—sentiment. It penetrated his thick skin, dissipated his cool and welled up into worry Saturday morning. To speed the time before the game he tried to balance his check book. It was a futile effort but it brought the clock to game time.

He was perspiring as the whistle blew. Years ago, when he was on the field, the funny feeling in his stomach disappeared on the first play. Now, as a helpless spectator, it remained.

His son, who came to watch with him, laughed in disbelief at his father's state. But it was the son who went to the bathroom a half dozen times during the game while the gray head lived through every play.

His bride had gone to the bedroom at the opening kick-off. "I can't stand seeing a grown man suffer," she said.

She came down once to say, "The cat is caught in the vacuum cleaner."

"Oh no," I yelled. "The extra point was blocked. How could they?"

Later she came down again to say, "The house is on fire."

"Can't you see I'm concentrating."

Finally it was over. The Browns had hung on. The gray-haired fellow was drenched. He took a cold shower.

Hours later he sat with his bride at dinner, feeling warm and mellow. "What were you saying during the game, dear?" he asked.

"I'm leaving town during the playoffs," my bride said.

Yours, too?

Throwing out the first pitch

July 17, 2000

I don't know why I said "yes" but I guess it was I just couldn't say "no" to Cleveland Indians vice president Bob DiBiasio. He's always been so helpful to me.

It was about two weeks ago when he asked me to throw out the first pitch at Sunday's game between the Cleveland Indians and Houston.

I had seen thousands of games, watched others throw out the first pitch, from Hall of Famers to show biz celebrities. I didn't pay much attention to them except when they goofed up and bounced one to the plate or threw it embarrassingly wild.

Now I had put myself in a position to embarrass myself. I hadn't thrown a ball in 20 years. As a sandlotter I had done some pitching. As an umpire I prided myself on throwing the ball back hard to the pitcher.

After I quit playing and umpiring I stuck to basketball. Not even a soft toss. But it shouldn't be so tough, I told myself. Just get out there and throw it.

Then I remembered that last attempt back in 1980.

My wife and I were going to an evening show. Our son, Neil, was player-manager of a slow pitch softball team that was playing for the championship. I suggested to my wife that we stop on the way to the movie and watch a few innings.

When we drove up to the field Neil rushed to the car and said, "Dad, we're one man short. Can you fill in for an inning until the guy shows up? Otherwise we might have to forfeit."

I said, hopefully, "The other team won't allow it."

He said he'd try to get permission from the opposing captain and, surprisingly, he got it, much to my chagrin.

He put me in as catcher, where I could do the least damage.

After each pitch I simply couldn't throw the ball back to the pitcher. I was sure everybody was watching and laughing. I was so happy when the missing player showed up. I got out of there fast.

That memory caused me to sweat. I was about to make a fool of myself before 40,000 fans.

I immediately found an old baseball and took it with me to the John Carroll football field where I jog each morning. Before the run I got on the goal line, would up and threw, hoping the ball would go to the 20-yard line, 60 feet away.

It went less than five. I couldn't believe it. My muscle-mind connection was zilch, just as it was in that softball game. When you quit a sports activity your skills erode. If you don't believe it, try throwing or fielding a ground ball. Better yet, don't and keep fantasizing about the past.

I continued to practice. The ball kept going farther, but the accuracy was laughable. Balls that did go as far as 30 feet were so scatter-armed I had to chase them off the field.

I was about to call DiBiasio and beg off, saying I had to go on the disabled list. My son said he would come over and coach me.

We began to throw in the backyard. My wife got a tremendous kick out of our workouts. She remembered, "When Neil played Little League you warmed him up. Now he's warming you up."

He worked on my release point and follow-through and I got a little better. Last Wednesday I took a ball again to John Carroll and began to throw 60 feet, with occasional accuracy. Maybe there was some hope I wouldn't be a total fool.

The next day I tried again. I was awful. I thought about the four bases on balls Bartolo Colon gave up at the start of a recent game. I'd never criticize a wild pitcher again.

But that didn't help my morale. Friday night I watched Scott Hamilton, the ice skating star, throw out the first pitch. That was a mistake. He threw it miles from the catcher. Since he was an entertainer, he made some comical gestures and the crowd loved it.

But I'm a sportswriter. I'd be throwing before my peers in the press box and readers.

The players whom I critiqued would be watching.

I was starting to choke.

My son came over for one final workout, kept reminding me of my release point and the follow-through.

Les Levine, with whom I do a weekly TV show, said, "When Willie Mays throws out the first pitch he says he never gets on the mound. He pitches from just in front of it."

Just before we—my wife and son—went to the ball park yesterday my daughter called.

She said, "When you stand out there just think of all the great pitchers you have seen. Visualize how they threw the ball and just do it."

I was hoping for rain. The skies remained clear. Before I was escorted to the mound, my son said, "Remember your release point. Scouts are watching. You might get an offer."

I walked to the front of the mound, flash bulbs popped and somebody said, "Throw."

I forgot everything: release point, great pitchers I had seen. With a blank mind I threw.

A miracle. Perfect pitch. I had not thrown one like that in practice.

As I walked up the stands fans said, "Nice throw."

I floated up the steps, totally relieved.

Somebody up there put wings on that pitch. I know I never could duplicate it.

And if I'm ever asked to throw out the first ball again I fully intend to say no.

Sept. 11: another day to live in infamy

September 16, 2001

My birthday—a milestone one—was last Tuesday, September 11. My friend Gib Shanley, the former TV sports anchor and outstanding radio voice of the Browns, always ribbed me, "It's easy to remember, 9/11, nine-one-one."

On my birthday, I always celebrate by running my regular number of laps and doing an extra one as sort of a present to myself to prove my body can do it.

After each birthday lap, I look up at the sky and say, "Thank you, Lord.

Finding no parking space near the track around the John Carroll University football field where I usually run, I drove to University School nearby (the lower school), which has an excellent new track in an emerald green setting just off a street of lovely homes.

A beautiful spot for a morning celebration run. I schlogged along, listening to my walkman radio. The birds were singing and the kids in their gym class were playing soccer on an adjacent field, their excited voices adding to the joy of being alive. "Thank you, Lord."

Suddenly, the radio program was interrupted. A plane had crashed into one of the tall towers of the World Trade Center in New York City.

Soon, another plane flew into the other tower. This no longer was an accident. The announcer, his voice quivering, said the obvious: The work of terrorists. The lives of some 50,000 who worked there were in danger. Many, certainly, already had died.

The birds continued to sing. The unsuspecting kids continued to kick the soccer ball. Now it was surreal. I mumbled my extra-lap "Thank you, Lord," and then said a fervent prayer for those at risk and their families.

As I drove home, in shock and disbelief, a bulletin revealed the Pentagon in Washington had been hit by a third plane. On our own soil. Our nation had been violated. All of us.

September 11. Nine-one-one.

We personalize catastrophes and tend to remember dates and details of them more so than happier times. The shock makes them indelible.

When John F. Kennedy was shot, November 22, 1963, I was in my office in the *Plain Dealer* sports department. Next door was the office of the Associated Press. When a major story broke, the bells on the machines that spewed out copy would ring as an alarm to alert the editors nearby.

The alarm went off and I rushed in. The President had been shot. Time stood still as we hovered over the printer.

On the bombing of Pearl Harbor, December 7, 1941, called "a date which will live in infamy" by President Franklin Roosevelt, and now being echoed for September 11, 2001, I was heading for a basketball officials meeting when the radio reported the bombing.

I recalled looking around the meeting room at my fellow officials and thinking how our lives never would be the same. Surely, many would be in a different uniform shortly and shipped overseas.

Then there was September 5, 1972. It was about 7 A.M. when I was awakened by the ringing of the telephone. A friend, Dr. Ben Berger, had broken my reverie. He and his wife, Dorothy, are two of the sweetest, kindest people I have ever known.

"Did you hear or see the news?" asked the doctor, abnormal concern in his voice.

I turned on the TV. Scenes were coming in from Munich, Germany, site of the Olympic Games. Hooded terrorists had commandeered a building housing members of the Israeli Olympic team.

The Jewish athletes were being held hostage. Berger's 28-year-old son, David, an Israeli citizen, was a member of the weightlifting team.

"Can you find out if David is among the hostages?" asked the doctor.

I said I would check with Associated Press, dressed hurriedly, rushed to the office, read all the AP dispatches, put in a query to seek further information on David.

Soon a dispatch indicated David was not in the hostage group. I immediately called Dr. Berger and Dorothy to convey the good news. Their relief was beyond words.

Four hours later, AP reversed the earlier information. It had confirmed that David indeed was one of the 11 hostages still under siege.

I had to call the Bergers again, ending their vigil of hope.

Several hours later, the TV screens showed the tragic conclusion. The terrorists had made a deal with German police to get out of the country by air, with their hostages. The police were convinced they could thwart the terrorists before they took off.

Instead, a grenade thrown by the terrorists into the helicopter killed David and his fellow Olympians in what became known as the Munich Massacre. The games went on as we mourned.

Dr. Berger and Dorothy still live in Greater Cleveland. They identify with the families of those killed September 11 by the suicidal terrorists and their hearts go out to them.

"We know their ordeal, the waiting for word, the frustration, the inability to do anything but just wait," said the doctor. "The fear and anxiety are impossible to describe."

For a while on that awful September 11, they were more than sympathetically involved.

Their daughter, Barbara, now a resident of Portland, Maine, gave them two grandchildren, David Berger Gulac, 21, and his sister, Palit, 18.

David is interning for Maine Senator Olympia Snowe in the Senate wing of the Capitol.

A plane had gone into the Pentagon. There were reports another might be heading toward the White House or the Capitol.

"Were we worried? Worried sick, you know that," said the doctor, admitting to flashbacks of another tragic time.

Not until David called to say the building had been evacuated and he was safe were the Bergers able to breathe almost normally.

But not quite, until they heard that their granddaughter, too, was safe. That morning she was to take a flight out of Boston's Logan Airport for Costa Rica, where she was to teach English to children in a remote area of that country.

Logan Airport was the same one where the terrorists hijacked the two planes they flew into the World Trade Center, killing themselves and all their passengers.

She got there just as the airport closed. Some of the terrorists had driven to the airport from Portland, on the same road she did, but earlier, thank God. She called her grandparents to say now she would have to drive to Houston next week and board a plane there for Costa Rica.

She has the fearlessness of youth and none of the trepidations of her grandparents who have nightmarish memories they'll never erase.

"It was almost 30 years ago," said the doctor, "and the most frustrating thing is there's not a heck of a lot you can do, just as those suffering today from the destruction in New York and Washington. You want to punch somebody, but the perpetrators are just ghosts. You can't.

"Terrorists are killers. They don't represent any country. They enjoy being terrorists. Life is meaningless to them. Including their own."

As you have noted, this is not the usual Sunday "A little bit of this and a little bit of that" column. In deference to our nation's suffering, all major sports events in the United States were postponed last week. There were few worthy sports bits and bites.

I didn't want to write a column.

But I was told readers didn't want this space empty today, and I did have an emotional urge to convey the above.

Advisers I respect suggested more—something in a sports vein, something to help us return to normalcy. Normalcy? Life never will be quite as normal.

I must confess I had hoped the major sports contests would resume earlier, at least by today. I felt the void of sports, trivial though they are in comparison, added to our emptiness, hence delaying our healing and the return to relative normalcy.

But I couldn't argue with the decision of the respective sports commissioners to delay their return to the playing field. Logistical factors were involved as well as emotions among the players. There was no right date to commence the games, but playing later than sooner had "right" on its side—and less criticism.

Still, to write about sports during this time of mourning and moratorium? For a disinterested public?

Each Thursday at 6 P.M. I share the microphone with Les Levine, host of the cable TV show, "More Sports and Les Levine." I dreaded going to the station that week, believing viewers still would be focused on their TV sets for more information on the catastrophes. Our audience would be minimal, and certainly there would be few, if any, callers.

Les and I would be looking at each other trying to make small talk and watch the minute hand go round for 60 agonizing minutes.

To my amazement, we had a most spirited program. The calls were constant. They were mostly good ones. All pertaining to sports. The hour was too short to handle all of them.

It spoke loudly that all of us need the outlet, we need a relief from repeated pictures of the planes crashing into the tower and its consequences.

We'll never forget that. But as a prominent psychiatrist said during one of those TV sidebar reports on the tragedy, "We need an outlet, too. We need a diversion we can get involved in. Something possibly to smile or chuckle about in the midst of our grief. That's the avenue toward healing, the best therapy."

So I decided, as advised, to put some sports into this space. But what? Nothing has happened. "Tell a funny sports story," my daughter suggested, "one of those you've told us."

I feared some readers might be offended, thinking I'd be trivializing the events of the week and running counter to the deep feelings that caused me to write the earlier paragraphs. Such a reaction would devastate me.

No, I was told by several whose judgments I respect: There now is a hunger for a smile.

So putting personal trepidation aside, let me tell you about "The Other Feller."

Everybody knows what an exceptional pitcher Bob Feller was, perhaps the greatest ever to wear an Indians uniform. Everybody knows, or should know, how great a patriot he is, enlisting in the Navy almost moments after the bombs were dropped on Pearl Harbor, erasing four prime years of a magnificent pitching career. He almost certainly would have been exempted from service for several valid reasons.

The other Feller, in his younger days, was an inveterate practical joker, a side unknown to sports page readers.

Often he would set off firecrackers in the clubhouse, especially when he saw a teammate dozing. He couldn't pass a novelty store without browsing inside for gimmicks and tricks.

An example: He bought several plastic "ice cubes" with fake flies imbedded, and he would drop one into the glass of an unsuspecting restaurant companion and then wait for the scream.

He tipped with a 50-cent piece that stuck to the table and then gave the waitress a real tip after she failed to wrestle away, amid her own giggles, the tricked-up coin.

Ed McAuley, the baseball writer for the *Cleveland News,* told me this story: When traveling with the team, after dinner in the train's dining car, his habit was to go into the lounge car and light up an after-dinner cigar.

One evening, during his smoke, the car became heavy with ashes, the stuff flying all over the room. The embarrassed McAuley, apologizing profusely, quickly put out his cigar.

The next day he learned Feller had stood behind him with a gadget blowing an ash-like substance.

He had another gadget that blew fake cobwebs. Invite him to your home for dinner and your wife, who had spent all day cleaning, would come into the dining room and, to her horror, see cobwebs all over the place.

For me, his crowning joke was concocted in Tiger Stadium. In the visitors' clubhouse was a cooler loaded with ice cream sandwiches—vanilla ice cream bars between two Nabisco wafers. Feller took a bar of soap—are you laughing already?—got two Nabisco wafers, placed the soap between them, wrapped it properly to make it resemble the others in the cooler, and placed it inside—right on top.

Who should come along but Satchel Paige. Through all his traveling years eating at greasy spoons, he ruined his teeth, eventually requiring plates, upper and lower.

He reached into the cooler, took out the "bar" and bit into it. When he opened his mouth, his teeth were no longer there. They were stuck in the soap.

One of the most hilarious sights I ever saw. So funny that even the good-natured Satch grinned a toothless grin. He simply put his teeth back in and grinned some more.

Nine-one-one, 2001, and its incomprehensible horrors will remain with me until my last breath. As it should. And no doubt with you. But a respite is not unhealthy. Let the games begin—and perhaps a laugh or two.

In this case, a little bug . . .

March 2, 2003

Strictly personal:

The phrase, "The Lord works in mysterious ways" is no cliché to me. About eight months ago, I saw a bug on our kitchen ceiling. I got up on a chair to reach it. The chair began to slide on the slick linoleum. I flew backward and landed hard on the floor.

In pain, I forced myself to get back up and kill the bug.

I knew I had cracked a rib, and the X-ray confirmed it. But it also indicated a shadow on my upper left lung. Talk about fear. I had it.

Our internist, Dr. Donald Junglas, appeased me by saying since I had never smoked and jogged regularly and I felt "great," it might be old scar tissue. He advised a CT scan, which was more definitive than the X-ray.

The spot showed up again. How long it had been there was pure conjecture.

He suggested a second CT scan in six months to see if there was any change. The second one made him more suspicious, and he advised a PT scan, in which a nuclear substance would be injected. This would show if the spot was cancerous.

It was. The news was devastating.

Dr. Junglas sent me to a thoracic specialist, Dr. Julie Clayman, a meticulous diagnostician and surgeon not much taller than a jockey. Junglas told me: "Every patient I've ever sent to her came back better."

Dr. Clayman gave me a few more tests, all indicating the PT scan was right. She said she would recommend surgery, except that at my age, 86, it was extremely risky and I should talk it over with Dr. Junglas.

He gave me some physical tests and said: "You're in good shape. Go for it."

He's been my medical quarterback for nearly 40 years, and I wasn't going to check off his call this time, although I wanted to, fearing I might never get off the operating table.

Our 65th wedding anniversary was coming up Feb. 20, and I hoped to make it, so the surgery was scheduled for Feb. 13. If all went well, I would be out of the hospital in six days.

I trained for the surgery the way a boxer would for a fight. I increased the speed and distance of my treadmill and pumped iron daily.

Dr. Clayman, my jockey, proved to be the giant Dr. Junglas claimed. She removed a lobe and the pathology affirmed the spot was malignant, but it also showed my lungs were now completely clear.

I was home in four days, and on the 20th my wonderful bride and I and our loving son and daughter celebrated the most precious day of our lives. One friend had sent in a delicious meal, another a cake. We had champagne. It was a perfect evening.

Thank you, Lord, I'm back and feeling stronger each day. So you're still stuck with me—if you haven't already turned the page.

I shouldn't have killed that bug. It saved my life.
